D1226776

AFRICAN KINGDOMS

AFRICAN KINGDOMS

Lucy Mair

CLARENDON PRESS·OXFORD

1977

Oxford University Press, Walton Street, Oxford OX2 6DP

OXFORD   LONDON   GLASGOW   NEW YORK
TORONTO   MELBOURNE   WELLINGTON   CAPE TOWN
IBADAN   NAIROBI   DAR ES SALAAM   LUSAKA   ADDIS ABABA
KUALA LUMPUR   SINGAPORE   JAKARTA   HONG KONG   TOKYO
DELHI   BOMBAY   CALCUTTA   MADRAS   KARACHI

© *Oxford University Press 1977*

British Library Cataloguing in Publication Data
Mair, Lucy
   African kingdoms.
   1. Ethnology—Africa, Sub-Saharan   2. Africa,
   Sub-Saharan—Politics and government
   I. Title
   301.5'92   GN645

   ISBN 0-19-821698-X
   ISBN 0-19-874075-1   Pbk

*Printed in Great Britain by
Fletcher & Son Ltd, Norwich*

CONTENTS

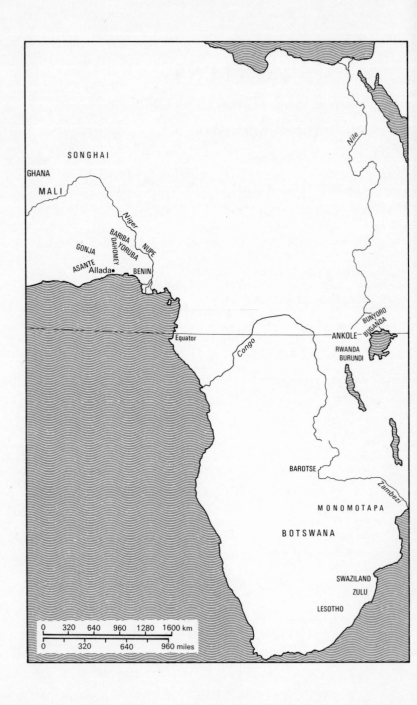

CHAPTER I
THE RISE AND FALL OF AFRICAN KINGDOMS

IT was from Africa that we first learned how the necessary minimum 'rule of law' which makes social life possible could be secured in a quite extensive population without the recognition of any formally constituted authority. Presumably there was a time when this was the case in all human societies, and this must have lasted for many millennia. As the pre-history of Africa is reconstructed, it seems often possible to trace the imposition of chiefly authority by outsiders on 'tribes without rulers'. And the earliest historical records tell of kings who controlled the entry of strangers into their domains, mulcted them of payments in return for safe passage and permission to trade, exacted tribute from their subjects and made war on their neighbours. Most of these records come from people who visited the tropical parts of Africa for the sake of trade, and particularly in search of precious metals. Some travellers were interested also in the governance of the countries they visited, but many were concerned only with what affected themselves. From their writings we can learn at least that in most of Africa, wherever there was any valued article of trade, there were kingdoms, and that once there were kingdoms, they competed for the control of trade routes. With the great interest that has grown up, since most of Africa became independent, in tracing the history of the years before the appearance of Europeans, a surprising number of documents have been discovered. Oral traditions have been collected, and have been found much more reliable than used to be thought. Some of what is told can be checked from the findings of archaeologists; occasionally dates can be fixed by the memory of an eclipse.

Nearly every African kingdom that we know of has been described by some writer as a 'vast empire'. Both these words need qualification. If any political system established by conquest is an empire, then one could use the word of nearly all. If we mean by empire a political unit that is organized from a single centre which effectively controls its whole area, it is much more difficult to be sure how far this has been true of African kingdoms. The historian Vansina, writing of kingdoms which he would not call empires, refers to 'states, all of which had a nucleus which was tightly controlled by the central government, and all of which had outlying provinces, where the authority and power of the central government faded away more and more the further one went from the centre toward the boundary. Thus boundaries between the states were vague, sometimes even overlapping' (1966: 155–6). This is his comment on a particular group of kingdoms in central Africa, but it is of much more general application.

This book will not attempt the impossible task of making an inventory of African kingdoms. It is concerned rather to examine, from the best-documented examples, their organization and the basis of force, consensus, and ritual sanction on which this rested; what sort of reciprocity—if any—there was between rulers and subjects; how authority was divided, and whether despotism could be checked; how administration was organized; what happened to royal authority under colonial rule, and whether there is anything left of it now. The account must be set in a chronological framework, so as to give some idea what kingdoms were dominant in the major areas of Africa in different centuries, who were the rivals and which were victorious, and what areas they covered. But the examples chosen for political analysis will not necessarily be those best remembered in history; the existence of adequate data is very much a matter of the choice of field made by individual inquirers.

In so far as African history depends on the records of travellers, it falls into two sections: that which we learn from Arabs journeying across the Sahara to the savannah country on its southern fringe and that which we learn from Europeans—initially the Portuguese—approaching Africa by sea. It is to this latter section that most of the oral traditions belong. Nearly all of them lead to the calculation that the kingdoms to which they refer had their origin some time in the fifteenth century;

and nearly all of them describe their first founder as an immigrant. What this means will need to be discussed later. It would certainly not do to ascribe the foundation of 'empires' to conquerors who brought with them some ready-made recipe for 'the arts of government'. It is much more likely that modes of government were devised in the process of extending and maintaining control, and in some cases this process, or stages in it, can be traced. For whatever reason, there seems to have been a general movement of peoples in the interior in the fifteenth century comparable only to the European *Völkerwanderung* of the Middle Ages.

The Sudanese Empires

It seems possible that really effective control over wide areas was maintained in the kingdoms bordering on the Sahara, where it is relatively easy to travel, and where horses were introduced by the Arabs and could be used for quick communications and for war. From the eighth century onwards we know of empires there, the first being Ghana, which was a long way to the west and north of the present Ghana; the latter took the name as a symbol of the emergence of African independence. We know of Ghana from the writings of Muslim chroniclers and the travellers who followed the trade routes from the Mediterranean coast that were first developed in the search for gold. A Moorish invasion of Ghana, no doubt an attempt to discover where the mines were and get control of them, is recorded in the eighth century (Bovill 1968: 69). Ghana was ruled by the Soninke, one of the peoples of the region between the upper Niger and Senegal, in the interior of the present Guinea. At its greatest extent it reached from the home of the Soninke to the Niger at about the present Macina. Its capital, Kumbi, about 300 miles from Timbuktu, was said in the eleventh century to be the largest market south of the Sahara. The traveller El-Bekri described the gorgeous gold ornaments worn by the king and his attendants, and the wells of sweet water around the town. To the north Ghana was constantly harassed by Berber nomads, but at its greatest extent, when the Berbers were fighting among themselves, it took from them the control of Audoghast, the market in the south of what is now

Mauretania, to which Arab traders came for the gold that they judged to be the best in the world. When the Berbers were united under an Almoravid leader preaching holy war, they reconquered Audoghast in 1055 and sacked Kumbi in 1076. But although the empire of Ghana disintegrated after this, the Almoravids did not build one in its place to the south of the desert.

In 1203 Kumbi was again captured by the Sese, a people formerly subject to Ghana, who also dominated the Malinke chiefdoms between the upper Senegal and the upper Niger. It was a Malinke chief, Sundjata, who created the next empire, a much larger one. He began by a successful rebellion against the Sese, after which the other Malinke chiefs swore allegiance to him. Towards the end of the thirteenth century his son moved east and north and conquered Timbuktu and then Gao on the Niger, and Walata on the edge of the desert, which by that time had superseded Audoghast as the principal desert market. It was in the fourteenth century that Timbuktu, with its access to river communications, replaced Walata as the terminus of the desert trade, and it was in 1433, when it was seized by the chief of the Tuaregs, that the decline of Mali began. At its greatest it controlled both banks of the Niger as far down as Kukuya (now Bentia), while in the west the kingdoms along the Senegal and Gambia rivers as far as the sea became its vassals.

The empire which succeeded Mali was that of the Songhai, the people of Gao, who rebelled soon after the loss of Timbuktu to the Tuaregs. In 1468 the latter threw off their own overlords and offered Timbuktu to the Songhai king Sonni Ali. He in his turn extended his domain nearly to the Atlantic, covering much of the former Mali, drove the Tuareg out of Air and made vassals of the seven Habe (Hausa-speaking) kingdoms that had been established from the eleventh or twelfth century across what is now the north of Nigeria. No such extensive empire existed anywhere else in Africa before the colonial period.

The principal trade of all these empires was in gold (and later slaves); in return they acquired salt from deposits in the desert, textiles and brass pots from the Mediterranean. Arab traders were not allowed to deal direct with the producers of gold, and indeed all through these early centuries whoever controlled the mines kept their location a secret—so successfully, indeed, that it is still not certain where they were. It is thought, however, that they were probably at Bambuk and Bure near the river Faleme, where gold is still being mined by Africans; the French colonial administration did not allow foreign prospectors there.

In the period of Malian dominance only Malinke traders were allowed to buy gold for export, and a numerous trading class grew up. They came to be known everywhere as Dyula, a Malinke word for trader which has sometimes been taken for a tribal name, and many of them settled permanently at points along the trade routes, which became towns with a majority of Dyula in their population.

It was in the sixteenth century, when Songhai had succeeded to the power of Mali, that an ambitious Sherif of Fez, al-Mansur, conceived the aim of conquering the country and so gaining direct access to the gold-mines. In 1590 his army set out across the desert on this enterprise. This was the first time that firearms (some of them supplied by Elizabeth I of England) had been used in the interior of Africa, and Songhai bows and arrows gave no defence against them. The Songhai army was utterly defeated, and the Moors put a garrison in Timbuktu which they maintained until 1660. But they had no control away from the Niger valley.

To the east of them now was a congeries of small warring states, with Kanem as the furthest. Kanem has been called the first empire east of the Niger (Urvoy 1936: 321-3), though it was nowhere near the magnitude of Mali or Songhai. Its rulers spoke Kanuri, a different language from that of its Hausa neighbours to the west. The original centre of their kingdom was to the east of Lake Chad, with its capital at Njimi near the south-eastern end of the lake. Thence they extended their power northwards along the route across the Sahara, and also to the west of Lake Chad, in the country that was then, and still is, called Bornu. At the height of their first period of expansion they exacted tribute from the kingdoms of Kano and Katsina.

Royal princes were made governors of newly conquered territories, and it seems that as soon as there were no more worlds
to conquer, they began to fight among themselves for the succession. While they were at odds they were constantly raided
by the Bulala, their neighbours to the south-east, who eventually annexed Kanem (about 1380) and held it for more than
a century. But the ruler, Omar, took refuge with a large number of followers in Bornu, and his successors gradually restored
the kingdom. In the middle of the fifteenth century Kano and
Katsina again paid tribute to them. Kanem itself was reconquered in the reign of the great warrior Idris Aloma (1580–
1617). Under him the territory of Bornu reached an extent
which was maintained until the beginning of the nineteenth
century.

The last power to appear in Sudanese Africa before the
colonial period arose in a curious fashion. We begin to hear of
the Fulani, a people of nomad herdsmen, in the eighth century,
when they pastured their cattle in the Fouta Toro mountains
south of the Senegal river, among the Tekrur or Toucouleur.
Early in the eleventh century the Tekrur turned them out, and
from that time on there was a steady, gradual, uncoordinated
movement of Fulani eastward across the savannah region. With
them went marabouts—Muslim holy men—who taught and
proselytized in the different cities. Gradually more and more
Fulani gave up their nomadic life and settled in the towns, and
in many places they eventually overturned the rulers and set up
small Fulani states.

Of these movements of rebellion the last successful one was
what is known as the Fulani jihad led by Othman dan Fodio,
who in 1804 took control of Sokoto and thence gave his support
to the subversion of the other Habe kingdoms; the new rulers
accepted him as their suzerain. This latest African empire
covered Northern Nigeria as far south as the line of the Niger
and Benue, and for a few years it controlled Bornu; but Bornu
reasserted its independence and maintained it until the time
came for the country to be divided between Britain and
France, the greater part being included in Nigeria.

A later holy war was launched in 1878 from the hinterland of
Sierra Leone (as this part of the west coast had now become)

by Samory, 'the Mahdi of West Africa'; but although his conquests reached as far as the western part of Asante, he was
defeated by the French before he could establish an empire.

The Kingdoms of the Forest Area

The stimulus to political ambition in the forest area was the
seaborne trade which began with the appearance of the
Portuguese on the Guinea Coast in 1471, still, at that time,
seeking gold; and among the means to power were the weapons
which the European traders brought with them. The earliest of
these southern empires was that which had come by about 1680
to be known as Asante. Its nucleus was a number of Twi-
speaking migrant groups whom the British envoy to Kumase,
Bowdich, writing in 1819, called 'enterprising or discontented
families' (cited Wilks 1975: 110). Moving northwards from the
Adanse region, they had to fight for the control of the gold-
trading town of Tafo, and they combined under a leader of the
Oyoko lineage which became the dynasty of the Asantehenes,
as their kings were called. The first Asantehene Osei Tutu
launched a number of successful campaigns, and built a new
capital at Kumase a few miles from Tafo; at the same time
were founded the towns which gave their names to 'the five
great states' surrounding the capital, which Wilks has called
'metropolitan Asante'.

In 1701 Osei Tutu attacked and conquered Denkyira, which
up to then had treated its northern neighbours as vassals, and
thus opened the way to the coast and to sea-borne supplies of
fire-arms. By the mid-nineteenth century his successor had extended Asante control along the coast from the Komoe (now in
the Ivory Coast) to the Volta river, and had made the kings of
Gonja and Dagomba in the north his tributaries. With a thous-
and miles of coast-line and a population of three to five million,
Asante at its greatest covered an area of 125,000–200,000
square miles, and could challenge comparison with the savannah empires. But it never effectively controlled the southernmost Fante states, and in the nineteenth century the British
supported them against Asante power. A series of wars were
fought between Ashanti (as it was then officially called) and the
British, the last in 1900. At first the British sought influence

rather than direct control; they made, and tried to enforce by punitive action, agreements for the promotion of trade and missionary activity, they defended their Fante allies against the Asante, or, as the Asante would have put it, subverted their subjects, and they tried to persuade the Asantehene to give up the ritual execution of condemned criminals at his annual great festival. But when Chamberlain became colonial secretary he thought it essential to bring Asante under direct British control, and in 1896 its king surrendered without fighting to a British military force.

Further east, between the Grand-Popo and the Niger, were the rival kingdoms of Oyo, Dahomey, and Benin, whose legends give them a common origin. Such traditions have some significance in that we can see in historic times how members of a ruling dynasty, with their followers, have sometimes moved out from the original base and either attained complete autonomy or recognized different degrees of dependence on the kingdom from which they originated. As a means of expansion this was an alternative to military conquest by a centrally controlled army, and it is typical of many parts of Africa outside the region of the ancient Sudanese empires. Traditions often tell of the dispersal of the sons of an original founder after some quarrel about succession or inheritance. But what actually happened was not a once-for-all event but a repeated process.

The first significant event in the rise of Oyo that is recalled in legend is the king's refusal to pay tribute to a ruler in whose land he had settled (a story also told of Dahomey). By the fourteenth century Oyo had successfully established its independence of Nupe to the east and Borgu to the north; Borgu, with its official capital at Bussa on the Niger, enters history in its own right some time later, when it successfully resisted attack from Songhai.

The tradition of Benin is that its royal dynasty was founded by a prince given to its elders, at their request, by the ruler of Oyo. Benin was at the height of its power in the sixteenth century, when its authority extended along the coast beyond Lagos and in the north-west as far as the Ekiti area of the Yoruba. We do not know exactly when it began to decline. It lost its northernmost territories in the Fulani invasion in the early nineteenth century, while to the south those vassals who found the payment of tribute irksome could seek aid from European traders.

Oyo and the much smaller Dahomey to the south-west of it were rivals in the eighteenth century, each seeking to extend its control of the slave trade. Oyo seized territory from both Bornu and Nupe, and made tributary vassals of the Yoruba states through which the trade route ran to the coast, Egba, Egbado, and Ketu. Oyo conquered Allada, which had already been subjected to its cousin-kingdom Dahomey. At one time it demanded a share of the spoils taken in Dahomey's wars. But it never took from Dahomey the slave-trading port of Ardrah (now Porto-Novo).

The power of Oyo began to decline in the late eighteenth century, when its armies were defeated first by Borgu (1783) and then by Nupe (1791). An army leader rebelled against the king and set up an independent headquarters in Ilorin, and vassal Yoruba states began to reassert their independence. The Egba built a new capital in Abeokuta, which became the equal in importance of Oyo, and defeated the Dahomeyans after they had succeeded in rejecting Oyo's claim to tribute. Thus Oyo was already in disarray when the Fulani invasion which subdued the Hausa kingdoms reached Ilorin.

All through the nineteenth century there was fighting between different Yoruba states, a condition that the Yoruba historian Samuel Johnson calls 'civil war'. But if civil war consists in attempts by opposing armies to gain control of a unitary state, the term is not a good description of a 'war of each against all' in a vacuum of power. Many African kingdoms have been rent by civil wars between contenders for the throne, but the wars between the Yoruba city-states were analogous rather to those between Greek or Italian city-states.

With the weakening of Oyo, Dahomey became the most powerful state of the Slave Coast. Its king Ghezo refused tribute to Oyo and several times attacked Abeokuta, though never successfully. But he was able to march his troops through Ketu, from which it may be gathered that this state had become independent again; and to the west he extended his power over the hinterland of the present Togo so as to come into conflict with Asante. His son Glele dealt as an equal with British and French envoys, and died before the French decided to impose their authority by force.

The Atlantic Coast

When the first Portuguese explorer landed at the mouth of the Congo in 1482, he found himself in the kingdom of Kongo (after which the river came to be called). This had been founded in the fourteenth century, possibly by immigrants from the neighbourhood of Stanley Pool. When it confronted the Portuguese it extended about 100 miles along the coast from Cabinda southwards to the river Loje, and inland for some 200 miles; and peoples further south as far as the Cuanza—another 100 miles—would send tribute when the ruler, the *manicongo*, was able to enforce his demands upon them. Portugal regarded him as a king who was powerful enough to be treated as an ally. He for his part embraced Christianity, though not without backsliding, and his successor Affonso from 1506 sought to remodel his kingdom on Christian and Portuguese lines, and renamed his capital San Salvador. The Portuguese sent him missionaries and all kinds of craftsmen; his return was to grant them a monopoly of trade. Very early the principal item of trade came to be slaves, and not much later the Portuguese conceived the idea that the *manicongo*'s country contained vast mineral wealth, and began to press him to disclose its where-abouts and authorize them to exploit it. More and more Portuguese settled in the country, and although the official policy was to support the *manicongo* against his enemies, rivals in economic competition allied themselves with rebellious sub-jects. Yet the fiction of an independent ruler in alliance with the Portuguese was maintained right up to 1883. But the first Kongo kingdom was destroyed about 1570 by an invasion from the interior of the unidentified people whom contemporary writers called the 'Jaga'.

The kingdom of Angola grew up after the Portuguese presence had been established on the Atlantic coast. Around 1500 the chief of Ndongo, the southernmost vassal of the *man-icongo*, gave himself the title of *ngola*, and he and his successors extended their authority southwards until it covered the area between the Dande and Cuanza rivers. In 1556 he defeated the *manicongo* in battle, and having done so, invited the Portuguese to give him the same help that they had earlier given to the latter. This time there was no question of an alliance of independent rulers. The Portuguese wanted to maintain their own security against the invaders who had destroyed the *manicongo*, and they believed that somewhere in the *ngola*'s kingdom there were fabulously rich silver-mines. They decided in 1571 to make Angola a colony and sent out the first settlers in 1574. But they could not effectively conquer Angola without African allies.

The Interior of central Africa

In the interior of central Africa the first foreign traders in the late eighteenth century came into contact with kingdoms ruled by chiefs of Lunda origin, which together covered a very wide area. This has been called the Luba-Lunda empire, and it certainly had the feature typical of an empire, that a small ruling class with a common culture imposed its authority over a great number of different peoples. But it is not so easy to be certain that the whole area was centrally controlled from a single capital; it seems more likely that outlying princes made themselves independent and refused to pass on the tribute which they collected from their subjects, and then embarked on their own conquests, as others did in the Zande state to the north of the Congo.

The germ of the 'empire' is supposed to have been the arrival around 1500 in Luba country, between the Bushimai and Luapula rivers, left-bank tributaries of the Congo, of an immigrant hero Kongolo. He and his son Kalala welded a number of chiefdoms into a single unit. Kalala's son Cibinda Ilunga, according to tradition, married a Lunda princess in the country to the west of the Luba, and *their* son is remembered as the initiator of Luba expansion.

Later generations of princes, though they called themselves Lunda, gave Luba titles to their chiefs and preserved elements of Luba ritual; the political institutions by means of which, according to Vansina, they maintained their supremacy, were Luba. The expansion of this royal lineage was going on right up to the mid-nineteenth century, when Arab slavers arrived in the country, though by that time Lunda chiefs were fighting against one another as well as against the Arabs. A recent writer maintains that the 'Jaga hordes' who destroyed the Kongo kingdom and so terrified the Portuguese were in fact the westernmost offshoot of the Lunda, who finally settled at Kasanje in northern Angola. Many different peoples in Zambia and Malawi, as well as in Zaire, say that their chiefs are of Lunda origin. The largest of the Lunda kingdoms was the latest to be formed, that of Kazembe of the Luapula. It covered the Katanga Province of today's Zaire and much of the North-Eastern Province of Zambia, and was the dominant power in central Africa for a century after 1750.

Further south was the fabled empire of Monomotapa, the ruler in whose dominions the still undiscovered King Solomon's mines were believed to lie. The story was founded on the fact that gold dust in small quantities was traded with Arabs or Swahili from the coast who penetrated up the Sabi river, and seem to have established regular markets even before the coming of the Portuguese. Monomotapa is a praise-name which has been translated 'Master Pillager'; it was bestowed on Mutota, a Kalanga chief of the Rozwi lineage, in the course of his ten-year reign of conquest. The original centre of the Rozwi kingdom was west of the Sabi river in the present Rhodesia. In the fifteenth century Mutota invaded the lands on the right bank of the Zambezi in the northernmost part of its course, where it now flows through Rhodesia and Mozambique, and moved his capital there. His son Matope extended Rozwi conquests further, until they covered the whole area bounded by the Zambesi in the north, the Munyati in the west, and the Sabi in the south, with a strip 100–200 miles broad reaching to the Indian Ocean. In modern terms Rozwi chiefs now (about 1480) ruled the whole of Mashonaland, the northern part of Rhodesia. But within a few years of Matope's death the kingdom was divided among three successors who were already fighting one another before the Portuguese appeared, and Matope's descendants held only the northern area close to the Zambezi. However, it was the son of a later invader who signed over all the minerals in his domains to the British South Africa

Company, and whose domain was held by them to cover the whole of Rhodesia.

South-Eastern Africa

The most famous kingdom in the south-east of Africa, that of the Zulu, arose only in the nineteenth century. Its expansion was chronicled by near-eye-witnesses, traders who had established themselves on the coast under the protection of the Zulu king, were treated by him rather like vassal chiefs, and sometimes went with him on his campaigns. Its earlier history was written by a missionary, A. T. Bryant, who arrived in Africa in 1883, but although he was dealing with events much more recent than those that historians are now seeking to trace in other parts of Africa, the stories he was told were just as mythical, just as much concerned with the deeds of heroes, and he accepted them without any of the scepticism of the twentieth century. What we know is that around 1800 a number of petty chiefdoms which had been roughly equivalent in power began to be dominated by one man, Dingiswayo of the Mtethwa. South African historians disagree on what prompted his conquests. Professor Monica Wilson, arguing from the history of the Ngonde kingdom in Malawi, suggests that he wanted to monopolize trade with the Portuguese; and there is no reason to rely on a single analogy for the view that that has been a common motive for expansion by conquest, in Africa as elsewhere. Leonard Thompson, however, finds no evidence of any development of trade between Dingiswayo and the Portuguese (1969: 340). Gluckman (1963) offers another hypothesis, based on the recollections of the few castaways who were stranded on the coast around the turn of the eighteenth century. He envisages an initial stage of the kind that anthropologists have observed in many places, in which lineages would divide as their numbers increased, and when a dominant lineage so divided the seceding section would take their followers with them. A population recognizing a chief from a dominant lineage was, in Gluckman's terms, a tribe, and its numbers might be anything from 'a few hundred to some thousands'. Tribes raided one another's cattle but did not seek to conquer their neighbours or drive them off their land. About 1775, however, according to Gluckman's calculation, later migrants began to find that there was no longer unlimited space for new settlement, and the more successful fighters established permanent domination over their neighbours. Of these Dingiswayo's Mtethwa confederacy, which developed into the Zulu kingdom, was the most successful of all.

If we reject the hypothesis that Dingiswayo was interested in the control of trade, this seems the only plausible alternative. But Thompson (1969: 341) reminds us that we know far too little about man–land ratios to be able to identify a critical point at which one group *must* encroach on the territory of its neighbours.

The facts of the history of Zulu expansion, however, are reasonably clear. It was initiated at the end of the eighteenth century by Dingiswayo, the chief of the Mtethwa, whose homeland was in the lower reaches of the Mfolozi and Mhlatuzi rivers, in the northern part of today's Natal, which is still called Zululand. Dingiswayo organized the manpower of his chiefdom into a standing army, and increased its numbers by taking contingents from his conquered neighbours. When he died in 1818 he was the paramount in a kind of confederacy of chiefdoms reaching southwards to the Tugela river and inland for sixty or eighty miles. The Zulu at that time were a small tribe acknowledging the paramountcy of Dingiswayo. About 1816 the latter organized the assassination of the Zulu chief who had recently succeeded, and installed Shaka, the chief's illegitimate half-brother, in his place. When Dingiswayo died a few years later (some say through Shaka's treachery) Shaka made himself paramount over the Mtethwa and all the (subordinate) allies. Then he himself extended his conquests inland, to the Buffalo river in the west and the Pongola in the north. Thompson estimates the number of his soldiers at that time at about 40,000. In his further campaigns he did not seek to subject the peoples he defeated, but to drive them away and lay their country waste in the most literal sense, seizing their cattle and burning their crops. Within a few years he had devastated the land from the Tugela to the Mzimkulu and inland as far as the Drakensberg mountains (just the area of Natal apart from Zululand). Thompson interprets this strategy, peculiar to

Shaka among African conquerors, as a means of creating a 'buffer zone' without resources, which might be hard for migrant white men to penetrate. He did not attempt to attack the populations further south who he knew would be defended by the British.

Shaka was assassinated in 1828 by a conspiracy among his kin, and was succeeded by his half-brother Dingane, who continued the policy of offensive warfare, but not always victoriously. By this time the British government at the Cape had become interested in him and his country, and the existence of a depopulated area seemed to the British in Cape Town a reason for annexation rather than a deterrent. Discontented or fearful Zulu subjects were taking refuge with white men on the coast as elsewhere they might have with rival African chiefs, and this led to clashes between Dingane and the white men. The first parties of Voortrekkers began in 1837 to cross the Drakensberg and move southwards towards the sea, travelling in wagons that could be formed into a square for defence, armed with muskets and riding on horses, those two implements of war that turned the scale in so many African battles. For a few months Dingane tried to reach some kind of accommodation with them; then he decided that the presence of any white community was a danger. His armies attacked and almost annihilated the easternmost Voortrekker encampment and razed Port Natal to the ground. But in December 1838 a new Voortrekker commando, this time bringing with them a cannon, utterly destroyed a Zulu army at the river which has ever since been known as Blood River. There were more Zulu wars after the British annexed Natal, but by that time it was the British and not the Zulu who dominated south-eastern Africa.

From about 1822 refugees from the wars of Dingiswayo and Shaka began to roam the high veld country in bands, spreading the devastation further and further, like the ripples on a pool. Historians of South Africa call them 'hordes', a word that evokes other examples of barbarian irruption into ordered communities. They plundered what and where they could, fought with one another, and the more successful gathered followers from the peoples they overran or from other wanderers.

Out of these heterogeneously composed warring bands there eventually arose two kingdoms and a conquering army which have had significance in African history; one of the kingdoms is an independent state today. These were the Ndebele under Mzilikazi, the Ngoni under Zwangendaba, and the kingdom of the southern Sotho under Moshweshwe. The last-named founded the state that is now called Lesotho from a base on a flat-topped hill in the lower Caledon valley. Here there came for refuge groups of people from many of the Sotho tribes which had been dispersed by marauders, and the amalgam came to be known as *the* Sotho (Basuto in English writings).

Mzilikazi was a Nguni subject of Shaka, who preferred to assert his independence and so be able to keep his war booty to himself, but then had to move out of reach of Shaka's vengeance. He too attracted followers by his success in war, and in ten years he increased his force of fighting men from 200 or 300 to some 5,000. By 1832 he had come to dominate the high veld, and had outposts as far away as the Limpopo, Crocodile, Vaal, and Molopo rivers, so he covered an area of about 30,000 square miles. Within this kingdom Nguni were rulers, Sotho subjects. In 1838 he crossed the Limpopo to escape the encroachments of the Voortrekkers, and built his capital at Bulawayo. Today's Matabeleland is the southern part of Rhodesia.

Zwangendaba was a subordinate chief of the Ndande, the kingdom to the north of the Mtethwa which was conquered by Shaka in 1819. He escaped north-eastwards towards Delagoa Bay, and made his way to the north, increasing the number of his forces partly by taking captives from the countries through which he passed, and partly, like Moshweshwe, by attracting other refugees who sought his protection. Barnes (1954: 13) guesses that the original seceders numbered about 1,000. They moved up the Limpopo from Delagoa Bay, entered the Shona country where they destroyed what was left of the Rozwi kingdoms, and went on, crossing the Zambezi, in 1835. Of course we do not know how often they may have paused on their journey, but it is recorded that their first halt north of the Zambezi lasted for only four years. In 1842 they reached the country of the Fipa west of Lake Rukwa, and there

Zwangendaba died. His successors separated in the manner with which we have become familiar. Two small groups went northwards, one to the east and one to the west of Lake Tanganyika. A little later two more broke off from the main body and went southwards, one to the east and the other to the west of Lake Malawi. The leadership of the main body was contested between two sons of Zwangendaba, Mpezeni, the eldest, and Mombera, who was more popular. Mpezeni's followers went south-westwards into the present Zambia, moving on until about 1856 the Bemba succeeded in resisting them. They later returned across the Luangwa river and finally settled in the neighbourhood of the present Fort Jameson, whence they sent out bands of warriors to raid the peoples around them. Mombera's, who formed the main body, settled in the present Mzimba District of Malawi, and another branch, Gomani's, in the area which is now divided between the Dedza District of Malawi and Mozambique.

Margaret Read (1956: 3–4) classified the Nyasaland Ngoni into the northern kingdom with three, and the central with four, 'separated states'. Thus we cannot speak of an Ngoni empire, or even of large Ngoni kingdoms. Their interest lies in the fact that we can trace their history in more detail than that of earlier migrants, and can see several remarkable features in it. The speed with which Ngoni bands sometimes moved on—a stay of only a few years at one base and then a long journey—is striking; it is quite different from the gradual trickle of small numbers that Vansina convincingly sees as characteristic of most African migrations. The existence of an organization that has all the essentials of a state, except the territorial base that has usually been regarded as the most essential, is again of great interest. Ngoni kingdoms, small as they are, must figure in any discussion of modes of organization. It is also worth noting that the unidentified 'Jaga' who attacked the Portuguese and their African allies of the Kongo kingdom were described in contemporary accounts in terms that might well fit the Ngoni. Vansina (1966: 57) draws the comparison: 'They lived permanently on a war footing in fortified camps. They would kill their babies [not recorded of Ngoni] so as not to be hindered by them in their march, but they adopted youngsters of both sexes from the areas they overran and incorporated them into their camps. Vast numbers of people could thus be aggregated quite quickly.' He quotes from Andrew Battell, the English sailor who lived for two years in a Jaga band, the statement that out of 16,000 people in the camp only fourteen or fifteen were Jaga by origin. Jaga kingdoms—if we can so call them—were dispersed, like those of the Ngoni, not, as in so many cases, contiguous with their parent states.

Between the Great Lakes

The interior of East Africa was not visited by literate travellers until the nineteenth century, and if there were early empires there, their existence can be known only by asking whether archaeological remains give support to oral traditions of the distant past. Such traditions tell of a great kingdom of Kitara, ruled by a dynasty of light-skinned supermen, the Cwezi; they do not agree as to exactly where it was. The name is claimed today by the people of Bunyoro, which is now a single administrative district of Uganda. Bunyoro was the dominant power in the Interlacustrine region in the early nineteenth century, but not all writers agree that it was the centre of the earlier Kitara. In Mubende district, the southern part of Bunyoro, which was included in Buganda under British administration, there is a line of great earthworks which has always been associated with the Cwezi; whoever organized their construction was in a position to mobilize considerable manpower. Radiocarbon tests ascribe the earthworks to the period 1350–1500. The historian Roland Oliver interprets them as a defence against invasion from the north, and concludes that the centre of Kitara was in Ankole, south of Bunyoro, that its effective power was in the south, and that the Cwezi ruled Bunyoro for only about fifty years.

Ankole tradition makes them masters of the present Bunyoro, Toro, Ankole, Karagwe (in Tanzania), and at least the northern part of Rwanda. But Rwanda has no tradition of subjection to Kitara. The Nyoro say that after only two reigns the Cwezi miraculously disappeared; Oliver considers that this story masks their defeat in war and retreat to the south from their northern outpost.

There is no doubt that their successors, the Bito, based their 'empire' on Bunyoro. Speke, in the map which he published in 1862, shows Bunyoro as 'the ancient kingdom of Kitara'. 'At its zenith', says Beattie (1971: 28), 'it is said to have extended over most of present-day Uganda, and beyond it into Tanzania, the Congo and the Sudan.' To the north of Bunyoro, the Acoli and Alur have traditions that their chiefs had to be confirmed in office by the king of Bunyoro, and the Alur also claimed the Bito kings as their kinsmen. One could take such statements as evidence of effective suzerainty of the kind exercised by the Sultan of Sokoto over the other Fulani emirs in Nigeria, or of a ritual supremacy of the kind exercised by Oyo over the Yoruba states, or of an outward dispersion of members of a ruling class of the kind described among the Lunda.

This last interpretation seems the most probable, since the traditions say that Rukidi, the first Bito king of Bunyoro, appointed his kinsmen to rule provinces, and that they or their descendants threw off his authority and made themselves independent. In the reign of Rukidi himself, the story goes, his twin brother whom he had made governor of Buganda repudiated his allegiance. (The Ganda reject this version of 'history' and say that their royal dynasty was much older than the Bito.) Later Busoga (east of Buganda), Ankole and Karagwe seceded in the same way (and also Rwanda if it ever had a Bito chief). Many wars were fought against Buganda and some against Ankole.

At the time of Speke's visit (1862) the King of Bunyoro was suzerain over a great part of Buganda, much of Toro and Ankole, and of Karagwe to the south of them. As late as 1892 Gessi Pasha referred to a powerful Acoli chief in the north who 'gave to Kaba Rega all the ivory he collected'. It is possible that the balance had begun to tilt in favour of Buganda when that country was acquiring guns through trade with the Arabs, but the ultimate supremacy of Buganda was a matter of its alliance with Britain.

To the south of Ankole lies Rwanda, a kingdom the history of which has been microscopically studied by Belgian scholars through its rich corpus of traditions. The reconstructed history of Rwanda is of extreme interest for the understanding of processes of state-building, but the kingdom as such was never an African great power.

This brief survey is intended to provide a few fixed points in time and space for readers who may be new to the vastness and variety of the African continent and its societies. It mentions a number of kingdoms that will not be discussed again, and does not mention some that will be considered in detail. The reason is that an anthropologist's choice of an area for study does not necessarily lead him to a people who have played a great part in recorded history or to rulers whose ancestors have conquered empires. The Azande, the Lozi, the Swazi, to give some examples, have been admirably documented by anthropologists who combined an interest in the past with the techniques of participant observation, but they do not occupy many of the pages in histories of Africa. It is to the peoples whose political structure has been thoroughly studied, so that the outlines which are all that tradition gives us are filled in from direct acquaintance with what is left today of royal people, that we must look in seeking to identify the characteristics of African kingdoms.

CHAPTER II

THE BUILDING UP OF KINGDOMS

ONE theory of the rise of African kingdoms is that the notion of kingship somehow spread from a single source in Egypt. It appears from archaeological evidence that the technique of iron-working originated in Meroe on the Nile and was gradually diffused throughout the continent. But it is hard to picture kingship as a technique which somebody has brought with him to practise in a new place. The argument rests largely on similarities in the ritual of kingship in widely separated places; it presupposes behind these rituals an idea of 'divine kingship' the precise nature of which is taken for granted. All peoples surround royal office with ritual, and we can find instances far from Africa in which miraculous powers are attributed to kings. The word 'divine' seems to have been taken over from *The Golden Bough* without much thought about what corresponds to it in the view of the peoples who are alleged to view their kings as divine. Modern structuralists might well ascribe the similarities in royal rituals to those unconscious mental structures that constrain all human thought. If one is concerned with the secular aspects of kingship, which rituals or ideas about divinity cannot replace but at best underpin, one has to envisage gradual processes of securing and consolidating power. Of course there is a stage, as kingdoms grow into empires, when the latest conquest is fitted into an existing system, but this is not and cannot be how kingships originated. What we want to know is how individuals were able to make themselves kings, how they manoeuvred and improvised in order to maintain and improve their positions; the later stages can sometimes be followed from recorded history.

In every African kingdom a tradition is preserved of the origin of the ruling dynasty. This tradition asserts the claim of a single descent line to sole right to rule, and in that respect is

what Malinowski called a 'mythical charter', an account of the
past that serves to justify the present. Sometimes, as in the case
of the Chwezi stories, the original rulers are indeed endowed
with miraculous powers. Sometimes such first kings are supposed to have brought 'civilization' to people who were living
like animals, hunting for their food, knowing nothing of cattle,
fire or any of the useful arts. An example is the Rwanda myth
of Kigwa, who fell from heaven and in that sense could be
considered divine (Vansina 1962: 43). The Nyakyusa story of
the coming of Lwembe, the hero-ancestor of their kings and
chiefs says, in one version, that at his arrival they were already
cultivators, but, knowing no fire, they ate their food raw.
Lwembe also brought them iron, which of course would have
been no use to a people without fire (Wilson 1959: 3, 13). But
for the majority of the Nyakyusa, the heroes brought grain food
with them too.

These stories reflect the tellers' idea that it is 'uncivilized' to
be without a ruler. Others conceal a break in dynastic continuity by forging, we might say, a link of indirect kinship between the displaced lineage and its successors. Where the
political function of a tradition is so obvious there is reason to
suspect its factual truth.

But there are other traditions that are so to speak neutral.
There is not much political capital to be made by claiming
descent from an immigrant without claiming extraordinary
powers for him; yet a number of traditions lead back to a man
who headed an immigrant group, and after becoming dissatisfied with a situation of dependence, rebelled and seized
political power. It is after this initial act that the period of
conquests, often attested by evidence from other sources,
begins.

It is clear that there must have been a time when there were
no kingdoms in Africa, or indeed anywhere in the world. In the
beginning all men were hunters, moving about in small bands.
When they learned to domesticate plants and animals they
formed larger autonomous groups within populations recognizing in common the elementary norms of respect for life and
property. Among nomad pastoralists such groups are usually
based on patrilineal descent; settled cultivators too may be

organized in this way. All these different types of society still exist for our observation, but what is harder to see is the slow process by which one lineage establishes domination over the rest and comes to be regarded as the one with unquestioned right to fill the office of chief or king. Indeed it had already become impossible to follow such a process by the time that anthropologists had realized the importance of close first-hand observation, since European rule everywhere either destroyed or distorted the political systems of independent Africa. In the corpus of African ethnography there are only one or two examples which may bear on this question.

One of these is Philip Mayer's (1949) study of the Gusii in western Kenya, a people divided into seven tribes, and these again into clans, each of them autonomous in its own territory. In every tribe except one, there was a lineage of 'owners of the land' and others attached to it by affinal or matrilateral ties, but there was no significant difference of status between them, and all were regarded as ultimately akin. The seventh tribe consisted of the people of Getutu. For whatever reason, Getutu was a place of refuge for people driven from their homes by raiding Masai or Kipsigis, the pastoral neighbours of the Gusii. These exiles would attach themselves to individuals who would give them protection and cattle to marry with; accordingly they were called 'bought people', and sometimes one would repay the cattle and go home. But those who stayed, and their descendants, were never 'adopted' as were immigrants to the other six tribes; they were political subjects of the 'owning' lineage, Nyakundi. Whereas among the other six tribes claims for debts or compensation were matters to be dealt with by the lineage representatives of the parties, in Getutu the different Nyakundi lineages acted on behalf of their 'bought people' in such disputes, and elders of one Nyakundi lineage would be recognized throughout the tribe.

This does not get us very far, particularly as Nyakundi, though in a sense jointly rulers, were not a minority but over half the population of Getutu, with their dependants a fringe of miscellaneous immigrants. What is perhaps more significant in the light of what we have learned about the origin of some kingdoms is a negative point: the apprehension of all Gusii that a lineage of strangers might oust the rightful owners of the land. 'If a sister's child is buried at our place', they say, 'his house will become many and ours will die out' (Mayer 1949: 28). In other words, be careful not to let him forget his stranger origin. The proverb may well spring from fear rather than experience; but when one reflects that the immigrant lineages of the historical traditions must have intermarried with their hosts—they could not otherwise have lived with them in amity—one can only comment that, as they say, 'There's something in it'.

Evans-Pritchard (1940: 185–9) offers another conjecture as to the process by which a central authority might be created in a population divided into autonomous and often mutually hostile segments. In the southern Sudan at the time of the Mahdist revolt against Egyptian rule, which was also a movement of Arab aggression against the Nilotic peoples, prophets arose among the Nuer who called on them to unite against their external enemies. The prophet who gained the most widespread influence, Ngundeng, appeared later, in 1906, as an opponent of British authority. He had been a 'leopard-skin chief', to use the name applied to such ritual experts by British administrators, or an 'earth-priest' as Evans-Pritchard came to call them later. Thus he belonged to a lineage believed to have the monopoly of a certain kind of ritual power. His fame spread all through the eastern half of Nuer country, and a great pyramid, made of ashes and other debris from cattle camps, some sixty feet high and surrounded by a ring of ivory tusks, was built by his followers in his honour and that of the sky-god by whom he was supposed to be possessed. If this was an organized enterprise, we must assume that Ngundeng had acquired considerable powers of command. If, on the other hand, the pyramid was just added to by the individual contributions of people who came to pay their respects to the prophet, as, on a smaller scale, passers-by add pebbles to a cairn, it is not evidence of effective political authority. There is no doubt that Ngundeng's fame spread far and wide, but when we ask what forces he could muster for the rebellion that he preached, the answer is that the largest on record consisted of 300 men.

But the belief that ritual powers are hereditary, and so are the monopoly of particular lineages, is much older than kingship. Should we then expect the founders of kingdoms to have been ritual experts, or members of such specially endowed lineages? The myths rarely ascribe any such status to them, although the Nyakyusa Lwembe is said to have possessed the special medicines of chiefship. But kingdoms once founded are sometimes able to extend their rule over kingless peoples because the latter believe the ritual power of kingship to be something that they cannot generate from among themselves. Yet the first example that I have to offer does not illustrate such a situation.

The Rise of Rwanda

The richest oral tradition to have been examined by a historian is that of Rwanda, and the most detailed exercise in disentangling history from myth is the work that has been done on this corpus of records (committed to writing in recent years) by Jan Vansina (1962). He has reconstructed a picture of the country that is now Rwanda, as it seems likely to have been at the time when Nilotic herdsmen of the people who later became known as the Tutsi began to enter it. At that time the Hutu cultivators were organized partly in tribes of autonomous lineages and partly in tiny chiefdoms with hereditary rulers, a description that parallels what a contemporary anthropologist, Aidan Southall, observed among the Alur and their neighbours on the Nile–Congo divide just north of Rwanda. Where the Hutu recognized chiefs, the latter were held to have ritual powers; they controlled the weather, causing rain to fall at the right time and not in excessive quantities, and they combated disasters such as locust invasion. Such powers were ascribed to the Alur chiefs too, and the neighbouring acephalous peoples, believing that they were an inseparable element in the quality of chiefliness, sought the sons of Alur chiefs to rule over them rather than looking to leaders among themselves.

Again we cannot learn how a special ritual power came to be claimed in the first place: Vansina simply says that the heads of certain lineages came to be regarded as chiefs. They had little secular authority, and they could not prevent the waging of blood-feuds among their subjects. These chiefdoms had certain

ritual features that later characterized the kingdom of Rwanda;
the sacred symbol of rule was a drum, and the priests who were
responsible for royal burials were called *abiru*, a name that was
taken for similar people in the embryonic Tutsi kingdoms, and
later for Rwanda.

Into this country came the immigrant herdsmen from the
north. Some of them made no attempt to dominate particular
areas, but moved to and fro with their cattle as their descendants do to this day. But the others became the pastoral ruling
class that was maintained in authority first by the Germans and
then by the Belgians. As Vansina reconstructs the picture,
bands of herdsmen arrived together, recognizing one man's
leadership in the choice of route and of pastures. In matters of
internal authority the heads of descent-groups and their successors remained largely independent, and it would seem that
each group kept to its own grazing lands, since otherwise there
could have been no analogy between lineage heads and territorial chiefs. There early existed some kind of patronage
system whereby men with favours to offer, notably gifts or loans
of cattle, could gather a following of dependants who would
serve them and support them in a fight. The one who came to
be a king must have been the most successful of these. In the
central area, the nucleus of today's Rwanda, the herdsmen
settled cheek by jowl with Hutu populations, and seem to have
achieved domination over them by offering individual protection and the use of cattle in return for labour or tribute in grain
or beer—the *ubuhake* relationship for which Rwanda is famous.
Vansina states definitely that in these early days there was little
ritual attached to kingship.

At the time when the curtain rises on Rwanda's story, such
kings had begun to appoint their own brothers and sons as rulers
over divisions of the country in the place of lineage heads. This
policy strengthened a royal lineage in relation to the rest, but it
opened the way to secession for those who were far enough
from the centre of power, and had enough followers of their
own, to make themselves independent. Thus the germ of the
historical Rwanda was a chiefdom of Bugesera, a kingdom
founded by secession from Gisaka, itself a seceder from Mubari,
which the traditions say was the first kingdom to be founded.

All these places were on the eastern and south-eastern borders of the present Rwanda.

Two brothers, Mukobanya and Mutabazi, in the early sixteenth century, finally detached Rwanda from Bugesera and set about extending its power over neighbouring petty Tutsi kingdoms. They conquered Bumbogo and Rukoma, where the ruling lineages claimed ritual powers similar to those described as belonging to Hutu chiefs, and called themselves *abiru*. Mukobanya attached these lineages to his court, as guardians of the royal insignia and priests who carried out rituals in secret, the mystery of which enhanced the prestige both of the king and of the *abiru* themselves. Vansina asserts that the notion of the ritual responsibility of the king for the welfare of the country arose only after the incorporation of the *abiru*. They exercised secular as well as ritual power, since they continued to control their former kingdoms, now as fiefs from the king. Later kings created new *abiru* to reward favoured subjects, making them keepers of newly devised ritual objects, or in some other way giving each his special function along with their combined duty of preserving the ritual secrets and having the rites performed when it was time for them. The association of the individual person of the king with the welfare of the whole country came eventually to create an ideology of national unity which, though it could not prevent wars between contenders for the throne, did discourage ideas of secession among Tutsi.

But secular power cannot rest on ritual alone. Indeed it is not made effective at all without the delegation of authority to secular officials in charge of divisions of the kingdom; this is a necessary limitation on central power, and kings who wish to remain paramount must somehow counteract it. As long as territorial authorities recruit their own armies, rebellion is too easy; what the Rwanda kings tried to do—mainly, of course, in the interests of military efficiency—was to centralize the army.

The earliest fighting forces were bands attached to any man who could attract a following by his success in raiding cattle. Mutabazi was able to forbid the recruiting of warriors by chiefs who had not his permission. He and his successors soon after they came to the throne called on leading Tutsi to send their sons to court, where they were trained in the use of weapons and in the bearing appropriate to an aristocrat. About 200 young men were recruited at a time, and in a long reign new bands were formed at intervals. But these were a royal body-guard rather than a national army; they must often have had to fight for the king against his over-mighty subjects.

The centralization of all fighting forces seems to have begun in the late eighteenth century. According to a recent inter-pretation of some lineage traditions (Rwamukumba and Mudandagizi 1974) this was the time when the Tutsi began to clear the forests and claim hereditary rights to the pastures that they had created, instead of roaming at large through the country. By this time the king was strong enough to assert his authority to appoint the chiefs of new armies, though once appointed they expected to pass on the office to their sons. The king assigned to each army its pastures on the frontiers of the country, and required the warriors to live in camps at strategic points; this may have been a means of controlling recently conquered populations as well as of defence. The army chief was now made the authority over all the inhabitants of his area, not only the warriors.

The king himself had no army, and therefore had to find other means of securing his supremacy. Both to protect them-selves against the army chiefs and to consolidate Rwanda's hold over conquered territories, later kings built subsidiary capitals in different parts of the country, in each of which they would establish a queen and a retinue, with an official to see to the provisioning of the capital from the resources of the country around it. Eventually the whole of Rwanda came to be divided into districts—much smaller areas than the regimental provin-ces—under civilian chiefs who had no armies at their disposal. Only then, says Vansina (1962: 71), could the king really be called supreme. A yet further development was the division of district authorities into 'land chiefs' and 'cattle chiefs' respons-ible for tribute in grain and beer, and cattle, respectively. Rivalry between these paired officials for royal favour made them jealous keepers of each other's conscience, always ready to detect and report misdemeanours and quite unable to com-bine against superior authority.

Rwabugiri, who reigned from 1860 to 1895, had made himself powerful enough to disregard lineage claims to hereditary office, even those of divisions of the royal clan, and appoint his own creatures to all positions of authority. He freely dismissed chiefs from office and had them put to death, and even disregarded and humiliated the *abiru*. He himself was eventually assassinated, but his successors followed his example, and both German and Belgian administrations supported this version of royal power.

Such highly centralized control, however, was fully effective only in the oldest parts of the kingdom, where there was the largest Tutsi population and the Hutu had accepted Tutsi rule for centuries. In the areas conquered in the late eighteenth and nineteenth centuries the position was different. There, although no rival ruler was tolerated, both the nature and the effectiveness of administrative arrangements varied widely from one region to another. In some places an army chief was in charge of the collection of tribute from newly acquired subjects, in others a trusted local Hutu chief; occasionally such an official might be one of those Tutsi who, in the outlying areas, had lived side by side with the Hutu but not intermingled with them as in the centre of the kingdom.

The effectiveness of control depended very largely on the proportion of Tutsi in a given district, whether these were new colonizers or had been there before the Rwanda conquest. In many cases Hutu refused to pay tribute, and punitive expeditions were sent against them. This might be followed by the gradual substitution of the king's men for local chiefs at all levels of authority. Many of the revolts in the history of Rwanda, including some in the present century, were led by the representatives of lineages thus displaced. But until the final bloodbaths of 1959 and later years, we do not learn of rebellions against Tutsi domination in the central region where the *ubuhake* system of clientship—some call it serfdom—was most firmly established.

It is only from Rwanda that we hear of a deliberately created ritual relation between descent groups and the king. Writers on other Interlacustrine kingdoms (e.g. Fallers 1964) take this as something that has 'always' existed, and it is doubtless futile to ask whether a conqueror rewarded his followers with ritual offices as soon as his position was assured, or whether they were created in some other circumstances. In both the Ganda and Nyoro states certain clans had the right and duty of providing keepers of different objects of the royal regalia, of performing certain parts of the installation and later 'refresher' rituals of the king, and of undertaking the secular responsibility of supplying the palace with essential foodstuffs and objects of craftsmanship such as pots. In Buganda the senior of these were chiefs controlling large areas of land (*masaza* or counties), and up to the time of British overrule the three most important of these offices were effectively claimed by heads of clans. The rest came more and more to depend on the king's pleasure, but in the case of the three major chiefs the assertion of the king's supremacy had to be made in a round-about manner, by controlling the appointment of their subordinates. It was also possible to weaken the power of a clan head or any other chief without actually demoting or dismissing him, by carving out sections of his domain and allocating them to a queen or prince, or a favoured warrior or palace servant.

Buganda developed a national army only late in the nineteenth century. When guns were introduced into the country by Arab traders, Mutesa I created a new chiefship with the title Mujasi, which is derived from the Swahili word for 'brave'. Mujasi was responsible for the guns kept at the palace; he had scattered estates all over the country, unlike other chiefs, each of whom controlled a single block of land, large or small, and in each of these he raised a band of men who had already proved to be good fighters, and who were now available when summoned, unlike the earlier warriors who were recruited ad hoc by their territorial chiefs (Southwold n.d. [1961]: 14). But Mutesa did not attempt to control the acquisition of guns by other chiefs. His successor Mwanga created a palace bodyguard from young men who already had guns; some had received these from local chiefs and then left their service. This measure reduced the power of the chiefs versus the king, but it turned against him when the soldiers rebelled and the territorial chiefs were unable or unwilling to come to his aid.

The Story of Dahomey

The legends of a hero who marries a king's daughter and begets the founder of the current dynasty are certainly intended to legitimize the descendants of someone who may have been a usurper. It is not very likely that the fabled hero arrived alone in his new country. Vansina's reconstruction of the Rwanda story gives us the picture of a number of descent groups migrating into sparsely populated land or displacing the inhabitants, but not at first imposing themselves as rulers. The west African counterpart to Rwanda is Dahomey, in the sense that there too there were guardians of the royal traditions, whose duty it was to preserve them by memorizing them, and to recite them on prescribed occasions. Unlike the *abiru*, these bards were descendants of the kings whose reigns they celebrated.

In the Dahomeyan tradition it is a leopard and not a hero who marries the princess and founds a new dynasty, the Agassuvi. The actual story as it is envisaged by Newbury is what must have been typical of many of the later-founded African kingdoms. The migrants from Allada, the original home, were 'roving bands of raiders under war-chiefs who acquired land rights by the generosity of their neighbours or by force' (Newbury 1961: 10). One of these war-chiefs 'staked out a *de facto* claim to paramountcy by his qualities of leadership in the struggle of the Agassuvi for new land and water rights'; on this interpretation he had no hereditary claim at that stage. The immigrants ingratiated themselves with their hosts by making them presents, but as more and more people from Allada followed them, the local chief began to be concerned about their power, and eventually he sent his messengers to root up their crops. At this they rebelled and killed him, no doubt with the support of those of his subjects whom they had won over. Argyle (1966: 8) injects a sense of proportion into the story by reminding us that at the death of Dako, the rebel leader's successor, the Agassuvi 'were in possession of an area of about five miles' radius from the point where they had first settled'. These small conquests took them about twenty-five years.

Dako's successor, Wegbadja, collected a tax from his subjects to buy guns from the coast, and he is said to have abolished the right of private vengeance for homicide and required all capital cases to be brought to him. This last is everywhere a criterion of effective central rule, though sometimes, as in Buganda, the royal power is asserted merely by the requirement that persons seeking vengeance must have royal authorization. We do not often find the insistence on the royal monopoly of capital punishment ascribed to a particular ruler. It is of course a part of the assertion of the primacy of royal power over lineage autonomy.

The Dahomeyan kings had to be wary, like all hereditary rulers, of competition from their own kin. Tradition holds that at no time was any member of the royal clan appointed to a position of authority; thus an unusually large number of people were excluded, and Dahomey appears as the polar opposite of the south-eastern Bantu kingdoms in which all territorial offices were held by royals. At the same time, the commoner officials in Dahomey never established a claim to pass on their office to their sons.

In this respect Dahomey contrasted sharply with the southern cousin-kingdoms of Allada and Whydah, where the Agassuvi left a considerable measure of autonomy to the autochthonous lineages among whom they settled. The twenty-six provinces of Whydah—none a very large area—were subject to hereditary governors, doubtless the heads of such lineages, who were able independently to collect tolls on trade caravans passing through their land. As the state of affairs was seen by an eighteenth-century traveller (Labat, 1730: 98), the immigrant kings were still regarded as intruders to such an extent that they were afraid to confront any of the lineage heads for fear of provoking a general rebellion.

Another contrast was in military organization. Although there does not seem to have been a standing army comparable with those of the Zulu and of Rwanda, the fighting force of Dahomey did not consist, as it did in Allada, and until a quite late date in Buganda, simply of bands led by their territorial chiefs. It was recruited territorially, but the soldiers were then allotted to a right and left wing which were not territorially based. The commanders of the right and left wings were the two chief ministers, whose office was hereditary.

Some Other Kingdoms

The founding of the Basuto nation is a matter of historical record; it grew up by the accretion of tribes or sections of tribes, or fleeing individuals, displaced from their homes by the devastations of Shaka, in the period of ten years from 1822. But the events that are recounted—raiding for cattle, migrations, the making and breaking of alliances, offers and repudiations of allegiance—are just what must have been typical of the anarchic conditions in which earlier kingdoms were created. According to the old men whose memories were recorded by the missionary Ellenberger, Moshweshwe had had from his youth the ambition to be a great chief; but although he early demonstrated his prowess in successful raids, it was by offering protection to those who sought it that he built up his power. At first these refugees were victims of the roaming hordes who, driven out by Shaka, drove others before them. Later there were added to these Africans turned off their land by migrant Boers. Geography helped Moshweshwe; after moving once or twice with a few thousand followers, he settled on a flat-topped mesa, Thaba Bosiu, that was almost inaccessible. He knew when to make alliances with other chiefs of small groups and when to buy off powerful enemies by paying tribute. As the number of his subjects increased, he had to be able to distribute the largess in cattle that they expected, and for this purpose he raided his neighbours. But he was constantly harassed by attacks on his own cattle, and on the people who lived at the foot of the hill and took refuge in the chief's place when the enemy approached. His principal enemy was Matiwane, one of the chiefs whom Shaka dispossessed, and at one time he sought a counterpoise to Matiwane by offering allegiance to Shaka. But eventually, in 1827, he finally defeated Matiwane without foreign aid. Then he had to face invasion from the Griquas who came from the Cape Colony with horses and guns. He set about arming his own men, getting the fire-arms by barter, by capture, by sending young men to work in the Cape Colony and bring guns back.

He consolidated his control over his heterogeneous subjects in part by appointing his brothers and sons as headmen of villages of miscellaneous immigrants, but also by recognizing the chiefs who came with bands of followers as his subordinate authorities. By 1843 he had come to be recognized by the British as a stable element in a still disturbed situation, and he was made responsible for keeping order among his people and handing over fugitive offenders from the Cape, and paid a small salary. He was now said to be the ruler of all the land between the Orange and Caledon rivers. Successive delineations finally left him in possession of only two-thirds of the arable land that he claimed. Nevertheless the Basuto kingdom exists to this day (1977) with the name of Lesotho.

Kings whose ritual power is not taken for granted by their new subjects may take various courses. The Rwanda capture of the *abiru*, though a rare event, is not unique. The much less powerful Manganja chiefs of the Shire basin in Malawi seem to have taken over and gradually transformed through the centuries the cult of a hero called Mbona, whose shrines they found when they entered the country. The typical policy in West Africa was to form an alliance with the existing ritual leaders, the 'owners of the land' as such men are called in different languages over a wide area. Here there was no question of taking over ritual power; the political conquerors were dependent in the ritual sphere on the men who alone could communicate with the spirits of the earth, ensure the welfare of the inhabitants and make the necessary atonement if some disaster struck them. Jacques Lombard tells us what happened when Bariba immigrants from the east established their control over Borgu, in the north-east of the present Dahomey. The 'owners of the land' asserted the right to preside over the installation and funeral ceremonies of the new chiefs, the moments, as Lombard points out (1965: 183), when political stability is most precarious. An 'owner of the land' was always a member of the king's council, sometimes its most important member; he took the king's place if he was away at war, and during the period of seclusion before his enthronement. These are cases among many where the king makes no claim to be 'divine'.

But something more needs to be said about the ritual power that is ascribed to many kings. We say that ritual is symbolic, and so it is. But the use of the word tends to reinforce the spontaneous feeling of sceptics and positivists that it is somehow not 'real'. The observer is satisfied that its significance is expressive and not instrumental, but those who believe in its efficacy do hold it to be in some way instrumental; and this provides a real support for political power. The subject of a chief whose anger is held to prevent the rain from falling *really* thinks twice before challenging his claims, and this enhances the chief's *real*, secular power. All chiefs have a claim to a share in precious objects found on their domains, and it is from this that they have been able to acquire that monopoly of foreign trade which in turn makes their subjects dependent on them for valued goods. At the outset they must have relied more on the belief in ritual punishment for sacrilege than in their ability directly to punish those who did not bring them the tribute due. Godfrey Wilson (1939) showed for the tiny kingdom of Ngonde, with its area of 3,000 square miles and population of 40,000, at the head of Lake Malawi, the operation of factors that could be found at work in larger and more famous ones. The starting point here was the king's claim to one tusk of any elephant killed within his domain. This is a very common type of royal prerogative. It may be a claim to the hide of large game animals such as leopards; the petty chiefs of the Banyang in the east of Nigeria claim the whole carcass of a leopard killed in a hunt, and failure to present it is a declaration of independence (Ruel 1969). Everyone has heard that a Nuer earth-priest has the right to wear a leopard-skin over his shoulders. In many different contexts one can see the symbolic association between the power of fierce animals and ritual power, but the real political effect of ritual power is not so often emphasized.

The traditions of Ngonde tell how it has 'always' traded ivory for iron goods, which might have come from other African peoples, and cloths and 'white crockery', which could only have come from overseas. It was believed that if any hunter tried to cheat the Kyungu of his ivory he would be punished by the wrath of the royal ancestor-spirits and would never kill another elephant. This belief did effectively maintain the king's right in the low-lying country around the capital, and no doubt the foundations of his wealth were laid in that way. But in the hills of the interior the territorial chiefs were expected to receive and pass on this tribute, and if one failed to do so a force of warriors led by a prince or one of the nobles of the plain would be sent to 'burn him up'.

But those who handed over the ivory received in return gifts of the cloths for which the Kyungu bartered it, and which he distributed on other occasions as a mark of his favour; they were worn as turbans, and thus proclaimed the royal favour to all.

All these were small kingdoms—Rwanda and Lesotho nearly equal in area, each the size of Belgium, and Ngonde less than one-third as large as the other two. More questions must be asked of the 'empires', whether or not they deserve to be called 'vast', that did extend over considerable distances. How were they held together?

In writing of the Luba-Lunda 'empire', Vansina makes much of the principle of 'perpetual kinship' which was identified by Cunnison as a feature of the chiefdoms of north-eastern Zambia and Malawi. Where this is the rule, the successor to any political office is held to stand in the same kinship relation to other office-holders as his remotest ancestors did. Thus, if at one time the headmen of two villages were actually brothers, their successors for ever are said to be brothers; in other cases two village heads are linked for ever as father and son, or mother's brother and sister's son. This, as Vansina says, early linked the migrating Lunda groups into 'a loose political unit' (1966: 78). But most of the Zambian and Malawian peoples who follow this principle have never become anything more than loose political units; and I would guess that something more is needed to make political control from one centre effective.

What is needed surely is some arrangement for the maintenance of authority in those fields where the dominant population has something to gain: tribute, tolls on trade, the provision of manpower. The most banal way to secure this is of course 'indirect rule'—one of the oldest political devices in history, although it is now popularly believed to be a peculiarly wicked invention of the British. The ruler of some small unit is either defeated in battle or seeks protection, and is confirmed in his position subject to the payment of tribute and possibly also raising a fighting force when called upon. African rulers, being committed neither to economic development nor to the improvement of the morals of their subjects, did in fact leave the subject chiefs to govern in their own way much more than their European successors did.

But some other methods are interesting enough to be mentioned. 'Direct rule', the appointment of an outsider from the dominant power, is one. This was the method of Alafin Abiodun of Oyo in the late eighteenth century, when he was in competition with Dahomey for the control of communications with the coast. He placed princes or commoner or slave officials in all the towns where trading caravans used to halt, and the explorers Lander and Clapperton found that there were considerable numbers of Oyo officials concerned with the collection of tolls. He also protected his western marches against possible intrusion by sending men to colonize them.

The method of the kings of Barotseland was different again. They appointed representatives to live near the subject chiefs 'to watch over the districts for them and to forward tribute' (Gluckman 1951: 17). In addition conquered populations, along with the 'true' Lozi, were allotted to 'sectors' each under the ultimate control of a senior member of the king's council, who together with all the other councillors belonging to the sector held a court where cases between sector members were tried. In the centre of the kingdom sector membership was not based on residence, but had rather the effect of breaking up territorial groups. But conquered peoples on the periphery would be attached *en bloc* to one or other. People were summoned in sectors for war or for large-scale public works, but according to Gluckman (1951: 39) such calls were rare.

At an early period each division of the Asante state had its own war organization, with chiefs of the right, left, centre, and rearguard. But the campaigns which extended its borders all through the eighteenth century were waged by a combined force in which these four commands were held by the war chiefs of different divisions. In the course of this period it came to be accepted that the Asantehene could call on the forces of any *omanhene* (chief) to fight on his behalf.

Side by side with this reorganization of the army went the

kind of internal change that has been described earlier in this chapter. Osei Kwadwo, who succeeded in 1764, replaced the lineage heads who had traditionally formed his council by young men brought up at court; some of these, however, succeeded in asserting the right to pass on their office to their heirs. Osei Kwadwo also created a personal bodyguard; and doubtless he relied on them to enforce, as we are told he did, peace between divisions whose armies could previously have fought against one another. Like the rulers of Oyo, the Asantehene appointed officers on the trade routes who not only collected tolls but controlled entry into the kingdom.

In Asante there was a two-way communication between centre and periphery. Proconsuls, as a nineteenth-century writer called them, resident commissioners as Wilks (1967: 222) calls them, using a British title, were appointed to live at the capitals of the subject chiefs and keep an eye on them, though doubtless not possessing the executive powers that the Roman or British empires would have given them. Such commissioners were also appointed to reside at the Danish, Dutch, and British trading-posts. In addition each of the subordinate chiefs was attached to one of the officials of the Asante court who was his intermediary in dealings with the Asantehene, and who also, as Wilks (1975) interprets the record, was responsible for suppressing any attempt at rebellion that he might make.

The aim of this chapter has been to trace, where the data allow it, the steps by which the builders of kingdoms have first asserted their power in competition with rivals on their home ground and then secured their control over conquered areas, a matter which may be more difficult than the actual conquest. Inevitably at certain points it has anticipated a description of the devices by which African kingdoms were administered, but later chapters will examine these in detail.

CHAPTER III

ROYALTY AND RITUAL

EVERY African king has traditionally undergone at his accession a *rite de passage* whereby he entered on the unique status that set him apart from all his subjects, and was endowed with the qualities that he needed in order adequately to play his role. Such a rite is clearly parallel to a European coronation, and where there are still kings in Africa, no doubt there are still rites, even if they are done in the truncated form which is all that remains when a man who has adopted Christianity and had a western education ascends a throne. But much traditional ritual has gone by the board, above all that which is not connected with accession. In those African kingdoms that did not rest on Islam, rites were traditionally performed by or for a king at intervals throughout his reign. Those of southern Africa were associated with the eating of first-fruits; the most famous of these, the Swazi *incwala*, also simulated the cleavages within the kingdom and the triumph of the king over internal enemies. Some annual rites reiterated the myth of the founding of the kingdom, and these too gave their appropriate place to persons representing divergent interests. Some were directed to the renewal of the king's power, or of that of the ritual objects with which he was invested at his accession. These often involved the taking of human lives; the 'annual customs' of Dahomey are the most spectacular example.

Some kings were themselves ritual rainmakers as well as secular rulers. On the whole this is typical of those smaller states that are usually referred to by the less imposing name of chiefdoms. But the Zulu and Swazi kings make a striking exception to the rule that, with the expansion of kingdoms, there appears a pantheon of gods, each with his specialized power and each with his own priests, to whom the king sends the appropriate offerings. Mercier (1954), writing of Dahomey, convincingly explains the multiplicity of gods by the adoption of the divinities of conquered peoples, but such an explanation

has not been offered in all cases. A specialist priesthood may
become a counter-power to the king, as did the Yoruba
diviners who annually consulted the oracles to learn whether
the Oba still had the favour of the gods, a clearly political
function.

A recently published short history of Africa (Oliver and Fage
1962) gathers all these different rituals and some others
together in a paragraph describing 'divine kingship' as a set of
customs which we are told were characteristic of ancient Egypt,
and could only be found in countries so widely separated if they
had all originated in a single source. Such a composite picture
might be thought of as an 'ideal type', though its components
are much more specific than those of a Weberian ideal type
would be. It would, I think, be hard to find a complex of royal
ritual that included them all. What historians have been able
to trace of the founding and expansion of kingdoms, as it was
summarized in the previous chapter, gives little ground for
supposing that ambitious kingdom-builders carried in their lug-
gage a blue-print from ancient Egypt. Nevertheless, some items
of royal ritual are very similar to those of ancient Egypt,
notably the act of real or symbolic incest between a king and
his sister or mother. Certainly the association of royalty with
incest, where this is regarded otherwise as a heinous offence, is
a way of asserting the uniqueness of the king. But does it make
him a god, if this is what it means to call him divine?

Sir James Frazer did not ascribe the origin of 'divine kingship' to Egypt, rather to a universal stage in the intellectual
development of mankind. He rightly perceived that persons
supposed to be endowed with more than ordinary power have
more often been priests than secular rulers. But he also held
that all peoples at some time believed that the life of a nation
was literally embodied in its king, and that not only his death,
but any diminution of his health, was directly reflected in the
welfare of his country as a whole. Hence, Frazer asserts, some
kings had to pass tests at regular intervals, and some were
allowed to reign only for a limited time. He quotes the Yoruba
kings as an example, since it was said that if the divination was
unfavourable, a king could be asked to die, but he does not
demonstrate that the oracle was concerned with the state of his

health, and a hard-headed anthropologist might say that what was of more interest was the state of the nation. This may also be true of the many other African traditions that kings were put to death when their physical powers were failing; perhaps the national misfortune came first and was explained by the failure of the king's powers. But it is certain that the ultimate blessing, life in the fullest sense of the word, was believed by many peoples to be given them and maintained for them through the medium of a king derived from the right line of descent, and consecrated in the right manner. Indeed, kingship seems to be inseparable from the belief that the potential for rule is the possession of a particular lineage, and this to be much more fundamental than the idea of the kingdom as a material possession.

Accession Rites

Detailed accounts of accession rites show them to have a number of features in common. They all confer *power*—not divinity—on the king. They include a statement of his obligations towards his people. All the main recognized groups among his subjects co-operate in the performance of the ritual, and so commit themselves to the maintenance of the kingdom under his rule. The ritual dignifies by association with ultra-human beings a procedure analogous to the taking of a coronation oath in the presence of the peers of the realm—that too a ritual process, though we have forgotten today why an oath is supposed to be sacred.

The power that a king received at his accession was not necessarily, or wholly, a gift of wonder-working like the medieval 'royal touch', or the control of the weather that a few rulers with secular powers were believed to possess. The Alur of the Nile-Congo divide had a concept that sums up, I believe, a more general attitude. Their word for chiefship—for the status of chief—meant at the same time the qualities that a chief must have. The word was *ker*. To say that *ker* had 'become cold' meant either that an individual had proved unable to assert his authority, or that his rain ritual had been unsuccessful. To the Alur political success was no more and no less 'magical' than the powers that we should describe by that word.

No more and no less; but both kinds of power were—or it might be better to say this undifferentiated power was—held to derive from the potency of the medicines with which the king was treated and from the regalia the possession of which was essential, along with his descent status, to make his rule legitimate. It had to be kept at full strength not only by rituals to renew it in the king's person, but sometimes also by others directed to the regalia; and it was because the power was that of life in the widest sense that these rituals might involve the taking of life. Sometimes, as in the Swazi first-fruits ceremony, the king's power and the life of the nation were renewed together.

Accession rituals, like many of the puberty rituals through which ordinary people were launched on adult life, included admonitions to the new ruler on his responsibilities to his people and his kingdom. These might be made in public ora-tions on the occasion of his installation, as they were, for example, in Asante. Or, in a closer parallel to the typical initia-tion ritual, the new king might spend a longer or shorter period in seclusion being instructed both in ritual and secular matters. The king of Dahomey spent a short time 'meditating on his newly acquired responsibilities in a special recess of the palace' (Lombard, 1967a: 85). The king of Parakou, one of the Bariba rulers, spent three months at the home of the chief priestess, and it was there that he performed the actions through which he cast off his previous personality, though we are not told what else occupied his time; his instruction came later on, and it seems to have consisted less in moral principles than in giving him a sort of verbal map of his kingdom showing what persons or groups had claims to particular rights or privileges. A Bariba prince, like the sons of many other African kings, was brought up away from the capital lest he should intrigue against the ruler, so that this was more than a repetition in solemn circum-stances of facts that he already knew. A king-elect of Dahomey was led through a series of rooms each containing sacks of pebbles which purported to represent the population of the country, increasing in every reign, and admonished that he too must contribute to this process (Argyle 1966: 98).

The king of a Yoruba town was 'captured' in his house and

taken to the bush for instruction. He was one of many who were supposed to be so reluctant to succeed to office that they had to be seized by force. Frazer interpreted this as the very understandable misgiving of a man who knew the dangers of kingship and the likelihood that he would not be allowed to live out his days. This may have been true of some kings, particularly those who were primarily priests; something very like it is remembered of the 'divine king' of the Nyakyusa (Wilson 1959: 21). But it is as likely that the simulated reluctance was held to show that the king-elect was not (or ought not to be) an ambitious man seeking an office which he would turn to his own advantage.

Another aspect of accession ritual that has sometimes been noted shows that this possibility was much in the minds of African kingmakers. This is the kind of symbolic action which impresses on the king that he is king only by the choice of his people; something that is expressly stated in a Swazi proverb. Thus a Yoruba king-elect was beaten and dressed in rags before being inducted into the position in which his person would be sacred; without the goodwill of the elders, perhaps, the message was, he would be no higher than anybody else. Victor Turner (1969) describes, in more detail than we have for the accession ceremonies of many more powerful chiefs, a similar ritual for the Kanongesha, the senior chief of the 17,000-strong Ndembu in Zambia. The original Kanongesha was one of the leaders who extended Lunda rule so widely in central Africa, and his domains were once much wider than any he could claim now. A new Kanongesha was secluded in a small hut about a mile from the capital, where he was said to 'die', as initiands at puberty so often are. He entered the hut with a ritual wife, both of them clad in rags. They had to crouch in a posture of respect while they were treated with the medicines of chiefship, and later were ordered to do menial tasks. The 'owner of the land', the representative of the conquered people, harangued the new Kanongesha in abusive terms. He was not merely told how a chief should behave, but credited with evil ways which he must abandon in the future. Anyone who claimed to have suffered injury at his hands could come and revile him. Thus protest against the abuse of power that all men know to be its

inherent danger took a more dramatic form than mere injunc-
tion. From that time on public protest would be silent.

The transition from the status of one prince among many to
that of a unique ruler was marked by the usual symbols of
discarding, notably head-shaving, washing and (in Bunyoro)
nail-paring. Those kings who were clothed in rags during their
seclusion had of course already shed their normal garments.
The king of Parakou presented his prince's robes to the 'owner
of the land', who shaved him in a house that he entered by one
door and left by another, one more symbol of transition. This
king also performed in a symbolic action that repudiation of
the past which the elders demanded of the Kanongesha. He
had to bestride the body of a sacrificed bull, and thereby trans-
mit to it his whole past personality, including whatever malign
influences might be attached to him. The beast was then eaten
by 'the representatives of the autochthonous element'—that is
the 'owner of the land' with unspecified others—who, says
Lombard (1965: 326), would inherit part of the unlucky
influences from which the king had been cleansed.

The procedure of installation must include some specific act
that confers upon the king the legitimacy that comes from
continuity with his predecessors. The most striking example is
the 'possession' of the Reth of the Shilluk by his ancestor
Nyikang. More often the continuity was expressed by the king's
association with some material object, and sometimes this
object was said to have been brought to the country by the
founder of the dynasty or some famous king of the past. These
regalia—'things of kingship'—both expressed and conferred on
him his uniqueness, and some were publicly shown only during
the accession rites. *Only* a king or queen of England may sit on
the Coronation Chair, and that *only* during the ceremony of
crowning; at other times it is kept in the ritual centre of the
Anglican Church, Westminster Abbey. Closely resembling the
Coronation Chair is the Golden Stool of Asante, the sacred
shrine of the Asantehene's ancestors, in which—not in the king
himself—the soul of the nation was held to reside (Rattray
1923: 290). The king never even sat on the Stool but rested his
arm on it at his installation, and it was seen only at an annual
ceremony.

In those states in which it was taken for granted that there would be a contest for the succession, the winner was he who held the significant emblem; and a usurper must capture it to make his conquest secure. In an interregnum it embodied the kingship. In the Interlacustrine kingdoms this most precious emblem was a drum. In Ankole the drum Bagyendanwa was supposed to have been brought to the country by the founder of the dynasty which ruled until Obote's destruction of all the kingdoms. It had its own shrine where people came with supplications, and, unlike other drums, it was never actually beaten; other drums were beaten in its honour. Ankole was one of the states where, on the death of the ruler, claimants to the throne were expected to fight it out; victory went to the one who secured control of Bagyendanwa. The Ganda royal drum could not be beaten during an interregnum; it was silent during the two years when the last Kabaka was exiled by the British government. That of Rwanda was kept in vigour by sprinkling on it the blood of animals killed for the divination ritual which preceded a war; it also was too sacred to be beaten at all. In Bunyoro a false pretender would not be able to make the drum sound when he beat it at his installation.

What might be called the constitutional aspects of installation are given especial solemnity by their association with the calling down of divine blessing on the new king. One could say of this part of the ritual what a recent writer has said of the annual renewal ceremonies of the South African Bantu: 'Representatives of the people address the ruler in a national dialogue about high office' (Sansom 1974: 261). Even though it contains a tantalizing reference to 'other ceremonies which it is unnecessary to include here', the account of his own accession ritual which was written by the last king of Bunyoro at the time of the coronation of George VI illustrates these themes in remarkably full detail ('K.W.' 1937). The public part of the ritual consisted partly in exhortations and partly in the presentation to the new king of objects which symbolized his various functions. Each of these objects, and the person presenting it, had its proper name; there is a rich field here for the study of etymology in relation to symbols. The duty and honour of making these presentations fell to representatives of different clans. On his first appearance before the assembled populace the king was 'made to swear that he will never frighten his nation, he must rule his people peacefully, he must admit foreigners to settle in his country, he must equally love his subjects however poor they may be, he must look after the orphans, and that he must justly "cut cases" (i.e. give judgments)'. The gifts included a spear (to kill rebels), a dagger and shield, both symbolizing the protection of the country, a stick and whip for minor punishments (to remind him that he should not 'frighten his nation' by inflicting savage penalties), a hoe for plentiful crops, a bow and arrows and an alarm whistle for offensive warfare, a bag made of leopard-skin (which symbolizes success in trade), and a hammer for making spears and hoes (victory and prosperity). A man representing foreigners [conquered populations?] showed him an elephant tusk which 'denotes that he is the head of all rainmakers'. Some of the objects used are said to have been handed down from the founder of the dynasty or even from remoter rulers, and some of the actors claimed descent from forebears who performed the same actions in those distant days.

Another typical address that has been preserved is the one made at the accession of an Asante chief (Rattray 1929: 82). 'Tell him', his leading subordinates say to the 'spokesman', the official through whom he communicates in public with lesser folk, 'We do not wish that he should disclose the origin of any person [since some are descended from slaves]. We do not wish that he should curse us. We do not wish greediness. We do not wish that his ears should be hard of hearing. We do not wish that he should call people fools. We do not wish that he should act out of his own head [without consultation]. We do not wish things to be done as in Kumase. We do not wish that it should ever be that he should say "I have no time". We do not wish personal violence.' This text calls for a commentary which unfortunately Rattray has not given us. The chief himself called down dire penalties 'if I with you [his subordinate chiefs] do not rule the people as well as my forefathers and you ruled them, and if I do not listen to your advice'.

Among 'refresher' rituals the most fully described is the *incwala* or first-fruits ceremony of the Swazi, which was witnessed three times and recorded by Dr. Hilda Kuper (1947), and has been interpreted and reinterpreted by later anthropologists. This renews at the same time the political power of the king and his warriors, and with it that of the nation, and the fertility of the land, which the king assures as he initiates a new year by spitting to east and west the medicines with which he has himself been treated. His political authority is strengthened even in this latter context by the belief that disaster will befall those who eat of their own harvests before he has performed the rite.

The *incwala* fell into two parts, in each of which the king was first treated with medicines and then conveyed the power they had given him to his people and country by spitting to east and west, an act that was called 'stabbing' or 'biting' the new year. The features of the ritual that have given rise to discussion are two: the fact that at certain stages in it songs expressing hatred for the king were sung, and the fact that at those same stages categories of persons who might be expected to be particularly hostile to him—namely, his own clansmen (potential rivals) and aliens not fully integrated into the Swazi polity—were excluded from parts of it. Gluckman (1954) bases on these two points a theory that this was a 'ritual of rebellion', in which the hostility that all authority must provoke was admitted and at the same time kept within the bounds of prescribed ritual behaviour. It strengthened the kingdom in the political sense by admitting the existence of conflict and then enacting the ultimate triumph of authority.

Beidelman, however (1966), interprets the *incwala* in a manner that makes it more analogous to other African 'refresher' rituals, and also disposes of the difficulty that it was *not* the people most likely to resent the royal authority who sang the hate songs; they had to be absent while the songs were sung. Was it the singers, the general populace, who were expressing hatred, when a little later, after the 'stabbing of the new year', they would be bursting into songs of praise? They did not sing 'We hate', but 'they hate'. The hate songs, as Beidelman points out, are sung while the king is being doctored, when his powers are about to be renewed to their maximum strength. Beidelman does not offer an explanation for what remains a peculiar feature of this particular ritual. But he explains the exclusion of the royal kin as part of the process of separation and transformation that can be seen in many rituals affecting the status of individuals. Again, in the second phase of *incwala* the king had to walk naked through the people, and this has been interpreted as a humiliation; this too Beidelman sees as the expression of the denial of social personality characteristic of that part of a status ritual when the subject of it has cast off an old self and not yet assumed a new. He does note, however, that the warriors who were throughout closely associated with the king were, like him, detached from divisive lineage relations and dedicated, as he was, to the kingdom as an entity.

No other royal ritual has been directly observed and recorded in detail by an anthropologist. The performances that Hilda Kuper witnessed were done in 1936–8, a time when already the great majority of such rites had been abandoned or seriously modified. Many of the records of the past refer to the taking of human life both in accession and refresher ceremonies, and the significance of these has been interpreted in different ways. In the case of the Nyoro the purpose is said to be 'to strengthen the kingship'; the life sacrificed by the subject contributed in some way to the life of the ruler. Bradbury (1973: 75) says of Benin that the human sacrifices there impressed upon the people the sole right of the Oba to take human life; but this is usually the monopoly of a supreme ruler, whether or not royal rituals involve human sacrifice. Elsewhere, however (ibid.: 50), he refers to the great increase in such sacrifices at the time when the kingdom was losing its power as giving 'a hint of desperation'; this would surely suggest the idea of strength obtained from the lives that were taken. The Oba's 'mystical energy', which he was expected to deploy for the benefit of his kingdom and people, must, one supposes, have been considered in some way to be recharged by the lives sacrificed during the rituals. Bradbury refers also to the Festival of the Beads at which royal and chiefly regalia were 're-dedicated, by human sacrifice, to the common purpose'.

In the accounts of the most famous of these ceremonies, the 'annual customs' of Dahomey, little emphasis is placed on such an interpretation. The nineteenth-century eye-witnesses were too indignant to ask the meaning of the sacrifice of captured slaves, and the anthropologist-historians of our own day have been more interested in the effect of the ritual in reinforcing secular power. J. Lombard does remark, however, that sacrifices offered to the ancestors infused the kingdom with a new spiritual force (1967a: 85). The political aspect of the ritual is apparent in the regular reaffirmation of the king's supreme authority, the display of his wealth and military power, the rewarding of those he delighted to honour. As with the Swazi eating of first-fruits, so here the ultimate supremacy of the ruler is emphasized in the prohibition of the performance of private or local rituals of any kind before the 'annual customs' had been completed. Since their overt aim was to commemorate the royal ancestors, they asserted the legitimacy of the king's descent and recalled the past glories of the kingdom. But the annual gathering at the capital of all the leading chiefs, and of many subjects bringing tribute, also had the purely secular aspect of a quasi-parliament, or, perhaps, of those courts that the Plantaganet monarchs held on the occasion of the major Christian festivals. New policies and laws were announced, political appointments made, tribute received and redistributed, military campaigns planned.

Generally such rituals not only replenished the royal power, but also gave religious sanction to the total political system, on the one hand by requiring the presence of the holders of subordinate authority and on the other by letting them participate in the renewal of the kingdom. Sometimes they re-enacted history so as to show the victory of the king over rivals, as in the Benin festival in honour of the Oba's father, when he used to defeat in a mock battle the *Uzama* or king-makers, the descendants of the elders who are believed to have brought the founder of the dynasty from Oyo.

Royal Women

Royal spouses seldom played ritual roles, but royal mothers and sisters frequently did, and at the same time exercised secular authority equivalent to that of senior chiefs. Beattie (1971: 102 ff.) describes the ceremony of appointment of the

Nyoro king's 'official sister', the Kalyota; she was presented with the characteristic insignia of office, drank milk from the royal herd and kissed the king's hand, as leading chiefs did on their appointment. Her duty was to keep the peace among the women of the royal clan, and, like the other chiefs, she had an official estate—an area of land over which she exercised authority in just the same manner as they did. The Ganda and Ankole also recognized a royal sister, and also a royal mother (so did the Nyoro, but Beattie tells us little about her). These were offices which had to be filled; they were essential to the continuance of the monarchy. Each king at his accession installed his own mother and chose his official sister, but if the royal mother died before her son—as was most likely—a substitute was installed in her place. The royal mother in Ankole wielded considerable secular power. She was a member of her son's council, her consent was necessary before anyone could be put to death, and envoys from foreign rulers had to approach her before they could see the king.

In these kingdoms it had traditionally been the rule that succession to the throne was decided by a war between the potential heirs in which the defeated were eliminated; hence, in theory, the king had no brothers, and in practice he would have been unlikely to have relations of confidence with them. Oberg (1940: 160) suggests that his closest female kin gave him the advice and support that other rulers got from their male agnates, but there is really no reason why he should not have looked to men on his mother's side, and he did have a 'favourite councillor' or 'prime minister' whom he chose for himself.

Moreover, royal mothers and sisters figure in kingdoms where there is no question of the elimination of the king's brothers. In the Lozi kingdom, as described by Gluckman (1951), the 'princess chief' controlled the most potent of all royal shrines, the grave of the king Mwanambinji, who seized from a conquered enemy the drums that became the major insignia of kingship.

In the Hausa kingdom of Maradi, a royal lady, not necessarily the king's mother, was appointed to preside over rituals involving royal women. She was the official head of the prostitutes, a recognized profession in Muslim societies, and also of the adepts of the pagan *bori* spirit possession cult. She had a say in all public rituals. She had her own slaves and clients and her own armed following which went to war at her command; she collected market tolls and taxes from the prostitutes. In Oyo not only the Alafin but every official in the palace had his 'mother'; these women had ritual responsibility for the palace shrines, and the most important of them were also 'mothers' of the principal city-wide cult organizations. The Alafin's own official mother had to be with him whenever he gave audience to one of his chiefs, and the heir apparent, the king's eldest son, had to be accompanied by *two* 'mothers' when he visited the palace (Morton-Williams 1967: 65).

The capital of Dahomey was similarly organized. According to Burton every man at the court had an official mother, and other writers confirm that this was so in the case of the two leading officials, the *migan* or prime minister and the *meu* or war chief. These ladies had authority over the great number of women who inhabited the palace, the first over commoners, the second over royal women. As in Oyo, a minister's 'mother' had to be present when he was in conference with the king. European visitors to Dahomey had 'mothers' attached to them for the same purpose. It was their responsibility to remember what had been said at the audiences.

From the meagre information that we have about these royal sisters and mothers it seems that most of them exercised some kind of secular authority, and the question may be asked why they should be discussed in the context of ritual. Where we are concerned with great concourses of women far exceeding the numbers to be found in any ordinary household (nearly 8,000 in Dahomey), it is merely common sense to observe that some authority among them must have been necessary, and that this could more appropriately be vested in a woman than a man. But this does not account for all the cases in which a sister or mother 'reigns with' her son or brother, nor for the fact that a king's wife *never* does so; and those writers who have discussed the subject agree that the institution had a symbolic as well as a practical significance, though they are by no means unanimous as to what this was. It need not, of course, be the same in all cases, just as the role of the sister or mother was not the same everywhere.

Argyle (1966: 64) associates the Dahomeyan institution with the opposition that was recognized between the 'inside'—the palace—and the 'outside'—the rest of the kingdom. The 'mothers' of the ministers and of other visitors to the court paralleled in their secluded feminine world the men of affairs whose activities were carried on outside. But in addition, there was a need for some mediating term between the king 'inside' and his ministers 'outside', and this was supplied by the official 'mothers'. This explanation might apply also to Oyo, where there was a similar division between palace and town, and the Alafin was supposed never to leave the palace.

But these women's motherhood was no more than metaphorical, and they present a different problem from that of the mothers and sisters who were expressly stated to 'reign with' a king. The explanation of their status which has been offered by Luc de Heusch (1958) turns on the theory that most African accession rituals include an incestuous marriage which may involve a real or symbolic act of incest. His prototype case is that of the Nyoro Kalyota, whose ritual of installation was described by Roscoe as a marriage; Beattie's discussion of this rite shows that it does not at all closely parallel a Nyoro marriage. However, de Heusch adduces many more cases in support of his argument than have been cited here. He maintains that for the king to be not only permitted but enjoined to commit incest—an act regarded among ordinary folk as abhorrent—emphasizes his uniqueness in the most extreme manner possible. It also, by making the incestuous union a *marriage*, combines concepts that are diametrically opposed. And by doing this it sacralizes sexual relations, and so fertility, throughout the kingdom. Monarchy, says de Heusch, is here founded on the sacred triad of king, sister, and mother.

Beattie (1971: 103), after he has effectively demonstrated that there was no rite of incestuous marriage in Bunyoro, rather dodges the issue by simply saying that the queen-sister's role is 'as the female expression or counterpart of the kingship'. This theme is developed by Balandier (1974) in a discussion of the various ways in which the opposition and complementarity of the sexes are perceived in Afrrican societies. For him the queen-sister's authority over other women is the essential of her position, and he compares her with the queen-mothers of smaller African kingdoms in Cameroun. In the Nyoro case the queen-mother, the third in the triad, is said to 'protect' the king, though it is not entirely clear what this means. But if it is a matter of magical rites, Balandier argues, the two royal women, who together represent the 'feminine society', are then differentiated and opposed in terms of the complementary opposition between sacred and secular power. Balandier's explanation does not invoke the symbolism of fertility. He stresses rather the assimilation of these female chiefs to men: 'When I go into council', said a princess chief to Gluckman, 'I change; I am a man'. As the West African 'mothers' mediate between the palace and the 'outside', so the de-feminized female chiefs effect a 'marriage' between the two sides in the basic, ineluctable division between the sexes.

CHAPTER IV
COURTS AND CAPITALS

No anthropologist has been in a position to write an eye-witness account of an independent African court or capital. But it has been possible to piece together from the records of travellers and the memories of old men a reasonably satisfactory picture of some of them.

Different writers have concentrated on different aspects. Evans-Pritchard (1971) put together a pretty full description of the court of Gbudwe, the last independent Zande king, by combining travellers' accounts, texts taken from old men who had been royal soldiers or pages when they were young, and what he could see himself in 1927 of the diminished splendour of Gbudwe's son. R. E. Bradbury spent six years in Benin and collected both documents and oral traditions as part of a project for a history of the kingdom; he died before he could publish a full-scale ethnography, but he has given us an admirable picture of palace organization. Beattie (1971) describes the numerous officials, many with purely ritual functions, to be found at the relatively unelaborate court of the king of Bunyoro; the prestige attached even twenty years ago to such offices was often sufficient to prevent their holders from seeking more lucrative employment elsewhere. M. G. Smith, more interested in political processes than in descriptive detail, used for his description (1960) of Zazzau (now called Zaria) a chronicle of nineteenth-century Abuja, the kingdom founded by the Hausa ruler of Zazzau when he fled from the Fulani conquest, which was made by the brother of the then Emir of Abuja; to this he added a history of the Fulani state of Zaria recounted to him by a grandson of the conqueror and some other elders.

Every court or capital comprised a greater complex of buildings and a larger population than would be found elsewhere in the king's dominions. There was therefore need for a category of officials concerned specifically with its organization and provisioning. Buganda had a king's cook and butcher: actually important men holding hereditary offices, whose duty it was to procure the necessary supplies of meat and vegetable food. Some kings also had ritual specialists who were responsible for foreseeing and warding off danger. Every king had great numbers of wives—women who had been given to him but did not necessarily become his consorts, were servants of his actual wives and might be given by him to favoured subjects. The women's quarters had their own authorities responsible both for supplies and the maintenance of order. Most kings had elaborate regalia for the upkeep of each of which, again, a specific official was responsible. In addition the highest political authorities under the king would have their residences at the court or in the capital.

Zande kings and princes still had their courts when Evans-Pritchard was there in 1927. Though it was but a shadow of what it had been in the days of Gbudwe's greatness, his son's court had the traditional lay-out. The buildings were round mud huts with thatched roofs, as were most of those of eastern and central Africa, but within this limitation there is room for considerable difference in elegance of construction and attention to upkeep. The public part of the court was an open space where people who came to present petitions or have cases judged could sit in the shade of some large tree. About twenty yards from the open court was the 'court of whispers', an unwalled building where the king would discuss secret business with his intimates. Along the path which connected the two were the houses of the royal pages, who could bar the entrance of unauthorized persons to the 'court of whispers'; and on one side of the open court were housed the military companies. The actual dwelling place of the king and his wives would be separated from this complex by a space of grassland. They covered a large area, in the case of King Gbudwe 'several miles' (Evans-Pritchard 1971: 77). Here there was a separate homestead for every wife with a garden round it, and one for the king himself somewhere in the middle. Behind this complex, at some distance, was a hut where the royal diviners consulted the poison oracle on his behalf.

Oberg (1940), who about 1935 reconstructed a picture of an

independent Nkole king's capital, follows the missionary Roscoe (1923) in calling it a 'kraal'. Earlier writers meant by this word an enclosure for cattle, later ones what might be thought of as a large homestead or a small village; it always implies the presence of cattle, and this makes it seem appropriate for the residence of the Nkole king, who was the owner of a large herd and moved with it from place to place. Oberg describes the capital as itself consisting of a number of kraals, each apparently a cluster of huts with a fence round them. The royal residence was in the centre, its gateway always guarded. In the open space inside the gate the king received visitors and suppliants and tried minor cases. But what might be called the throne-room and audience chamber, comparable to the Zande 'court of whispers', was a large hut in which serious matters of state were discussed and cases of murder and treason were tried. This was also a centre of public ritual; the installation of a new king took place in front of it. Around it were smaller huts where guests could sleep, and one to store the beer that was always offered for their refreshment. A large enclosure housed the women of the court. This was subdivided into quarters for favourite wives, for concubines, for immature girls who might or might not become royal consorts; a girl chosen by the king was fattened by being made to drink enormous quantities of milk while living in a special hut set apart for the purpose.

Outside this royal residence were the dwellings of court officials and servants. According to the Nkole historian S. R. Karugire (1971) the closest to the royal enclosure were those of regional chiefs, who were also war leaders, and who, like most of their counterparts elsewhere, were expected to show their loyalty by spending much of their time in the capital. Commoner chiefs were nearest the king's quarters; princes, who might harbour thoughts of assassination, further away. At an equal distance in a different direction lived the ambassadors/ hostages of conquered rulers. Oberg does not describe any cattle enclosure within this complex, and Karugire says the royal herd was kept some distance away.

It has commonly been from among the palace attendants, whose qualities and loyalty the king could judge at first hand, that the holders of political office were chosen, so that the

question of their recruitment and promotion is of some significance. From the kingdoms of Uganda we get the general impression that men would send their sons to serve at court as
pages in the hope of launching them on successful careers; in
particular fathers who were themselves chiefs would do so.

According to one of Evans-Pritchard's informants, Kuagbiaru, who had been a royal page and then a warrior, a
Zande king would himself pick out the boys whom he wanted.
There is an apparent contradiction in a later statement that
boys chose to serve at court because the king would provide
their bridewealth. It may be, of course, that they or their
fathers were free to refuse the royal invitation and that this was
a motive for accepting it. In any case the poison oracle was
consulted to find whether the invitation was propitious, and an
unfavourable answer might be held to justify a refusal.

A select number of pages were the king's constant companions, and the youngest of these were allowed to enter his domestic quarters, from which all other males were excluded.
Hence they might learn a good deal about his private affairs,
and the first requirement of such a confidential follower was
the ability to keep his mouth shut. These pages went with the
king to court, to war, to a hunt, to consult the poison oracle or
on a journey, and slept within earshot so that he could summon
them at will. Pages guarded the entrance to the 'court of whispers' and kept out those who had no right of access to it. They
carried out into the public place the huge bowls of food that
were prepared every day for all the men at the court. They
were sent with messages, and were also expected to be spies.
Kuagbiaru said the king told them: 'Anything you may hear
anyone say about me, do not hide it from me in any circumstances. You must know the names of everybody who attends
court, for if I ask you who is in the court you must be able to
name every one of them correctly' (Evans-Pritchard 1971:
184). Older pages shared in the work of hoeing the king's
extensive fields, where the grain was grown that provided for
the lavish distribution of food and beer, and younger ones
might help the royal wives, who had each her garden like other
Zande women. They were threatened with ferocious punishment for any dereliction of duty, and, according to Kuagbiaru,

when a prince died all his pages at the time were put to death.

The greatest elaboration of courts and capitals was naturally to be found in those West African kingdoms—some call them empires—that were built on the control of trade. We know more of Asante than of any other, thanks to the records of visitors to Kumase at different times in the nineteenth century. But it is from Rattray, the Gold Coast Government Anthropologist in the period between the two world wars, that we learn just what kind of a labyrinth the residence of a royal personage might be. When Rattray was at work, the Asantehene had recently been allowed to return, as a private citizen, from a long exile, and his studies of the nature of Asante kingship were made by visiting the different chiefs and collecting their versions of remembered history. When with the chief of Kumawu he drew a plan of the palace there and numbered each of the separate rooms according to its use. Asante buildings were rectangular, with mud walls and roofs which in the present century are made of corrugated iron or thatched with straw, but earlier had been of leaves stitched together. This palace was a large rectangle the external wall of which consisted of rooms divided by partitions, while inside there were courtyards and free-standing buildings.

The entrance was at a corner, not in the middle of a wall. Since the most striking item of a chief's insignia was the large umbrella carried over his head, the doorway had to be wide enough for one of these to pass through. Immediately inside was the open court where the chief held audience and tried important cases. This was called *gyase*, a word that refers to the cooking-hearth and the space around it where, in ordinary houses, women and servants work and children play. Domestic slaves slept there, and were called *gyasefo*, 'people of the hearth-place', and in a large establishment one was set in authority over the rest as *gyasehene*. This, therefore, was the title given to the official in charge of the multitude of servants in the king's vast household. At the further side of the *gyase* was an open-fronted room where on important occasions the chief would sit and serve out wine. Opposite him was the room where his drummers sat, and, on the two other sides of the square, rooms where the drums were kept. In a smaller court leading out of this to the right he dealt with cases among his own servants; only members of his household had access there. It was flanked by his bathroom and rooms for his bath attendants, who in this case were also cooks, and his youngest servants. To the left, separated by a wall, was the court where lived the *Barimhene*, the official responsible for the ceremonies that commemorate the chief's ancestors, whose souls were believed to be enshrined in the stools that they had sat on in their life-time, which were blackened and kept in a shrine-house when they died. A chief himself, the *Barimhene* had his own stool-house. The Kumawuhene's stools were in a court to which there was access both from this and from the *gyase* court. Along the outer wall of this were dwellings for those responsible for the care of the stools and for menial services during the rites. In the middle was a place for heralds and musicians to sit at ceremonies, and at the further end a room containing the skeletons of dead chiefs and one for the chief to sit during rituals directed to them. Behind the *gyase* was another court where 'all the lesser ordinary' cases were tried; the chief sat on one side and his two leading subordinates opposite, and his 'linguists' at the further end. Further back was the room where the chief ate, and in front of it a small space where visitors were given food and drink. Across from this was the room where the chief slept; this looked out on an open space flanked by a room for wives who came to visit him and store-rooms for his clothes and eating utensils. Further back again was another large court, at one side of which was a room for the chief to be alone, and one near it for wives who came to see him. At the back of this were a number of store-rooms, each of which was intended for particular classes of object; but from the photographs that Rattray took it would seem that the rule 'A place for everything and everything in its place' was not strictly adhered to. At one side of this court were kept the chief's magical charms. Parallel with this court was a small one for private discussions between the chief and his elders; at one side of this the state umbrellas were kept, at another the goldsmiths in his service did their work. Here there was yet another small room for the chief to sit and rest in and 'hear complaints from his wives'. A narrow passage led from the *gyase* court to a wide space 'where small boys attending the chief's wives play', and from this there was a way into the women's area, houses along the whole interior of the side wall, garden patches along the whole of the back. Behind the room with the skeletons of dead chiefs, outside the main wall but close to it, was one for the relics of dead wives of chiefs.

The city of Kumase was divided into seventy-seven named wards, some of which were the homes of the king's servants, including those of his leading councillors, the senior of whom, the *Gyaasewahene* or treasurer, held a court of his own. His house was close to the entrance of the palace on the west, and the head of the executioners and police lived immediately to the south of the palace. Most other senior officials also lived close to the palace. The 1,000 or so Muslim merchants and mallams had their own wards; so did the goldsmiths, while the blacksmiths and umbrella-makers lived in two small hamlets outside the city. Whether inside or outside the palace, every person holding any kind of public authority had an open room facing the street, in front of his domestic dwellings, where he transacted business. One way of establishing a claim to a hereditary office up to quite recent times was to demonstrate that an ancestor had had such a *dampan*.

The palace of the kings of Dahomey at Abomey epitomized the history of the kingdom, since every king was buried in his house in the capital, and his successor had to build a house next to it. It was therefore a ritual as much as a political centre, and this may be one reason why the palace as 'the inside' was expressly opposed to all that was 'outside', and this opposition was conceived in terms of the opposition of the sexes, a leading theme in Dahomey religion. In the late nineteenth century it was estimated to have 8,000 inhabitants, the great majority being the royal wives and their slaves, who here worked the gardens and fetched water. Even the king's bodyguard were women, the 'Amazons' of whom Burton and others wrote. Senior officials were generally eunuchs; not all of them actually lived in the palace. One had the duty of making the king's path straight by removing sticks and stones in front of him, and was also in charge of the palace night-watchmen. Another controlled entry to the palace and dealt with misdemeanours among the other eunuchs. A third was in charge of the royal stores, including 'cloth, cowries and rum', and ammunition. The palace was conceived as a sort of mirror of the rest of the kingdom; within it there was for every chief who had responsibilities of government a 'mother' whose title corresponded to his own, and who was present whenever he had audience of the king. When the king appeared in public, a line was drawn on the ground by laying down bamboo sticks, which no one from the 'outside' might cross.

Again, in Oyo, the senior of the Yoruba kingdoms, the leading court officials were three eunuchs. They, however, had responsibilities outside as well as within the palace. One was responsible for the ritual of the god of thunder and could curse offenders in his name. One judged disputes between vassals of Oyo, and the third, who went to battle in the place of the king, also had authority over the collection of tolls. Actual daily duties were largely performed by slaves.

The most complex palace organization of which we have record is that of Benin. Here the palace was divided on the ground into three sections, each the residence (though not the home) of a different association of officials. In the administration of palace affairs each of these had a different sphere of responsibility. The *Iwebe*, the highest in rank, had charge of the throne and of the Oba's ceremonial garments and other insignia, and their head chief was the senior palace official; they were also responsible for his stock of trade goods. The *Iweguae* was the section of the palace where the Oba lived. Its association provided pages, messengers, domestic spies, cooks, and other servants, and it was to its members that individuals addressed themselves when they wanted a private audience with the Oba. They organized the feasts at which the Oba entertained his chiefs. In this part of the palace were stored the medicines and other magical objects used in rituals to protect the king's health and maintain his power, though the experts who manipulated them lived outside in the town. Then came the *Ibiwe*, where the Oba's wives and children lived. The *Ibiwe* chiefs were responsible for the provisioning of this large population, for keeping the peace among them and reporting on them to the Oba; and also for buying animals for sacrifices. When the wives were sick or pregnant they were taken to the home of some *Ibiwe* chief outside the palace; in such homes, too, the princes were brought up, since they were sent away from the palace as soon as they could leave their mothers. Palace chiefs had charge of the different wards of the town, some of which were allotted to the practitioners of the different crafts which supplied the palace. They were not maintained directly from the Oba's resources, but had allotted to them villages from which they drew tribute and labour, and over which they exercised the same authority as any territorial chief. Nor were their duties confined to palace affairs; they were constantly being sent, as the Oba's emissaries, to summon levies from villages other than their own, to deal with complaints, and to represent the Oba, who was expected to take part directly or indirectly in all village rituals.

The division in Benin between 'inside' and 'outside'—here called 'Palace' and 'Town'—was associated with the supposed foreign origin of the ruling dynasty; the kings were reminded in various ways that they were not wholly members of the Edo population who were their subjects. While the Palace Chiefs were first and foremost retainers of the Oba, the Town Chiefs were thought of as spokesmen for the people at large. One of them, the *Esogban*, was the 'elder' of the whole kingdom, maintaining on its behalf the same ritual relations with the dead that fell in each village to the actual oldest man. The shrine at which he officiated stood immediately outside the palace, across the broad highway that separated it from the town. Thus it confronted the shrines of dead Obas, which were directly behind the front wall of the palace. The town chiefs included the war leaders and the principal ritual functionaries of the kingdom, but we do not read of specialized administrative offices attached to their position.

The Career open to Talents

Earlier it was argued that an essential element in the consolidation of central power was the assertion by a ruler of the right to choose his subordinates without regard to hereditary claims, and oral traditions often name the ruler who first did this. He had of course to make the choice from those known to him, and in the nature of things these were most likely to have

been court servants, though no doubt chiefs of lower rank
might sometimes commend a follower to him. The belief that
any free man—and sometimes any slave too—could rise to the
highest office if he had the luck to be noticed by his superiors,
and the merit to deserve their notice, was current in many
African kingdoms; stories were told to illustrate it, and here
and there it is supported by authentic life-histories.

It is usual to find that fathers could offer their sons as servants to their immediate chiefs, if not to the king himself, and
that these authorities or their emissaries on their travels could
pick out likely lads for court service. A most striking example of
theoretically open access to high office was to be found in
Benin, where every free man inherited from his father membership in one of the three palace associations. As with many such
rights, only those could exercise it who could afford to do so.
But quite a number did 'enter the palace', and stay there until
they gave up hope of preferment and went back to their villages; young men from the capital, one suspects, less often had
to give up hope. The three associations (*otu*) were similar in
structure to the cult and other associations which have been
described among the Ibo-speaking peoples; the latter have
many characteristics in common with the Edo-speakers of
Benin and the surrounding country. One entered any such
association by paying fees to the existing members. Everyone
had the right to enter his father's *otu*, but it was possible to
transfer later on, and brothers were not usually found in the
same *otu*; hence there was no concentration of lineages in any
association. On entry a new member was given seven days'
instruction in his duties and swore to be loyal to the king and
not divulge court secrets; and evidently there were also rites of
initiation. He then became the servant of higher-ranking members of the association. By making more payments and taking
part in further rites he advanced through a series of grades to
that of messenger, when he would be sent, by this time no
doubt with followers of his own, on various missions on behalf
of the king.

When he reached this grade he had the right to apply for one
of the limited number of titles to which were attached certain
villages as 'fiefs' or sources of tribute and labour. The titles did

not carry specific responsibilities. They were ranked in order, but there was no ladder of promotion; anyone of the appropriate grade could apply to the Oba for any title that became vacant. Again he had to pay fees to the other title-holders and ask their blessing one by one, just as a man in the village wishing to be promoted to elderhood (still) makes gifts to each of the elders and seeks their blessing. His title was not confirmed until he had been formally installed by the senior Town chief (the *Iyase*); so there could be many a slip before he actually entered upon it. Promotion was, then, an expensive business; but every advancement brought with it more sources of wealth. Town titles were sometimes given to men who had not passed through the palace ranks but had acquired wealth as traders or craftsmen, or distinguished themselves in war; this was the background of several who held the position of *Iyase*.

The annals of Asante are full of records of the creation of new chiefships—stools—which seem to have sometimes been treated as hereditary. On the other hand, from Bowdich's time onwards, we hear how the Asantehene 'raised his favourite captains to the vacant stools, uniting three or four in one', and 'extend[ed] his prerogative by dignifying the young men brought up about his person' (cited Wilks 1975: 445). Bonnat in 1870 noticed how young men came to Kumase to offer their services in the hope of advancement. Bowdich recorded one individual success story, that of Asante Agyei. He worked in the salt trade on the Volta and was noticed by the chief of Akwamu, who enlisted him in his bodyguard. He was in the chief's retinue when the latter was summoned to Kumase to answer some charge against him. He spoke for three hours, so it is said, in defence of his master, and so impressed the Asantehene that he took him over as a retainer. Eventually he achieved another triumph in a negotiation between the Asantehene and some councillors who opposed his views, upon which he was appointed to the rank of *okyeame*, a word translated as 'linguist' by the older writers and 'counselor' (*sic*) by Wilks. He again supported a minority view in defence of a chief whom the king proposed to despoil of his property, and, surprisingly enough, was yet further advanced for this. Next he was sent with an army against the rebel chiefdom of Akyem, as the civilian responsible for concluding the peace terms, and from then on was entrusted with all negotiations with foreign states.

Equally impressive is the story of Opoku Frefre, who as Gyaasewahene (treasurer) was one of the Asantehene's four 'privy councillors', and whom Bowdich described as holding every day 'a sort of exchequer court'. According to the Asantehene Prempeh II 'Opoku Frefre had no family. He was a slave' (Wilks 1975: 461). He went to court in the retinue of one of the Kumase chiefs and was noticed by the Asantehene, who had him taken into court service as part of the share of his master's estate due to be paid as 'death duty'. He was attached to the then Gyaasewahene, and when the latter was executed for treason he was appointed in his place; he was then about thirty. He commanded armies in campaigns against rebellious southern provinces and was one of the two officials who took charge of the capital when the Asantehene was away.

CHAPTER V
ARMY ORGANIZATION

NEARLY every African people had some form of military organization.

There is an obvious contrast between those kingdoms in which soldiers were raised locally and fought as bands from their home area under a territorial chief, and those in which they were amalgamated and then divided on some other than a territorial basis; and another between those in which a 'citizen army' was summoned from its everyday avocations when it was needed, and those in which some men at least were given a special training. It might be expected that the contrast would be associated with that between the 'empires' of Zande and Luba type, in which members of a royal lineage set out on their independent conquests and recognized only a nominal supremacy of the descendants of the original head, and those in which the conquests were additions to the domains of a single ruler. But this does not always hold good. The kings of Asante, for example, although they claimed the right to demand troops from any of the chiefdoms that acknowledged their rule, also allowed some of these to raise their own armies and prosecute their own wars.

The Zande organization is the most informal to have been described in any detail. Zande warriors were unmarried youths who were recruited into companies in each of the districts administered by a representative of the king, either a prince of his own family or a commoner governor; each of these had its own commander, one of their number and so not an official with any authority outside his own company. There was no compulsion to join a company, though the young men's fathers maintained that they offered their sons' services as a form of tribute. According to Evans-Pritchard, however, it was the youths themselves who insisted on joining the companies, and their fathers could not prevent them (1971: 198). When not required for fighting, they could be called on to work the king's

extensive fields; they were summoned through their local commanders. Each company had a barracks—a single very large
hut—at the royal or provincial court, where the commander
spent most of his time, while the others came and went, but
were not expected to stay away for long periods. Individuals
left when they wanted to marry. Married men joined companies in their own districts. When fighting was called for all
able-bodied men, not only members of the companies, were
expected to take part. Each one brought with him a spear and
shield, but only the companies had the many-bladed throwing-
knife, a weapon issued by kings and governors to their followers. A king also distributed additional spears to favoured
warriors.

Zande warfare, as described by Evans-Pritchard, did not
have the conquest of territory as its aim but simply the destruction of the enemy's possessions; movable goods were looted,
women and children made captive, huts and storehouses destroyed. Captured weapons were brought to the king, and were
one source from which he supplied his warriors in later campaigns. In Evans-Pritchard's view the material gains were less
important to the Azande than the lowering of the enemy's
prestige. But warfare was not confined to the single raids which
the rulers of provinces were free to mount on their own; what
they called 'sit-down' wars might last several weeks. Yet these
wars, though they were fought between rival Zande kings and
princes, were not, it seems, intended to establish or restore the
political authority of any one of them. Auspicious times for
attack were found by consulting the poison oracle, but also by
spies who would report when an enemy population was preparing a feast and could be caught off guard. There were famous
spies; some were named to Evans-Pritchard.

From the point of view of organization what is interesting is
the supply of provisions for large numbers of men away from
home. The warriors brought an initial supply with them, and
those who were not too far from their homes went back for
more when they needed it. In addition they might 'live on the
country', even one which they were supposed to be defending.
Each man foraged for himself. Evans-Pritchard refers to
famines caused by the demands of Zande armies.

The centralization of the Rwanda army has been mentioned. The army organization created for the Zulu by Dingiswayo and Shaka resembled it in some respects, though its starting-point was a different one, the principle common to so many African peoples that all young men must pass through a period as 'warriors' immediately after their formal initiation into manhood. As with the Azande, it was the youths of one territorial division who fought together when their leaders summoned them. In southern Africa chiefs took charge of the initiation process, and a son of the chief would be made a leader in each of the 'regiments'—the word that has been favoured by South African writers for more than a century—that were formed in this way. In time of peace the men lived in their own, not necessarily contiguous, homes, but they fought as a body when their leader summoned them. They could be, therefore, a source of support in power struggles and so of division within the realm, as the Zande companies certainly were. Evans-Pritchard argues that what others might call internecine wars were the expression of loyalties to the immediate superior, and one which assured the maintenance of his authority. It is part of his argument that the Zande did not seek territorial expansion at one another's expense; any of them who did must surely have been driven along the same path as Dingiswayo and Shaka.

The first modification in the common type of organization was made by the former. He gave up the initiation ceremonies, supposedly because of the danger of enemy attacks when numbers of young men were away in the bush, and instead left it to his chiefs to assemble youths of the right age and give each set a regimental name. But they did not remain under local command. Each regiment was assigned a rallying-point at one of the royal households which were distributed over the country, and here age-mates from different areas collected and went to battle together. Shaka made the regiments into a standing army. They now lived in six settlements, some of them very large; one was reported to contain 1,400 huts (Isaacs, cited Omer-Cooper 1966: 34). Each was commanded by a commoner appointed by Shaka. No man could marry until the king disbanded his regiment. They spent much of their time in military exercises. Shaka introduced the use of a short spear for stabbing in place of the assegai which left the soldier defenceless as soon as he had thrown it; he employed his own blacksmiths to make these. Shields as well as spears, and all military insignia, were issued by him; another means of centralization. The regiments were trained to manoeuvre in close formation. A division of the royal herd was attached to each to supply them with meat and milk; the warriors were responsible for herding them. During the short period of Shaka's despotism he employed his army not only in the conquest and devastation of the neighbouring country but also in the massacre of any subjects whom he suspected of disloyalty.

The Asante empire consisted originally in an alliance of Twi-speaking peoples, each under its own chief, who looked to the chief of Kumase for leadership and regarded him as ritually supreme; hence his title, Asantehene, head of Asante. Each chiefdom had its own fighting force, but they accepted the obligation to join in the Asantehene's wars; failure to do so, like failure to pay tribute, constituted rebellion. All armies were organized on the same principle; there was a right and left wing, a centre and a rearguard (obviously a very usual form of organization). The special feature of Asante was that the commander of each of these divisions was a hereditary official, and the titles describing their commands were the same in every division. Bowdich wrote in 1819 that when contingents were raised from different chiefdoms, each was given one of these positions and its supreme commander held the appropriate title. But by 1870, when British military intelligence was interested in Asante armies, these commands were held by Asante chiefs, not those of non-Asante subjects. A force of 20,000 attacked the coastal peoples twice in the nineteenth century, and that which fought the British in 1873–4 was estimated at 60,000, the same number that the Emperor Charles V in 1539 planned to launch against the Turks.

From the beginning of the expansion of Asante, quotas of men were imposed on conquered chiefs. According to Bowdich a contingent from the most recently conquered people formed the vanguard in the next campaign. Another way to obtain soldiers was the mass transfer of conquered populations. Dissatisfaction with demands for troops was one reason why so many chiefs threw off their allegiance to Kumase after its defeat in 1874. But even after this, some chiefs were required to hand over slaves for the small standing army, equipped with modern weapons, that was created as a *corps d'élite*.

When the Asantehene was preparing for war in 1873, the two captive missionaries in Kumase whom the British mission had come to rescue (among other aims) noticed people drying corn and cassava and making up packages. Bowdich observed that every soldier had a bag in which he carried his rations. But unlike the Zande armies with their campaigns of a few weeks, Asante troops were often in the field for many months, and their wars were financed by the expenditure of the gold dust which was collected in tribute and by various forms of taxation. Halfway through the war of 1873–4, the Asantehene informed his council that it had cost the equivalent of £48,000 at the rate then current. Ten times as much was lost in an earlier defeat when the treasure chest was captured. A large part of these funds must have been expended on arms and ammunition; some, perhaps, on securing the support of allies or safe passage through a neutral chiefdom. Brodie Cruickshank, writing in 1853 of a war fought in 1806, refers to a chief who 'undertook to sell provisions to the Ashantee army, provided they came to his town without their arms' (1966: 66–7); and Reindorf, the Ghanaian historian, wrote of 'ammunition' spent in buying provisions (1966: 127). Conquered towns were destroyed. Cruickshank and Reindorf describe famine in the wake of Asante armies; Wilks refers to famines in Asante caused by the diversion of man-power from cultivation, something that is not mentioned in accounts of any other army.

As at all times when weapons were relatively ineffective and sanitary notions rudimentary, the heavy losses in campaigns were due as much to epidemics as to casualties in battle. A count of the number of troops under arms was 'ascertained or preserved in cowries or coins'. Ramseyer and Kühne, the captive missionaries, wrote that on returning from a battle 'every chief who passed before the king threw into a vase as many grains of corn as he had lost people' (cited Wilks 1975: 81). This was evidently a long-established method of computation, for an Arab gold dinar was reckoned to weigh 72 such grains. The Asante authorities knew the estimated strength of each province; this was reported by intelligence to the British in 1873.

Dahomey was famous for its 'Amazons', the women soldiers who were recruited by summoning to the royal palace on a fixed day the daughters of all the king's subjects and choosing those who looked most promising from among them (Skertchly 1874, cited Argyle 1966: 87). They were actually a bodyguard, necessarily female since only women lived in the palace, and there are varying accounts of them, some saying that they rarely went to war, others that they had done so from the early eighteenth century. There were two war captains, of the right and left wing, with their female counterparts. Leaders of local groups brought their followers with them, and these were combined in different ways, but the groups themselves do not seem to have been broken up as were the corresponding ones among the Zulu.

War was as normal a part of the routine of Dahomey as planting and harvesting the crops. A campaign was fought every year. The word for 'war' meant 'man-hunt' (Argyle 1966: 81), and its sole purpose was the taking of captives, which had a ritual as well as a material purpose since many were put to death at the great annual festival—the 'Customs'—so that their blood should 'water the graves' of the king's ancestors. For these ritual reasons a territory was not held to have been effectively conquered until its king had been killed. The Dahomeyan spies had magical rather than practical functions; their duty was to destroy the power of the spirits on whom the enemy relied for protection.

It was only the kingdoms on the borders of the Sahara that could employ cavalry; on the one hand horses are effective only in open country, and on the other they cannot live where diseases carried by the tsetse fly are endemic. Horses, unlike soldiers, consume food, even in peace time, which they do not help to produce (since sub-Saharan Africa did not know the plough). A description of the cavalry force of the short-lived (1818–62) Fulani empire of Masina, in the interior delta of the Niger, tells us that there were mounted soldiers in all the principal towns, as many as 10,000 at the capital. The whole population was liable to serve in the army—not all, of course, in the cavalry. Horsemen were given an allowance for weapons and harness, and on campaigns they had rations for themselves and their horses, and an allowance of food was given their families; so that the generalization that cavalry fighting must create an aristocracy because of the high cost of gear and horses does not seem to hold good here. Smiths and leather-workers went with the army on campaigns. Although the numbers of the horses themselves could be kept up and increased through war captures, the food had to come from home production, and it was largely grown by the slaves who fell to the share of the royal treasury in the distribution of spoils (Johnson 1975).

CHAPTER VI
INTERNAL ORGANIZATION

As soon as an appreciable area comes to be controlled from a single centre, problems arise of the delegation of authority; and where the control is extended over populations already organized in states, the new ruler has to decide whether he will leave the existing one in a vassal relationship, get rid of him altogether, or exercise some form of surveillance and control over him. In the nature of things the most recently conquered areas will be the furthest from the centre, and where communications are limited to the speed of a horse or even that of a fast runner, it will be over them that it is hardest to maintain authority.

On the furthest fringes vassal kingdoms and subject populations must have revolted and been reconquered, or brought to order by force when rebellion was threatened, more than once in a kingdom's history; and of course rebellions that could not be put down marked stages in the decline of empires. We hear, for example, of seven campaigns by kings of Rwanda against the Tutsi chief of Gisaka, and of Hutu populations in the north who were never effectively subdued until the king had the support of German troops. Eighteenth-century records of Asante refer to several expeditions for the reconquest of peoples who had earlier given their submission.

But what is more interesting is the way in which continuous relations were maintained between the dominant authority and populations with different degrees of autonomy. There was usually a central core in which the descendants of conquerors and conquered were together subject directly to the ruler through the medium of chiefs appointed by him. Where this is so, the criterion of distinction between core and periphery is the source of local authority—essentially, whether this is in the hands of bureaucrats or of subject rulers. From East Africa we learn more about the substitution of bureaucrats for lineage heads in the dominant population than we do about relations with tributary vassals; the history of the establishment of authority in Rwanda which was summarized earlier is one of the removal, not the control, of rival authorities. The least centralized kingdom that we know of is Ankole, despite the fact that it seems to have been expanding throughout the nineteenth century, when its authority over petty kingdoms whose relations with it were ambiguous was confirmed by the British government in Uganda. The periphery, as our sources describe it, consisted in the border areas of Ankole itself, where chiefs appointed from among the king's retainers were mainly responsible for defence, but had to rely largely on warrior cattle owners who had offered to the king an allegiance that they were able to withdraw if they felt strong enough to protect their own interests, or preferred to attach themselves to a neighbouring king.

The Core and the Periphery

It is, however, in West Africa that we are able to see clearly the distinction between core and periphery and the kind of relations maintained between superior rulers and their vassal states. Attached to the Habe kingdom of Zazzau (which has been called Zaria since the Fulani conquest that was launched in 1804) in the days of its independence were four small vassal states. The king of Zazzau had the formal right to appoint the rulers of these states, although there is no record of any interference with hereditary succession as this was understood by their own subjects. But a vassal on his succession had to be formally confirmed in office, either by an envoy of the king sent to receive his allegiance or by the king himself if he came to the capital to offer it. The king presented him with the insignia of office, of which, here as in so many places, the principal was a drum. He described himself as a client or dependent of the king, as some among his subjects would call themselves his own clients, and was required to pay tribute and supply soldiers when called upon.

The Fulani conquerors were themselves vassals of the Sultan of Sokoto, the direct descendant of the leader in the holy war, and were linked to him in much the same way. The Emir of Zaria was expected to visit Sokoto, taking the due tribute with him, at the two great annual Muslim festivals. The amount demanded was steadily increased, and by the end of the century an Emir was expected to make gifts in addition, on his own accession and on that of a Sultan. A third of an Emir's property went to the Sultan when he died. The Sultan claimed the right to dismiss the rulers of Zaria as well as to appoint them, and this right was exercised on a number of occasions. What made this burdensome allegiance worth while was that, from the time of the Fulani conquest, there was competition for the throne between the members of three lineages, in which the Sultan's support was an important factor. There is record of a rebellion of another vassal of Sokoto in 1850, when Zaria and three other Emirs sent troops for a campaign against him (which was unsuccessful). But on other occasions Zaria was entitled to ask for military aid from Sokoto.

The southward expansion of Fulani rule was effected not by combined forces directed from Sokoto but by the independent enterprise of those Fulani whose domains bordered on pagan lands. Thus Zaria itself added to the number of its vassals, and sometimes vassal states were exchanged between neighbouring Fulani kingdoms. Both in Habe Zazzau and in Fulani Sokoto a court official was responsible for dealings between each vassal and his overlord. Affairs in Zaria were in charge of the Sultan's senior official, the Wazir, who in time came to demand a separate tribute for himself when he visited the city once a year.

The Dahomean method of keeping the periphery in subjection was unusual. When a people were defeated in war, their villages were destroyed and the population driven away; if they came back they were attacked again. But if their king was killed the king of Dahomey appointed an official to replace him and allowed them to stay where they were or, if they had fled, to return to their homes.

The 'core' of the Asante empire consisted of Kumase with five states close to it (the 'five great peoples') which are said to have offered their allegiance to the conqueror Osei Tutu when he made it his capital. Hereditary succession to the headship of these states was and still is recognized, though the Asantehene, like the British in their 'indirect rule' territories, could remove individuals and could influence the succession. Superficially their position resembled that of subordinate chiefs anywhere; they levied tribute from their own subjects as well as that required by the Asantehene, they tried cases with an appeal to him. Just as the great Nyoro chiefs wore beaded crowns like the king's, they wore 'the little silver circles like buckles which distinguish the sandals of the king' (Bowdich, cited Wilks 1975: 113). But they and their descendants were always conscious that they had not received delegated authority from the Asantehene but had surrendered elements of their own power. The British consul Dupuis in 1820 thought the chief of Dwaben (who had been described as the Asantehene's 'brother king') was 'an independent ally', and was sharply rapped on the knuckles by the Asantehene for saying so; but it is just possible that the Dwabenhene thought the same. Mampon and Dwaben both went to war on their own, and at first at any rate levied their own tribute from the peoples they conquered; the Asantehene eventually took over Mampon's rights in payment of a debt owed him. These two states fought each other over their northern conquests, but the Asantehene asserted his right to settle the dispute, though nobody knows what the settlement was. In 1831 Dwaben had to be reduced by fighting. From the beginning there was a centrally controlled army in the sense that each of the five chiefs had a title designing the place of his contingent in it. Later, taxes of different kinds were levied directly on individuals and no longer in the form of tribute assessed on an area; this is referred to by several writers as 'exemption from tribute' and is taken by Wilks as a defining criterion of incorporation. Nevertheless, it can only have been because they preserved their sense of autonomy that all these chiefdoms toyed with the idea of secession after the defeat of Asante by the British in 1874.

Boundaries between the metropolitan region and the inner provinces, and between these and the outer, were marked by posts where travellers were stopped, might be refused passage, and had to pay dues, on each of-the 'great roads' that radiated outwards from Kumase. This in itself tells us little about any difference in political relations with Kumase between the inner and outer provinces. An ingenious calculation by Wilks, based on Asante statements about the number of days a journey to various different points was supposed to take, leads him to relate the effectiveness of control to 'message-delay'. He concludes that the minimum message-delay from Kumase—the time taken to send a message *and get an answer*—was six to twelve days in the metropolitan (the 'core') region, about a month in the inner provinces, and up to seven weeks in the outer provinces to the north. In this connection he remarks that messages had to be memorized by their carriers. But early in the nineteenth century written documents, carried in boxes, were becoming common.

The distinction made by the nineteenth-century writers between subjects and tributaries corresponds to that made elsewhere in this chapter between subjects and vassals. Although Dupuis wrote of the 'tributaries' as being 'left to the government of their own caboceers' (cited Wilks 1975: 63), this hardly seems to be a crucial distinction when we recall that even the five 'great peoples' had their own chiefs. What is more significant is that in the more distant provinces an emissary from the metropolis resided permanently. These men were nominated by the great chiefs of the Asantehene, who here, as in Zazzau, were each made responsible for certain of the outlying areas.

Nadel (1942), writing of the Emirate of Nupe, describes a very much more fluid situation, one in which the core was hardly more effectively controlled than the periphery. Within the kingdom proper the princes and other office-holders fought among themselves or raided 'outer peoples' who, having paid the tribute due from them in slaves, had a claim to be left in peace. Moreover, the Emir might countenance raids on these 'protected persons'; all they were in fact protected against was raids from other states. Nadel refers to chiefs 'put in charge' of these districts, but his not very clear statements seem to imply that the sole 'charge' was the responsibility to go with an army to collect the tribute.

The principle followed in Dahomey, that conquered peoples were not allowed to return to their homes unless they surrendered the head of their king, was hardly compatible with the recognition of tributary vassals. According to Le Hérissé (cited Argyle 1966: 29–30), after the conquest of the related kingdom of Allada the king's chief minister was made responsible for it, but he did not have to go and live there. We are also told, however, that Dahomean kings sometimes appointed heads of conquered towns from among the population and sometimes from among their own followers.

Territorial Authority

While these differences in modes of controlling peripheral populations are interesting, the possibilities of greatest elaboration are to be found in the government of the people who are held to be directly subject to the king. The simplest way of delegating authority within such a realm would be to carve it up (notionally) into a number of geographical areas, each with a single head responsible to the king for law and order, and for the organization of whatever services and payments were required. This was what the kingdoms in Uganda looked like when they had been streamlined by British authorities who were supposedly maintaining the traditional system with just a little tidying up. It is, apparently, what Asante really was like, since all its states kept their traditional boundaries and the Asantehene's sanctions against their hereditary rulers took the form of fines. But in many places, kings were constantly creating new chiefdoms to reward their followers, and these could not always be found in newly conquered territory. In Buganda it is recorded that the twenty-second Kabaka created a new kind of chiefdom called *butongole*, by placing loyal followers whom he wished to reward in authority over sections of the wider areas that have commonly been called counties in English. These posts were not hereditary, so that it was not absolutely necessary to keep founding new ones, but their numbers did continually increase. The holders were subject to the general authority of the county chiefs, but were clearly in a different relation to them from that of the subordinates whom they chose themselves. They raised troops from the areas under their control, but these were not part of the county chief's contingent; they led their men directly to the capital. Father Gorju, writing in 1920, compared them to a parasitic organism attached to the county chief; their direct relation to the Kabaka implied the obligation of spying on other authorities and was one way of restricting the power of the greater territorial chiefs, as was the appointment of paired chiefs in Rwanda. Estates allotted to queen-mothers were under the authority of chiefs, who may perhaps have been included among the *baton-gole*. Others again supplied revenues for chiefs with duties at court. In addition, in the nineteenth century further areas were given to the military chiefs who were mentioned in Chapter II.

There was a recognized rank order among the ten great chiefs, but there was no 'promotion ladder' such as existed in some West African kingdoms. Nor could there have been as long as it was possible for them to maintain a claim to hereditary office, and the kings who refused in the nineteenth century to recognize such claims were not likely to tie themselves to any other formula that would limit their freedom of choice.

In some kingdoms even major chiefs were not given authority over large contiguous areas. Bradbury describes the divisions of Benin as 'tribute units', villages or groups of villages from which various individuals were responsible for collecting tribute and providing manpower for public works or war; most of these went with chiefly titles, though they could be transferred from one title to another, and the areas under any one title might be scattered all over the kingdom. Similarly in Fulani Zazzau the 'tribute units', or 'fiefs' as M. G. Smith prefers to call them, consisted of numbers of small towns with the hamlets attached to them. Each of these had its own head, a member of the local community, and the actual execution of orders from above was in this man's hands. A large fief-holder would have agents in charge of different parts of his estates, and he could appoint and transfer them at will. They were his clients as he and the other fief-holders were clients of the king, and for both categories a title was the evidence of right to authority. Some titles in Zazzau were claimed as hereditary, but in the main the king disposed of them as he pleased, and in Smith's view transferred or demoted the holders less in the interests of efficiency than in that of rewarding his followers; this fact is connected with the rule that the kingship rotated between lineages, each of which did its best for its own members.

As Gluckman describes the organization of Barotseland it

was individuals who were set under the authority of different titles, and when a new title was created its holder was given resources and responsibilities by attaching to it 'people scattered over Barotseland'. Such a division of the population was called a *likolo*, a word which Gluckman translates as 'sector'. The chief of any sector had subordinates, among whom the sector members were not necessarily distributed individually; people could 'take affairs' (1951: 33) to any chief of their sector, but whatever these affairs were, in judicial matters they went to the capital, where all the chiefs of the sector held court as a body. People were summoned by sectors for public works, or war, or for large communal hunts. Only on the periphery of the kingdom were non-Lozi populations sometimes attached *en bloc* to one sector, and even there this was not done systematically. For purposes of tribute payment there was yet another arrangement; people were allocated, again as individuals, to a number of 'storehouses' for which 'stewards' were responsible. How this system could have been maintained over the generations in a society which did not recognize unilineal descent groups it is very hard to see, and Gluckman only tells us that it was 'extremely difficult to work out the framework of this very complicated administrative system', but that every Lozi knew exactly where he fitted into it (1951: 39). But however the system came into being, it had the same result as the less complicated one in Benin, that there were no territorially based political units of a size to constitute a threat to the royal authority; and it was valued by the Barotse people, who were indignant when it was destroyed by British authorities in the interests of efficiency. The councillors who agreed to the change, Gluckman tells us, writing shortly after the event, 'have been discharged by the whole nation'. How? That he does not tell us.

The practical need to distribute authority over divisions of a kingdom is obvious; in addition this distribution could sometimes solve the problem of satisfying (or neutralizing) the ambitions of members of royal lineages. In such kingdoms as that of the Azande or the Luba princes this problem was solved by territorial expansion, a process that went on until fixed boundaries were imposed under colonial rule. In the

Interlacustrine Bantu kingdoms princes were kept under strict control, occasionally massacred lest they attack their royal brothers. In Asante sons of kings, who in this matrilineal society had no direct claim to the kingship, were often appointed to bureaucratic positions; rivalry between members of the royal lineage seems to have been confined to competition for the succession. In Benin during the period of its expansion members of the royal lineage, usually the sons of the king's brother, were given an authority over outlying districts which was then recognized to be hereditary; they did not displace the village heads who held their position by right of seniority but exercised varying degrees of control over them. The implications of the Zaria rule of rotating succession have been mentioned, and will be discussed again in connection with various types of political competition.

If the need to create subordinate authorities offered kings a way of rewarding their supporters and endowing their kin, the need to reward supporters and endow kinsmen could lead to the proliferation of offices. The most remarkable example of this is the system which developed in Lesotho after the kingdom became a British colony. As a colony Lesotho (then Basutoland) had fixed frontiers and a rapidly expanding population, not least among the royal lineage with its many wives. British authority there for a long time was confined to supporting the king (now Paramount Chief) and maintaining order; it did not seek, as elsewhere, to reorganize the administrative system until as late as 1938.

Out of the very common idea that princes should be set in authority over outlying districts, and the by no means uncommon idea that the heir to a chiefdom or kingdom should serve an apprenticeship in administration, there evolved the practice of 'placing' not only all the king's many sons but those of the senior chiefs (themselves descended from him) in authority over areas from which they derived revenues, and a belief on the part of these royal sons that they had a claim to be maintained in this way. When a chief's son was 'placed' the existing chief was not dismissed but became his subordinate, with the legal consequence that cases tried by him could be appealed to the newcomer. Only the humble headmen or village chiefs who were originally members of the small local community were eventually crowded out by royal kin, so that the number of chiefs continually increased.

When a royal son was 'placed' he traditionally built his own village, the land for which had to be provided by the chief already in authority over the area. The latter was asked to designate the 'place', but in practice he might find he had to give up half his domain, and within this area the new chief could himself 'place' kinsmen and followers. Then he would begin to require the chief who had been demoted to make room for him to provide him with services—ploughing and gathering firewood, the latter a service customarily demanded by Sotho chiefs. In a case recorded by Ashton (1952: 201–2) the earlier chief ultimately lost one-third of his subjects. Boundaries were not clearly drawn, except in cases where disputes were referred to magistrate's courts, and the new chief would be constantly trying to extend the area under his direct control. Where both the senior chief and his subordinate had sons to 'place' there was even more competition.

A report made in 1935 on the administration of Basutoland was highly critical of a system under which chiefs could be said (by one of their subjects) to be 'as many as there are stars in the heavens', and shortly afterwards the British authorities decided to cut down the number whose authority they would recognize. Such a policy, though clearly desirable for administrative efficiency, only increased the anxieties of the lower level chiefs whose position was already insecure. At the time when it was being implemented there was an outbreak of murders committed in order to use the victim's flesh for magical purposes, and some of these were undoubtedly organized by chiefs who thought that to have such medicines would strengthen their position.

Specialist offices: Asante

The more complex the organization of the kingdom, the more necessary it was to create specialized offices concerned with particular aspects of national business. As was indicated in the previous chapter, specialized military officials can sometimes be found in kingdoms where other special responsibilities are confined to the upkeep of the palace and the control of its population. Other specialist officers were generally based on the capital, and if they were in charge of activities outside they might nominate henchmen to represent them on the spot. But a striking exception is to be found in connection with the control of trade in those West African kingdoms that depended on it. We learn how this was managed from the records of traders which go back to the seventeenth century.

Bosman wrote in 1700 of Dahomey: 'For every Affair that can be thought of the King hath appointed a Captain Overseer, also a great many Honorary Captains'. He specified as the Grand Captains, whom he also called Vice-Roys, the Captain of the Market, the Captain of Slaves, the Captain of the Tron (prison), and the Captain of the Shore; though he did not describe the duties of the last-named, he must have been in charge of transactions with the trading ships, as were two of the Benin palace officials. Later the four Vice-Roys were described as being responsible for dealing respectively with Portuguese, English, French, and Dutch ships. They or their servants watched the landing of goods, and before anyone else could buy, they agreed the amount to be paid in customs, and then bought on the king's behalf such goods as he required, notably fire-arms and powder, over which he maintained a strict control; often he pre-empted as much as two-thirds of the cargo. Sellers of slaves were required to pay a tax on each man sold. Canoe trading by African middlemen was supervised in the same way.

As the organization of a kingdom becomes more complex, it can be expected that new needs will be met by assigning additional responsibilities to existing palace officials. This is what happened in the creation of the Asante king's company of traders. Its original members were the king's drummers and horn-blowers, men whose duties in the palace were not strictly limited to what was implicit in their designation. An Asante told Wilks that they 'did any job which the Asantehene required'. They accompanied the singers who on state occasions chanted the names of royal ancestors, and the horn-blowers every midnight played a sort of national anthem which, so Bowdich was told, represented the king's thanks to

his officers and people. But both they and the drummers also
kept the palace in repair and were responsible for royal burials.
Their leading members, like the Ganda royal cooks and but-
chers, were important persons. As early as 1714 a 'King of
Ashantee's Drummer' was visiting the coast to buy guns. As
Asante trade increased and the king imposed strict control
upon it, the chief of the horn-blowers became the head of the
traders, a 'company' or 'department' called the *batafo*. The
leading men of this company received advances in gold dust
from the Asantehene with which they bought their trading
stock, or, alternatively, paid for the guns and powder that they
bought from the coast. The gold-dust was given out at the
Adae ceremonies which were held every six weeks, and when
an expedition came back, its leader gave an account (both
financial and narrative) of its activities and a share of the profit
made was allotted to the members of the expedition. The
Asokwahene, the hereditary head of the company, an office
that went with authority over territory near Kumase,
nominated the leaders of different expeditions, and they collected carriers from the villages under his control, some of these
being slaves and some women; there would also be an armed
guard. A caravan might number two or three hundred people.

A participant's account of such an expedition was given to
Rattray by an old man who described the typical organization.
It is worth noting that he was talking of a caravan sent out not
by the Asantehene himself but by the chief of Mampon, since
this shows that the bands of functionaries at a subordinate
court closely paralleled those of Kumase. This old man recalled
an annual journey to the north to sell kola nuts, the one
stimulant permitted to Moslims, for which the demand rose
steeply after the re-establishment of orthodox Islam in the northern kingdoms by the Fulani conquest. The kola nuts were
bought in the forests between Mampon and Kumase. The
caravan would leave early in the season when prices were high,
accompanied by messengers whose golden-hilted state swords
showed that they were official emissaries, and, when it had
passed, the same messengers closed the road to other travellers
to prevent competition by private traders. When they had done
their business the road was opened, and a toll, in nuts, not in

gold-dust, was collected from any other traders who passed; one-fifth of this was kept by the collectors. The official traders were allowed to deal on their own account in small quantities of nuts in addition to the loads carried on behalf of the chief, which were of a standard size, 1,500 or 2,000 nuts. These expeditions may have had slaves with them carrying food, but Rattray's informant said 'it was no disgrace for a free man to carry a load while trading' (Rattray 1929: 109–111).

The royal revenues in gold-dust were in charge of a special company under the Gyaasewahene. The total reserves were kept in one enormous box, and according to tradition it was held to be desirable that this should be full. Wilks (1975: 419) calculated that it could hold gold dust to the value of £1,500,000 sterling at nineteenth-century rates. Its contents were kept in reserve, while wooden boxes and glass flagons were used for smaller, but nevertheless appreciable, amounts. Each held 1,000 peredwans (about £8,000), and each peredwan was separately wrapped in cloth, as were smaller quantities. It would be from these that the Asantehene made his advances to traders at the Adae. Goldsmiths (another company) worked in a room next to that in which the great chest was kept, reducing the nuggets to dust. Around 1870 about 100 men were employed in this work. Gold-dust was weighed when it was received or paid out; this was the responsibility of another company, the 'openers of the bag'; the bag, an elaborate decorated leather satchel with a padlock, was a container not of money but of implements for weighing. A rough account was kept by the simple method of putting a cowrie shell in the box whenever a peredwan was taken out, and removing one each time this amount was paid in. As Rattray points out, the people concerned in money transactions remembered them with remarkable accuracy, as those who have to get on without written records often do.

Two companies of officials were concerned with road communications. The *akwanmofo* were created in the eighteenth century 'for cleaning the roads and paths of the kingdom of nuisances', that is seeing that the authorities through whose land they passed kept them open. They had funds to pay for the work and were authorized to fine those 'committing a nuisance'—Reindorf's phrase, which Wilks interprets as 'failing to keep the ways cleared'. Just as collectors of tribute or other dues (of which there were many) were remunerated by keeping a share of what they collected, so the road inspectors were entitled to a share of these fines.

The *nkwansrafo* (police) lived permanently at points on the great roads—the points, says Wilks (1975: 48), where they crossed the boundaries of the metropolitan region. If the metropolitan region is defined as the area entry into which' is subject to control, this description is a tautology. However, the fact is that travellers who arrived at these posts were stopped and questioned, and not allowed to go further until a messenger had gone to the capital and come back with permission. It was the *nkwansrafo* who collected the tolls, and who closed the roads to individuals who might seek to compete with the official traders. At one time there were reported to be 500 or 600 armed men at one of these posts.

Along with the 'sword-bearers', whose presence guaranteed the official character of any mission, for trading or simply to convey messages, there were heralds (who sometimes seem to have been the same people) and 'criers'. According to Rattray the main function of the heralds was at court, where they would intersperse the speech of an important person with calls of 'Listen, listen' (something that was still being done to my knowledge in 1952), while the 'criers' went round the city beating the 'gong-gong', actually a not very resonant piece of metal struck with another piece of metal, to call attention to some announcement made from the court. Every chief had his own heralds and gong-beaters. Sometimes, it seems, they were sent all over the country to announce decisions if important.

Estimates were made from time to time of the numbers engaged in these different activities. The Gyaasewahene was said to have more than 1,000 men under him, and the company of heralds and gong-beaters to number 1,000. The 'official carriers'—of persons, not goods—numbered, in contrast, only 100. A senior official was entitled to build an open-fronted room (*dampan*) facing the public way in which he received people with requests to make, also to have a large decorated umbrella. European observers often counted the numbers of such umbrellas at meetings which they attended. Wilks (1975: 467) reckons that there were about 250 such notables, but these would include territorial as well as specialist authorities.

Although these bodies of men were called companies, they had little in common with the Benin associations. Theoretically appointment to posts of authority within them was in the gift of the Asantehene, but in practice they seem to have frequently passed from father to son. The general rule of succession in Asante was matrilineal, but a specialist official was expected to train his successor; if he chose a younger brother he would still be following the matrilineal rule, but it seems that when a set of brothers had been exhausted the next to succeed would be a son, not a sister's son, of his predecessor. As Wilks observes, the reason was that a post to which nomination was theoretically free would most likely be filled by someone who had acquired the necessary qualifications, and he again would most likely be one who had grown up in an official's household; but it is still not clear why these officials did not have sisters and their children living with them in the normal Asante family pattern. It is interesting too that when, under colonial rule, the titles describing the posts became purely honorific, they began to be inherited in the female line.

Highest of all in the state, after the king, were the men who have been called 'linguists' almost ever since anyone began to write about them in English. Rattray, the first anthropologist to write of Asante, called them 'spokesmen', a translation of their Twi name which more effectively indicates their functions. The *akyeame* spoke in the name of the king on public occasions, notably on the installation of chiefs and in trying court cases. It was also the *akyeame* who were the intermediaries between the Asantehene and subordinate chiefs (see Chapter III). A story recorded by Rattray (1929: 150) illustrates this duty. After the destruction of Kumase by Sir Garnet Wolseley in 1874 there was a general move to throw off the Asantehene's authority. Dwaben rebelled, and there seemed a danger that it would be joined by Bekwae. An *okyeame* and a sword-bearer were sent to summon the Bekwaehene to Kumase, where he asserted his loyalty and offered to commit his forces in action against Dwaben (a version which suggests that divisional chiefs did not

automatically obey the royal order). But the king did not allow
him to command his own troops for fear he should go over to
Dwaben. When such a rebellion was successfully put down, it
was for the *okyeame* to fix the indemnity to be paid. Every chief
at whatever level had his *okyeame*. Those of the chiefs of the
important companies were apparently appointed by the king,
and they exercised as much influence on their activities as the
chiefs themselves.

Specialist offices: Zazzau

The organization of the kingdom of Zazzau may well have
been as complex as that of Asante, though the records of it that
exist do not allow one to describe it in anything like the same
detail. Here the senior official was a man promoted from
among the palace eunuchs, who were recruited from a limited
number of villages. This officer, the Galadima, held ultimate
responsibility for all civil matters, including control over the
territorial authorities. He was concerned with the maintenance
of roads and ferries, with supplies to the capital, and in time of
war to the army. He controlled the police, who were drawn
from the king's slaves, and offenders who were tried in the
capital were punished in his compound. In time of war the king
went with the army and the Galadima acted as his deputy.
Next to him came the military leader, the Madawaki, whose
title means 'owner of the horses'. He too was appointed by
promotion from the household officials, but as a free subject of
the king he was rewarded for his services by the grant of fiefs, as
well as the right to distribute among his own followers half of
the spoils of any victorious campaign. Eunuch officials had no
such right; they received a share of the taxes that they collected
and were maintained as members of the royal household. Each
of these two officials had territorial control over one half of the
capital.

Next in rank to the Galadima were two other eunuchs,
Wombai and Dallatu. The latter took the place of the
Galadima on campaigns and was in charge of the army's 'civil
administration' (i.e. commissariat?) (Smith 1960: 45). The
Wombai is simple described as an assistant of the Galadima.
Slaves were employed in other public duties, unspecified, as

well as that of police, and titles were conferred on those holding authority in the different spheres. Collectively they were subject to the joint control of a subordinate of the Madawaki and of the head of the palace officials.

In the Hausa kingdom the mallams, the Koranic scholars, had purely religious functions, and should not be mentioned in a discussion of administrative organization but for the fact that a mallam could be appointed to a civil office, in which case he had to give up his priestly duties and his claim to be supported by alms.

The Fulani conquerors preserved certain elements of the traditional system, but with as much distortion as the British were later to make in their attempts to preserve such systems while adapting them to new requirements. In this case they had the initial advantage that most of the high officials of Zazzau fled with their king to Abuja.

In Habe Zazzau only three titles were held by members of the royal family, two of these being women. The third was the Dan Galadima, the king's chosen successor, who does not appear to have had any administrative responsibilities. Under the Fulani three lineages in turn were entitled to provide the ruler, an arrangement made by the Sultan of Sokoto to reward those who had taken major parts in the conquest. There was no strict order of succession, but it became the rule, a very rational one, that only a man who had held one of the senior titled offices could become king. Moreover the arrangement for the rotation of lineages implied that there were spoils of office of which each in turn should have its share. The king was now expected to appoint to 'offices of profit' one son of each of his wives, and in addition to find posts for other kinsmen and affines. The highest offices were considered to be appropriate for sons, others for grandsons, of a king; the latter category could not succeed. No longer were the highest offices rendered politically neutral by reserving them for men who could have no heirs; now they were key positions in struggles for power.

A comparison of the Fulani system with that which preceded it seems to indicate that there were fewer organizations directly dependent on high officials at the capital, and that instead all holders of territorial authority were general purpose officers.

They still lived at the capital, leaving subordinates in actual charge of their districts, which were in practice allotted as fiefs to persons whom the king wished to reward or favour. Some of these fiefs came in practice to be hereditary; others were re-allocated during the lifetime of the holders. The fief-holder had the ultimate responsibility for the basic requirements of political peace and the observance of Islamic law, for the collection of tribute and labour and the provision of manpower for civil and military purposes. The essential difference between African kingdoms in this respect was in the nature of the public works required. At the minimum what was called for was the maintenance of the residences of kings and chiefs; then the clearing of roads, something in which Buganda was exceptional in East Africa but which was normal in the west. Fulani Zazzau was concerned with the upkeep of town walls, mosques, and markets, the last item implying law and order as well as clearing weeds.

A major innovation made by the Fulani was to entrust judicial functions to the mallams as part of the restoration of the strict law of Islam which had been the motive of their crusade. Such a recognition of professional judges might be thought to imply that separation of powers which western nations have considered vital to civil liberties. The mallams were entitled to try officials for an offence called *zalunci* or maladministration, which is condemned by the authoritative exponents of Islam. But whereas the word had originally implied oppressive rule, it came to mean no more than failure to carry out the ruler's orders.

Slaves

Missing from the list of services that a fief-holder could claim is one that is conspicuous in all accounts from other regions of Africa: farm work as a contribution to the food supply of a king's or chief's capital. The reason lies in the major contrast between the west and the other regions, its reliance for manpower on slaves. Not that war captives were not made servants elsewhere, but they were attached to the households of their captors and little differentiated from the rest, except that the most disagreeable work would fall to them. But in West Africa

slaves were an object of wealth; rulers demanded them in tribute, Africans as well as Europeans bought them for whatever
was accepted as currency in different areas. One of the tenets of
Islam was that the faithful were entitled to enslave the infidels,
and in Zaria raiding for slaves in the non-Islamic subject areas
did not count as war or require royal permission.

Thus the slaves of an important man were far too numerous
to be treated as household dependents; they were a labour force
which freed him from the necessity of directly providing his
own subsistence; they were capital just as machinery is capital.
Both in Zaria and in Benin slaves were settled in villages where
they cultivated land for their masters, and in Benin they cultivated oil palms as an export crop. In Zaria the members of
the three royal lineages were entitled to create separate slave
villages and even sometimes small walled towns, which came
under their direct authority and on which they paid no tax or
tribute. But others, and everyone in Benin, had to get authorization—in effect, the right to occupy land—from territorial
authorities before setting up such villages, and in Benin there
might be bands of slaves of different masters in the same village.

Of Asante Bowdich wrote that slaves were employed 'to
create plantations in the more remote and stubborn tracts'
(cited Wilks 1975: 52), though when he wrote of Kumase he
said these remote parts were only two or three miles from the
town; there, the slaves produced the food for their masters'
large households in the town and also 'fruit and vegetables for
sale', and looked after some of their masters' numerous children. A significant occupation for slaves was gold-mining, the
very basis of the economy of the kingdom. The Asante held this
to be a profanation of the earth for which they themselves, if
they picked up gold, would suffer ritual punishment.

CHAPTER VII
THE RESOURCES OF KINGDOMS

Reciprocity or Exploitation?

DURING the period between the establishment and the withdrawal of European rule in Africa the attitudes of the thinking people among the ruling nations towards the political institutions of the subject ones went through a series of changes, and we see yet a new phase in the interpretation of those institutions now that it is for Africans themselves to judge how far they deserve to be maintained.

However much the expansion of Europe in Africa was dictated by material interests, some of the individuals who took part in it had other aims—the dissemination of Christian belief and with it of the values then held to be associated with 'civilization'. Of course it was reassuring for those who were seeking their fortunes to be told that this was an incidental part of the process, but they were not much concerned with details of the ways in which African institutions fell short of the civilized ideal. It was those responsible for the administration of African territories who thought it was their duty to introduce just rule and free Africans from oppression, an attitude which led them to interpret African rule in terms of injustice and oppression: Africans must be freed from arbitrary exactions in the economic sphere, arbitrary decisions in the political. In some places this led to the total suppression of African authority, in others—those from which most of the material in this book is taken—to attempts to improve standards of African rule.

A revulsion accompanied the recognition that European rule had been by no means wholly just nor self-denying in the field of exactions. This did not in itself lead to a revaluation of African rule, but it was associated, for those who wanted to know what African institutions were really like, with the functional theory of anthropology which asserted that the institutions that non-industrial peoples had developed for themselves were those best suited to their needs, and should not be arbitrarily modified by paternalist outsiders. At the same time some administrative officers were looking at the people for whom they were responsible with eyes that saw something other than abuses to be suppressed. Anthropologists began to talk in terms of reciprocity, the return that a king made to his subjects for the prestations that he demanded of them, and of consensus, the reasons that led them to accept his rule as legitimate. An element in their attitude was that they conceived it as their duty to present the institutions of the societies they studied without the adverse prejudices that were and still are widely current among the uninformed; and at the very least they were prepared to maintain that those institutions were valued by the people whose lives they regulated.

More recently a new trend has appeared, which is associated with the popularity of new interpretations of Marxism, though not all the writers who follow it would call themselves Marxists. In this interpretation, traditional African political systems are again represented as exploitative and oppressive and as resting on coercion rather than consensus; and this of course is consistent with the view that all political authority is so. This is the attitude at present of only a minority of anthropologists. But these alternative interpretations need to be examined.

Since the economic functions of government are essential to its organization, we should consider first the question whether the taxpayers and tributaries in African kingdoms thought they got, or did get, an adequate or fair return for their contribution to the upkeep of the kingdom. Where peripheral vassal states are concerned, it might sometimes be difficult to argue that they did. Yet Bowdich was quite clear about what was gained by Dagomba as tributary of Asante: 'at the expense of an inconsiderable tribute he established a commercial intercourse which, his markets being regularly supplied from the interior, was both an advantage and a security to him' (Bowdich 1819: 234, cited Goody 1968: 203). And when Asante authority was rejected after 1874, the prosperity of the trading cities declined. By that time, evidently, Dagomba made the calculation differ-

ently. To outsiders attempting objective assessment, the benefits of security would seem clearly greater where trade was
more important.

On the whole it is from small kingdoms or from the core
areas of empires that we can sometimes learn how subjects
envisaged the nature of their exchange with their rulers.
Sometimes this was an exchange of material for intangible
goods; taxes maintain the authorities, certainly at a somewhat
higher level than the majority of their subjects, though this
depends to some extent on the total resources of the kingdom,
and in return they receive institutions for the settlement of
disputed claims which make it unnecessary to seek private
redress. There is evidence that the law-enforcing function of
authority is valued. The neighbours of the Alur, chiefdoms so
tiny that they have not been discussed in this book, would ask
an Alur chief to send them one of his sons, who, they thought,
had the necessary hereditary ritual power, to live among them
and settle their disputes. Cynics have argued that traditions of
such incidents are merely inventions to justify Alur expansion.
But Elizabeth Colson, writing of the acephalous Tonga of
Zambia, is satisfied that they welcomed the coming of an over-
riding authority (in this case British) which made it unnecessary for them to rely on force to settle their quarrels. What they
valued was not so much, or not only, greater security, but a
method of decision that was more expeditious than the gathering of kin and friends, perhaps from a distance, to support one's
case in a discussion among equals. She cites other societies
which abandoned the pursuit of claims by force as soon as they
heard of the coming of administrative courts 'almost as if they
had only been waiting an excuse to give it up' (Sorrenson 1972,
cited Colson 1974: 65). Jacob Black-Michaud, writing of
Albania, where feuds were carried on till a later period than
anywhere else in Europe, notes that they repeatedly told
enquirers that 'what they really needed ... was a strong
government with an efficient army to compel them to abandon
the feud' (1975: 134). Of course everyone believes that unfair
judgements are given in individual cases, particularly cases that
he has lost himself, but this does not contradict the view that
judicial institutions in themselves are valued.

The second question to be asked is that of the economic returns for the tribute and services given. The Azande were very clear on this. *Ru ae*, gifts to a prince, should, they said, be balanced by *fu ae*, gifts to his subjects. 'If raw beans went into the royal residence they ought to return to court as cooked beans; if termite oil went into the royal residence it ought to return to court as a relish to flavour porridge; if malted eleusine went into the royal residence it ought to return to the inner court as brewed beer; and if the subjects cultivated their masters' eleusine, the harvest ought to be pounded, ground, and cooked as porridge for those same subjects to eat at court'. 'It was fully understood on both sides that labour and tribute were for this purpose' (Evans-Pritchard 1971: 215).

Bowdich described the distribution of food at the Asante court in 1819, where a peredwan of gold (£8 at the rate of the time) was spent daily on palm wine served to 'the retinue of all captains attending'; an element of royal ceremonial was the appearance of the king in public to drink with his people. Sometimes brass pans containing rum were carried through the street for the populace to drink. Here one can see the contrast between the circulation of commodities within a small population, those in attendance at a Zande court, and in one as great and as widely spread on the ground as that of Asante, where clearly a much smaller proportion got this sort of return for what they gave. But later writers on Asante, both British and African, emphasize the public purposes on which the royal revenues were expended.

Another kind of argument for the legitimacy of tribute is that summarized by Basil Sansom (1974: 148) as characteristic of the southern Bantu in general. 'The logic of tribute is that it is sent as "thanks" to an administrator for doing work to make production of the commodity represented possible.' He is referring to the function of a chief or headman in allocating land for production, in co-ordinating productive activities and perhaps also in performing ritual for propitious weather. This reverses the commoner description of this kind of reciprocity—he collects tribute but is expected to return it—in a very interesting way.

According to the recently published recollections of an old

Sotho, the subjects of Moshweshwe's successors had a clear idea of the services that could and could not legitimately be asked of them. A chief had three 'lands', the produce of one of which was reckoned to supply provisions for the army, while the other two were for his personal needs. His subjects were called on to plough these, and were not rewarded with beer or a meat feast as was common elsewhere. 'But they were pleased to do it; they knew they were cultivating their own land.' Jingoes recalls an occasion when a work-party finished the ploughing early in the day and were asked to plough two private lands of the chief's wives. They agreed as a favour, but when he wanted them to do still more work, they refused. 'Where does the food from these fields go? Not to us! Do you think we are going to work in your mothers' lands without getting food for our work?' (Jingoes 1975: 174–5).

The extreme opposite evaluation of the relation between tribute and return is that made by Jaques Maquet (1961) in his study of Rwanda. Certainly we are dealing here with a ruling and a subject population, and it could be argued—he would perhaps argue himself—that the whole Hutu population stood in the same relation to the ruling Tutsi as the tribute-paying vassals did in the more extensive empires, getting nothing back except protection from rival exploiters.

The sources of tribute in Rwanda were those typical of the Bantu kingdoms. A proportion of their cattle was taken from Tutsi, and vegetable food was collected at harvest from Hutu. Only Hutu were called upon for labour. Maquet calculates that the amount required was equivalent to one third of the time of one member of an extended family; all recent accounts say that the labour demand, though not the tribute in kind, was resented. As Maquet interprets the function of tribute, it was solely to 'provide the ruling class with consumption goods' (1961: 104), and to maintain it in power. The share of tribute retained by the collectors was no more than a reward for their loyalty to the king, and the services rendered by government, which to so many anthropologists, and, as my quotations indicate, to some Africans, have seemed to be identical with those that are the basic functions of any state, were nothing of the kind. They were legitimized not by the ideology of reciprocity but by that of divine right. Exactions, Maquet argues, were pushed to the limit beyond which the subjects would have either starved or moved to the realm of another ruler, a cynical inversion of the argument that a check on oppressive government was the need to conciliate followers who would otherwise transfer their allegiance. If the political system did provide a minimum of security from physical violence, this was merely incidental.

Oberg (1961), without going quite so far, says that the Hima (the Nkole counterparts of the Tutsi) 'endeavoured to keep [the Iru] in subjection' so as to be able to count on tribute from them. Herdsmen visiting the royal court expected to be fed on porridge all the time they were there. Some Iru craftsmen—makers of spears and milk pots—were attached to every chief as his servants (but presumably at least partially maintained by him), and some of the objects they made were distributed to Hima visiting the chief, a practice which, according to Oberg, limited the amount of free barter open to the Iru.

Naturally the most elaborate ways of obtaining resources for the state are to be found where total resources are greater, and products and occupations more varied. In the West African kingdoms there were far greater differences of wealth and poverty, and many of the wealthy—though not all—were holders of office who took their share of tax and tribute. If their economies are described as redistributive it is because every dignitary had his own retinue who received some reward for his services, some of them perhaps getting their whole subsistence. It is in this sense that the state was the largest employer, as indeed it is in many parts of independent Africa today. Behind the rational calculations of the balance of advantage which taxpayers must surely have made, there lay, of course, usually in some form an ideology supporting the claims of the king himself, of the sacredness of kingship carrying with it the belief in ritual sanctions against disobedience, though certainly these were never wholly effective. As a justification for the claim on the subjects' property this might be put in the form given to Herskovits (admittedly long after Dahomey had ceased to be a kingdom): 'If the king is fed Dahomey will not fail to prosper' (cited Argyle 1966: 102).

Writers on West Africa make a distinction which is not found in the literature on the Bantu, between tax and tribute. For them a tribute is a lump sum demanded from a subject area, a tax a payment levied on individuals, and nineteenth-century observers in Asante distinguished on this basis between subjects and tributary provinces of the empire. When the imperial power began to weaken after 1874, the states which broke away resented both the tribute which had been collected by force, with the destruction of villages if they failed to pay it, and also the demand for contingents of troops. Perhaps all this meant was that former tributary chiefs now kept for themselves all that they collected.

Revenues in Dahomey

From the point of view of organization, however, the interest lies in the kind of activity for which, or circumstances in which, a tax was held to be due. European traders were naturally most concerned with dues and tolls on trade, and so have described how they were collected; some aspects of this were anticipated in the discussion of types of state servant. These traders paid a customs duty before buying and selling could begin. Benin records do not tell us much of this process, but many of those who wrote on the Slave Coast, before and during the time when the port of Whydah was subject to Dahomey, have left descriptions of what happened. First the merchant stated what he had to sell and what he wanted to buy. In Dahomey, before the trade was suppressed, slaves were the only commodity; later the only export was palm-oil. Samples of the goods brought were chosen, and were sent to the king by a messenger bearing a staff marked with the emblem of the company offering them. The prices were fixed by bargaining. Then the customs due were paid in goods, the amount being calculated, as late as 1870, not on the quantity of goods or even on the tonnage of the ships but on the number of their masts (Skertchly 1874: 22). In addition a large portion of the cargo was bought by the king before any could be sold elsewhere, and his slaves were sold at a higher price, either in cowrie currency or in goods, than those of his subjects. Also the traders had to buy as many slaves as he wished to sell before they could deal with anyone else. In addition he collected from his subjects a gun and gunpowder from every slave they sold, and those who bought liquor from the European fort paid a proportion which was measured out in a coconut shell (this information comes from Le Hérissé, a French official writing in 1911; it is not easy to see how this tax in kind could have been transported, but perhaps it was part of the tax-gatherer's payment).

Like Asante, Dahomey collected tolls from traders passing certain posts. Those of Dahomey had a fence across the path with only a narrow space to go through, which could be easily closed. Bosman said the king had 'above one thousand collectors, who disperse themselves throughout the whole land . . . There is nothing so mean sold in the whole kingdom, that the King hath not toll for it.' The toll-houses on the roads are thought to have been taken over from the petty states that Dahomey absorbed; they had political as well as economic functions, in that everyone passing through had to swear that he planned no evil against the king. No doubt because the subjection of the coastal peoples was always in question, the control kept over their movements was even stricter than it was in Asante; every company of travellers carried a 'passport', which was either a bundle of pebbles equal in numbers to that of its members or a notched stick. Skertchly, travelling with a royal escort which was exempt from scrutiny, noticed as he left Whydah that his retinue had become unexpectedly large. The tolls were not heavy; the collectors kept a small proportion as their reward and had the rest carried, by slaves or hired porters, to the superior chiefs to whom they were assigned. Tolls were also collected at the local markets where foodstuffs, drink, pots, and magical substances, and even water, were sold; the proceeds are said to have gone to the upkeep of the royal tombs.

Every individual, including children old enough to run messages, was liable for a payment the name for which Le Hérissé translates as 'sleep money' (payment for existing?), and this was first imposed in order to buy guns from the coastal traders. A most elaborate census procedure for calculating the taxes due was described to Herskovits by informants telling what they knew of the traditions of a distant past. Men, women, boys and girls were counted, and for each individual a pebble was put in a sack marked by a design representing the appropriate category. An annual census was certainly taken, with whatever degree of accuracy. In addition there was a count of units of production of different kinds: grain stores for agriculture, palm trees for oil, forges for metal-working. Animals were taxed by numbers. According to the account given to Herskovits the owners made their own returns; that is, they were required to produce a cowrie for each animal. Hunters were enumerated on the occasion of an annual ritual for their protective deity, at which each was given a knife to offer to the god. On the basis of the numbers issued, leaders of different bands were required in turn to supply the palace with all the game they caught for a fixed period of time. After palm oil replaced slaves as the principal export a special tax was imposed on it, the yield of which was divided among the principal chiefs.

When Skertchly managed to get away from Abomey and spend a little time on the real purpose of his visit—collecting entomological specimens—he went north to a recently conquered area in the Kong hills. Here an 'old caboceer'—a resident representative of the royal authority—showed him the local tribute that he was about to send to the capital. 'It consisted of a few jars of palm oil, bags of cotton, cowries, Guinea corn and large calabashes of yams'.

Whereas both Asante and Fulani Zazzau obtained significant revenues from death duties, the portion of a subject's possessions which the ruler took on his death, the claim made by the Dahomean king seems to have been purely symbolic. According to Le Hérissé, a dead man's movable property was brought to the palace to be displayed and then at once returned to his heirs. Although a proverb says that the king inherits 'even the fly-switch of a leper', supposedly such a man's only possession, it seems unlikely that every individual's property went through this procedure.

Before the opening of the Annual Customs, at which every man in the kingdom was supposed to be present, a representative of every taxable group, territorial or occupational, was expected to appear before the palace and present the amount due. This ceremony was the reaffirmation of the relationship of king and people that is characteristic of so much royal ritual. Of course it was performed, like its counterparts elsewhere, after the harvest during the slack agricultural season, but the peculiarity of the Dahomean ritual was that it focused not on the fertility of the land but on success in war; its immediate occasion was supposedly the return of the army from its latest campaign. A great part of it consisted in the distribution of cowries and of imported goods, cloth, and liquor. Formal presentations were made to chiefs and to commoners who had distinguished themselves in fighting, and then, for hours at a time, and on several days, strings of cowries and lengths of cloth were thrown down from a raised platform to be scrambled for. When Skertchly witnessed this in 1871 nobles as well as commoners took part in the contest, and it may have had a ritual significance. Argyle notes that the objects distributed were those regarded as appropriate for sacrifice. It appears too that, despite the genuine ferocity of the struggle, there was an idea that everyone should receive a share.

The Dahomeans themselves believed that most of what was demanded of them was redistributed at the Customs and that the ceremonies which their contributions made possible were important enough to justify the demands. According to Polanyi, who presents a rather idyllic picture of this 'redistributive economy', the royal treasury, where taxes paid in kind were stored, contained materials for building and road-making and iron to be issued to blacksmiths, as well as the wherewithal for 'payment in kind to diverse craftsmen'. In terms of material return to those who carried on the business of government, we can see that, in Dahomey as elsewhere, those in high authority were given the resources that enabled them to support the followers who did the menial work or oversaw it.

What is of special interest here is that for some purposes payments, even at the lowest levels, were made in currency (cowries) and not in kind. Carriers or messengers travelling away from home were given cowries to buy food at the markets along their route, where only cowries were accepted in payment, a fact from which it follows that they circulated among the village women who brought their cooked food for sale as well as in more grandiose transactions.

Revenues in Asante

Whereas the Dahomean king's claim to inherit his subjects' property seems to have been no more than a ritual assertion of ownership of 'the land and everything in it', in Asante and Zaria it was enforced quite literally. Wilks estimates that in Asante it produced the greater part of the revenues; and he argues also that men who enriched themselves by trading were held to be actually serving the Asantehene because of the share of their wealth that would ultimately go to him. The amount due was calculated in gold dust, but sometimes equivalents were accepted or demanded. Villages were handed over, sometimes to the king himself, sometimes to a chief who made a payment which the dead man's property could not meet. It is hardly appropriate to call this, as Wilks does, 'dealing in real estate'; granted that the chief of a village had claims on objects found on uncultivated land and the right to allocate it, what was transferred was political authority with the prestige that it carried and the material advantages in tribute and labour. In special cases the king might take skilled servants, not necessarily slaves; for example, on the death of a chief of Bekwae he customarily took from his retinue one gold-weigher and one sword-carrier. The proportion taken does not seem to have been fixed; some records of past holders of chiefdoms mention a half or a third of their estate as due to the Asantehene, while in the case of the various state servants mentioned in the previous chapter the king, who had maintained and enriched them, took the whole. Divisional chiefs made corresponding claims on their subjects and servants. In turn king and chiefs made gifts at a dead subject's funeral, but these would be a small proportion of what they took from the estate. A successor to office made a payment, and in cases where the holder had been exempted from death duties as a special privilege the payment demanded was higher.

When gold dust was to be melted down to make ornaments, the king claimed one-fifth of the amount so used; his share may actually have been more, since the royal weights were heavier than those used by ordinary people. Gold nuggets were claimed by the divisional chief on whose land they were found, and from him by the king. They were reduced to dust by the royal goldsmiths in Kumase, after which the king took his share and returned the rest to be divided between the finder and his chief; according to some of Rattray's informants, chiefs and their elders took it all. Late in the nineteenth century the king Mensa Bonsu levied half the proceeds of all gold-mines.

A flat rate tax of one-tenth of an ounce of gold was due from every married man. In the late nineteenth century this was collected by emissaries from the capital, who received one-seventh of the proceeds in payment, the rest being divided equally between the king and the headman of the village where it was raised. Fines for letting the roads get blocked seem to have brought in considerable revenue; this was called 'sweeping money'. The king took a third of it, and the rest went to the road overseers and their head in Kumase. Tolls have been discussed in connection with the organization for collection.

Some kings raised special levies to finance military campaigns, but the payment that Wilks rather curiously calls a war tax was an indemnity imposed on defeated rebels and on peoples conquered for the first time. Another occasion for a special levy was the accession of a new king, and of some divisional chiefs, 'to replenish the treasury' as Rattray puts it (1929: 230), that is to let them embark on office with adequate resources, 'to feed them' as the Dahomeans would have put it.

From these revenues a bureaucracy that was apparently more numerous than that of any of the other kingdoms—unless this impression merely reflects the greater volume of information available—was rewarded essentially by commissions on what was collected. Records refer to arbitrary extortion only in the periods when control from Kumase was ineffective. Bowdich noted early in the century that royal messengers had been instructed to pay a fair price for the food needed on their journeys, though he did not ask whether this was paid to individuals or to local chiefs who requisitioned it. At times people complained of the obligation to supply men for the army, and the major count against Mensa Bonsu, the king who was deposed in 1883, was that he imposed excessive taxes and fines. But this complaint came from the wealthier section of the population, those who were frustrated in their desire to accumulate even greater wealth by the state trading monopoly and the levying of death duties.

In Fulani Zaria taxes were levied on grain, on hoes, and later on trade by means of tolls and market dues, including a tax on slaves sold. Kings expected to receive gifts from their officials on their own accession and on the latter's appointment, and this became formalized as a payment demanded (the king himself had to make such payments to the Sultan of Sokoto). They took a share of every official's property when he died, a claim that might be justified by the argument that it was the gift of office that had enabled him to acquire his property, and also from every vassal chief. From his own officials the king took one-sixth of their houses, cattle, and slaves, and from vassal chiefs a third of the slaves and cattle and half the childless concubines. When he dismissed an official he took half his property. He also claimed half of all booty taken in war.

In the discussion so far slaves have been referred to in passing as if they were just another commodity. Of course this is not so, and of course it was not only for the sake of the slave-trade that Dahomey fought its annual wars and that all the kingdoms demanded a quota of slaves as tribute from their vassals. Slaves played an important part in the internal economy. Wilks delicately refers to the employment of 'unfree labour' as carriers for trade goods as well as in production. Those who owned large numbers established them in villages where they produced food to support their masters living in the capital, and, later, export crops; the king of Dahomey's palm plantations were worked by his slaves. Kings of Zaria had slave settlements which were crown property and passed from one ruler to the next (it must be remembered that in Zaria three lineages claimed the succession in turn). Slaves too, then, formed part of the resources of the state, both in that the rulers everywhere disposed of those who were brought in as captives or as tribute, and, in Zaria and Asante, in that they were taken as death duties.

The revenues of Zaria had to meet the tribute demanded by Sokoto, the return for which was the payer's maintenance in office but no particular benefit for his subjects. They supported the royal household, rewarded officials, and maintained state property, including horses and weapons for the army. But they also served to enrich the lineage which was on the throne for the time being, and to reward the personal support, for example in backing the king's election from among the leading men of his lineage, of clients who had not been appointed to office. Perhaps it was not entirely hypocritical of the British to suppose that the proceeds of taxation might be expended in ways that would distribute their benefit more widely.

Which of the interpretations of the claims made by kings on their subjects mentioned at the beginning of this chapter is a sound evaluation must remain a matter of the reader's judgement. Those to whom the state is always and everywhere an organization for the extortion of surplus value will have no difficulty in deciding. Others face the difficulty of quantifying intangibles. Refusal to pay tribute could be punished by the burning and looting of villages and towns. Was it the 'common man' who instigated the refusal, or the vassal chief who preferred to keep the tribute for himself? Safe travel was an advantage for everyone, not only for wealthy traders; so were judicial institutions. African states did not reckon to provide their subjects with schools, hospitals, or clean water; from the time when their European overlords tried to persuade them to do so, there have been endless references to the high proportion of the budget devoted to salaries. For the period before the notion of social services reached Africa, however, the question to be asked is whether the common man had to pay too much for the minimum conditions of personal security; and nobody has yet produced a formula for a cost-benefit analysis of this kind.

CHAPTER VIII

THE BALANCE OF POWER

EARLIER chapters have discussed the process by which some individual claiming kingship has established a position of dominance over other leaders of groups, formerly his equals, who thus became his subjects, and that by which one ethnic group has extended domination over the territory of its neighbours. Of course these processes must have gone on side by side. There is a temptation to take the most recent account of any kingdom as if it described a constitution deliberately devised with checks and balances. Checks and balances there certainly were, but it may well be, as Peter Lloyd (1971) suggests, that they simply represent, as we know of them, the stage that had been reached, in the see-saw between king and chiefs, at the moment when colonial rule put an end to it—not, as with the earlier empires, by destroying the kingdoms, but by suppressing the power struggle and then imposing constitutional changes of a quite new type. It is true that such historical record as we have seems to describe a linear movement rather than an ebb and flow of central power; yet every time we read of the deposition of a king, or of the execution of conspirators against him, we are reminded that any particular contest could go one way or the other. And such rebellions as we read of are as likely, or more so, to have had their roots in the rejection of royal authority by chiefs defending their own privileges as in the resentment of oppressed peasants.

In most kingdoms, as anthropologists have been able to see or reconstruct them, kings have been expected to listen to the views of specified groups of people, forming councils which often have their distinctive names. In most kingdoms there have been specified persons with the right and responsibility of nominating the successor to a dead king, and even where succession is supposedly regulated by strict rules, the people in charge of the installation of the new ruler have *de facto* influence. In many kingdoms the ruler depends on the co-operation of priests whose ritual powers derive their validity from sources outside his control. A curious feature of many, which has already been discussed in connection with ritual, is the independent voice allowed, in particular contexts, to the king's closest female relatives, his mother and sister.

Although the Yoruba kings recognized a common ritual head in the Alafin of Oyo, he did not exercise political control over them, and no one of them controlled a very extensive domain; some were only heads of one town with its outliers, though the towns themselves, with populations of 10,000 or more, were large by the standards of pre-colonial Africa. Doubtless there is a connection between this fact and the narrow limits set to the authority of the kings. Peter Lloyd describes them as 'sacred'; this avoids the connotations that have been attached to the word 'divine' by readers of *The Golden Bough*. The firm basis of an Oba's authority was the sacredness conferred on him at his installation, which in itself guaranteed, in the eyes of the general populace, that he 'could do no wrong'. His sacredness could be diminished, however, if he was held to have lost the favour of the deities; and this question was answered by an oracle that he did not control.

The day-to-day conduct of public affairs was not in his hands, but in those of bodies of title-holders which were in some cases unusually representative. As Lloyd (1960) describes the organization of Ado Ekiti, there were five kingmakers, the Olori Marun, each of whose titles was hereditary within one of the major lineages. They formed the senior grade of an association of twenty chiefs, some of whom represented less important lineages while others were appointed by the Big Five in consultation with the Oba. This body itself was the highest of three grades of chiefs, the members of each of which held meetings at which they discussed public affairs, and then submitted their conclusions to the next highest grade. The Olori Marun themselves met daily in the courtyard of the palace, but usually without the Oba; their views were transmitted to him, and it was taken for granted that he would promulgate them, thereby giving them the support of his ritual authority.

Commonly, though apparently not in Ado, important ritual

powers were exercised by the *ogboni*, a cult association whose myths and rites were kept strictly secret, as were also its discussions of secular matters. The name *ogboni* is derived from words meaning 'elder'. Senior holders of secular titles had to join *ogboni*, and so did the members of trading associations where these existed.

The political activities of *ogboni*, and its relation with the kingmakers—here called Oyo Misi—in Oyo, have been described by Morton-Williams (1960). At the time of his inquiries a Muslim Alafin had recently disbanded his *ogboni*, but they were still flourishing in the Egbado kingdoms. The Oyo Misi, like the Olori Marun in Ado, met daily by themselves, not in the palace but in the house of their own leader, and then went together to give their advice to the Alafin. But every sixteenth day they joined in discussion with the rest of the *ogboni*, and in these gatherings they were cut off from the lineages of which each was the political representative and merged in a larger body whose deliberations were kept strictly secret. Differences of view within it could not be made public, and the Oyo Misi, like all the other members, were under the obligation to support its decisions. In the Egbado kingdoms the ritual head of the *ogboni* was also the priest of the oracle which was consulted every year to see whether the king still stood in favour with the gods and so should continue to rule; and in the smaller of them the *ogboni* had themselves taken over the functions of the Oyo Misi.

Not every king was content to be a mere mouthpiece. How far a king could assert himself depended largely on the strength of his palace following, particularly of slaves. The 'citizen army' which fought in foreign wars was recruited by the different chiefs from among their own followers. Intrigue, says Lloyd (1960), was a king's chief weapon. He was able to reward his loyal supporters by the grant of titles, and this could not be formally opposed by bodies of chiefs as it could in Benin. So his subjects sometimes found they had more to gain by revealing plots against him than by joining in them.

Ado chiefs might boycott the palace, if they could all agree— but there was no *ogboni* association there to compel agreement. Such action implied a boycott of the rituals which were performed in the palace. Hence it was a double-edged weapon, for if the chiefs prevented the performance of rituals on which the general welfare was believed to depend, they could themselves be held responsible for anything that was going wrong.

A Yoruba Oba, then, was not a priest-king whose main significance lay in his ritual activities. He had ritual powers not shared by any of his subjects; he could curse those who disobeyed him and forbid them entry to the palace, thus (in some cases) debarring them from political discussions. He was the symbol of established order, so that an Oba could say without contradiction—as one did on the death of George VI— 'When we try to dispense with the position of king we immediately find the town with the people concerned thrown into confusion; we find lawlessness and general disorder'.

Another country where a body of ritual experts was the main counterbalancing force to the king's power was Rwanda, where the college of *abiru* was responsible for his installation and for the rites he was expected to perform for the general welfare. Exceptionally, the Rwanda ritual was secret; but the nation had to be told that it had been successfully carried out, so that here too neither the king nor any of the *abiru* could afford to be intransigent in blocking them. It also rested with the *abiru* to name the lineage from which the king should choose his royal consort, ostensibly in accordance with an ancestrally ordained rotation.

Yet another category of ritual experts on whose goodwill a ruler might depend were the earth-priests or 'owners of the land', who in many parts of West Africa tended shrines that were reputedly older than those of the reigning dynasty. Their position has been described most fully in the context of the Bariba kingdoms in the north of Dahomey, kingdoms founded by the emigration from Borgu of bands of mounted huntsmen led by princes who, like the Zande or Luba chiefs, constantly sought to set up their own principalities independently of their fathers. The populations over which they established their rule recognized ritual heads, perhaps with minimal political power but with a monopoly of access to the local deities. As Lombard (1965: 183) puts it, the conquerors never sought to take over those ritual functions. One might say they hardly could, so

universal is the belief that local divinities 'belong to' those who
have lived longest under their protection—were it not for the
annexation of the *abiru* by a Rwanda king. But the 'compact'
recorded in Bariba traditions, whether it was historical or
mythical, left to the 'owners of the soil' their religious authority
and also gave them the right, as priests of the earth in which
Bariba kings would be buried, to conduct their funerals and
also their accession rites. In practice the kings looked to the
earth-priests as their intermediaries with the spirits for
whatever purpose; and made gifts to them which included
insignia of office, sandals, Arab-style clothes, and sometimes
even a horse.

In Rwanda we are not told much about the discussion of
secular matters. The accounts of most kingdoms describe councils which gathered at the royal capital, but there are differences in their 'constitutional' status—in the extent to which
they could claim a right to be heard and in the degree to
which, like the Yoruba secular councils, they could be considered to represent the views of different sections of the
population.

In Buganda the chiefs who were expected to maintain houses
at the royal capital brought news to the king of events and
conditions in the areas they governed, but the most recent
studies indicate that they did not constitute a formal council
until they were 'recognized' as a law-making body by the
British authorities. There was not here any obligation on the
king to consult them. Sir Apolo Kaggwa, who around 1900
compiled a history of the kings of Buganda, records an occasion, probably in the seventeenth century, when King
Mutebi planned to dismiss two important chiefs who had been
appointed by his predecessor; he summoned a council to ask
their advice, and it was that this would be a difficult thing to
do (cited Southwold n.d.: 9–10). Since the kingdoms were not
thought of as the property of a royal lineage, there was equally
no obligation to consult close agnates, as there was in some
Southern Bantu chiefdoms. In the Interlacustrine Bantu kingdoms, the king's sons were required to live at a distance from
the court, and only summoned to the capital when the time
came to nominate a successor; and some Ganda kings had their

brothers put to death as soon as they had sons to make the succession secure.

Nevertheless, these kings did not bear the sole weight of decision, or exercise untramelled despotism, whichever interpretation one prefers. Each of them had a 'favourite counsellor', a commoner who has often been described in English as a 'prime minister'. A new king retained his predecessor's adviser and was expected to be guided by him. He would eventually be superseded by someone of this king's own choice. But this need not imply that such a man was a mere sycophant.

The Ganda Katikkiro, however, was the most important man in the kingdom after the king himself, and had territorial authority over a wide area. He was responsible, as was the Nkole *nganzi* (literally 'favourite') for the installation of his master's successor. Maquet remarks that one of the most important functions of the 'favourite counsellor' was to take the blame for any cause of dissatisfaction, leaving the king himself out of reach of criticism; and it is certainly interesting that many people who were wedded to the idea of monarchy— including some in quite recent centuries in Europe—have liked to believe that whatever goes wrong is the fault not of the king but of his 'evil counsellors'.

The kings of Rwanda are said to have summoned their leading chiefs for consultation, though Maquet (1961: 128) holds that this was to get their views on how to implement decisions already taken rather than on what should be done. In such a council the men who had to be listened to were the *abiru*, the guardians of ritual secrets who have been mentioned in Chapter II. Although, as was pointed out there, it was an effective political move to take over the *abiru* as guarantors of royal legitimacy, the price paid for it was to give them an influence that was not easy to resist. The first *abiru* had been hereditary rulers who were confirmed as subject authorities, and though later ones were the creation of Rwanda kings, they could effectively claim hereditary status since the secret knowledge that each of them possessed was preserved by passing it on within his lineage; it was not politically possible to transfer the office of a *mwiru* to a more amenable individual. Their most powerful weapon was their knowledge of the correct ritual for the installation of a king; they might use this retrospectively to argue that a reigning king's position was not valid. Also it was for them to say from what lineage the queen must be taken. Logically, they might thwart the king's designs by refusing to perform the rites for which they were responsible, but the value of this strategy was limited by the fact that they could themselves be blamed if they delayed some ritual that was held to be necessary for the general welfare.

The Ngambela of the Lozi was his king's chief *induna*, to use a Zulu word that became current further north as a result both of Ngoni and of South African expansion. In a kingdom where princes were not debarred from political power it was important that he could not be a member of the royal lineage. Gluckman (1951: 46–7) interprets his role as that of the people's representative to the king; his homestead was a sanctuary for anyone who had incurred the royal anger. But the king himself was also, in a manner that Gluckman does not specify, the protector of the people against the Ngambela. He was not the king's sole adviser, for there was an elaborate council organization; but he presided over the full council and reported its deliberations to the king, who returned his answer to them through him.

Unlike many ethnographers, Gluckman gives an indication of the kind of matter that the council might discuss. The most momentous of all were questions of war and peace, but if large public works were planned, such as digging a canal or building one of the mounds on which Lozi made their villages, the council would have to consider whether there was enough food available for the workers. Then there was appointment to titled offices, which one might guess would be the most hotly disputed of all. But Gluckman remarks that the divisions of the council which deliberated separately were not based on opposed economic interests; so that whether their conclusions did or did not coincide would be a matter of individual views. This would seem to have been true of most of the kingdoms with multiple councils, though M. G. Smith (1960) writes of Zazzau as if its two councils did represent different interests.

The full council of the Lozi had three divisions known as 'mats' from the placing of the mats on which the members sat.

On the right of the royal dais were the senior indunas, men who had judicial and executive authority over divisions of the Lozi people (these were not territorial divisions, a peculiar feature of Lozi polity); on the left were the 'stewards', officials responsible for the collection of tribute, for which purpose the general population was divided in a different way; and still further to the left were the royal princes. The councillors of each 'mat' sat in strict order of the seniority of their titles, and they spoke in order from junior to senior, so that no one was ever in the position of contradicting a senior. Out of this council were formed three bodies in each of which there were members of every 'mat'. Two of these, the Saa and Katengo, represented respectively the senior and junior members of the three 'mats', and so might be expected to come to different conclusions on some matters; the head of Katengo, however, was a member of Saa. The third included the highest chiefs of all, the Ngambela and the Natamoyo, the latter the only prince to sit on the mat-of-the-right; his title means 'giver of life', but Gluckman does not describe his functions. With them were 'an undetermined number' (Gluckman 1951: 50) of senior chiefs. Messages would pass between these councils, and their aim was to reach an agreed view to put before the king.

In the West African cases which are on record, separate consultative bodies were not expected to agree, and M. G. Smith envisages in Zazzau a process in which either the two such bodies were in agreement to oppose the king, or he got his way with the support of one of the two (of course there is no reason why all three should not sometimes have agreed). The total number of people whom the king of Zazzau was expected to consult was small: first the four senior officials of his own household and then the holders of the four senior public offices. The only kind of business that Smith mentions is the conferment of titles and appointment to offices, and it is clear that this was a matter of much more interest than administrative decisions, while one might almost say that there were no issues of general policy. Public offices might be filled either by the promotion of existing public officials or by transfer from the royal household. It was by infiltrating the public offices that the palace officials could increase their influence, but it is not at all clear what would be the issues that would interest them as a body. One might suspect that individuals of both sections backed men from whom they expected personal favours. Where the two councils disagreed, Smith tells us, the king could do as he chose; but it would be instructive to follow the fortunes of a man appointed to any post against the wishes of those senior in authority to him.

Bradbury (1973) had the advantage of being able to draw on the memories of living men for his record of the power struggles that went on in Benin in the context of the elaborate structure of separate yet interlocking councils described in Chapter IV. No doubt the complexity of the system as it was described to him reflected the outcome of such struggles in a past too distant to be traced. It is clear from his account that they were pure power contests, focused on the control of titles and the resources that went with them and not on any general issues such as would deserve the name of policy. The opposition between the claims of king and subjects that is found in some form in all kingdoms had its own mythical charter in Benin: the story that the ruling dynasty was founded by a prince brought from Oyo, who had to leave his kingdom after begetting a son because the Edo would not endure the rule of a foreigner. Hence the opposition between town and palace chiefs was represented as the defence of the Edo against the foreign ruler and his retainers, or, in terms of principles, the defence of 'the commonalty against the threat of palace autocracy' (Bradbury 1973: 79). Bradbury does see the three orders of chiefs as corporate bodies each trying to extend its own influence; and in contexts in which each order was called on to express a collective opinion they would have to agree on a common line. But he also takes account of internal rivalries and of the common interests that might link members of the different orders, and concludes that in actual conflicts the alignment of factions was very fluid. Nevertheless, crises in the kingdom were represented in tradition as confrontations between the king and *Iyase*, the senior town chief, who alone had the right to oppose the king in public. The town chiefs, as well as the hereditary *Uzama*, the official 'guardians of custom', had ritual responsibilities on the performance of which the sacred aspect of the Oba's power depended. Although the ultimate validation of his sacredness was his royal descent, the mystical power to maintain the welfare of the nation that only he possessed could not be sustained without periodic renewal through the many ceremonies which punctuated the year.

In earlier days, it is said, the *Uzama* chiefs were the Oba's principal opponents, and the eventual assertion of royal supremacy over them was commemorated in a ritual that included a mock battle ending with their submission. Their formal assent was required for all royal decisions, and their part in the installation of a new king was indispensable. At one time they had actually chosen the king, but by the nineteenth century the rule of primogeniture had come to be recognized, and although this did not prevent wars for the succession, it much reduced the influence of the *Uzama* over the choice. One of them, the *Ezomo*, was a war commander, and as such the equal in power of the *Iyase*. But each of these had a deputy from another order. The *Uzama* as a body did not take much part in public discussion.

There was yet another form of power-sharing, in connection with foreign trade. Police authority over the beaches where trading canoes put in, and over the port of Ughoton where European ships called, was in the hands of two senior palace chiefs from the *Ibiwe* association. But the trade itself was in the hands of other associations, each controlling one of the routes, and these contained members of all the chiefly orders, who did not depend for their membership on appointment but simply on ability to pay the necessary fees. This trade was a more important source of wealth than the tribute or gifts of villagers; from it came the resources that enabled men to buy slaves. It was men who had been successful in these associations who obtained rapid promotion into the ranks of the town chiefs.

It is from Asante, where we have rich documentary records going back before the nineteenth century, that we know most about the actual issues that divided the makers of decisions. Those of which we learn most are matters of foreign relations, as we should expect since most of the documents are the work of Europeans dealing with Asante kings. From early times English writers have discussed Asante politics in terms current at home. This illustrates a conception of the kingdom that was appropriate at the period when Europeans dealt with African states by negotiation and not dictation. But when Asante institutions are described in a twentieth-century vocabulary, as they are by Wilks, one is baffled in the same way as one would be if it were applied to the Tudor or Stuart monarchies. Nevertheless it is possible to see past Bowdich's references to 'three estates', the 'aristocracy', and the 'Privy Council', and Wilks's to government of opposing parties, to a fairly clear idea of what qualified the holders of particular positions to have a voice in decisions.

The 'assembling of the nation', as the word that Wilks renders by 'parliament' is literally translated, did not consist, as did the councils previously described, of people living permanently in the capital. It included, in addition to the senior Kumase chiefs, the heads of all the states of which metropolitan Asante was composed. These were summoned once a year on the occasion of the great yam festival (*Odwira*), as were the rulers of vassal kingdoms, who, however, sometimes sent representatives. The council could also be called together at other times; one such occasion arose when Dwaben rebelled. As Wilks sees it, a major matter for deliberation was the apportionment of responsibility for providing men and gold for war campaigns; and this could well lead to argument about mounting a campaign at all. Bonnat, the French trader who was held as a hostage in Kumase from 1869 to 1874, wrote that the Asantehene 'must attend to all the petty affairs of his kingdom, and furthermore to religion, to commerce, to agriculture, to weights and measures, to prices and tariffs of all kinds' (cited Wilks 1975: 392).

Even the capitals of the 'five great towns' were two days' journey from Kumase; not only was it a time-consuming process to summon the council and gather it together, but all those who had a right to be there did not always care to make the journey. This in itself would be likely to lead to the development of the smaller body that Bowdich called the 'Privy Council', and Wilks calls the Inner Council which, he says, later became the Council of Kumase. Bowdich said in 1821 that there were four councillors 'whom the king always consults on the creation or repeal of a law; whose interference in foreign politics or in questions of war or tribute amount to a veto on the king's decisions . . . and whose power as an estate of the government always keeps alive the jealousy of the General Assembly' (Bowdich 1821: 22, cited Wilks 1975: 395). These officials were the heads of wards in Kumase; one of them was the Gyaasewahene or treasurer, whose responsibilities were described in Chapter VI. All these were appointive, not hereditary, officials. According to Bowdich the king could not decide matters of war and peace without their agreement (in practice he would need the agreement of at least two of them). But in other questions they would 'watch rather than share' in decisions. In addition there were two senior *akyeame* (see Chapter VI), and other chiefs with special knowledge of the matters under discussion would be invited to attend.

In 1870, when the Asantehene had to decide whether to hand over his three European hostages to the British or hold them for the ransom he had originally demanded, the council met every day except on holy days. By this time it was larger, and, as the missionary hostage Kühne understood it, the members were heads of the various bureaucratic organizations, not (or not primarily) holders of territorial authority. It now included (naturally) military leaders and the heads of the royal physicians (who were also practitioners of magic), the treasury and the sword-bearers, as well as a representative of the royal lineage and four *akyeame*. The queen mother, whose special position must be discussed further, also had a voice. There was no idea, however, that either the total number or the status of members was permanently fixed.

The West African kingdoms maintained their independence in relation to European states for much longer than most of the others, and the question of confrontation or negotiation and accommodation, of war and peace, was for them a matter of serious debate. This was doubtless true of Benin and Dahomey, but it is from Asante that we have the fullest records. If these do not necessarily support Wilks's interpretation of conflicting views as the expression of permanently opposed economic interests, they do show when conflicts arose and how decisions were reached. The many Europeans who recorded their observations could see that the Asantehene's councils were dominated at different times by the advocates of different policies, and that he was not in a position to reject views that had strong support despite the fact that by tradition he, like other monarchs, had the last word. There was of course room for diplomacy. 'I must do what the old men say', Osei Bonsu told Dupuis in 1820; but the same Dupuis records that he was determined to have his way.

There was certainly no absolute commitment to the principle of democratic discussion. More than once a king's opponents plotted to depose him, were discovered and large numbers put to death; though it is not always certain that their motive was their attitude towards the question of war or peace. As has happened in other parts of the world, the king's enemies would attach themselves to his presumptive successor, and in the choice of a new Asantehene, a matter that was not determined by strict rules in Asante any more than in the other kingdoms, a candidate's attitude on this question was of some importance. We should need more evidence, though, to be sure that this was the crucial division between the supporters of rival princes.

The special status of the mothers and sisters of kings has been considered in connection with royal ritual, and their secular importance was inevitably mentioned in that context, but it deserves a little more discussion here.

In Asante, where, under a system of matrilineal succession, it was through his mother and not his father that a king derived his claim to the Golden Stool, one would expect the queen-mother to have an important position. But the woman who held the title generally so translated—that of Asantehemaa—obtained it as one who was qualified to be, not one who actually was, the mother of a king. The first Asantehemaa was the daughter of Osei Tutu's eldest sister, the second the daughter of his second sister; all the later ones traced their descent through their mothers to her. The actual successor to the office was chosen from a number of princesses, as the king was from a number of princes. She might be the king's sister. Once appointed she would use her influence to secure the succession for one of her own sons. The queen-mother was a respected member of the council, and presided over it when the king was away with his army. Several queen-mothers are on record as speaking on the side of peace in the debates of the nineteenth century. But they also sometimes joined in plots against their royal 'sons', and some lost their lives as a result.

The 'mothers' of Yoruba and Dahomey officials are not described as exercising any particular political influence. But the Bariba kingdoms offer us a remarkable instance of a royal woman whose ritual functions had political implications. This lady was called the 'senior princess'. She was not in fact the eldest of the king's sisters or daughters, but had the title conferred on her by the king with the agreement of his close kin. Usually she was chosen from a branch of the royal line other than that of the reigning king. Her title literally meant 'the elder of the razors', and it referred to the fact that at the annual national ceremony it fell to her to shave the heads of the young boys (about seven years old) of the royal lineage and to give to each the name of one of his ancestors. The name supposedly indicated that the fortunes of its bearer would correspond to those of his predecessor and so foretold his chances of success in competition for the kingship; conferred as it was on a ritual occasion, it was regarded as an expression of the ancestors' choice, not simply that of the princess. To have a propitious name did not guarantee the succession, since in the Bariba kingdoms this was contested by force of arms, but it was one of the considerations that secured support for a candidate, and to that extent the senior princess did have an influence in politics.

Among the Bantu kingdoms the most interesting from this point of view is that of the Lozi. They had two capitals of identical construction twenty-five miles apart, which represented a division of the kingdom into north and south. The southern one was ruled by a sister of the king whom Gluckman calls the 'princess-chief', and was a sanctuary from the king's anger. The princess-chief had her own chiefs and councillors and her own army, and she was consulted on all matters of importance. But the princess-chief of Gluckman's day told him that though she might argue against the king she would not hold out against him; nor would she try to get her way by refusing to perform her ritual duties.

It is in this context more than in any other that one feels the absence of written records contemporary with events. The contrast between the lively picture of Asante politics and the stylised accounts of constitutional arrangements remembered when the kings had lost their independence is striking. Outside Asante we know of principles, we can talk of possibilities, some writers have been able to interpret such meagre evidence as records of the succession to chiefly titles. But we know enough to see that no monarch was absolute and that positions of countervailing power were generally recognized, possibly because no king was able wholly to destroy them. It is perhaps most instructive to see the importance of religious belief not only as an ideology but as a check on political power; if access to spiritual beings is a resource, it is of a very different kind from those that are commonly considered in the discussion of power struggles.

CHAPTER IX
SUCCESSION CONTESTS

EVEN where there are ostensibly precise rules of succession to kingship, people will find means to contest it as long as the office is desirable. It would be an exaggeration to say that the strict rules which hold in Britain were not established until the throne ceased to be a source of political power, but it is only since that time that monarchs have stepped into their predecessors' shoes without any argument about claims. In African kingdoms it was exceptional for succession rules to designate a single individual; in the majority of cases a choice was made between a number of eligible candidates, and in some of them the contest was expected to be one of armed force. Wherever there was to be a contest, princes would be gathering support some time ahead, perhaps all through their adult lives. A further complication in some African kingdoms was that the succession went in turn to different branches of the royal lineage, or even to different independent lineages. Where this was the rule, a candidate would have to seek support within his own descent group, by pacific means and not by fighting, but there was still sometimes argument between the branches as to whose turn was next.

Succession Qualifications

Although a prince could not become a king without going through a rite of passage of the kind described in Chapter III, the belief that only a member of the royal lineage could be qualified could have its ritual aspect. Thus the Yoruba held that a pretender who went through the accession ceremonies would die—that is that only a legitimate successor would be ritually strong enough to receive the powers that they conferred. But very many people might have the basic ritual qualification, whatever it was, that went with royal descent, particularly since kings and princes, with their many wives, had many sons. The number of possible claimants could not be allowed to increase indefinitely. It was usually limited by the rule that only a man whose own father had reigned could be a claimant—and this rule might stimulate competition among the sons of kings, each aware that, if he failed, his descendants would be disqualified for ever.

In many African states there were kingmakers, who selected one of the eligible royals and presented him to a gathering of the people. Sometimes they purported to be acting on the wishes of the dead king, as did the leading *abiru* in Rwanda. In Buganda the successor was chosen by the senior chiefs, purely secular officials with no hereditary status. Benin provided for the nomination in advance of the chosen heir, who should then have been included among the *Uzama* (see Chapter VIII), with the title of *Edaiken*; but in fact most kings of Benin were afraid to appoint a son to a position from which he might challenge their authority, and no Edaiken was appointed during the nineteenth century. Tradition said that strict primogeniture had been established early in the eighteenth century with the deliberate aim of avoiding contests; but in fact there are a number of recorded instances of such contests. In Dahomey too the kings were said, at any rate by some authorities, to nominate their successors, and the rule of succession from father to own son is said to have been introduced at the time when in Allada to the south, as in Borgu to the north, a number of lineages claimed to provide the king in turn. The heir had to be the son of a commoner woman, and must have no physical defect (left-handedness was regarded as one such). According to Argyle (1966: 58), oracles were consulted on his future prospects; M. A. Glélé (1974: 94), a member of the royal line, writes that the consultation was made at the time of the prince's birth, and the oracle then named the ancestor who would have an especial responsibility for him, and from whose life-story his destiny could be predicted. In such a case it would be for the king to take the prediction into account when he made his choice. Argyle tells us that it needed the approval of the two leading officials, the Migan and the Meu, though the evidence that he gives is the record of an occasion when these two set aside the chosen heir after his father's death, not quite the same thing.

The heir apparent shared power with his father. Of course there was rivalry for the office. M. A. Glélé refers to 'intrigues going as far as poisoning', and quotes a proverb which said 'The throne is always contested and seized in a struggle' (1974: 87).

Circulating Succession

In a number of West African kingdoms it was the rule that the kingship should circulate among several branches of the royal house, and in one, the Fulani kingdom of Zaria, four independent lineages claimed this right in virtue of the contribution of their founders to the conquest of the country. Zaria was a special case in that, as a vassal state of Sokoto, it had to accept the intervention of its overlord in matters which elsewhere were settled by internal power struggles. But we know so much more about the actual course of these struggles in Zaria, from the research of M. G. Smith (1965), than we do in relation to other kingdoms, that this system, anomalous as it is, deserves to be described first.

In Zaria, although the rule that a king should not be succeeded by a member of his own line was generally followed, there was not even a theoretical order of rotation, and two of the four eligible lines held the kingship for most of the nineteenth century. According to Smith, conventional rules of succession had come to be accepted after about fifty years of Fulani rule, but his own account shows that these were by no means always followed. Three officials were recognized as kingmakers: the senior non-royal territorial chief, the senior Muslim priest and the chief justice. They seem sometimes to have made their own nomination of one candidate and sometimes to have left it to Sokoto to choose from three candidates, the men they judged to have most support in each of the eligible lineages. The number of competitors was limited not only by the rule that only a man whose father had been king could succeed to the throne, but that to be eligible he must also have held a senior territorial chiefship; this rule led the kings to appoint as many of their sons as possible to such offices so that they should have a chance of the succession.

Records and memories tell little of the power struggles

within lineages which led to their choice of one man as candidate, though Smith mentioned that the chance of success in competition with rival lineages was a consideration. But we know a good deal about the means by which a king, once on the throne, made hay while the sun shone. In Zaria the conception of the kingship as a source of profit outweighed such considerations of duty to their subjects as we find among longer-established dynasties. On the death of a king who had reigned for only a few weeks, it was argued that his lineage had not had their share of power, and Sokoto supported the claim of a successor from the same line. As far as they were able, kings, on their accession, dismissed incumbents from the leading offices and substituted their own close kin.

But after a time their power to do this was restricted by the interference of Sokoto in appointments to superior chiefships as well as in the succession itself—a 'divide and rule' policy in the only meaningful sense of that phrase. From about 1880 Sokoto sought to weaken the king's power by keeping senior offices in the possession of other lineages than his. But since it did not specify the individuals to be appointed, a counter-measure was available in deliberately appointing weak characters. This, however, had the disadvantage that the duties of the office were not done efficiently, and the king could not rely on the exercise of the chief's authority, even though he might be sure he would not be actively sabotaged. Sambo, the king at this period, tried to secure his position by making a Habe client governor of Zaria as well as Galadima (the senior non-royal chiefship). He thought he could count on the loyalty of a man who owed everything to him, but he had merely created an over-mighty subject who eventually rebelled against him.

For various reasons, not all connected with rivalry for the succession, Sambo was deposed by Sokoto and succeeded by Yero, whose father Abdullahi sixty years earlier had been deposed, reinstated, and then deposed again. The property of a deposed ruler was divided between the Sultan and his successor. Thus Yero, though he had lost an earlier individual inheritance, had had his share of Sambo's wealth. However, he determined to recover what he could of his father's possessions by plundering the lineage to whom they had gone, and to this end he built up a force of slaves armed with guns which he bought from the Royal Niger Company. They did not confine their attentions strictly to Yero's rivals. However, as Smith indicates (1965: 192), their activities simply carried to a logical extreme the principle that the estates of a rival lineage were liable to confiscation as its members were dismissed from office. Yero expected his successor, whoever he might be, to retaliate in kind, and he evaded this crude form of death duty by giving a large slave village to his son. It is hard to guess what this practice might have led to if Zaria had remained independent, but Yero's successor, Kwassau, appealed to the British to defend him against his neighbours, and so found himself under a more demanding overlord.

The British, while purporting to recognize traditional rules of succession, did not follow them closely, and they appointed three successive kings from the same lineage, all of them men whose fathers had not ruled. But they severely cut down the number of territorial chiefs, and as they regarded administrative experience as an important qualification for the kingship, this imposed a new limit on the number of candidates. Now there developed the same demand for rotation between the segments of a single lineage as there had been before for rotation between lineages. So, within a narrower range, the same process of eliminating rivals and rewarding supporters went on. The approved reasons for dismissing a chief from office had changed. For the British, only shortcomings in bureaucratic or financial probity could justify it. But it was not hard to find grounds for charges of this kind. At the same time, a great many new bureaucratic offices were created as technical services (health, education, agriculture, veterinary) were developed; the senior posts were filled by the king from his kin and clients, the lower ones by the heads of departments on the same principle.

The Muslim kingdoms alone in Africa possessed a specialized judiciary in the mallams with their expert knowledge of Koranic law. They were in theory politically neutral, and they were largely so in fact. But they were never conceived as a countervailing force to royal power. This was what the British meant by the independence of the judiciary; and in addition they developed a system of courts which called for the appointment of many more judges. The post of chief justice soon came to circulate among a number of lineages.

It was now possible for supporters of the king to be dismissed by a judge on grounds that would be upheld by the British authorities. The king could not dismiss the chief justice, and only the chief justice could appoint and dismiss his subordinates. So the king had to find means of protecting his kinsmen and followers. The readiest was to promote the chief justice to a post outside the judicial system. Another stratagem was to appoint kin of the chief justice to departmental offices, thus making them in effect hostages for his compliance with the king's wishes.

In Allada succession went in turn to five different lineages, and Glélé, in arguing the merits of direct succession in Dahomey, remarks that the French were able to establish their control there by intervening in a dispute between rival claimants. Lombard shows how in Borgu a similar rule contributed to the process of endless division that was still going on at the time when France and Britain partitioned the country. He has reconstructed from oral tradition a picture of endless power struggles between princes who devoted their entire adult life to the contest. They were seeking the royal status which only a king could pass on to his heirs; not, like Zande or Luba princes, an autonomy that they could achieve by conquering new territory.

The aristocracy of the Borgu kingdoms had entered their present home as horsemen living by hunting and pillage, and the sons of a king maintained this way of life up to the moment when one was chosen to succeed his father. The many who were unsuccessful could be appointed to administer divisions of the kingdom, and could pass these lower-ranking offices to their sons; and some gave up the struggle early and sought offices of this kind. Those who favoured their chances, however, gathered followers from their matrilateral kin, who could not be their rivals, and from anyone else who was attracted by the distribution of booty. When the choice came to be made, prestige in fighting and the actual command of power played a significant part.

But a prince's success did not depend entirely on his own efforts. Likely winners were marked in childhood, at the annual Gani festival when all nobles, princes and office-holders assembled to do homage and bring gifts to the king, and to 'salute the drums' in which dwelt the spirits of the royal ancestors. Each brought with him his young children to have conferred upon them by the senior princess (Gnon Kogi) an ancestral name which would predict for each a destiny similar to that of its previous holder. The prophecy of success might well be self-fulfilling; and in addition an illustrious name was believed to carry with it that ritual efficacy which is so widely believed to be essential for secular achievement.

If this represented a first selection, one which limited the contest to two or three candidates was made through the conferment of a high-ranking title by the king. These titles, passed down in the royal lineage, carried no authority, but the highest, those which were said to 'open the door' to the throne, entitled the holders to ride caparisoned horses and use the copper stirrups of the ancestors who first held them. Rivals would fight or poison one another for nomination to these titles, for which they were put forward by the elders of the descent line which 'owned' them. The title designated the holder as the official choice of his branch of the royal line when its turn came for the kingship. But, like the Gani name, it was also held to confer an additional element of the ritual power to command success. Although the titles were supposedly ranked in order, a holder might try to enhance his status by going ahead of his turn to salute the ancestral drums; this too is remembered to have led to fighting.

Nor was the rule of rotation between the five branches of the royal line always strictly kept. The branch whose turn it was could be ousted by force, and the 'usurpers' would then maintain that they had followed what was really the correct order. This was the strategy of a candidate who had the support of his branch but was afraid he might not live till his turn came round; it was risky, because it made enemies, and he might, as Lombard (1965: 322) delicately puts it, lose by premature death what would have come to him if he had waited for it.

The system of rotation among the Gonja of northern Ghana,

as it is described by Jack Goody (1966), seems to have worked as smoothly in designating the successor as any system of primogeniture. Lineages succeeded in turn to territorial chief-ships as well. Five territorial chiefs, each belonging to a differ-ent lineage, were entitled to succeed in turn to the kingship. Any office which fell vacant was filled by the senior man—not the oldest, but the holder of the senior title—of the lineage whose turn it was. A ritual assertion of the claim to succeed was made at a new king's installation, when, as he mounted his horse to return to the capital, the territorial chief whose lineage was next in line seized his bridle and led his horse on. At the lower level a chief was selected by the existing chiefs of his division; thus all the eligible lineages had their say, and the divisional chief could not favour his own kin as did the Fulani in Zazzau. Goody does mention the possibility of a disputed succession, though only in the case of divisional chiefs, for whom the system was still in operation when he was there in 1964. He sees it as having many advantages. In Gonja the territorial chiefs must stay in their own divisions up to the time when one becomes king and moves with his family and fol-lowers to the capital. But, because they all hope to succeed to the kingship, they are not tempted to assert their independence as, for example, the Zande princes were. They 'have a stake in seeing that the kingship to which they might eventually succeed is not damaged by attack from without or by succession from within' (Goody 1966: 162). The counter to any attempt by a ruling lineage to perpetuate its power would be not seces-sion but rebellion by a combination of the rest. So it may be that those who regard direct succession as preferable are simply committing the error of ethnocentrism, of assuming that what is done in their own society must be best. Certainly there is no reason why a conflict between claimants in any system should not lead to foreign intervention.

The Nomination of the Heir

In Asante the rule of succession was matrilineal, that is a king derived the right to reign through his mother and not his father. It has been mentioned that the Asante recognized, alongside the Asantehene, a 'queen-mother', the Asantehemaa—not a mother of the ruling king but a sister whose son would be the next king. The rule that an Asantehene must be the son of an Asantehemaa was never broken. In this system the sons of kings were not themselves of royal lineage. But by marrying his sons to royal women—or rather by requiring royal women to marry his sons—a king could make his grandsons eligible for the Golden Stool, and in fact the kings of Asante did follow their grandfathers in a direct line. But since a son could not succeed his father two lines alternated. The second Asantehene, Opoku Ware, was the son of the first Asantehemaa, who was a sister's daughter of the first Asantehene Osei Tutu. Down to the eighth king the Golden Stool was held in turn by descendants of these two. Each king nominated as his successor a member of the other line—though this by no means always guaranteed the succession. It came to be taken for granted that senior women of the royal lineage should marry into one or other line. But early in the nineteenth century a lady who never expected to become Asantehemaa married a man of neither. Her son Kwaku Dua I succeeded in 1834, apparently without opposition. He nominated two heirs apparent, one from each of the claimant houses. But he did not let his sisters' daughters marry into these houses, so they were effectively barred from the succession; and he married six of his own sons to royal women.

To name an heir apparent was in itself hardly more than a gesture, since a dead king's wishes were not regarded as sacrosanct, and more than once a king died while his nominee was still a child. The formal procedure for the choice of an heir was for the Asantehemaa, after consulting with various persons in high authority, including the head of the treasury and the head of the police, to offer three names, in order of preference, to the council of Kumase chiefs—who, however, could reject them all. One would suppose that the choice would depend on their estimate of the candidates' support, and some of the records show clearly that this meant not popularity, let alone voting support, but military support. Perhaps this was how the succession was decided on the occasions when no contest is recorded. But eight out of fifteen kings of Asante up to the present day secured the Golden Stool by fighting.

Regents and Caretakers

One way of contending a succession, even one that has been ostensibly decided, is to claim that the king is in fact a caretaker appointed in the minority of a rival. Two of the more controversial of the Asante kings, Kofi Kakari (1867–75) and his younger brother Mensa Bonsu (1874–83), who were both removed from office, were described by Captain Barrow, a British envoy to Kumase, as having held their posts only 'at pleasure' of the grandson of Kwaku Dua I, whom he had nominated as heir apparent but who was only seven years old when he died. Barrow's report was made at the time when the charges that led to his destoolment were being brought against Mensa Bonsu, and one might guess that there was an element of hindsight in this assessment of the two brothers' status.

A better documented illustration of this kind of argument comes from some Tswana chiefdoms which have not been discussed in this book because their extent and organization did not seem to qualify them for the designation of kingdoms. These are the Rolong chiefdoms in one of the Bantu 'homelands' of South Africa, where J. L. Comaroff worked in 1969–70. The rules of succession of the Tswana, the group to which the Rolong belong, were such as to make a minority almost inevitable, since a chief's heir had to be the son of a woman whom he had married after his own accession. Their annals are full of wicked uncles who would not step down when a nephew came of age. Perhaps at any given time as many holders of office were regents as substantive chiefs. While in theory a substantive chief cannot be deposed, it is recognized that a regent may be, and that it is for the people to decide when he must give way to the recognized heir. The effect of this principle is that the status accorded to a chief depends upon genealogical argument. If it is agreed that he had in fact the right qualifications when he succeeded, well and good; if not, then he must only be a regent usurping the place of a 'rightful heir'. People may question whether his mother was in fact his father's principal wife. More difficult is the question whether a man is to count as the son of the man who begot him, or as the son of that man's deceased elder brother on behalf of whom this

man begot him through the institution of the levirate, the 'raising up of seed' to a man who dies without heirs. Successfully to
claim that your genitor was in fact the surrogate of a man
much senior to himself can substantially advance you in rank.
Of course no one can verify the facts; the acceptance of the
claim is the measure of your political weight. If you are sufficiently widely recognized to be the successor of the actual
incumbent of a chiefship, he will 'turn out to have been' merely
a regent who must make way for you. It is this that led an
informant to say to Comaroff (1974: 40): 'Many chiefs are
born, and some are robed with the leopard skin, but few die as
chiefs.' No doubt this continuance of the contest after the
investment of a chief becomes less likely as kingdoms are established and power is concentrated at the centre; and it becomes
impossible in practice once the power of the ruler is guaranteed
by an external authority. In theory superior rulers are responsive to the dissatisfaction of their subjects' subjects; in practice
they incline to support the man to whom they have committed
themselves, and when chiefs have been dismissed from office
under colonial rule it has usually been for some shortcoming in
their role as bureaucrats.

CHAPTER X

CONQUERED KINGS

WHEN a kingdom with any organized hierarchy of authorities is conquered by an outsider, it is rational for the conqueror to maintain this hierarchy in being as the most convenient way of attaining his own ends. The aims of African conquerors were very similar to those of their new subjects; in essence they were to extend the area from which resources and manpower could be obtained. In the main, vassal chiefs ruled their subjects as they had when they were independent. The contrast between Zaria under Sokoto and Zaria under Britain makes the point. The Fulani conquerors altered the rules of succession, the ranking of titled offices and the principles of recruitment to office; but the functions and activities of fief-holders were what their predecessors' had been. The British sought agents for all sorts of policies that had never been heard of before; they demanded the renunciation of lucrative and, before their coming, respectable practices such as slave-raiding and slave-trading, and they sought to establish new principles in such matters as tax-gathering and the administration of justice. It is the uneasy coupling of political systems with divergent aims and principles that gives its interest to the history of kingdoms under colonial rule.

British and French attitudes towards indigenous rulers have often been sharply contrasted, but where they were dealing with kingdoms of substantial proportions the contrast was not as great as might appear at first sight. The French feared that kings would lead rebellions; they deprived them of all but their ritual functions, but they kept the administrative framework of the kingdoms in being. The British deposed those kings whom they conquered but replaced them with men who had a claim to succeed in traditional terms, and they usually maintained the boundaries that they found. They held that law and order depended upon the continuation of traditional authority; that

African ideas of legitimacy would be outraged by the rejection of traditional claims to rule and the substitution for their own kings and chiefs of mere nominees of the new conquerors; that Africans were inherently predisposed towards hereditary rule. The term 'indirect rule', to refer to a system in which subject kingdoms are administered by their own rulers under an overlord, was first used in the context of Nigeria. It is a cliché nowadays to say that it was an expedient which later become a philosophy, and to ascribe the policy to the fact that in the early days in Nigeria there were very few administrative officers. It would be more accurate to say that the British in northern Nigeria did just what their predecessors had done and what any intelligent person does who takes over a highly organized going concern. Indirect Rule became a philosophy when it was held that *every* African political unit must be administered through its traditional authority, and petty chiefdoms of a few thousand population or even village groups with no single head were stretched to fit a Procrustes' bed originally made for the Sultan of Sokoto. Yet it is the fact that people whose chiefs or kings had previously been disregarded were gratified when they were given recognition, and that there has often been dissatisfaction, sometimes even rebellion, when a 'native authority' was appointed who was not considered to have the appropriate qualifications. As Lombard (1967: 104) points out, it was particularly in the early period, when both king and people saw the new ruler as a victorious enemy, that their solidarity was complete. Later, when the co-operation by virtue of which the kings were able to survive began to be seen as a betrayal of their subjects, they became the object of criticism and political opposition.

It was assumed that under European rule African kings would cease to be arbitrary rulers moved only by their 'whims'—as Europeans perceived them—and become benevolent monarchs dispensing impartial justice and devoting themselves to the welfare of their subjects. They lost the power of life and death which many had exercised freely both for ritual purposes and to punish disobedience. Their judicial powers were limited, sometimes very narrowly, and their decisions were subject to appeals to European authorities. They were required to replace tribute in kind by regular taxation in cash at fixed rates; though, as before, they passed on a portion of the tax collected to the superior government. Lugard said that a tax must be imposed because it was the traditional symbol of subjection, but of course it had more practical reasons.

More far-reaching in its effect on the position of kings was the endeavour to enlist them on the side of progress in the sense of improved living standards. The people listen to the chief, was the argument; let him be our mouthpiece in persuading them to send their children to school, to contour-ridge their fields, to plant new crops and plant them where and how the agronomists recommend, to dig latrines . . . and so on. The larger the kingdom, the less the king himself could be expected to pass on the message directly to the people; in such a case the advice would be given to his subordinates, but he would be expected to use his influence in the same direction.

In one sense the indirect rule principle worked best in the great kingdoms where it was first introduced. The tax-gathering and judicial organizations were efficient, the revenues were large simply because the populations were large and in Kano, the wealthiest of them, they were expended on impressive modern-style installations, piped water, electricity, a printing-press, a well-equipped hospital, and a number of schools. Critics remarked that expenditure on activities of this kind was concentrated in the capital, but only at a very late date in the colonial period was it found possible to increase the share of tax collected that was to stay at village or district level.

Asante had a peculiar history. After British authority was extended over it in 1896, its separate chiefdoms were treated as independent units, Kumase being merely one among many, and the Asantehene in exile. Only in 1932 was he brought home and restored to his position as head of the Asante Confederacy, as it was now officially named. During the period of interregnum the Gold Coast, as it was then called, depended for central government revenues entirely on customs duties, and the chiefdoms met their internal needs from rents paid by cocoa farmers and, if they were fortunate, mining royalties. They had a new incentive for extending their boundaries, no longer by war but by litigation. As the British saw it, they squandered on these contests money that they raised by *ad hoc* levies on their subjects; on one occasion the government took control of a Stool treasury because it was bankrupt. But it was only in 1936 that all Stool finances were made subject to accounting and supervision; and much later than that Asante chiefs were managing to keep their revenues separate from public funds.

Kings, once recognized by the overlords, had their full political support. Dissent of a kind that would have been possible before—whether or not it was regarded as rebellion—was now treated as subversion. The manpower demands that could be made on subjects, however, were defined, limited, often commuted for a money payment; in British territories there were not complaints that government authorized undue exactions.

The theory that kings and their chiefs, having been persuaded of the desirability of changes in their mode of life, would impose on their people regulations requiring these changes to be made, led to two alternative results; either the 'native authorities' avoided making themselves unpopular by not enforcing the regulations, or they did enforce them and so came to be more and more identified with the alien government. Nowhere did they pass on to their subjects the arguments for innovation, which they very likely did not fully understand themselves. Agricultural regulations often involved harder work than traditional methods required, and their value was not immediately apparent. However, in British territories direct compulsion to labour was not a normal form of exercise of chiefly authority.

In Rwanda the traditional claims of king and chiefs on the labour of their subjects were heavier than anything recorded elsewhere in the Interlacustrine kingdoms (and of course heavier than in those kingdoms where kings and chiefs commanded the labour of slaves). They had required one day's labour in five, but up to 1933, relying on the support of Belgian authority, they increased this to two or three out of six. In that year their claims were commuted for a money payment, but both before and after this date they were required by the Belgians to impose compulsory labour for the cultivation of cash crops and for re-afforestation and the terracing of slopes (Lemarchand 1970: 122) and could be punished if they failed to do so. Here was a specific local reason to add to the dissatisfaction with traditional authority that became vocal in most of the kingdoms after the second world war.

In French West Africa policy was directed first to the diminution of the authority of kings by removing from their control populations which had recently been conquered; and also by deposing or pensioning off such monarchs as the king of Dahomey and placing other members of the royal family in charge of divisions of the kingdom. Later the French found that they could rely for their administrative needs only on 'chiefs who were listened to'; but they never believed, as did the more romantic among British thinkers, that the kingdoms could be modernized and remain a permanent feature of the political scene. One governor described the role of the Sultan of Baguirmi as that of an agent of French policy with no right of independent initiative (Lombard 1967b: 129).

The opposition to kings and chiefs from their own subjects followed a parallel course in British and French territories. The general populace may have suffered from abuses of power, but it was the educated commoners who began to assert claims to be the true élite in the modern world which their schooling and experience enabled them to understand. Indeed it was they who were referred to as the élite by the French authorities. Profoundly committed as they were to the values of their own culture, the French emphasized the mastery of their language in the schools and encouraged the most successful pupils to go to France for further study. When they came back with advanced political views, authority was alarmed and fell back on the argument—which had some substance in this case—that the young politicians were alienated from the mass of their people, that the true spokesmen of the masses were the chiefs. Hence, as late as 1932, French policy turned to reinforcing chiefly authority, though this hardly went to the length of restoring deposed kings.

If 1932 was too late to recreate kingship, it was early to be confronted with political demands. In the British territories these only began to be heard during the Second World War, and they took the form of demands for elective institutions to replace those based on heredity before the question of independence began to be mooted. Kings and chiefs were represented as illiterate and out of touch with modern developments, a stereotype which did not conform to the facts, since most of them were literate and many had been in some form of employment before their accession.

The role of chiefs and kings was much debated in the discussions of political evolution which began during the war and continued without interruption until all the British territories were independent. The Aitken Watson Commission, sent to the then Gold Coast after the riots of ex-servicemen in 1948, stated in its report that 'the star of the chiefs has set.' But the locally based Coussey Commission which made the first proposals for constitutional advance was by no means eager to do away with them, and produced a constitution which found a place for chiefs in representative institutions. African politicians favoured the substitution of elected local authorities on the English model for 'native authorities', but with the proviso that kings and chiefs should be ceremonial heads who would open a session and then withdraw. In Ghana, where the revenues of the Stool—not of the individual incumbent—had never been effectively brought to account in native treasuries, chiefs were paid salaries intended to enable them to live in an appropriate style and perform their ritual responsibilities.

Although, in the period of constitution-making before independence, African politicians seemed to be not wholly dedicated to the destruction of royal or chiefly power, the new rulers soon found that they could not tolerate any potential focus of opposition. In English-speaking West Africa kings and chiefs still exist, but they play no formal part in the government of their subjects, let alone that of the nation as a whole. Local administration is in the hands of nominees of a single party or a military government. The great Emirates of northern Nigeria have been broken up, as their neighbours were by the French, into smaller units, each directly responsible to a centrally appointed superior.

The history of the kingdoms in Uganda illustrates the difference between the British attitude to kings and that of indepen-

dent African leaders. Nowhere, except in Basutoland and
Swaziland, did a king's dominions extend to the frontier of a
colony which was to become independent. In all the rest of the
new states, there were populations which owed no allegiance to
a king, and very often the new political leaders were drawn
from these. The story of Uganda just before and after independence dramatically illustrates the relations between kings and
their own subjects, kings and the British authorities, kings and
politicians who were not their subjects. Of the four Uganda
kingdoms, Buganda was by far the richest and most populous,
though of course its population was a minority in the country as
a whole. Many Ganda, looking back to their traditions of conquest, assumed that they would dominate an independent
Uganda—just what the peoples of the north feared and
resented. In the years before independence the kingship and its
incumbent had been criticized from within Buganda, and the
king was perceived by some of the politically-minded as a *fain-
éant* foisted on them by the British. But when a British Governor
deposed him because he refused to implement a democratic
reform, he became a martyr overnight; and from that time on
he was the symbol of his country's prestige. He was restored as
a 'constitutional monarch', and as independence approached
he and his supporters succeeded in obtaining a large degree of
local autonomy for Buganda and a smaller degree of independence from the centre for the other kingdoms. By this time, it is
clear, what was at stake was the status of the unit symbolized
by the king, not devotion to monarchy as a form of government. The Kabaka of Buganda became President of Uganda,
but with narrower powers than most presidents have; there was
a moment when he and the elected Prime Minister—Obote, a
man from the kingless north—each claimed to have dismissed
the other. But the final collapse of kingship was sudden. Obote
suspected the Kabaka of plotting a military coup and took
the initiative himself; and his army drove all the kings into
exile.

Even more dramatic was the end of the kings in Rwanda,
which was brought about not by a *coup d'état* but by a popular
revolution (tacitly assisted by a Belgian administration which
had swung from support of traditional authority to that com-

mitment to the democratization of Africa which Harold Macmillan called 'the wind of change').

Many African kings, then, are living, or have died, in exile. But some are still on their thrones, and one must ask what their status means today. The Hausa kingdoms in the north of Nigeria have been broken up into districts and sub-districts under authorities directly appointed by the military governors of the six states that were created by General Gowon. Through Ghana's history up to the present the Asante kings Prempeh II and his successor Opoku Ware II have remained in office, the former first supported by the British but reduced to the status of an elected local authority, then losing all political recognition when elective bodies were dissolved, the latter the chief custodian of the Asante tradition which is now being so diligently studied by Ghanaian historians.

In Yoruba country the kings are still believed by the general populace to hold the power that was long since taken from them in fact. When during the Nigerian civil war taxes were steeply increased, rioters attacked the palaces of several Obas, and one was killed. But the attempt to introduce elected authorities who would administer welfare services and local amenities has left behind it only a local bureaucracy—still called 'council officials'—who run their districts in colonial style.

Nowadays in Africa there are more dictators than kings.

BIBLIOGRAPHY

ARGYLE, W. J. (1966). *The Fon of Dahomey*, Oxford.

ASHTON, E. H. (1952). *The Basuto*, London.

BALANDIER, G. (1974). *Anthropo-logiques*, Paris.

BARNES, J. A. (1954). *Politics in a Changing Society*, London.

BEATTIE, J. H. M. (1971). *The Nyoro State*, Oxford.

BEIDELMAN, T. O. (1966). 'Swazi Royal Ritual', *Africa*, xxxvi. 373–405.

BLACK-MICHAUD, J. (1975). *Cohesive Force*, Oxford.

BOVILL, E. (1968). *The Golden Trade of the Moors* (2nd edition), Oxford.

BRADBURY, R. E. (1973). *Benin Studies*, Oxford.

COLSON, E. M. (1975). *Tradition and Contract*, London.

COMAROFF, J. L. (1974). 'Chiefship in a South African Homeland', *Journal of Southern African Studies*, i. 36–51.

CRUICKSHANK, B. (1853). *Eighteen Years on the Gold Coast of Africa*, London (reprinted 1966).

DE HEUSCH, L. (1958). *Essais sur le symbolisme de l'inceste royale*, Brussels.

EVANS-PRITCHARD, E. E. (1940). *The Nuer*, Oxford.

—— (1971). *The Azande*, Oxford.

FALLERS, L. A. ed. (1964). *The King's Men*, London.

GLÉLÉ, M. A. (1974). *Le Danxome*, Paris.

GLUCKMAN, M. ed. (1951). *Seven Tribes of British Central Africa*, London.

—— (1954). *Rituals of Rebellion in South-East Africa*, London.

—— (1963). 'The Rise of a Zulu Empire', *Scientific American*, 202.

GOODY, J. R. ed. (1966). *Succession to High Office*, Cambridge.

—— ed. (1968). *Literacy in Traditional Societies*, Cambridge.

GORJU, J. (1920). *Entre le Victoria, l'Albert et l'Edouard*, Marseilles.

JINGOES, S. J. (1975). *A Chief is a Chief by the People*, London.

'K. W.' (1937). 'The procedure in accession to the throne of a nominated King in the kingdom of Bunyoro', *Uganda Journal*, 4.

KARUGIRE, S. R. (1971). *A History of the Kingdom of Nkore in Western Uganda*, Oxford.

KUPER, H. (1947). *An African Aristocracy*, London.

LABAT, J. B. (1730). *Voyage du chevalier Des Marchais en Guinée, isles voisines, et en Cayenne, fait in 1725, 1726 et 1727*, vol. 2, Paris.

LEMARCHAND, R. (1970). *Rwanda and Burundi*, London.

LLOYD, P. C. (1960). 'Sacred Kingship and Government among the Yoruba', *Africa*, xxx. 221–37.

—— (1971). *The Political Development of Yoruba Kingdoms in the Eighteenth and Nineteenth Centuries*, London.

LOMBARD, J. A. (1965). *Structures de type 'féodal' en Afrique Noire*, Paris.

—— (1967a). 'The Kingdom of Dahomey', in Forde D. and Kaberry, P. M., eds., *West African Kingdoms in the Nineteenth Century*, London.

—— (1967b). *Autorités Traditionelles et Pouvoirs Européens en Afrique Noire*, Paris.

MAQUET, J. J. (1961). *The Premise of Inequality in Ruanda*, London.

MAYER, P. (1949). *The Lineage Principle in Gusii Society*, London.

MERCIER, P. (1954). 'The Fon of Dahomey', in Forde D., ed., *African Worlds*, London.

MORTON-WILLIAMS, P. (1960). 'The Yoruba Ogboni Cult in Oyo', *Africa*, xxx, 362–74.

—— (1967). 'The Yoruba Kingdom of Oyo', in Forde, D. and Kaberry, P., eds., *West African Kingdoms in the Nineteenth Century*, London.

MUDANDAGIZI, V. (with Rwamukumbi, J.) (1974). 'Les formes historiques de la dépendence personnelle dans l'État rwandais', *Cahiers d'Études Africaines*, 6. 26–53.

NEWBURY, C. (1961). *The Western Slave Coast and its Neighbours*, London.

NADEL, S. F. (1942). *A Black Byzantium*, London.

OBERG, K. (1940). 'The Kingdom of Ankole in Uganda', in Evans-Pritchard, E. E. and Fortes, M. eds., *African Political Systems*, London.

OLIVER, R. and FAGE, J. D. (1962). *A Short History of Africa*, Harmondsworth.

OMER-COOPER, J. B. (1966). *The Zulu Aftermath*, London.

RATTRAY, R. S. (1923). *Ashanti*, Oxford.

—— (1929). *Ashanti Law and Constitution*, Oxford.

READ, M. (1956). *The Ngoni of Nyasaland*, London.

REINDORF, C. C. (1895). *History of the Gold Coast*, Basel (reprinted London, 1966).

RUEL, M. (1969). *Leopards and Leaders*, London.

RWAMUKUMBA, J. (with Mudandagizi, V.) (1974). 'Les formes historiques de la dépendence personnelle dans l'État rwandais', *Cahiers d'Études Africaines*, 6. 26–53.

SANSOM, B. (1974). 'Traditional Economic Systems', in Hammond-Tooke, W. D., ed., *The Bantu-Speaking Peoples of Southern Africa*, London.

Skertchly, J. (1874). *Dahomey as it is*, London.

Smith, M. G. (1960). *Government in Zazzau*, London.

Southwold, M., n.d. (1961). *Bureaucracy and Chiefship in Buganda*, London.

Thompson, L. (1969). 'The Zulu Kingdom in Natal', in Wilson, M. and Thompson, L., eds., *Oxford History of South Africa*, Oxford.

Turner, V. W. (1969). *The Ritual Process*, London.

Urvoy, Y. (1936). *Histoire des populations du Soudan central*, Paris.

Vansina, J. (1962). *L'évolution du royaume rwanda des origines à 1900*, Brussels.

—— (1966). *Kingdoms of the Savanna*, Madison, Wisconsin.

Wilks, L. (1975). *Asante in the Nineteenth Century*, Cambridge.

Wilson, G. (1939). *The Constitution of Ngonde*, Livingstone.

Wilson, M. (1959). *Communal Rituals of the Nyakyusa*, London.

INDEX

Paape

INTRODUCTION TO IRAN

BY THE SAME AUTHOR

INTRODUCTION TO
IRAN

o()o---o()o---o()o---o()o---o()o---o()o---o()o---o()o---o()o---o()o

ELGIN GROSECLOSE

NEW YORK
OXFORD UNIVERSITY PRESS
1947

CONTENTS

CONTENTS

LIST OF ILLUSTRATIONS

PART ONE
THE PEOPLE AND THEIR LAND

I

THE LAND OF IRAN

TO DISCOVER the land of Iran on the map, one twirls the globe eastward, following the latitudes of Texas and California, or the South Atlantic States, through Gibraltar, the Mediterranean, and on east of Suez past the Arabian peninsula. Here Iran is found, bounded on the west by Iraq and Turkey, on the east by Afghanistan and British Baluchistan, while on the north lies the great political mass of Russia, like a slowly moving glacier pressing towards the warm waters of the Persian Gulf and the Arabian Sea which enclose Iran on the south. Iran is politically an enclosed land, to which the commerce of the world has access, without passing through the territory of other sovereign powers, only through two deep-water ports of the Persian Gulf on the south.

Iran is the country formerly known as Persia, the people of which, twenty-five hundred years ago, commanded an empire that embraced Lybia and Egypt in Africa, Thrace, and Macedonia in Europe, and all the lands eastward to the Indus in India and the Oxus and Jaxartes in Central Asia. The word *Persia* applies properly only to the ancient province of Iran, which gave the empire its ruling race and its dominant culture and language. Modern Iran includes those areas which have remained essentially Persian in speech and culture, and to a large extent in race, and as such it may be classed as one of the oldest national existences in history.

Modern Iran is still a vast territory of 628,000 square miles. This is an area equal to that of Texas, New Mexico, Arizona, and California combined, and the population is roughly equivalent to that of these states (approximately 16,000,000). The landscape and climate offer general resemblances to those of the American Southwest. There are the elevated plateaus, the vast stretches of empty land, ringed by silent, awe-inspiring ranges; there are salt deserts and imperial valleys rich in fruits

3

and produce, and in a few districts forests and jungles. The air is generally dry and bracing; the extremes of temperature are about the same. There is the same 'wind along the waste'—and it may be mentioned that the windmill, so common on the Great Plains, was first known in Iran. But Iran is more arid, more desolate, and has greater expanses of desert. Grazing and tillage by irrigation are characteristic of both.

The greater part of Iran is a vast plateau, or more properly a series of high valleys lying between mountain ranges, which also form a wall around the country, save on the east. The elevation of this tableland varies from 3,000 to 8,000 feet above sea level, while the mountains reach a height, in Mt. Demavend, of 18,602 feet. On the south the elevation drops sharply to a sterile sea-level coast along the Persian Gulf; on the southwest occurs an equally abrupt descent to the arid plains of Iraq; on the north the land drops to below sea level, where it meets the Caspian Sea,[1] in a region of luxuriant subtropical forest. On the east the elevation continues to mount until it reaches, in central Asia, the immense altitudes of the Hindu Kush and Himalayas. In southeastern Iran is a vast expanse of desert known as the Dasht-i-Kavir and the Dasht-i-Lut. The Dasht-i-Lut is one of the most sterile regions of the globe, an area of sand and salt marshes inhabited by neither bird, nor beast, nor reptile, and by not even the most audacious desert herb.[2]

The ascent to the Iranian tableland is an experience to enthrall even the most experienced voyager. The traveler leaves the plains and climbs up escarpments by trails so precipitous that in the Persian tongue they are called *kotal*, or ladders. He traverses mountain ranges of terrifying ruggedness and majestic grandeur; he passes the ruins of ancient cities by roads that were followed by Alexander and Darius and Marco Polo; he follows gorges, walled by rocky precipices shimmering in an ochre and purple mist, divided by the water foaming white

[1] The level of the Caspian Sea is 85 feet below 'sea level.'

[2] No meteorological observations have been made in the desert itself, but data gathered at neighboring stations indicate that the prevailing humidity is between 5 and 15 per cent. The word applied to this district, *Lut*, signifying the 'Land of Lot,' connotes its terrifying desolation.

between; but everywhere he views chiefly barrenness and desolation.

Yet such is the mystery of Nature that her most precious gifts are to be found in these seemingly barren wastes. The mountains serve the beneficient purpose of reservoirs, holding the moisture that descends as snow in winter, and releasing it as the advancing sun of summer melts it and sends it in rivulets down onto the plain, where it activates the rich soil and produces garden oases of unbelievable charm. From a distance, the oases, surrounded by sun-dried mud walls, above which the poplars wave their foliage, resemble jade and coral upon the ochre expanse: one approaches them with a sense of anticipation and excitement and mystery. Here is a spot in which to rest and enjoy a moment of solitary paradise amid the wastes. The nomads and the villagers, if wary at first, are quickly hospitable, and the traveler will be offered for refreshment *lawash,* or thin strips of whole wheat bread, of remarkable delicacy of flavor, goat's milk cheese, nut meats and raisins, and a delectable preparation of milk, known as *mast,* together with wild honey, *doshab* or grape sirup, and *sherbet,* or sweetened fruit sirup.

All the produce of the temperate zone burgeons in these gardens. The grapes—over fifty varieties may be found in a single vineyard, ranging from the sugar sweet *kishmish,* small as the tip of the little finger, to the massive *sahebi,* large as a man's thumb—are famous: ancient Persian tradition has it that here originated the art of making wine, which in old Persian is known as the 'sweet poison.' And the Bible tells of how Noah, descending from Ararat into what is now Azerbaijan, set out a vineyard, and, drunk with the wine, became the first inebriate in history.[3]

The modern Persians, who do not as a rule drink wine, have a way of hanging grape clusters from rafters so that they retain their juices throughout the winter. Sun-dried, they are exported as raisins, and it was from the grape cultures of Shiraz, transported by the Arabs to Spain, in medieval times, that the Sherry-wine industry was founded.

Wheat is grown in most districts of Iran, sufficient to meet

[3] Genesis IX: 20, 21.

the demands of the population, for whom it constitutes a staple of diet, and to provide a small surplus for export. About 80 per cent of the cultivated land is devoted to wheat and barley. Rice is also cultivated, and connoisseurs assert that no finer rice is grown than the Persian. Certainly, perfectly prepared as it is in Iran, with each grain separate and the whole light and fluffy, it makes a dish to entice the appetite even without the numerous sauces with which it is served.

Among the fruits and nuts which are produced in abundance are apricots, peaches, cherries, quinces, almonds, walnuts, and pistachios. Nuts are exported in considerable quantities.

Proverbial are the flowers, and justly celebrated in song. To the Persians we owe not only the names but probably the flowers themselves: rose, jasmine, lilac, narcissus, myrtle. The secret of pressing the oil from the rose was a Persian discovery, and the name of this oil, *attar,* is also Persian.

The melons too must be mentioned. Long before motor transport, caravans laden with melons of Isfahan wended northward to Teheran, a distance of 250 miles, and in recent years varieties have been brought to this country for propagation. The soil and climate of Iran is, however, so peculiarly adapted to their culture that only in Iran itself can the perfection of their flavor be tasted. The way of keeping melons, by bedding them in straw, together with the qualities of the Iranian climate, permits them to be served late in winter with all their original freshness preserved.

Everywhere, except along the northern coast, rainfall is scanty. On the eastern tableland the rain seldom exceeds 8 inches annually and on the western tableland averages 15 inches—about the same as in Salt Lake City. In the Lut, the rainfall does not exceed 2 inches.

Except in the Caspian lowlands, where mosquitoes are a danger, and the Persian Gulf littoral, the climate is healthful. On the tableland the weather resembles that of Iowa, Nebraska, and the Dakotas, except for the lesser rainfall. In winter, temperatures are low, although they seldom drop below zero. In summer they average between 70 and 90 degrees, sometimes soaring above 100, but the effect of such extreme temperature is modified by the dryness of the atmosphere. The range of temperature varies of course according to the altitude, and in the mountains the variations are extreme.[4]

In the south, along the Persian Gulf, where during World War II so many Americans of the Persian Gulf Command worked at unloading war material for transportation to Russia, the heat is unbearable, reaching as high as 123 degrees at times.[5] In the north, also, in the provinces bordering on the Caspian, the climate becomes subtropical, and as rainfall is heavy, luxuriant forests are found. These dense forests are called in Persian, *jangal,* from which the English 'jungle' is derived.[6] Likewise, from the leg wrappings which the natives of Gilan and Mazanderan wear as protection against the brambles, and which they call *paitava,* or *paitwa,* has come, by way of India and the British Indian Army, the English 'puttee.'

Besides unnumbered oases and villages nestled at the feet of the ranges, there are, at what were formerly enormous intervals of distance and time, cities of distinctive appearance, of fascinating interest, and formerly of considerable importance in world trade. The principal cities are: Teheran, the capital and the largest, with a population estimated in 1940 at 540,000; Tabriz, a great emporium in Marco Polo's time and today the second city, with a population of approximately 215,000; Isfahan (population, 205,000), of which a proverb says, 'Half the world is Isfahan'; Meshed, holy city and center of pilgrimage (population 175,000); Shiraz, birthplace of Hafiz and Sa'di (population 130,000); Resht, center of the silk industry (pop-

[4] In Teheran, the range of the monthly average high temperature for a 22-year period was from 44° in January to 99° in July; the average low temperature for this period ranged from 27° in January to 72° in July. The maximum recorded temperature was 109°, the minimum recorded was 4° below.—W. W. Reed, *Temperatures in Asia,* U. S. Weather Bureau, 1931.

[5] The temperature at Abadan over a 10-year period ranged between an average high and low of 113° and 81° for August, and an average high and low of 65° and 47° for January. Ibid.

[6] Or its Sanskrit equivalent. *The Oxford English Dictionary* gives the origin of *jungle* as Sanskrit *jangal,* meaning waste, desert, dry. Since the Persian *jangal* refers only to forest, and since Persian was the official language of the government of India from Mongol times until the middle of the nineteenth century, it is more likely that the English word was derived from the Persian.

ulation 120,000); and Hamadan, a rug-weaving center (population 105,000).

These are the only cities larger than 100,000 population. Remote from each other as these cities were before the advent of motor highways and railways, they manifest characteristics that are found in no other land, a similarity of aspect and composition that testify to a common inspiration and to the unity of the culture that produced them. Characteristic of them are the miles of arcaded streets, known as bazaars, in the dim aisles of which, protected from the heat in summer and from the cold in winter, the varied trade and handicraft of the East are conducted; the mosques without number, with turquoise domes and imposing high-vaulted gateways, covered with faïence of indescribable intricacy of design; and always a great public square, or *maidan,* the most famous of which, that of Isfahan, was renowned in the England of Shakespeare's day and is still the largest public square in the world, with the exception of the Kremlin.

On the trade routes that connected these cities, in earlier times passed immense caravans of camels, several hundred in a single line, coupled in queues of six or seven, their bridles and harnesses ornamented with turquoise to ward off the Evil Eye, and hung with many bells, the tinkling of which made haunting music in the silences of the wastes. Upon their backs was borne the prize merchandise of the East—silks and carpets and spices—and in late modern times such bulky articles as pianos and glass chandeliers to grace the houses of the rich.

At stages along the route were inns for man and beast, caravanserais built in a square about a courtyard, in which the merchandise unloaded from the camels was protected from thievery and pillage, while the camels, brought to kneel outside, resembled at night dark hummocks on the plain. The erection and maintenance of these caravanserais were often the concern of shahs and princes, for the Persians have always been a principal trading people, and the merchant a highly regarded member of society. Many of the caravanserais, especially those built by the great Shah Abbas, a contemporary of Queen Elizabeth, still exist, some still used and others standing as ruins to evoke sad contemplation:

Think, in this batter'd Caravanserai
Whose Portals are alternate Night and Day,
How Sultán after Sultán with his Pomp
Abode his destined Hour, and went his way.

Today, air transportation across the great spaces of these uplands takes no more in hours than the caravans required in weeks, and from the transport plane can be seen the ancient trails threading their way across the plain and among the mountains. But now upon them the patient camel line is seldom seen; rather, motorcars and trucks and wayside garages take the place of battered caravanserais, and to the *bul bul*, the Persian nightingale, which sings in the gardens by night, must now be added the *bulbul rang*, which is the Persian way of saying 'ball bearing,' which sings a new song upon the wastes.

The motorcar and truck, and the railroad that now pierces and gashes the mountains on its way north from the Persian Gulf have brought a new aspect to the country, without changing its essential character. In the cities, broad avenues cut like a knife through the maze of winding streets, and along them automobiles stand parked bumper to bumper. Modern houses with glass windows and open terraces now display what was formerly concealed by high walls of sun-dried mud; the covered bazaars are giving way to modern store fronts of plate glass, behind which are arranged the curious wares of the West. The people wear European dress, and they listen to *Radio Teheran* giving forth the newest dance music and the latest dispatches from the capitals of the West. But a few miles away, life is still undisturbed by the march of civilization. The peasants plow their fields as their ancestors did; upon the hillsides the nomads pitch their black tents and follow their flocks in search for grass, as did Abraham and Lot and the sons of Jacob.

II

THE PEOPLE

A. THE ARYANS

THE WORD 'Iran' means 'Land of the Aryans.' The Aryans were the people from whom were derived the language, culture, and ethnic characteristics of most of the peoples of Europe. It is in Iran that the Aryans first appeared in history as a people of definable racial, linguistic, and cultural identity. The Iranian tableland, with its extensions, was one of their earliest homelands, and may have been their original homeland. The first knowledge of them, in pre-history, was of their appearance in Iran some two thousand years before Christ. Where they came from is still an unsolved question, but the most recent research indicates that it was not from far—from around the Caspian, either in what is now Khorasan and Turkestan, or the Russian Caucasus, and possibly the Crimea. They came into historical notice when they settled in the valleys and plains of the Zagros Mountains on the borders of the Sumerian, the Babylonian, and the Assyrian empires. They appeared at intervals and in several groups, among the best known of which are the Medes and the Persians. Another branch had moved down into India to become the Brahmins of that country. Though anthropologists classify the prehistoric Aryans as a 'warrior' people, from the custom of barrow-burial with the battle axe and drinking beaker, the Aryans who appeared in Iran did not come as conquerors, for it is known that they crossed to the eastern side of the Zagros to avoid conflict with the Urartu, who lived around Mt. Ararat. They seem to have come very much as the later settlers of the American West, looking for new land and opportunity, bringing with them their herds and their families and their household gear laden in horse-drawn or oxen-drawn covered wagons.

Racial Characteristics

The kinship of culture between the Aryans of Iran and the Americans is indicated by similarities of language and the familiar ring of many Persians words: *padar* corresponds to 'father'; *mader* and *barader* to 'mother' and 'brother,' *do* is 'two,' and *shesh* is 'six.' The Aryans of Iran are generally of darker pigmentation than is common here, but their ethnic characteristic is closer to the Nordic mean than to that of the normal Mediterranean type.[1] Similarities will be found in the tendency to spareness, in the long heads, the level eyes, high foreheads and narrow (leptorrhine) noses of the pure Persian and the typical American or Englishman. Similarities of temperament are particularly noticeable between the nomadic Aryans of Iran (who have preserved in greatest purity the ancient Aryan characteristics) and the frontier Aryans of the American West. A love of horses, dexterity in their management, and a capacity for long hours in the saddle [2] characterize both. Hospitality, amiability, quickness of wit, a droll, sometimes rather dry, humor—not to overlook a common tendency for the 'tall story'—are traits that are also familiar among both. A love for the open spaces, a fondness for design and embroidery, a great reverence for the mystic and unseen powers of the Universe, and, formerly, a great preoccupation with questions of sin and human destiny: all these mark the disposition.

There are others that might be mentioned, though parallelism begins to part: a common addiction to hot drink—in one case, tea; in the other, coffee—but not to hard liquor, which is unfamiliar and forbidden among the Persians; [3] an ancient regard for chastity and the sanctity of the home, defended on the Great Plains by the traditional buck-loaded shotgun and among the settled Aryans of Iran by the institution of the *andirun,* the veil and the high wall.

[1] See Coon, Carleton Stevens, *The Races of Europe,* New York, 1939, pp. 418 ff.

[2] An Iranian army colonel of my acquaintance told me that as a youth he rode every week end from Teheran to Kasvin and back in visiting his betrothed. Kasvin is 96 miles distant from Teheran.

[3] Wine is celebrated by the Persian poets, despite the Koranic interdiction to its use.

They were great horse breeders, the early Aryans of Iran, the earliest peoples in history to employ the horse for drawing wagons, and it was from them that the civilizations of Sumeria and Babylonia became acquainted with its use. They were also the first 'cow punchers' of history. Their Gathic hymns speak highly of the herd and herdsman, and in India today the cow is sacred to the Brahmins. They were also addicted to cattle 'rustling,' as the art of pillage is called in the Southwest, and it was against this practice that Zoroaster, their first great prophet and teacher, devoted much of his preaching, urging the people to take up agriculture and husbandry instead of seeking excitement and spoil in rapine.

The Aryans, though perhaps not the inventors of the wheel, must be identified with its early development for it is after their appearance that the wheel in its various applications became a familiar implement of civilization.[4] They made of the wheel what the Egyptians made of the lever, a principal tool of culture and a symbol of the moral order, and in the movement of the wheel in history may be traced the underlying influence of the Aryan spirit in human culture. *Charkh* it is called in Persian, and *car, cart, chariot, caravel,* and *carousel* are its variants in English. It is found engraved upon the foot of Buddha as the symbol of eternal existence, and in the mechanical civilization of the West it has become the key to mortal existence, employed to capture the essence of time, to conquer the distances of space, to grind our bread and to clothe our backs. The first-known highways for wheeled traffic were the 'royal' roads built by Darius the Persian.

[4] The origin of the wheel is a question on which archaeology as yet offers inconclusive evidence. On a painted vase, excavated in the lowest strata of Tell Halaf, in northwestern Mesopotamia, is to be seen what, if usual interpretation is correct, is the earliest known picture of a chariot. The chariot has great eight-spoked wheels and carries a man. The Tell Halaf site comprises remains from several archaeological periods, the earliest of which had its beginnings well back in the fifth millennium B.C. (Finegan, Jack, *Light from the Ancient Past,* Princeton, 1946, p. 15.) From a cemetery at Ur, in southern Mesopotamia, dating probably around 2500 B.C., was found by C. Leonard Woolley in 1934 a wooden panel on which is clearly represented four-wheeled chariots drawn by what appears to be horses. The chariot wheels are solid rather than spoked. (Ibid. p. 35 and Fig. 16.)

Moral and Social Traditions

The early Aryans that settled the Iranian uplands, like their later kinsmen of the American frontier, were a restless, roving people; but they were not a rootless people, blown like tumbleweed before the wind. They were a home- and family-loving people, and they were soon accustomed to tillage and the settled ways of civilization. There is some basis for believing that they were the first wheat growers. Their songs, which have come down to us in the Vedic hymns of the Sanskrit, speak of 'stabled cattle' and of 'grass piles' and 'autumn harvests,' and give us a picture of farm life and hamlets, a people who prepared their grain for food with 'grinding stones of the mill.' There are references also to 'kith and kin,' to 'wife and child and home,' in the same nostalgic accents as a cowboy lament; and we hear of 'kings and chiefs,' of 'anointed priests' and 'physicians and healing medicine,' from which we know they were not a primitive people, but one that had reached a high level of social organization at this early period in their history.

Here is their concept of the ideal life, as described in their religious books:

It is where one of the faithful erects a house with a priest within, with cattle, with a wife, with children, and good herds within; and where the cattle continue to thrive, virtue to thrive, fodder to thrive, the dog to thrive, the wife to thrive, the child to thrive, the fire to thrive, and every blessing of life to thrive. It is where one of the faithful cultivates most corn, grass, and fruit; where he waters ground that is dry, or drains ground that is too wet.[5]

They were a devout people, too, these early Aryans, who looked up to one God, 'heaven-dwelling father'—*dyas-pitar*, or Jupiter, as he was later known to the Romans. There is something especially significant in this, in the idealism and sense of mission which is found alike in the man of the West and pioneer traditions, and this older kinsman, the Aryan of the Persian uplands of thirty-five to forty centuries ago. They sensed the mystery of sin, and looked to their God to deliver them from its clutches. We may imagine that among their camps and settled habitations, as among the villages

[5] *The Vendidad*, Fargard III.

and rural districts of our West, the voice of the evangelist and itinerant preacher was often heard, lifted in honor of the heavenly Father, calling upon men to war against the forces of evil and darkness.

For this we know, that time and again in history have issued from these uplands and these people great seers and prophets proclaiming new revelations and calling men to a new right-eousness, and founding religious systems that were more than local, extending far beyond the land of Iran and which, in instances, have profoundly influenced European religious thought: Zoroaster, Mani, Mazdak; and in modern times the Bab and Baha-Ullah, are among the best known.

First Aryan Kingdoms

From the eighth century, B.C., through the sixth, the Aryans developed increasingly as a military force and state. Among the several Aryan tribes or groups that had settled on the plateau and among the mountains of Iran were the Medes and the Persians. The Medes occupied the regions of what are now Kurdistan and Azerbaijan, on the borders of the Assyrian Empire, the capital of which was at Nineveh, near modern Mosul. The Persians settled farther south in what is now the province of Fars. The Medes established a kingdom with its capital at Ecbatana (now identified as modern Hama-dan) and in 606 (612?) B.C., in alliance with the Babylonians, attacked Assyria. The ferocity of this assault, in which the horse and the wheel first appear in history as major instru-ments of warfare, is described in the Bible:

The noise of a whip, and the noise of the rattling of the wheels, and of the pransing horses, and of the jumping chariots. The horse-man lifteth up both the bright sword and the glittering spear: and there is a multitude of slain, and a great number of carcases; and there is none end of their corpses; they stumble upon their corpses.[6]

Nineveh fell, and the empire of the Assyrians disappeared from history. Meantime, the Persians, until then a subordinate branch of the Aryans, had been growing in power, and within 56 years from the fall of Nineveh they established their ascend-ancy over the Medes. The kingship passed to a Persian family

[6] Nahum III: 2 and 3.

known as the Achaemenians; the capital was transferred from
Ecbatana to Persepolis, and the kingdom was now known as
that of the Medes and Persians. Under a line of Achaemenian
kings, among whom the names of Cyrus I, Cambyses I, Cyrus
the Great, Cambyses II, Darius, and Xerxes still awaken the
imagination, the kingdom became an empire exceeding that
of the Roman in extent. The language of the land now became
that of the Persians; the country itself came to be known as
Persia; and though the Persian Empire lasted for only two
hundred years, it fixed a national tradition that has persisted
throughout subsequent vicissitudes and remains a living stream
of national consciousness, nourishing and activating the spirit
of the people of Iran today with a sense of their cultural and
political unity.

The First 'Great One'

This cultural tradition, this national spirit of the Persian
Aryans, its peculiar and distinctive features, and the qualities
and characteristics of the people, may best be explained by
reference to certain great personalities that have appeared at
intervals in the history of the land. The greatest of them—
greater than Cyrus or Darius, one to rank with Moses and Elias
and Mohammed as lawgiver, prophet, and teacher—was Zoroaster, purifier of the ancient Magian faith, founder of Zoroastrianism.

We do not know a great deal about the man Zoroaster, and
for many years scholars doubted his historic existence. It seems
fairly certain now that he was born in what is now Rizayeh
(formerly Urmiah) in northwestern Iran, about 660 B.C., and
died about 583 B.C.[7] This was some hundred years later than
the Hebrew Isaiah, a hundred years before the Hindu Buddha,
and two hundred years before the Greek philosopher Socrates,
and at a period in Iranian history when the first great Aryan
kingdom, that of the Medes, was in the ascendancy.

Like Isaiah and Socrates, Zoroaster perceived the great fact
that the essential problem of the universe was that of sin, and
that God could be approached only by the soul that is pure.
Evil was not to be propitiated by offerings to the spirit of dark-

---

[7] Some modern scholars now lean to a date between 580 B.C. and 510 B.C.

ness. Man was a creature of dignity and worth, and the duty of man was to wage war, under the banner of Ahura Mazda, the Lord of Great Knowledge, upon all the forces of darkness, until the blessed day, at the end, when eternal goodness would triumph, and Ahura Mazda would reign in peace over heaven and earth.

Such also was the exaltation of Zoroaster's inspiration that he taught the resurrection of the dead, the immortality of the soul, and the heavenly Paradise, or 'Abode of Song.' It is believed by some scholars that these ideas first appeared in Hebrew thought as a result of contact with Zoroastrianism during the Babylonian Captivity.

Kings and Conquerors

As Zoroaster manifests the capacity for spiritual exaltation of these Perso-Aryans, so in certain great ones of war and dominion are exhibited qualities of another sort, qualities not unfamiliar in the civilizations of the West. Of Cyrus and Darius and Ahasuerus, or Xerxes—we have vivid pictures in the Bible, and on the uplands of Iran the solid but forlorn vestiges of their majesty. It was Cyrus the Great who with broad tolerance returned the Jews of the Captivity to their homes and aided in the rebuilding of their temple. It was Ahasuerus who made the Jewish Esther his queen. It was Darius who built Persepolis, regarded as among the most ambitious and awe-inspiring works of architecture, the ruins of which, standing in their lonely grandeur on the Persian wastes, still lure the traveler and sadden him with contemplation of the futility of greatness and the transitoriness of fame:

> The Palace that to Heav'n his pillars threw,
> The Kings the forehead on his threshold drew—
> I saw the solitary Ringdove there,
> And 'Coo, coo, coo,' she cried; and 'Coo, coo, coo.'

It was Darius whom, the Bible tells, the prophet Daniel served as counselor, and who condemned Daniel to the lion's den for the decree he had made and could not revoke, because of 'the law of the Medes and Persians which altereth not.' And it was this Darius who with the arrogance of a Caesar caused to be smoothed off the face of the mountain Bisitun, and to be carved upon it the glories of his reign—and with the humility of a Lincoln to attribute these glories to the grace of Ahura Mazda, his protector. It is an enormous tablature, three hundred feet above the plain—columns of cuneiform writing, so carefully executed, so cunningly glazed, that they stand today in their original freshness after twenty-five centuries. Above the writing is an image of the Great King, majestic as he stands before his throne, shielded by a parasol, his left hand holding a bow, his right hand raised in pronouncement of sentence, his visage fierce and awesome. Before him stand the kings of the earth in chains, whom he has made captive, and above him is the symbol of his God, Ahura Mazda, the Lord of Righteousness. The inscription recites the names of the kings and the countries the Great King has conquered, recounts the blessings of his reign, and admonishes his posterity against Ahriman, the Lie, and, again and again, acknowledges the sovereignty of Ahura Mazda. But first of all, the strong racial pride of his kind:

I am Darius the King, the King of Kings, the Great King of the provinces, the son of Hystaspes, the grandson of Arsames, the Achaemenian. From antiquity have we descended; from antiquity those of our race have been kings.

Such was the majesty of the Great King Darius.

By the grace of Ahura Mazda I have become king of them: Persia, Susiana, Babylonia, Assyria, Arabia, Egypt; those which are of the sea, Sparta and Ionia, Media, Armenia, Cappadocia, Parthia, Zarangia, Asia, Chorasmia, Bactria, Sogdiana, Gandara, the Sacae, the Sattagydes, Arachotia, and Mecia, in all, twenty-two countries.

There is much else, besides, done by me [says the Great King], which is not written in this inscription; on this account is it not written, lest that which I have done may seem exaggerated to him who shall hereafter read this inscription, and may not appear to him true and may seem to him to be a Lie.

And if this seems proud and boastful, recall that nowhere does Darius attribute his success to any other than the grace and protection of God. Neither with Cyrus nor Darius, or in the later generations of Persian kings and emperors, do we find that which the early Christians combated in the Roman world—the assumption of godhead—*Caesar divus*. And although it is generally reported that the deification of kings was something Alexander the Great found in Persia and introduced to the West, it is a fact that there were no altars to the Persian kings; there were no oblations offered to them: they might be kings, but they were not God.[8]

'A great God is Ahura Mazda,' says Darius in his Susa inscription, 'who created this earth, who has created that heaven, who has created man, who has created good things for man, who has made Darius king, unique king of many, sole commander of many.'

And though in later Iranian history, much that is dark and depressing must be written of the absolutism of the monarchy, the foul deeds of kings, and the pitiful debasement of their subjects, yet this sense of moral responsibility and of accountability of man to God, and the ancient Aryan tradition of human dignity, persist, like a ray of candlelight in a cavern, and to them may be attributed in part the fact that in the twentieth century Iran was the first of the lands east of the Nile to rise in democratic fervor, depose its monarch, and establish a constitutional and parliamentary political system.

Of Shapur, who defeated and held captive the Roman Emperor Valerian (A.D. 260); of Shah Abbas the Great (1587-1629), contemporary of Queen Elizabeth, who made Isfahan 'half the world' and erected the caravanserais one still sees throughout the country; of Nadir Shah, who conquered India in 1738 and brought home spoil estimated at nearly $500,000,000 value, including the famous gold and gem-encrusted Peacock Throne, only mention may be made. They were conquerors, but their conquests did not equal in extent those of Cyrus and Darius, nor did they display those personal attributes of greatness and dignity history associates with the Achaemenians. The characteristic quality of these later Iranian rulers may be illustrated by the story told by Sir Thomas Herbert, who spent some years in the court of Shah Abbas. The king, he recounts, was hunting one day, and seeing something stir in the grass he sent a

[8] Later dynasties of kings, down to Moslem times, took the title 'whose lineage is from the gods' in imitation of the apotheosis of Hellenistic kings, but claims to godhead were perfunctory, and not in the national tradition or belief.

shaft into it, only to discover that he had shot a peasant who had curled up for a nap. As he rode on he remarked, 'I did the man no wrong; I found him sleeping, and asleep I left him.'

The Poets

Along with prophets and seers, and monarchs whose names in their times have caused generations of men to tremble, must be mentioned geniuses of another cast, singers of sweet songs and composers of martial epics. Chief of these is Firdausi (935-1020), who stands among the immortals with Homer and Vergil, and Dante and Shakespeare, and in some ways is more distinguished than any of these. Firdausi is the author of the epic poem, the *Shah Namah,* or 'Chronicles of the Kings,' which was completed in A.D. 999 and it is his distinction that his verses are still recited, after over nine hundred years, around campfires and in the bazaars by wandering troubadors, in the tongue in which they were composed; and even unlettered porters can quote couplets from his sonorous cantos. For Firdausi fixed the Persian language as it may be said that the King James version of the Bible fixed the structure of the English language; and modern Persian is nearer to the Persian of Firdausi than modern English is to the English of Chaucer. Such, moreover, is Firdausi's renown, and the esteem in which he is held throughout the world, that the millennium of his birth was celebrated in London, in Paris, and in New York, with expositions and ceremonies.

And there are others, whose names will only be mentioned here, that are read in English in translation: Omar, Hafiz, Sa'di, Jalal-ed-Din Rumi, Nizami, Jami.[9]

And thus, as exemplars of the Perso-Aryan genius, we have a list of names that include prophets and seers to rank with those of the Old Testament; monarchs and conquerors remembered like Alexander and the Roman Caesars; poets whose songs are sung in many languages. And in this diffuse and variant florescence one may observe the stature and breadth of the Aryan spirit as it expanded in the Iranian uplands.

[9] *The Thousand Nights and a Night,* sometimes called the *Arabian Nights Entertainment,* familiar to every child, is a collection of Persian tales brought into Arabic literature and thence into English.

B. OTHER CULTURAL STRAINS

Other racial and cultural strains have, of course, contributed to the composition of modern Iran. Among the peoples whom the Medes and Persians brought into subjection were races that cannot now be classified ethnically, such as the ancient Sumerians and Elamites, whose civilization flourished in the Tigris-Euphrates Valley a thousand years before the appearance of the Aryans. Besides these there were the Hittites, the Hyksos and various Semitic peoples to the west, such as the Assyrians, the Chaldeans, the Akkadians, the Phoenicians, whose highly developed cultures blended to form the compound associated with historical, or classical, Persian civilization.

Arab Invaders

Later racial incursions, also, gave new characteristics and flavor to the Iranian race and culture. Greek influence appeared with the conquest of Persia by Alexander the Great in 331 B.C., but though Alexander remained a great name among the Persians, and as Iskander became a legendary figure, and though Greek dynasties ruled the land for a hundred years, Greek influence in Iranian culture is less than is generally believed. During the Sassanian Empire, Greek influences were submerged under a renascence of Achaemenian and purely Iranian culture.

In the seventh century arose the great prophet of the Arabs, Mohammed, destined to found a religious system which in its virility and zeal is today the chief rival of Christianity and claims more followers than Jesus Christ. Islam in its early years was spread by the sword—'The fires of Hell shall not burn the legs of him who dies in Holy war,' Mohammed had proclaimed—and in A.D. 642, at the battle of Nehavend, the Sassanian Empire of Iran disappeared under the Arab onslaught.

The Arabs did not colonize Iran; there is little Arab blood in the modern Iranian. The Arabs took the highly developed Persian culture—its art and architecture, its literature and science—and dispersed it throughout the Islamic world, a world which soon extended from the Oxus in the East across North

Africa to the Pyrenees in Spain. In return they left the Persians
a book—the Koran. This book is written in Arabic, a language
unrelated to Persian and belonging to the Semitic group, which
includes Hebrew, Aramaic, and Syriac. Of the influence of that
book more will be said later, but it may be remarked here that
its influence was greatly to affect the vocabulary of the Persian
language (though not its structure), with the result that probably half the words in common use today are of Arabic extraction. Arabs today populate the southwestern plains of Iran
(Khuzistan) and the southern seacoasts, where they live as
growers of dates and as fishers.

Turanian Invaders

Repeatedly, from the ninth through the fourteenth centuries,
Iran suffered from incursions of various Turanian peoples
from the East, of whom the principal were the Seljuk Turks,
the Mongols, and the Tartars. By the Mongol Genghis Khan
(1162-1227) and the Tartar Tamerlane (1335-1405), the land
was devastated, cities were razed, and vast pyramids of human
skulls erected. Mongol and Tartar khanates and overlordships
were established in various parts of Iran, and their followers
settled in the land. Today, in a belt across northern Iran, the
Turanian element can be observed in the racial types, and in
Turki-speaking villages and communities. In northwest Iran
(Azerbaijan), Turki is the common language of speech, though
it is not written, and all written communications are in Persian
(Farsi). Turki is linguistically unrelated to Farsi, but belongs
to the Ural-Altaic group which includes Turkish, Finnish,
Magyar, and the Mongol tongues of Central Asia.

The Turanian influence did not modify the main stream of
Persian culture and tradition. Indeed, there occurred during
this period an artistic and literary florescence comparable to
that of the Renaissance in Europe. It was during this period
that the mosque of Gauhar Shad in Meshed was built, regarded
by some as the finest piece of mosque architecture to be found
anywhere; that Firdausi composed his national epic, and
Persian poetry found its finest expression in the works of
Sa'di (b. 1176), Jalal-ed-Din Rumi (1207-73), Hafiz, and Jami
(d. 1492); and that the philosophical system known as Sufism
developed.

In addition to the ethnic grouping by linguistic affinities, presented above, a classification by religion, occupational tradition, and by geography is necessary for an understanding of the present composition of the Iranian people. The principal stock is, of course, the Persian-speaking Aryans, descendants of the ancient Medes, Persians, Parthians, and other Aryan peoples. These Persians are found in villages and towns throughout the central plateau. They provide the dominant culture, the language, and the political cohesion of the country. The least-mixed Persians are found in the province of Fars, the ancient Pars or Parsua, where they originally settled, and from where the language of the country, Farsi, derives its name. The land of the Medes, who were also of Aryan stock, was principally what is now modern Azerbaijan, the fertile region of the northwest lying around Lake Urmiah. It is the *Arayana Vaego,* or the Old Iran, of the Avestic writings; later it became a seat of government of the Mongols and is today colored by Mongoloid types. The language commonly spoken here is Turki.[10]

The Kurds

In the mountain ranges that fringe the country on the west and in the ranges and uplands of the east are various tribal or racial groupings, of ancient lineage, which form an important element in the national characteristic, though culturally their contribution has been relatively negligible. The people most famous in legend and story are the Kurds, and they may be mentioned first. Darius lists them among the peoples he subdued; they are the Carduchi of the *Anabasis,* whom Xenophon and his Ten Thousand encountered on their adventurous return to Greece after serving as mercenaries in the armies of Cyrus II (*c.* 401 B.C.). The great Saladin of the days of the Crusades, familiar to readers of Scott's *Talisman,* was a Kurd. The Kurds range from the slopes of Mount Ararat in the north, southward as far as Hamadan and Kermanshah in the ranges of the Zagros Mountains. They are herdsmen of

---

[10] This is the area that Russia continued to occupy after World War II, and where an autonomous 'republic' was fomented on the ground that Azerbaijan was not really Persian in speech or culture and had no vital connection with the rest of the country.

sheep and goats and they are migratory with the season, though many among them have adopted settled life, living in villages of dried mud houses in which livestock are stabled with their owners. They are independent, and resentful of control by others than their tribal chiefs. Dwelling as they do on the boundaries of Iran, Turkey, Iraq, and Soviet Armenia, they find it easy to pass from the territory of one to that of another as occasion demands, and consequently they have never been under more than nominal control by any of these sovereignties.

The racial origins of the Kurds are obscure, but they are probably of Aryan stock. Their language, while distinct, is related to Persian, with a large admixture, however, of Arabic and Turkish. In appearance they are distinct from the typical Persian, being stocky, with aquiline features, strong noses, dark eyes with beetling brows, and generally swarthy complexions. Their women have never veiled; they are handsome, vivacious, and good humored. The men are often bloodthirsty, and fond of depredations upon their more sedentary neighbors.

The Kurds in Iran number probably five hundred thousand. In the sixteenth century Shah Abbas transported a colony of them to Khorasan, in northeastern Iran, as wardens of the marches, and they constitute today a sizable element in that district.

Lurs and Bakhtiaris

Dwelling to the south of the Kurds, and in the same Zagros range, are important tribal groups, probably descendants of ancient Aryan stock, of whom the principal are the Lurs and the Bakhtiaris.[11] The Feili, or Little Lurs, live in the region of Kermanshah, through which one passes in following the ancient Darian highway from the Persian plateau down to Baghdad; farther south and east are the Bakhtiaris, the Mammassani, and the Kuhgeluhje, sometimes grouped as the Great Lurs. The Bakhtiaris graze their flocks in a region of rich oil deposits, the discovery of which, early in the century, produced major modifications in their tribal life and customs.

The chiefs of the tribes received substantial blocks of stock

11 The Bakhtiaris lack some of the ethnic characteristics of the Irano-Afghan, being generally brachiocephalic. (Coon, op. cit.)

in the Anglo-Iranian Oil Company, which exploits the area, and retired to the ease of Teheran, where their sons became scholars and gentlemen and amiable conversationalists, as well as patriotic servants of the government. Many of the tribesmen accepted employment with the oil company in their favorite occupation of riding the range, now as guardians rather than as disturbers of the peace, and many others have learned the lucrative craft of oil-well drilling.

Still, the migratory habits did not disappear, and twice yearly the tribes strike their tents, load their babies and household gear on the backs of donkeys, round up their flocks of goats and fat-tailed sheep, and set off in search of greener pastures. In the spring, they go northward, from the Mesopotamian plains of Khuzistan to the mountain slopes and valleys of the Zagros. In the autumn, when the grass is turning red and brown, and the mountain peaks become shrouded with a pall of gray, and as the first snow flakes begin to fall in the upper passes, they return to Khuzistan.

The trek northward in spring is especially hazardous and calls for the highest courage and perseverance. The snows in the mountains are now melting; rivers are bankfull, and the gorges are like millraces, foaming with whitish spume. The tribesmen do not carry boats with them: these torrents must be crossed by fording, or, in the broader, deeper channels, by a device as ancient as the oldest inscriptions on the rock walls: primitive rafts of inflated sheepskin. By human lung power the empty skins are filled with air; they are tied together; household gear, babies, the infirm, lambs and kids are piled upon them while the men, swimming alongside, push them to the farther bank. Beyond the rushing waters are still greater hazards. In the mountain passes lie the fields of snow. Up these the tribes plod, driving the flocks ahead of them—from a distance they resemble a line of ants on the dazzling snow expanse. Up rocky escarpments, where footing is held by hand and toe thrust into the crevices, they inch their way, carrying the young of man and beast upon their shoulders. Only the hardy and the young survive: the infirm, who will not be left behind, fall by the wayside, for like the seagull beating against the lighthouse, they are driven by an inner urge and an outward fascination, and by the inexorable demand of their way of livelihood—pasturage for their flocks, grassy terraces for their tents—and they are stayed only by the exhaustion of physical energy.

Fortunately for the edification of civilized man, to whom too often heroism is something to be captured only on the field of battle, a record of these journeys has been preserved by a party of intrepid cameramen and writers in the motion picture *Grass* and the book of the same name.[12]

The Lurs and Bakhtiaris are horsemen by nature, and they have provided the cavalry of both ancient and modern Persian kings. They never adopted, however, many of the customs of the Persian court, such as the veiling of women and the harem.

Miscellaneous Tribes

The principal other nomadic peoples of Iran may be grouped as Turanian, with racial origins in central Asia and allied in feature and language to the Mongol-Tartar-Turkish peoples. Among their representatives in Iran are the Kashgais, probably of Turkish origin, who occupy the highlands to the east of the Bakhtiari country; the Turkomans, to be found in the eastern provinces of Khorasan and who are to eastern Iran what the Kurds are to western; and the Baluchis of southeastern Iran (Baluchistan and Seistan).

Besides the tribes of Iranian and Turanian origins, there are also, as has been mentioned, a number of Arab tribes. They are to be found in southwestern Iran, where Iran merges with the Mesopotamian plain, and along the Persian Gulf littoral as far east as the Indian frontier. The Arabs of Iran, however, are not to be confused with the Arab Bedouin of song and story. They are not migratory; they are date cultivators, fishers, and traders. A principal tribal group is the Khamseh, found chiefly around Shiraz. They are of Arab origin mingled with old Iranian, and their language is a mixture of the two linguistic strains.

Of the total population of Iran, the nomadic tribes constitute probably a fourth, or between three to five million. They are of considerable economic importance to the country for they produce a number of principal articles of com-

[12] Cooper, Merian C., *Grass*, photographs by Ernest Schoedsack, New York, 1925.

merce, namely, rugs, lambskins, dyestuffs, and medicinal herbs. Some of the finest Persian carpets are woven by these people.

They are also of prime political importance, and few dynasties of Persian kings have been able to sit for long on the throne without their support. It has been classical statecraft in Iran to draw levies from the tribes; the great Shah Abbas relied regularly upon his tribal adherents; the Kajars, who ruled the country from the middle of the eighteenth century until 1925, began as chiefs of the Turkish tribe of Kajars; and much of the trouble that besets Iran at the moment arises from tribal dissatisfaction with the government and the mismanagement of tribal relations from Teheran.

Lesser elements in the Iranian population are the Armenians, numerous in Azerbaijan and in Isfahan; the Nestorians, of particular interest to Americans since American missionary activity in Iran first began among them; the Parsees, adherents of the ancient Zoroastrian faith; and the Jews, remnants of the Babylonian Captivity.

PART TWO

THE CULTURE OF IRAN

I

CULTURAL CHARACTERISTICS

A. DESIGN

THE EYES of a traveler, as he approaches an Iranian city, in whatever district he journeys, will be attracted by sunlight glinting upon a dome. The dome will generally be that of a mosque, and there may be many of them. As he draws nearer, he will observe that these domes are covered with tile, and that the tile is worked into a marvelous pattern of line and color. As he enters the city, and passes through the bazaars, observing the handicraft of the country—the rugs, the embroidered fabrics, the silver and brass work, the precious inlay, and the marvelously illuminated books—he will recognize that here is a cultural expression characteristic of the land, distinctive and unique, to be found nowhere else in the world so highly developed, so perfectly executed, so laden with the veritable spirit of a people.

Design as Cultural Expression

This spirit is one that is primarily artistic, and finds its medium in line and form. Persian culture represents a completeness of specialization, a concentration of all the faculties and inspiration of a race upon that which is beautiful, and the expression of this beauty in a fashion that is at once infinitely narrow and infinitely varied. This expression is called in the West the art of decoration or embellishment, but the term fails to convey the depth and magnitude of that which produces it. For as it evolved in Iran, it is the substance rather than the attribute of art. The beholder feels that the dome exists only to display the arrangement of line and color, that the carpet is less an article of utility than a vehicle for the expression of the pattern, and that the pattern itself is again only the means by which the weaver reveals a thought too vast and too exalted for words. The mathematician, gazing at the

symbols written on a blackboard, and seeing in them the clue
to the structure of the material universe, can appreciate the
meaning of pattern to the Iranian.

It is not necessary to go to Iran, of course, to appreciate the
uniqueness of Persian art or to feel its impact upon human
culture. The Persian rug has been prized for centuries throughout the civilized world: it is found in the throne rooms of
monarchs; in houses of Christian worship; in the homes of
those who invest in beauty. The variety of design of which the
Iranian craftsman is capable is as wide and rich as the notes
of the *bul bul:* it is literally without limit. To observe the
infinite variations of line and color, it is only necessary to visit
the nearest Oriental rug shop. Except for rugs woven in *juft,*
that is, in pairs, no two are alike, and there are few of them
that are not completely satisfying to the artistic sense.

Cultural Origins of Persian Art

It is commonly believed that Islamic influences are responsible for the Iranic emphasis on design as an artistic expression.
The Koran forbids the making of idols, and Koranic law or
tradition prohibits the representation of human or animal
figures. Artistic expression was therefore confined by Moslem
doctrine to abstract line, or the depiction of flowers and foliage, which tended to become formalized designs.

While Islamic influence may have been an important contributing factor, Islam was not the source of this interest in
abstract design among the Iranians. The Islamic prohibitions
were generally ignored, and Iranian artists continued to depict
flowers, animals, and even human figures in their rugs, minia-
tures, pottery, and murals. Moreover, long before the Islamic
conquest, the Persian artistic genius had shown an especial
aptitude for design. In the archaeological museum of Teheran,
in which is contained a comprehensive array of Persian archaeological discoveries, from the most ancient times to the present,
the earliest potteries and bronzes display curious and interesting designs. With each successive age the designs show
increased complexity, character, and substance. Attention to
design becomes more apparent after the appearance of the
Aryans, that is, from the second millennium B.C.; but whether
it is innately Aryan, why this facility for design should be so

characteristic of the Perso-Aryans and not of the Aryans of, say, India or Europe, what were the inner forces of the genius that called for this preoccupation with the abstract, are questions that require the further researches of scholarship. The opinions of the fascinating Chardin, who traveled in Iran in the seventeenth century, are of interest:

There is such an exquisite Beauty in the Air of *Persia,* that I can neither forget it my self, nor forbear mentioning it to every body: One would swear that the Heavens were more sublimely elevated, and tinctur'd with quite another Color there, than they are in our thick and dreary *European* Climates. And in Those Countries, the Goodness and Virtue of the Air spreads and diffuses it self over all the face of Nature, that it enables all its Productions, and all the Works of Art with an unparallel'd Lustre, Solidity and Duration; not to speak how much this Serenity of Air enlivens and invigorates the Constitution of the Body, and how happily it influences the Disposition of the Mind.[1]

Power of Abstraction

An appreciation of the significance of design in Persian culture is helpful in understanding modern Iran and its people, for the same qualities of temperament, the same tendencies and cast of mind, are still important in coloring the Iranian character, even though the manifestations are less virile today than formerly. Essentially, it is a faculty for dealing with the abstract, a capacity for idea as an existence *sui generis*. It is the same faculty that produces philosophy and theology, and that lies behind the developments of mathematics, science, and pure poetry.

Of this faculty, E. G. Browne states as follows: 'The most striking feature of the Persians as a nation is their passion for metaphysical speculation. This passion, so far from being confined to the learned classes, permeates all ranks.'[2]

Some mention has already been made of the theological and eschatological contributions of Persian culture to the total of human comprehension of the divine order. In the grand concept of Ahura Mazda, the Lord of Righteousness, and Ahri-

[1] Chardin, Sir John, *Travels in Persia* (N. M. Penzer, ed.), London, 1927, p.134.
[2] *A Year Amongst the Persians,* London, 1893, p. 122.

man, principle of evil—or the Lie (Druj), as it was called in early Zoroastrianism—Zoroaster presented what is still perhaps the most rational statement of the problem of evil in the world: the doctrine of the warring principles, and in the Avestic scriptures appears the foreshadow of the awe-inspiring scene portrayed later in the Apocalypse: 'And there was war in heaven: Michael and his angels fought against the dragon; and the dragon fought and his angels, . . . And the great dragon was cast out, that old serpent, called the Devil, and Satan, which deceiveth the whole world. . .' [3]

Zoroaster, also, like the Egyptians, grappled with the profundities of immortality and resurrection, and his teachings, transmitted into Judaism by means of the Captivity, may have been part of the divine scheme of preparation of the human spirit for the coming of the Saviour. Later in history, Mithraism, while for a time a challenge to Christianity, served as a leaven in the Roman world, fermenting a broader interest and readier acceptance of the Christian revelation. From then on the great light passed to the West, but the Persian sense of the mystery of the godhead, and preoccupation with the problems of abstract being, did not cease, but produced Mani and Mazdak and the Sufi school of mystics. Sufism, communicated to Europe in late medieval times, influenced Christendom, then sinking into formalism and ecclesiasticism, and restored its mystical view of life, and through Eckhardt and others prepared the way for the Protestant Reformation.

In applied science, the Persian contribution has been less notable. Nevertheless, it is worthy of mention that the astrolabe is a Persian invention, that the works of Abu ibn Senna, or Avicenna (b. A.D. 980), were the standard treatises on medicine in Europe from the twelfth to the seventeenth century, that the science of algebra is greatly indebted to the poet, Omar Khayyam, who was also a mathematician and astronomer.

B. POETRY

It is in poetry that the Persian faculty for pure abstraction finds, as in decorative design, its greatest expression, and

[3] Revelation XII: 7, 9.

by which it is today chiefly known and still unsurpassed. Poetry was congenial to the Persian temperament, a more facile medium than the sciences for its peculiar approach to the abstract. Omar turned with relief from contemplation of the mysteries of the heavenly sphere to the greater mysteries of the human spirit and dwelt upon them with affectionate but forever baffled interest:

> Ah, but my Computations, People say,
> Reduced the Year to better reckoning?—Nay,
> 'T was only striking from the Calendar
> Unborn To-morrow, and dead Yesterday.

Omar is only one of a long list of Persian poets whose verses, translated into English and the tongues of Europe, have enriched our Western culture. Firdausi, Jami, Hafiz, Sa'di, Jalal-ed-Din Rumi, Nizami, these names have already been mentioned; the list might be extended by the addition of Rudagi, Muizzi, Anwari, Farid-u-Din, all of whom may be known, in part, in English translation. What is significant is the fact that they still dominate the Persian temperament and outlook, and if one would sense the spirit of modern Iran, he must be acquainted with these poets, for they are familiar to the Persian in a way in which even Shakespeare is not familiar among us. The English language is embroidered with phrases from Shakespeare, but in Persian the songs of the poets are the woof and warp of language. To listen to a Persian speaking is to hear the veritable music of discourse: the Italian does not surpass Farsi in the rhythm of its accents, the sonority of its cadences, the water-like purity of its tones, the general melodiousness of its movement.

While the musical values of Persian poetry are largely lost in translation, the import of its content, the abstraction of idea, remain, though likewise greatly diminished in force. The word and the phrase are the vehicle of the idea, and, in Persian poetry especially, are almost inseparable from the thought. The word is more than a symbol, it is an evocation of a cultural and racial tradition; it is freighted with the experience of the race. Thus, the lines of Omar so admirably rendered into English verse by Edward Fitzgerald, '. . . a momentary taste of Being from the Well amid the Waste—' are touchingly

evocative, but to sense in full their terrifying force, their bewildering mingling of sadness and joy and exaltation, one must
have experienced the rigors of a caravan journey across the
sterile Iranian *lut*.

Likewise, one must have felt the winds of the Iranian uplands to understand the flavor and the inner meaning of the
passage: '. . . as Wind along the Waste, I know not Whither,
willy-nilly blowing'; and one must have known both the Persian passion for poetry and the paradisiacal quality of a Persian garden in the midst of the desert to sense the ecstasy of
this: 'A Book of Verses underneath the Bough . . . and Thou
Beside me singing in the Wilderness.'

Sufism

Except for the *Shah Namah* of Firdausi, the principal and
the finest productions of Persian poetry are associated with
Sufism, which employed poetry largely as the medium of its
expression. Sufism may be described as the search for God as
disembodied spirit, the attempt to realize all existence in its
purely abstract and spiritual essence. Sufism derives much of
its inspiration from Neo-Platonism, which developed as a
school in Alexandria in the third century, and spread its influence into Iran. As a philosophical system, however, it was
given structure in the teachings of Abu Said ibn Abul Khayr,
and appeared in the tenth century indirectly as a revolt of the
Aryan spirit [4] against the narrow dogmatism and materialistic
eschatology of Islam. Abu Said's doctrine is summarized as
follows: 'What thou hast in thy head—thy ambitions—resign;
what thou bearest in thy hand throw away; and whatsoever
cometh upon thee, turn not back.' [5]

The mood of Sufi thought and the imperative necessity of
the poetic form for its expression are admirably summarized
by E. G. Browne, the English authority on Persian literature:

[4] 'A host of heterodox sects born on Persian soil—Shi'ites, Sufis, Isma'ilis,
philosophers—arose to vindicate the claim of Aryan thought to be free, and
to transform the religion forced on the nation by Arab steel into something
. . . widely different from that . . . intended by the Arabian prophet.'
Browne, E. G., *A Year Amongst the Persians* (London, 1893), 1927 ed.,
p. 134.

[5] Quoted in Sykes, op. cit. vol. II, p. 146.

There is the fundamental conception of God as not only Almighty and All-good, but as the sole source of Being and Beauty, and, indeed, the one Beauty and the one Being, 'in whom is submerged whatever becomes non-apparent, and by Whose light whatever is apparent is made manifest.' Closely connected with this is the symbolic language so characteristic of these, and, indeed, of nearly all mystics, to whom God is essentially 'the Friend,' 'the Beloved,' and 'the Darling'; the ecstasy of meditating on Him 'the Wine' and 'the Intoxication'; His self-revelations and Occultations, 'the Face,' and 'the Night-black Tresses,' and so forth. There is also the exaltation of the Subjective and Ideal over the Objective and Formal. . .[6]

Better than any treatise of Persian poetry is an example of its charm and beauty and insight, and the following verses by the sweet singer Hafiz, even in English translation, afford, far more adequately than this brief discussion, an aroma of the true fragrance of the flower that has blossomed on the Iranian uplands:

MYSTIC ODE

In wide Eternity's vast space,
    Where no beginning was, wert Thou:
The rays of all-pervading grace
    Beneath Thy veil flamed on Thy brow.
Then Love and Nature sprang to birth,
And Life and Beauty filled the earth.

Awake, my soul! pour forth thy praise,
To that great Being anthems raise—
That wondrous Architect who said,
'Be formed,' and this great orb was made.

Since first I heard the blissful sound—
    'To man My Spirit's breath is given';
I knew, with thankfulness profound,
    His sons we are—our Home is heaven.
Oh! give me tidings that shall tell
When I may hope with Thee to dwell,
That I may quit this world of pain,
Nor seek to be its guest again.

A bird of holiness am I,
    That from the vain world's net would fly;

[6] Browne, E. G., *History of Persian Literature Under Tartar Dominion*, London, 1920, vol. II, p. 267.

Shed, bounteous Lord, one cheering shower
From Thy pure cloud of guiding power,
Before, even yet, the hour is come,
When my dust rises toward its home.

What are our deeds?—all worthless, all—
  Oh, bring Devotion's wine,
That strength upon my soul may fall
From Drops Thou mad'st divine.
The World's possessions fade and flee,
The only good is—loving Thee!

O happy hour! when I shall rise
From earth's delusions to the skies,
Shall find my soul at rest, and greet
The traces of my loved one's feet:
Dancing with joy, whirled on with speed,
Like motes that gorgeous sunbeams feed,
Until I reach the fountain bright
Whence yonder sun derives his light.[7]

Modern Literature

Persian poetry is not a thing of the past but is still a vital and favorite form of expression in Iran; among modern poets may be mentioned Pizhman-i-Bakhtiari, Bina, Hekmat, Shafaq, Lahuti, Sarmad, to give only a few. That poetry is not an esoteric art but one that men of affairs do not disdain may be indicated by the fact that Hekmat, who has not only written poetry but has translated several of Shakespeare's plays into Persian, is a distinguished public figure who has served in various ministerial capacities, including that of minister of justice. Shafaq, known as a philosopher and mystic, is also a noted Iranian patriot, who was one of the group who fought the Russians in Tabriz during the Constitutional movement of 1906; he is today professor at the University, and in 1945 served as member of the Iranian delegation to the United Nations Conference at San Francisco. Lahuti is a social reformer, one time chief of gendarmerie in Tabriz, who employs the poetic form to advance the cause he supports. As a result of his pro-Russian activities, he was exiled in 1923 by the late Riza Shah Pahlavi, and has since lived in Russia. One of his

[7] Translated by Sir William Jones.

best-known poems is entitled *Kirimil,* or 'Kremlin,' the opening lines of which have been translated as follows:

How long shalt thou shed tears over the throne of Nurshirvan?
O Heart, read the secrets hid in the Kremlin.[8]

The characteristics of modern Persian poetry have been appraised by Mohammed Ishaque as follows:

(a) Ornate style of the past has been supplanted by simple and natural diction;
(b) Poetry is personal and the poets display greater individuality than heretofore;
(c) Considerable originality of theme;
(d) Amatory themes are less common today;
(e) Nature, formerly only a background in poetry, is now wooed for its own sake;
(f) Exclusively personal feelings have become less conspicuous in favor of themes dwelling on the life of the community in its political, social, and economic aspects.

c. MUSIC

Only a word can be said about Persian music. Music, even more than decoration or poetry, is the quintessence of design and the abstraction of pattern. Because of this very ethereality —the fact that music is even more insubstantial than the air upon which it palpitates—what exists today of Persian musical art is only a vestige of what it once must have been, about which we are left to guess from fragments of research. It is likely that Persian music influenced Byzantine, and that the strange, evocative music of the chants and litanies of the Eastern Churches was largely derived from Persia. This much we know: music was highly favored by Achaemenian and Sassanian monarchs, and it was the custom—a custom that still persists in Iran—to greet the rising and the setting sun with music of strings, drums, and cymbals, performed above the principal gate of the cities. There has come down to us also the legend of the two famous singers of Chosroes Parviz—Serguesh (Ser-

[8] Ishaque, Mohammed, *Modern Persian Poetry,* Calcutta, 1943. The Soviet Press for Foreign Languages (Moscow) published in 1946 a volume of Lahuti's poems entitled *Divan of Abol Qasim Lahuti.*

gius) and Barbedh, the latter of whom is said to have had three hundred melodies at his command. Masoudi, the Arab historian, attributed to the Persians the invention of modulations, of rhythms, and of divisions, and the seven Royal Modes that express the sentiments of the soul; but how much of what Masoudi attributes to the Persians was typically Persian and how much was of Greek or other influence is not certain.[9]

The word 'guitar,' used generically for stringed instruments that are plucked, though generally considered to be derived from the Greek *cithara*, may have come originally from the Persian *si-tar*, meaning a three-stringed instrument.

It seems fairly certain that the lute (Ar. *berbat*) came from Iran, and was dispersed eastward as far as China. Other ancient Persian musical instruments were the flute, mandolin, hautboy, and harp.

Use of Modes

The chief characteristic of Iranian music, as of Arabic and Indian music, is the employment of modes, as distinct from harmony. Modal music exemplifies the purest abstraction of design. A mode may be defined as a group of notes related to the tonic and all other notes of that group and summarizing in their organization the conditions governing the composition of a particular type of melody. The octave, or scale, was divided into either 17 intervals (in Khorasan) or 24 intervals as is found in Indian music. The intervals were not fixed, however (as on a piano keyboard), but the value of each note or interval could be modified as the creative genius of the musician dictated. Besides half tones, as in the chromatic scale, the musician employed quarter tones, eighth tones, and smaller divisions of the interval. The same melodic line accordingly could be executed with an infinite variety of mood and feeling. Thus, in the same way that a basic line pattern of a Persian rug remains unmodified, while variety is achieved by embellishment, so a thematic line could be embellished by modal treatment.

Possibly as many as a hundred standard modes were employed, and the names of thirty modes employed by Barbedh

[9] Huart, M. Clement, in Lavignac's *Encyclopédie de la Musique et Dictionnaire du Conservatoire*, Paris, 1922, vol. v.

have come down to us. There were, it appears, originally twelve basic tones, which were said to correspond to the zodiacal signs, and were to be used in accordance with the time of day, and each of these conveyed its own recognized mood. These twelve tones could be continued or modified by six *âvâz* and 24 *cho'ba*, which again could be divided into 48 varieties, called *goûché*. Because of the abstraction of language, the precise meaning of these terms is not clear, but their general effect was to permit the production of an almost infinite number of gradations in the tonal structure.

This abundance of modes may be contrasted to the seven classical modes of the Greeks, the eight modes (four Authentic and four Plagal) of the Gregorian system (6th century), the twelve modes of Glareanus (16th century), and the two modes to which modern secular music is largely confined. Modal music as a form of musical expression in the West is found chiefly in liturgical compositions, though a revival of interest in modal expression is found in a number of modern compositions.[10]

Much of what must have been in former times a marvelous florescence of musical form has been lost in modern Iran, owing largely, it is probable, to the repressive influence of Islam, which is not a joyful or exuberant faith.[11]

Still, if the ear is attentive, and one is prepared to explore the fascination of what at first seems sad and plaintive, he may hear Persian music on the *si-tar,* the three-stringed lute, and on the pipes, in village hamlets, behind high walls, in corners of the bazaar, or on the wastelands where the shepherd keeps watch over his flocks. And as one listens, and the ear grows accustomed to the melodies, it will be discovered that Persian musical art today is not dead, or completely sterile, but retains a mysterious power to soothe and exalt.

[10] For a brief discussion of Western modal music, see Scholes, Percy A., *Oxford Companion to Music,* art. 'Modes,' London, New York, 1943.

[11] The doctrinal view of Islam towards music has been a subject of controversy among Islamic theologians, some holding that the Prophet disapproved of music, others contending that he approved it. In any case, music has never become in Islam the adjunct to worship that it has been in Christendom ever since the disciples sang hymns together on the eve of the Crucifixion.

D. ARCHITECTURE

Persian architecture also displays a characteristic genius. This genius attained its artistic heights in structural form and embellishment during the Safavid dynasty, from the sixteenth century through the eighteenth. Isfahan, capital of the Safavid kings, is rich with magnificent examples, as are Meshed, Qum, and Shiraz. Curiously enough, the finest example of Persian architecture, expressing the very essence of the Persian spirit, a structure accounted by many to be mankind's greatest triumph in architectural form, a work of passionate beauty and inspiration, is to be found in India and is the work probably of an Italian architect. This is the Taj Mahal, built by Shah Jehan at Agra, 1631-53, as a tomb for his favorite queen, Mumtaz-i-Mahal.

Characteristic Features

The principal features of this architecture, apart from the decorative detail, are the domes and cupolas, of ethereal grace; the imposing, ogive gateways, and the ogive vaults. While the dome is usually associated with mosque architecture, a more common, more utilitarian, and less imposing use is in bazaar construction. The bazaars are covered streets, the roofing of which is vaulted by a series of joined cupolas. Light is admitted through apertures in the apex of the cupolas. Bazaars are distinctively Persian and nowhere else in the world will their like be found.

The ogive arch, familiar to the West in Gothic architecture, is found everywhere. It is said to have originated in the use of unfired brick, and when constructed of that material affords a sense of lightness and grace which equals that of the finest Gothic. An architectural use of the ogive vault, unique in Iran, is the *ivan,* which may be described as a structure roofed but open on one side. Vaulted *ivans* were employed originally as throne or audience chambers, and their modern descendants are found in the band and concert shells of parks and open-air theaters. From a structural standpoint, the principal contribution of Persian genius was a method of setting a dome on a square, by a device known as the squinch, at once ingenious and satisfactory. Oddly enough, this practical method never found its way into Europe.

Magnitude of Scale

For pure grandeur in structure, however, one turns to the work of the Achaemenian and Sassanian kings, of which only ruins exist today—but such ruins! Persepolis has been mentioned. Here, on a stone platform 40 feet high, 1,500 feet in length, 900 feet in width, was erected a collection of palaces of a size and grandeur to stupefy the imagination, which, in the view of some travelers, are the most imposing architectural work in history, save possibly the Pyramids.

A paradoxical feature of the Persepolis constructions is that, unlike the Pyramids, they were preceded by no transitional architecture, but issued directly from the wooden dwellings which were their structural antecedent.

Again, in the Sassanian period, appears a great architecture, conceived and executed on the most imposing scale. This architecture developed first in Fars, the native province of the Achaemenian rulers, and was definitely a revival of Achaemenian traditions in reaction to Arsacid Hellenism. The castle of Ardeshir (A.D. 224-41), founder of the Sassanian dynasty, which Ernst Herzfeld rediscovered in 1925, was constructed on a more sumptuous scale than any in Europe and was one of the parents of all those great structures that were erected by the castle builders of medieval times. It was built on the summit of a mountain 1,600 feet high, near Firuzabad: the ground plan covered an acre and a half, the walls were 100 feet high. Even more grandiose was the palace of Chosroes, probably Chosroes II Parviz (590-628), near modern Kasr-Shirin, on the Baghdad-Teheran highway. The palace was 1,220 feet long and 623 feet wide and was built on a terrace that extended an additional 935 feet before the palace. The magnitude of the construction can be appreciated by recalling that the greatest length of St. Peter's in Rome is 718 feet, and that the Cathedral of Sts. Peter and Paul in Washington (D.C.), when completed, will be 525 feet long and 275 feet wide at the transept.

The largest in scale of all Sassanian royal residences was the palace at Ctesiphon, built probably by Nurshirvan, or Chosroes I (531-79), near modern Baghdad. The superb, vaulted hall, in which the Great King sat on his golden throne in view of his subjects, can still be seen for miles across the Mesopotamian plain. It is the highest masonary arch in the world (90 feet) and spans a width of 84 feet. The use of vaulting, which was characteristic of Sassanian architecture, and remains characteristic of modern Iranian architecture, had the advantage of providing a hall which, no matter how vast, was unbroken by pier or column, and offered a setting for kingly state that has no equal in architectural design.

II

SOCIAL LIFE AND ORGANIZATION

THE TRAVELER to Iran, coming from the abundance of the Western shores, will be struck by the evident and widespread material poverty of the Iranian people. If, however, he approaches the land from a sojourn in India, he is apt to be impressed by the relatively greater comfort and material well-being of the common man compared to his fellow being in India. Before an appraisal is made of a civilization by its material standards, some examination is due the intellectual, physical, spiritual, and moral factors that contribute to the material state. The eye of the Western man is, in any case, apt to be myopic on the subject of material progress, since its chief prospect and object of gaze in the West is a display of material production unexampled in history, a display so profuse that it conceals the underlying spiritual and intellectual humus by which it has been nourished.

Before the importance and the causes of the material poverty of the Iranian people can be assessed, or the cures prescribed, it is necessary to have some understanding of the various factors that have tended to produce or ameliorate this condition. Among these are the social organization of the people.

A. CHARACTERISTICS OF SOCIAL LIFE

A principal characteristic of the social life and organization of Iran today, as of yesterday, is its fluidity and individuality. In these it retains what may be regarded as a main characteristic of the Aryan cultural heritage wherever the Aryan-speaking peoples have journeyed, with the major exception of India. That is to say, in Iran, while there may be social classes, there is no caste, and the movement of an individual from class to class has been, and remains, relatively free.

The nearest approach to caste is found in the status of

women, who were, until within the last decade, a class apart, hemmed by arbitrary restrictions of custom and creed. The social status of women in Iran is a product of the Perso-Aryan tradition, but the restraints upon women were intensified as a result of Islamic doctrines and influence.

Fluidity of Social Movement

The traveler who approaches Iran with an appreciation of the individuality of the Iranians will quickly find himself at home among them and in possession of the surest key to an understanding of Persian culture. Such a traveler, for instance, was James Morier, who served early in the nineteenth century as secretary to the British Minister at Teheran. Returning home, he wrote a novel of Persian life called *Hajji Baba of Isfahan.* Partly satirical in nature, it recounted the adventures of a good-humored, likable rascal and adventurer, who started in life as a porter and peddler and ended by becoming a minister in the court of the shah. Possibly this rise to honor and position, by one who had no education, no position by birth, and was a rascal to boot, struck the Englishman as paradoxical: it may be a commentary on England of the early nineteenth century as much as on Iran. So characteristic was it, however, of the Iranian people and their ways that it was translated into Persian, in which it became a classic as it is in English. Many Persians believed it to have been written by one of their own countrymen, so revealing was it of a certain type of unscrupulous adventurer common in Iran.

Those who are inclined to regard Iranians as a species distinct from, say, the American, should read *Hajji Baba* and then Mark Twain's *Connecticut Yankee at King Arthur's Court,* and the essential similarities of the types portrayed will be obvious. In both cases the hero is practical, with a strong sense of humor and sentiment; shrewd and not above trickery; adaptable, opportunistic, intelligent, and showing a marked capacity for growth and advancement, but without any social, moral, or other disciplines.

Recognition of Individual Merit

The most recent example of the Persian success story is that of Riza Khan, who rose from the rank of private in the army to become the *Shah-in-Shah* of Iran. As one becomes acquainted with the Iranian scene, one will come upon numerous examples of those who have passed from poverty to wealth, from obscurity to renown, and, likewise, from the top of the ladder downward. From another and serener order may be mentioned the physician Seyyid Khan, who began life in a Kurdish village, was converted to Christianity as a boy, was compelled to flee the wrath of his kinsmen for having renounced his faith, who worked as a stable boy in the household of a missionary in Hamadan, obtained the rudiments of an education, and finally enough money to go abroad, where he studied medicine; he returned to his native land, rose in his profession, and became the mediciner to princes and poor, and died at an old age, one of the most renowned men in modern Iranian history. 'From one point of view,' commented Lord Curzon, a shrewd and realistic appraiser, if one not entirely sympathetic to the Iranians, 'Persia is the most democratic country in the world. Lowness of birth or station is positively not the slightest bar to promotion or office of the most exalted nature.' [1] It may be significant also of this characteristic of Iranian social life that the shahs customarily selected their grand viziers not from the nobility but from the obscurest, often the poorest, classes.

One who has spent some time in, say, India, and has become accustomed to caste distinctions there, has got used to hiring one servant to cook and another to sweep, has learned that in India, as in the army, a gentleman may not carry a parcel in the streets, will be refreshingly shocked on going to Iran. There a servant is like a member of the family, who is not afraid to correct his master's son, or volunteer his ideas to the master himself, and, in the homes of the moderately well off, does as many jobs as the proverbial 'hired man' on an American farm.

Americans, fresh from the democracy of the West, with its own peculiar lines of caste, which are likely to obsess a person with the idea of 'front,' and possibly to make him feel that to make an impression he must belong to an exclusive club, live in a house in the best suburb or an apartment on the best street, and wear the best tailoring the town affords, will be

[1] *Persia,* London, 1892, vol. I, p. 444.

equally refreshed by the nonchalance their Iranian friends
manifest in regard to such matters. They have a keen sense of
personal worth, and, like their counterparts here, are quick
to cut through sham. One of the highest born Iranian princes,
a man of great wealth and a general in the army, lives con-
tentedly in a made-over stable behind one of the palaces of
the shah. One of the leaders in Iran today, a professor on the
faculty of the University, a member of Parliament, and a delegate to the United Nations conference at San Francisco, began
life as a poor student in Tabriz. One of the most popular foreigners in Teheran during the days of World War II, when
the city was full of foreign army officers and officials, was a
young army captain, to whose modest three-room flat came
high and low of the Iranian government for tea and for conversation.

Lack of Social Outlook

While this sense of individuality in the Iranian has been a
source of freedom and opportunity, it has not been without
its attendant evils. Iran exhibits the virtues of a free society,
but it also displays all the evils of such a society unhampered
by the moral and social restraints that have been developing in
the West. It is, in a sense, an example of the decay of what is
called by economists the 'capitalistic system.' The principal
economic problems of the country—of landlordism, of commercial rapacity, of uninhibited pursuit of gain, of irresponsible
wealth and unrelieved poverty—may be attributed in large
measure to the effects of a rampant individualism. Marco Polo,
traveling in Iran in the thirteenth century, commented upon
the city of Tabriz as follows: 'The merchants concerned in
foreign commerce acquire considerable wealth, but the inhabitants in general are poor,' and these words are an apt summa-
tion of the economic condition and problem today.[2]

B. SOURCES OF THE IRANIAN SOCIAL SPIRIT

Among the factors contributing to the quality and character
of the Iranian social organization is the nature of the land.

[2] *Travels,* ch. IX.

The individualism of Iranian life, like the corresponding individualism of the American West, may be explained in part
by the vastness of the country and its sparsity of population.
Settled localities are separated by expanses of desert and grazing land, and the trammels of civilization are everywhere
challenged by the freedom of the uninhabited spaces. To the
Iranian, as to the American of the Great Plains, the openness
of the landscape is an invitation to movement and freedom;
it exercises upon the spirit the subtle effect of setting it in
rebellion against the restrictions of convention and the pressures of society.

Democratic Spirit of Islam

Second among the influences upon the Iranian social spirit
must be mentioned the religious faith of Islam to which the
greater part of the inhabitants adhere. The total effect of
Islam on the Iranian people will be taken up later, but here
it may be mentioned that it is a religion without a hierarchy.
There are no priests in Islam. A cardinal tenet of the faith is
that every man prays to God himself. He needs no intermediary. And so, while there is a sort of hierarchy, consisting of
mujtahids, mullahs, seyyids, and *hajjis,* it does not exist by
ordination or claim the attributes of authority and infallibility.
There is an essential democracy in Islam by which whoever
bows his head upon the earth towards Mecca, recites the
Creed, and keeps the Month of Fast, is a Muslim and a brother.
Less embrasive than Christianity, which teaches that all men
are brothers, it regards those outside Islam as outside the
domain of fraternity. Yet over those within the fold it throws
the cloak of unity in the peace of God, so that there are, in
true Islam, no distinctions between black and white, between
him who rides and him who walks, between him who speaks
fairly in tongues and him who is dumb, between him who rules
and him who is ruled. In Islam, only those who are of the
female sex are considered inferiors, or, as the Koran says,
'as a field to be plowed.'

A third influence making for social fluidity is the general
decay of administration and the absence of hieratical distinctions. A man may wrap a green girdle about his waist, put on
a green turban, go into another city, and there declare himself

a *seyyid,* a descendant of the Prophet, and if he is sufficiently assured in manner, he can carry off his deception, for genealogies are nonexistent or haphazard: there is no public register of *seyyids,* and no one to challenge the assertion of him who claims to be one. What is true of the *seyyid* is also true to a degree of the professional classes. The ranks of mullahs, who are the scribes of Islam, the expounders of the religious law, the preachers and the custodians of the mosques, increased so inordinately, and became such a parasitical group that among the reforms instituted by Riza Shah Pahlavi during the 1930's was a purge of the profession and the institution of government examination for admission to the order. Likewise, though in theory examinations are required for admittance to the practice of law and medicine, until recent years anyone with appearance and presumption was able to set himself up as a healer or advocate.

Commerce as Leavening Influence

Reference to the commercial character of the civilization has already been made. The bazaar, or merchant, element has always been important in the social structure, and generally is accorded a respect exceeded only by that of the landed nobility. Readers of the *Thousand and One Nights* will recall how often the heroes of those tales were merchants. In trade, fortunes accumulate and disappear according to the varying skill of the trader and the fluctuations of the market. By luck and diligence a small trader becomes a great merchant, before whom the doors of opportunity open, and about whom the supplicants clamor while equally the pitfalls multiply. This is true in Iran as well as on Wall Street.

Finally, among the elements in Iranian life that give it its characteristic democratic quality is the fact that there is no hereditary nobility, and no laws of primogeniture such as have perpetuated families in England and to a lesser extent America. Inheritance is uncertain, since polygamy is still legal though rare; and though under recent legislation women enjoy certain statutory rights of contract, actually their social and legal position is dependent largely upon the will of the husband. Under the Koranic law, a share of the estate must go to each heir, with the proviso that in such division a male shall receive the portion of two females.[3] The exclusiveness of nobility has been further affected by the freedom with which sovereigns in times past elevated favorites to position and honor by means of the gift of a title. A favorite barber, for instance, might receive a scroll—in lieu of his fee—decorating him 'The Exalted of His Profession.'

In this connection, the following from S. G. Wilson's *Persian Life and Customs* may be quoted:

> Men can readily change their social status. A ballet dancer was the favorite of Fath Ali Shah. The son of a *fellah* may be vizier tomorrow. Lowly birth is not a bar to the highest position. An adventurer presenting a rifle to a prince is dubbed *khan*. A carpenter, tailor, or photographer is paid for his services with a title. . . The official world has an infinity of titles conferred by the shah indicating some relation to the government, by the use of the words *Doŭlah, Mulk,* and *Sultanah,* as the Eye of the Government, the Guide or the Righteousness of the State, the Faithful of the Sultan. Physicians receive their titles such as the Sword, the Confidence, the Fidelity of the Physicians.[4]

Although this practice of the shahs has disappeared, one of the reforms of Riza Shah Pahlavi having been the prohibition, in 1935, of the granting or use of titles of any sort, except for the equivalents of 'mister' and 'madame' and, for high officials, 'excellency,' the abundance of names with the prefix or suffix of *Khan, Hajji, Kerbelai, Meshedi,* and the like, indicate how strong was the influence of the practice upon the social structure.

c. SOCIAL CLASSES

While the individuality and fluidity of the Iranian social structure has tended towards a general leveling and absorption of class, it also cultivates distinctions and differences, so that the Iranian scene is one of great variety, in which class and distinction are both apparent and important. That is to say, while the boundaries of class are shadowy, its substance is evident.

[3] *Koran*, Sura IV, *Women*.
[4] New York, 1895, p. 181 and footnote.

Landowners

Outside the royal court, itself a structure of fluid composition, the most important and the most solid class in Iran is
that of the great landowners. The Iranian agricultural system is predominantly feudal. This feudalism was produced
by some of the same factors which produced feudalism in
Europe. The fact that tillage is generally concentrated in oases,
called villages, requiring a common supply of water that must
be provided by means greater than an individual cultivator
can muster, has fostered a concentration of ownership. While
the cultivator is not a serf and is free to leave his land and
move elsewhere, in practice the land is farmed by family succession. The landlord owns the entire village, and a landowner's wealth is measured by the number of villages of which he
is proprietor. As landlord, he takes a fifth to a half of the crop
as rent, although this varies according to the general fertility
of the region, whether irrigated or not, and whether he provides seed and oxen. The prevailing rule of thumb is to attribute a fifth of the produce to the land, a fifth to the water, a
fifth to the seed, a fifth to the oxen and implements, and a
fifth to the labor of the cultivator.

The landowners often never see their villages, which are
managed by stewards. They prefer to live in Teheran, or the
larger cities, that are furnished with the comforts of civilized
life, and where they exist as a compact oligarchy, the most
powerful class in the country.

They live simply, that is, with a retinue of servants who are
like poor relatives, enjoying the pleasures of spacious gardens,
delicate viands, lively conversation, and, in recent years, such
added items as radio music, ball-room dancing and indirect
lighting. Large parties are infrequent, however, for despite
wealth and position, their social life is still patriarchal and
limited to relatives and members of the clan. They provide
officers for the army and administrators for the civil government. The Iranian parliament, or Majlis, is largely composed of landowners. While the landowners comprise the
principal ruling class, theirs is not a vested interest. The political tradition for centuries has been one of monarchical absolutism, and the shahs have customarily regarded as a per-

quisite of office the enrichment of their private fortunes by exactions from the landowners. Even the progressive Riza Shah Pahlavi, whose reformations of the Iranian social system will be noted later, did not hesitate to sequester vast estates to his personal enrichment.

Merchants

Generally apart from the landowner is the merchant class, or the bazaar, as it is universally known, though wealthy merchants will invest their wealth in villages, and landowners may embark in trade. In the case of the bazaar, wealth is more fluid, and the merchant class ranges from the peddler with his wares upon his back, and the tradesman with no more than a ledge in the bazaar, on which he squats with his merchandise within reach of his hand, to the powerful *tajir* and *sarraf* who, like Antonio in the *Merchant of Venice,* may have their argosies in a dozen distant ports, their agents in New York, London, and Shanghai.

The bazaar is well organized into guilds and 'chambers of commerce.' It is the vocal element in Iranian society, and being in constant touch with affairs of the world is more alert to the winds of change. News travels in the bazaar like fire on a prairie, and bazaar sentiment is a great molder of public policy. In times past, and even more recently, the power of the bazaar, particularly when united with that of the clergy, has been sufficient to unseat ministers and to cause the throne to tremble. So potent was the bazaar that in 1294 it compelled Kai Khatu to abandon a project for the issuance of paper money; in 1891, in alliance with the mullahs, it carried out a boycott in protest against a tobacco monopoly that Nasr-ed-Din Shah had granted to foreigners, and compelled that monarch to rescind the concession. Again, the constitutional movement in Iran, which obtained the grant of the Constitution in 1906, was largely stimulated by bazaar agitation for reform.

Clergy

The Moslem clergy [5] was until recent years a more powerful element in the political, social, and economic life of the coun-

---

[5] Properly, there is no Moslem clergy, since ordination is not an element of Moslem theology. The term *clergy* is here used to indicate collectively

try than it is today. A principal duty of the Moslem is the giving of alms, as a result of which a great body of wealth and estates has become the property of various shrines and religious foundations. Furthermore, until modern times, the Koranic law was the fundamental law of the land, and as expounders of this law the mullahs exercised enormous influence in affairs of state. Islam has been declining in influence, however, particularly since the revolution of 1906; in recent years the application of the *Shari'a,* or religious law, has been limited; the pious foundations have been brought under State control; and the power and influence of the clergy have been restricted in other ways. Consequently the importance of the clergy as a class has greatly diminished.

Cultivators and Artisans

The cultivators of the soil are the most neglected though not the most unfortunate class in Iran. Stalwart, patient, frugal, unlettered, and sometimes brutalized, they tend the fields and grow the crops of wheat and barley and rice, the grapes, melons, and the various sorts of nuts and fruits, which feed the cities and are to some extent exported. Since the adoption of military conscription they have provided men for the army.

The artisans of the town suffer a poverty greater than that of the cultivator. They work in wood, leather, silver, and brass; they weave rugs and execute the fine *khatam,* or 'nailhead' inlay work, all in cramped quarters where the light and ventilation are poor; their food is dear and their diet limited. Nevertheless, since industry is primarily individual and household, they enjoy a relative independence, and as they generally market their wares direct, they are quasi-members of the merchant class and share its opportunities. A depressing element of Persian crafts is that children are put to work at an early age. This is largely due to the poverty of the people and the necessity of winning a livelihood early in life. An important factor, however, is the characteristic of this craftsmanship, its fineness of detail, for which the tiny fingers and delicacy of touch of children are particularly suited. This is especially so in rug weaving, and the finer the weave the more certain one

the members of the various hierarchies, such as *mullahs, mujtahids, ulema,* and their like.

SHRINE OF FATIMA AT QUM

Photo courtesy United States Army Signal Cor

2a. VILLAGE ARCHITECTURE

b. VILLAGE COBBLER

Photo by auth

may be that the rug was woven by little children. There is, of course, no effective prohibition of child labor in Iran.

Beneath the artisans are the mass of unskilled or semi-skilled laborers: porters (for man is still a beast of burden in Iran), donkey drivers, house servants, masons, gardeners, laborers, and scavengers, who exist on a pittance, live in hovels, and yet, for all their miserable poverty, maintain a certain independence and insouciance that elevate them above their fellow beings of similar class in neighboring countries, such as Egypt or India. Among the members of each of these professions—for an occupation, however lowly, constitutes in Iran a 'profession'—exists a freemasonry, a form of guild solidarity, which yields them a certain pride and standing. Nowhere in Iran will there be encountered the cringing and servile class of touts such as those that assail the visitor to Cairo with their improper solicitations; nor will there be found the abasement of human dignity that is encountered among the lower castes of India.

Of recent years there has appeared in the Iranian cities, as a result of the attempts at modernization, a new class of society, the factory proletariat. State-owned or State-supported enterprise introduced a variety of mass industries—'mass' in a relative sense, of course—and the determination of the Shah to magnify his reign brought a great influx of population to the cities—Teheran doubled in size in two decades—all with the effect of creating a large new social element: people fresh from the hinterland, unfamiliar with the disciplines of factory work, easy prey to exploitation. Unhinged from their traditions, baffled by the perplexities of a world they had had no hand in making, they are today ready subjects for Communist propaganda, and, organized into political groups, they offer a continuing threat to the stability of the government.

D. WOMEN AS A SOCIAL CLASS

Until recent years women constituted a class in Iranian society that was subject to restraints, disqualifications, and prohibitions to a degree suffered by no other group of humanity. No more depressing sight met the eye of the traveler from the West than the funereal figures, shrouded in black, that flitted along the streets, silent, timorous, unreal. Passing a mosque by night, during the celebrations, one might see them crouched outside, among the dogs, listening to the mullah within describing to the Faithful the joys of a paradise to which they could never hope to be admitted, since woman was, according to the Koran, an 'inferior being.' [6]

Custom of the Veil

Not only were women required to veil in public, but their private life was equally restricted by a veil of brick and the veil of convention. A wall surrounded the garden. Another wall closed off the *andirun,* or women's quarters, access to which was the privilege only of the head of the house. A visitor never saw the females of the family, nor did he dare inquire even about their health. A woman's existence, except in relation to her husband, was restricted to her kind. The more elevated her husband's status, the more secluded and abject her condition. In the countryside, she might work in the fields with the men, though even here she carried a corner of her shawl in her teeth to conceal her face. Among the tribesmen women were freer, and there the veil was not worn. But in the towns, among the well-to-do, the life of a woman was terrible and lonely, full of bitterness and envy. Though she might be loaded with jewels and brocades by a doting spouse, she never knew when his favor would be shifted to another. Confined to the company of her sex, she became a prey to gossip and adept at intrigue. She knew nothing of the world beyond the wall; her faculties withered, her soul was dispirited.

The institution of the veil is ancient in Iran and is probably of Aryan origin. The earliest picture of the domestic institution is found in the Book of Esther, in which is recounted how the Great King Ahasuerus commanded Queen Vashti to show herself to his guests. The queen refused; and because of her refusal, and lest her contumacity set an example to women generally, 'so that they shall despise their husbands in their eyes, when it shall be reported,' the Great King divorced her.

---

[6] 'Men are superior to women on account of the qualities with which God hath gifted the one above the other, and on account of the outlay they make from their substance for them.' *Koran,* Sura IV, *Women.*

The veil is a product of the same temperament that creates the sanctuary, that put the Holy of Holies within the innermost curtain of the Tabernacle, and fences off the altar by the Ikonostasis. It originated probably with the great value placed on the domestic institution by the early Aryans, coupled with a somewhat perverted notion of how best to preserve its sanctity. The advent of Islam worked a further perversion of good intentions. The Koranic law authorized polygamy and concubinage, and permitted a man to divorce his wife at will. By means of *muta'a,* or temporary marriage, a form of prostitution in the precincts of the holy shrines developed under clerical auspices, which was doctrinally justified by the necessity of refreshing the pilgrim and purifying his thoughts of lust before entering the holy place. In the rice fields of Mazanderan, S. G. Wilson recounts, it was the practice for a man to engage as concubines for the season as many women as were required to harvest the crops.[7]

Recently, however, a remarkable transformation has occurred in the outward status of women. Since 1936 the veil has ceased to exist, and in the cities women, who a decade ago never appeared in public, except in the enclosing *chaddar* and *pardeh,* may now be seen strolling down the streets in the latest Parisian or Hollywood modes. And while one may see the élite of society dancing in cabarets, sipping cocktails, and otherwise partaking of the freedoms of their sisters of the favored lands of the West, one may also find women of other classes busy attending schools, entering the professions, or earning a livelihood as clerks, typists, and factory workers.

In spite of these improvements, however, the legal status of women has been only nominally modified by the reforms. They may still be divorced at the husband's whim, and in such a case they have but limited claim to the children born of the marriage, while their property rights are limited to what may have been agreed upon as divorce settlement at the time the marriage was contracted. Moreover, the shah who abolished the veil and instituted reforms in the legal and social status of women did not hesitate also to take to himself wives and concubines.

[7] Op. cit. p. 263.

E. THE MINORITIES

Among the peoples of Iran who constitute distinct social classes are the members of the various religious minorities. These are the Christians, the Jews, and the Guebers or Parsees. The Christians consist of the Armenians, the Nestorians, and the adherents of the indigenous Christian churches. Of these, the Armenians are the largest element. They are to be found principally in Azerbaijan, where there are many villages predominantly Armenian, and in colonies in the principal towns and cities. The most considerable number of them outside northwestern Iran are found in Isfahan, in a suburb called New Julfa, which was established during the reign of Shah Abbas, when that Shah transferred a colony of Armenian artisans and craftsmen from Julfa, on the Araxes, to Isfahan, in order to provide skilled workmen for the embellishment of the capital. The Armenians have been a respected class in Iran, and it is a fair generalization that while they have been subject to some restrictions and disabilities, on the whole they have been accepted as an indigenous element.

Certainly the Armenians have never been persecuted in Iran as they have been in Turkey; individuals frequently occupy stations of prominence in the service of the State. During the celebration of Moharram, when fanaticism is fanned by the bloody spectacles, it has generally been safer for Armenians to remain indoors, but this celebration occurred only once a year, and now has been abolished.

The greatest sufferings of the Armenians have been due to the depredations of the Kurds, with whom, in Anatolia, they have long been at odds, partly because of the machinations of the Ottoman sultanate, and partly because of the willingness of elements of the Armenian population to support foreign intervention, particularly Russian, in times of national crisis. As in Turkey, the Armenians have been inclined to look to Russia as the protector of their interests, and, however justified, it has been a course exciting suspicion of their devotion to the national interest, and has had its effect upon the relations between them and the Moslem population.

This inclination to look to foreign powers for support was

not lessened by the policies of Riza Shah Pahlavi, who after 1925 intensified the restrictions upon the Armenians. Armenian schools were closed or hampered in their operations, and it became difficult for an Armenian to rise to any position of rank in the administration.

Nestorians

The Nestorians, remnants of the once populous Assyrian nation, adherents to what is perhaps the oldest Christian rite— the Church of the East, founded by the Apostles Thaddeus and Thomas—have been reduced to an insignificant number in modern times. Their principal concentration has been in the northwest, around Mosul in Iraq and the Urmiah plain in Iran. In appearance and modes of life they offer many resemblances to the Kurds. While the patriarch of the Church of the East is also the head of the Assyrian nation and endeavors to keep alive a national consciousness among his people, the Nestorians are too weak in number and influence seriously to cherish ideas of a national sovereignty of their own.

Other Minorities

Besides the Armenians and Nestorians, there are adherents to the Roman Catholic and indigenous Protestant Churches, drawn not only from the older Christian faiths but also from Islam and Judaism. Their position is about the same as that of other Christians, except that Moslem converts were subject frequently to persecutions of various sorts from relatives and former friends. In parts of Iran it is still a hazardous thing to forsake the faith of Islam for that of Christ, but the general feeling against apostasy has greatly diminished.

The Jews have been an element in the Iranian population since the time of the Captivity, and although they are distinctively Jewish in faith, tradition, and domestic life, in physical appearance they are hardly to be distinguished from the Persians.

In Hamadan, which for many years was suspected to be the ancient Ecbatana, summer capital of the Medes and Persians, the Jews maintain and revere what are asserted to be the tombs of Esther and Mordecai of Biblical history. Because of the lack of any archaeological evidence, the belief that Hamadan was the site of the ancient Ecbatana rested almost entirely upon the existence of this Jewish colony and its tradition. During the 1930's, however, exploratory shafts were sunk in the neighborhood, and the evidence unearthed has confirmed for most scholars what until then could only be surmised from tradition; and so, in this case, are shown the importance and endurance of tradition.

The Jews have in general suffered greater disabilities than the Christians, partly because the Jews, unlike the Christians, have not enjoyed the jealous interest in their welfare on the part of powerful nations. In the old days a Jew could not go in the streets in wet weather lest he contaminate one of the Faithful. In general, however, anti-Semitism has languished in modern times, though considerable revival of this feeling occurred during the period of Hitlerian ascendancy in Europe, when many Iranians adopted the views of the Germans.

The Guebers are adherents to the ancient Zoroastrian faith, descendants of those who refused to accept Islam at the time of the Mohammedan invasion. The greater number of them fled to India, where they comprise today the wealthy and influential sect of Parsees most generally congregated around Bombay. Those who remained in Iran have for centuries suffered various disabilities because of their faith, but after the ascendancy of Riza Shah Pahlavi their condition was greatly ameliorated. It was the policy of Riza Shah Pahlavi to revive the national spirit by recalling the ancient glories, and as the Parsees represented the purest strains of the pre-Islamic Persians and adhered to the ancient faith of Darius and Cyrus, they suddenly acquired new esteem and received the paternal interest of the State.

Under the Constitution of Iran, while Islam is declared to be the State religion, and Farsi the official language, all religions are tolerated and receive the protection of the State. The restrictions and disabilities endured by the several religious minorities are due less to official policy than to the influence of the Islamic clergy.

III

POLITICS AND GOVERNMENT

A. POLITICAL CHARACTERISTICS

THE MOST famous palace in Teheran, now used only for State occasions, is the Gulistan, or Rose Garden palace. In a series of great vaulted rooms opening onto the courtyard —a lovely garden with a pool surrounded by plane and poplar and cypress trees—are contained some of the most priceless treasures of Iran, if not of the world. Among these treasures are the famous Peacock Throne, brought by the conqueror Nadir Shah from the sack of Delhi in 1739, covered with gold and studded with precious gems, together with a second throne equally as gorgeous and as opulently jeweled. The casual visitor may stroll through the Gulistan and examine these masterpieces of the jeweler's art, as well as the many other treasures displayed in glass cases along the walls. A few uniformed attendants may be found standing about, but no armed guards. Even during the occupation of Iran by foreign troops in World War II, when the government was weak, its sovereignty uncertain, and at times a condition bordering on anarchy prevailed, the Gulistan stood open, negligently, or indulgently, watched over by its dingily clad guardians.

There is significance in this. The Peacock Throne is a symbol of the national greatness. It is protected by the same spirit of reverence that guards the furniture of a church, the sacred vessels of a temple. So long as the people prize their national history, so long may the Peacock Throne stand under its casual guard in the Gulistan; conversely, so long as the Peacock Throne stands under its casual guard one may be sure that the Iranian people still preserve and prize their nationhood. It is of interest that a neighboring power, which has not hesitated to filch a province when occasion offered, has never gone so far as to seize the Peacock Throne or the Crown jewels.

While the Peacock Throne thus symbolizes the national tradition, it also signifies the monarchical institution. The monarchy may eventually disappear in favor of a republic, but the temperament and tradition of the people suggest that its abolition would be undertaken with the same reluctance with which the Peacock Throne would be melted down for its metal and precious gems.

The place of the throne in Iranian political life is not easy for a Westerner to comprehend. Until the twentieth century, the monarchical concept in Iran had been one of absolutism. This absorption of all sovereignty in the personal hands of the king was a concept dating from Achaemenian times, from the days of the first empire of the Medes and Persians. This respect for sovereignty existed despite the fact that almost any person could aspire to the throne, and many times in history it fell into the hands of lucky adventurers. Between the sovereign and the people stood no intermediate class or interest, such as the nobility and the merchant guilds that restrained the medieval princes of Europe. This has been generally true throughout Iranian history, despite the powerful influence exerted by the clergy—the Magis in ancient times, the mullahs since the advent of Islam—and the not insignificant influence of the merchant class.

Likewise, as in the days of the Roman Empire, no principle of succession was ever established, though the crown usually descended within the family and was regarded as a family possession. However, as polygamy was customary, and as the various sovereigns, unlike the Roman, usually had a numerous progeny, the question of the succession often became a cause for sanguinary contest among the various sons. The history of the Iranian monarchy, as with most Oriental monarchies, is a repetition of parricide, filicide, fratricide: instances without number exist of whole families slain in order to make sure the throne. Mutilations and castrations of rivals were common.

The tradition of absolutism prevented any development of institutions or customary law even faintly resembling the system that appeared in Europe during medieval times. The structure of society became feudal, the feudal aristocracy was equally at the mercy of the throne, with the effect that even in modern times the landowning class, while economically powerful, remained politically subservient.

Inherent Tradition of Freedom

The nomadic tribes stood in a somewhat different relation to the throne. Among them existed a strong customary law, with a strong sense of personal freedom and independence. Leadership of the tribe, while frequently confined to a family succession, usually went by election or by general consent of the elders. The tribe dealt as a unit with the throne, and in exchange for a stated tribute to the State, including the supply of armed contingents, retained its traditional privileges.

The autocratic Mongols, for instance, never reduced the Lurs and the Kurds to more than nominal allegiance, and from the eleventh to the sixteenth century they were governed by their own *atabegs*. With the rise of the Persian Safavid dynasty, they were brought again into the political system; the Safavids and succeeding dynasties cultivated the support of the tribes, and chiefly relied upon them, rather than upon the landed nobility, for their military levies, and as late as the nineteen twenties the tribal contingents constituted the main element in the military forces of the Empire.

Among the tribesmen, therefore, as in villages remote from the capital, the typical attitude towards the throne was one of indifference if not disdain—an attitude well expressed by the following quatrain from the *Rubaiyat,* true today as it was nine centuries ago:

> With me along the strip of Herbage strown
> That just divides the desert from the sown,
> Where name of Slave and Sultán is forgot—
> And Peace to Mahmúd on his Golden Throne!

Thus despite the long tradition of absolutism, there existed an equally tenacious tradition of personal freedom and independence. The significance of this is considerable: it explains the paradox by which a people among whom the system of monarchic absolutism has been the most ancient in the East became the first people of the East to throw off the system in favor of parliamentary government. It explains, moreover, the relative facility with which they became accustomed to parliamentary government, and the relative virility which it has manifested in succeeding crises. More will be said later about this early ripened vigor and its manifestations; for the moment a brief survey of the constitutional movement is appropriate.

B. The Constitutional Movement

Coincident with the abortive Russian Revolution of 1905 a revolution occurred in Iran, but with greater success and with less bloodshed. Muzaffar-ed-Din Shah, who had come to the throne ten years before, was weak and corrupt: he had dissipated the revenues of the State and had mortgaged the national resources by foreign loans and grants of concessions. In 1905, demonstrations took place, instigated by the bazaar and the clergy. A customary form of protest, besides that of closing the bazaars in boycott, was that of taking *bast,* or sanctuary, in one of the shrines; in 1906, the leading *mujtahids* enforced their demands for reform by retiring in a body to the shrine of Fatima at Qum, and further by threatening to exile themselves to Turkish territory. Since the *mujtahids* administered the Koranic law, and thus constituted the principal judicial body, this was tantamount to an interdict.

Meantime, a still larger demonstration was occurring in Teheran. This was the famous *bast* in which over twelve thousand merchants and others camped in the grounds of the British legation and refused to leave until a code of laws had been granted. As a result of the mediation of the British minister, the Shah issued a rescript granting a national assembly. This was on 5 August 1906; the assembly convened in October and drew up a constitution, which was ratified at once.

Muzaffar-ed-Din Shah died within a few days after the promulgation of the Constitution. The terms of the Constitution did not seriously restrict the power of the shah, but they did provide for a consultative assembly, known as the Majlis. Muzaffar-ed-Din's successor, his son, Mohammed Ali Shah, a despot of the worst type, promptly undertook to nullify the instrument. In December, he attempted a *coup d'état,* which failed.

The success of the parliamentary regime encouraged the Turks to a similar movement, and in 1908 the 'Young Turks' obtained the restoration of the constitution which Sultan

Abdul Hamid had granted on his accession in 1876, but had promptly annulled.

The spread of democratic institutions on the borders of the Russian Empire caused great uneasiness in Moscow, and in 1908 Mohammed Ali Shah was persuaded to a new effort to overthrow the Constitution. With the aid of the Cossacks [1] and their Russian commander, he bombed the parliament building and dispersed the Majlis. The result was widespread reaction. In Azerbaijan the people revolted and the Shah had to send troops to besiege the provincial capital Tabriz. This siege was lifted when the Russians sent forces and intervened. Meantime, the Bakhtiari tribes under the leadership of Haj Ali Kuli Khan, Sardar-i-Asad, assembled in force and marched on the capital. Teheran was captured in July 1909; the Shah was deposed, and his 12-year-old son, Sultan Ahmad, was placed on the throne under a regency. Mohammed Ali Shah retired to Odessa under a pension from the government, payable so long as he remained out of politics, and the Russian government undertook to keep him under surveillance. In 1911, however, he made a further attempt to regain his throne and with Russian aid mustered a force at Astrabad; this attempt also failed.

Throughout the regency and subsequent reign of Sultan Ahmad Shah (1909-25), though the power of the government progressively decayed, the legal sovereignty of the Majlis within the government was unchallenged. Sultan Ahmad Shah suffered from obesity; he seemed, moreover, to be in constant fear of his life, and during the latter years of his reign spent much of his time in Europe. In the early years of the Constitution, the government was dominated by the Bakhtiari chiefs, who had been instrumental in securing the Constitution, but by 1912 their influence had been removed. The troubles that beset parliamentary government in Iran were not only the lack of political preparation among the people, but the failure of the Constitution to provide either a fundamental law or a system of administration under law. An elec-

---

[1] This was an Iranian military body that had been created in 1882, but it had always been officered by Russians, and was under Russian influence.

tive assembly of one hundred thirty-six deputies was instituted, but no election procedures were laid down.[2]

Power remained with various cliques in Teheran which, through control of the prime ministry, effectively disposed of public offices. The administration of the provinces remained largely unchanged; the provincial governors were practically absolute in their exercise of power, and the system of farming out offices to the highest bidder, which had prevailed since antiquity, was hardly modified.

From 1909 until 1925, the rule of Iran was exercised by a succession of prime ministers and ministerial cliques—always however, with the nominal consent of the Majlis. This was a period of political impotence, economic stagnation and declining prestige, in which Russian imperialism pressed for hegemony.

The fact that Iranian sovereignty did not disappear during this period is attributable to a number of factors. One of these was British diplomacy, which was interested in keeping Iran independent as a protection to British sovereignty in India. A second reason was the influence of world opinion stirred up in 1911 by the ultimatum issued to Iran by the Russian government regarding the American, W. Morgan Shuster, the incidents of which will be described later. A third factor was, of course, the sudden collapse of Russian power during the Revolution. A fourth factor was British inability, due to war weariness and the unwillingness of the British public to support further imperialistic activities, to fill the vacuum created by the Russian withdrawal. A fifth factor, the actual strength of which is now in the balance, is the virility of the national spirit of the Iranian people, of which the Majlis, however feeble, continued to be the political expression.

Whatever may be the ultimate destiny of Iran, the remarkable fact is that the Majlis, despite what may appear to Western eyes to be a travesty of the processes of democracy, not

[2] Ignorance of democratic procedures produced some ludicrous, as well as tragic, results. During an election in Riza Shah Pahlavi's reign (1937) the students in one of the mission schools were directed by the police to assemble and proceed *en masse* to the polling place. There, each of them was provided with a folded slip of paper and told to drop it in the ballot box. One of the students started to unfold his slip, but was cautioned by the police not to do so. 'This is a secret ballot,' the policeman explained.

only survived but to a large extent became the vocal expression of the spirit of the people. Whatever may be said of corruption, of nominal elections, of political ineptitude, when the record of the Iranian parliament is placed beside the condition and theory of monarchic absolutism, a fair and reasonable judgment must accord the Iranian people respect for the manner in which they adopted constitutional principles and continued to enlarge the application and strengthen the structure of parliamentary government. The success of the Iranian people in achieving constitutional government this early, and with so little bloodshed, is a phenomenon that has been overlooked by the world, even as it amazed students of Middle Eastern politics.

c. FOREIGN IMPERIALISM

The major factor in the modern political history of Iran has been the glacial-like movement southward of the political mass on the north; and whether Iran survives as an independent sovereignty will depend upon whether the force of that movement is melted by the sun of a more temperate international order or is blasted away by force.

The policy of southward expansion was promulgated in the early eighteenth century by Peter the Great, and that policy has since been consistently pursued by successive tsars, and more recently by the Soviet government of Russia. The policies that Peter the Great promulgated for posterity are contained in the famous will he is supposed to have left. This will was published in Europe in 1755 by the Chevalier d'Eon, who claimed to have obtained a copy while acting as reader to Catherine the Great, and though it has been challenged as spurious, the evidence is that it has been accepted in Russia as a political charter. Regarding Iran, this document states:

IX. To approach as near as possible to Constantinople and India . . . consequently excite continuous wars, not only in Turkey, but in Persia. . . And in the decadence of Persia, penetrate as far as the Persian Gulf.

Even before the time of Peter the Great, however, the Muscovites had been covetous of the shahs' dominions. In 1668, according to Chardin, the Grand Duke of Muscovy had picked a quarrel with the Shah and had invaded Mazanderan as far as the northern capital of Ferahabad.[3] Peter also had not contented himself with advice, but before the end of his reign had made a bold attempt to possess the entire Caspian region.

At that time the dominion of the shahs extended as far as the Caucasus mountains and was defended on the north by this formidable barrier. The Shah, however, had fallen into difficulties with his neighbors to the east, the Afghans, who in 1722 had penetrated as far as Isfahan, his principal capital. Seizing upon this opportunity, Peter assembled an army at the mouth of the Volga, sailed down the coast and attacked the port of Derbend. The city fell, and Peter proceeded along the coast towards Baku. At this juncture he was met by the Ottoman ambassador who warned him of a Turkish attack unless he withdrew.

A year later, Peter resumed his enterprise by attacking Resht, on the southern coast of the Caspian. The province of Gilan fell into his hands and later in the year Baku was taken. The Shah now came to an understanding with Peter whereby, in return for aid against the Afghans, the towns and dependencies of Derbend and Baku, as well as the provinces of Gilan, Mazanderan, and Astrabad, were ceded to Russia.

Subsequently, however, the Caspian provinces were surrendered, although Baku and Derbend were retained. This may have been due to Peter's death in 1725, following which the Russians became embroiled in domestic dissension over the succession. The insalubrity of the southern Caspian climate may have been a factor, as well as the rise of the powerful and war-like Nadir Shah.

In 1813, war again broke out between Russia and Iran, and again in 1827. By the Treaty of Gulistan, in 1813, which concluded the first of these wars, Russia acquired the quasi-independent territories of Georgia, Imeritia, and Mingrelia, in the Caucasus, as well as Daghestan, Shirvan, Ganjeh, Karabagh, and parts of Talish, more properly Iranian dominion, while Russia was given the sole privilege of maintaining ves-

[3] Chardin, Sir John, *Coronation of Solyman III* (printed as Supplement to his *Travels*). pp. 152-4, cited in Curzon, op. cit. vol. 1, p. 186.

sels of war on the Caspian Sea. The Treaty of Turkomanchai, signed in 1828, which concluded the latter war, ceded to Russia the Armenian districts of Erivan, Nakhitchivan, and a war indemnity of thirty million silver rubles, or approximately $15,000,000. A commercial treaty was also concluded which limited the customs Iran could levy to an ad valorem 5 per cent.

The Treaty of Turkomanchai is significant in Iranian history, for by it attributes of sovereignty were taken from the government which were not restored for a hundred years, among those being the power to fix its own customs dues, and to execute law and justice on all within its territory. This latter cession, known in Turkey under the name of Capitulations, granted the Russian consuls either joint or absolute jurisdiction in all civil and criminal cases involving a Russian subject. These privileges were extended as a matter of course to other foreign powers, and the fixing of customs tariffs also became a matter of negotiation and agreement with other powers maintaining relations with the Iranian government. The re-establishment of customs autonomy and the abolition of the Capitulatory privileges were finally achieved by Riza Shah Pahlavi in 1927 and 1928.

Ten years after the Treaty of Turkomanchai, without the formality of declaring war, Russia seized the island of Ashurada, at the mouth of Astrabad Bay, and established a naval base there. Subsequently, other points on the Persian Caspian were seized, including Hasan Kuli Bay, Chikishliar, Cheleken Bay, and Balkan Bay.[4]

British Interests in Iran

Russian aggressive tactics now subsided, partly because of preoccupation elsewhere, principally in expansion in Trans-Caspia and elsewhere in Asia, partly because of the vigor of Nasr-ed-Din Shah, who came to the throne in 1848 and ruled until 1896, partly because of increasing British activity in defense of their interests in that part of the world. Following the Sepoy Mutiny in 1857, India, which had formerly been governed through the East India Company, was formally incorporated into the British Empire, and British influence be-

4 Curzon, op. cit. vol. II, p. 393.

came ascendant in Afghanistan. From the time of Shah Abbas, British merchants and British diplomacy had been active in Iran, and in 1800 a treaty had been signed with the Shah guaranteeing him aid in case of attack by the Afghans or by the French. Throughout Nasr-ed-Din Shah's reign, relations between Afghanistan and Iran were strained, and several wars occurred. Earlier, during the war of 1837, the British had intervened and occupied Kharak Island in the Persian Gulf, but later they had evacuated it. In 1856, on the occasion of the second Perso-Afghan war, Great Britain declared war on Iran and again seized Kharak, as well as Bushire, but once more evacuated these places at the conclusion of peace. These are the only instances of armed hostilities between Great Britain and Iran.

During the reign of Muzaffar-ed-Din Shah (1896-1906) and during the impotency of Iran following the establishment of the Constitution, Russian penetration became more pronounced. In 1907, as a means of restraining Russian expansion throughout Asia, and as a part in the total pattern of European politics by which the Triple Entente was formed among Britain, France, and Russia to counter Germany, a series of agreements was negotiated with Russia by Great Britain delimiting the respective spheres of influence of the two powers in Central Asia. The agreement with regard to Iran is known as the Anglo-Russian Convention of 1907. Although the powers professed every respect for Iranian independence, and denied any intention of interfering in the internal administration, the Convention divided the country into two spheres of influence with a neutral belt between, and provided that neither of the two powers should seek privileges in the sphere of the other.

The Russian sphere embraced all the productive northern half of the country, including Azerbaijan, the Caspian provinces, and Khorasan; it extended southward as far as Kermanshah and Isfahan; all the principal cities of Iran were within the Russian sphere, except Dizful, Shustar, Shiraz, and Kirman. The British sphere consisted of the southeastern desert bordering on Baluchistan, in which the only city of importance was Kirman. The chief advantage to Great Britain was that it excluded Russian influence from the Persian Gulf littoral, the control of which was of paramount importance to the security of India.

The Anglo-Russian Convention failed to accomplish its purpose of curbing Russian infringement on Iranian sovereignty. In 1910 occurred the famous Potsdam Agreement between Germany and Russia, by which Germany agreed to support Russian imperialism in Iran in exchange for similar support of German expansion in the Ottoman Empire. Russia therefore promptly resumed her aggression towards Iran. In 1911 the Russians encouraged and assisted the exiled Mohammed Ali Shah in an attempt to regain his throne. He was permitted to leave Odessa and to land at Astrabad with a consignment of arms and ammunition labeled 'mineral waters.' Moreover, to intimidate Persian resistance, the Russian legation announced that under its Capitulatory privileges it would arrest 'illegal Russian subjects who might take part in the events actually going on in the country'—a device that permitted the legation to arrest loyal Iranians who were supporting the Constitution on the pretext that they were suspected of being Russian subjects.[5] This whole attempt was, however, a failure.

The Shuster Incident

The Iranian government, meantime, in an effort to improve its administrative structure, had applied to the American government for the services of a financial adviser. W. Morgan Shuster was recommended and was engaged as Treasurer General of Iran, with extensive powers, and in May 1911 arrived in Iran with a group of assistants. The Russian government had informally protested to the American government against the appointment and promptly undertook to discourage Shuster's mission.

One of Shuster's measures that antagonized the Russians was his establishment of a special Treasury gendarmerie, charged with enforcing the internal administration of the country, primarily in connection with the collection of the taxes. At the time, the principal military force at the disposal of the government was the Russian-officered Cossack Brigade. Shuster

[5] Shuster, W. Morgan, *The Strangling of Persia*, New York, 1912, p. 109.

offered to a young Englishman the appointment as head of the gendarmerie. To this the Russians violently objected, as 'not compatible with their interests,' and the British legation co-operatively ordered the Englishman out of the country.

In the midst of these events occurred the attempt of Mohammed Ali Shah to regain his throne. With its failure, the Majlis ordered the confiscation of the estates of the ringleaders in the plot, including those of Shua-u-Saltana, the ex-shah's brother. The Russian legation declared a protectorate over these properties and posted a guard. This guard Shuster had the temerity to remove. There promptly followed a Russian ultimatum demanding an apology from the government, which was given, followed in November by a second ultimatum, demanding Shuster's dismissal.

A national uprising was provoked by these ultimatums, the second of which the Majlis rejected with the cry of 'Death or Independence,' and Russian forces stationed in Tabriz and Resht were attacked by the populace. In reprisal, Russian troops moved down on Tabriz, bombarded the city, massacred several hundred people, hanged several of the principal citizens, and threatened further to move on to Teheran. Typical of the spirit of resistance shown by the people was the appearance before the Majlis of a delegation of three hundred women, carrying revolvers under their shroud-like black garb; tearing aside their veils they declared their intention to kill their own husbands and sons and to leave behind their own dead bodies if the Majlis wavered in its duty of upholding the liberty and dignity of the Iranian people and nation.[6]

When neither threats nor bribes availed against the Majlis, Russia undertook to destroy the government by force, and on 24 December 1911, engineered a *coup d'état* by which the Majlis was dispersed. Shuster accepted the inevitable and left Iran early in January 1912.

In the south, the British had not been inactive in maintaining their interests against the Russians. While the Russians were marching about in northern Iran, the British had, on 10 October 1910, complained of the insecurity of the roads in the south, and practically demanded that a number of officers

[6] Shuster, op. cit. p. 198.

of the British-Indian army be placed in charge of the policing of these roads under the general supervision of the British government, the expense to be met from the Iranian customs revenues.[7] The British, however, had supported Shuster's proposal for the establishment of a gendarmerie (though not agreeing to the British officers), and as a result the gendarmerie, under Swedish officers, came into being—somewhat to Russian irritation.

The effect of the Shuster incident on British public opinion was to awaken it to the casuistry of the Anglo-Russian Convention and to produce a revulsion against British policy in Iran. Shuster's book, *The Strangling of Persia,* produced repercussions also in the United States. As a result of all this the Anglo-Russian Convention was allowed quietly to lapse, so far as British policy was concerned. In Iran, Shuster had become a national hero, revered to this day.

Russian interference persisted, however, and in March 1912, the Russians, determined to assert their power, found in eastern Iran—as they had in Tabriz the preceding December—a pretext for military action, in the course of which they bombarded the revered shrine of the Imam Riza at Meshed, and badly damaged its famous golden dome.

D. IRAN DURING WORLD WAR I

Such was the condition when World War I broke out. The government of Iran was helpless, disorganized, and bankrupt, and a sense of despair possessed the people. Since the revolutionary troubles of 1909, Russian troops had been stationed in Tabriz and elsewhere in northwestern Persia. This territory now became the theater of operations between Turks and Russians. In January 1915, Tabriz was captured by the Turks, only to be recaptured by the Russians. The Urmiah plain was devastated by Turks and Kurds, the Christian Nestorians slain or dispersed.

In the south, Great Britain had begun operations against the Turks in Mesopotamia in order to protect the oil fields and works of the Anglo-Persian Oil Company, and in November

[7] Shuster, op. cit. p. liv.

1914, Basra was captured; but British power was too weak to drive farther. In 1915, Turkish and German detachments moved up the Darian highway from Baghdad as far as Kermanshah in Iran, and a German mission was dispatched overland to Afghanistan.

In 1916, both Russia and Great Britain raised local levies to maintain a defense line against Turko-German advances. The Russians employed the existing Cossack Brigade, which was enlarged and re-equipped; the British created a new organization known as the South Persia Rifles. By 1917 these forces, nominally Iranian, but actually under Russian and British control, were in effective occupation of all Iran, and with the incorporation of the Swedish-officered gendarmerie into the British forces, in 1917, there disappeared the last military force at the disposal of the Iranian government. Iran had for all purposes ceased to exist as an independent nation.

Thus, during World War I, the sovereignty of Iran was violated with less compunction than that of Belgium, and with probably greater loss of life and property and disorganization of society. The most fertile province in all Iran, the Urmiah plain, was devastated, hundreds of prosperous villages depopulated, the orchards cut down, the water canals broken in, and a hundred thousand refugees left to wander about the country. The Urmiah district remains to this day semi-depopulated, its prosperity gone, its landscape showing ruins of once fertile villages, now sterile and lonely.

Despite the justness of their claims for restitution and indemnity, the Versailles Peace Conference, which was to establish a new justice in the world and a respect for small nations, declined, on the insistence of the British delegates, to admit the Iranian representatives or permit them to state their case. Collateral reasons for the refusal of the Conference to admit the Iranian delegates were the extravagance of the claims they were advancing and the fact that Iran had not been a belligerent.

In 1917, Russian power in Iran had collapsed as a result of the Russian Revolution, and while Great Britain hurriedly attempted to fill the political and military void this event created, the attempt never quite succeeded. In January 1918, a force was dispatched from Baghdad northward by way of

Iran in an effort to anticipate the Turks and Germans who were driving into the Caucasus. While British forces eventually reached Baku, they subsequently withdrew, and never succeeded in establishing in northern Iran a hegemony comparable to that which the Russians had abandoned.

Iranian nationalism began to reassert itself in 1918, stirred by the Russian debacle and by German successes at arms; and British overtures to an Irano-British *rapprochement,* made in March 1918, were rejected. The British government had proposed that the South Persia Rifles be recognized as an Iranian force and that British troops be allowed to occupy Azerbaijan until the end of the war; the British further conceded the abrogation of the Anglo-Russian Convention of 1907. The effect of the Iranian rejection of these terms was to cause defections from the Iranian-recruited South Persia Rifles, which had been the principal stabilizing force in the south, and at the same time to invite a rising of the southern tribes led by the Kashgais. This opposition to British authority was not quelled until the end of the year.

The end of the war established a new orientation in Iran. Russian influence had disappeared, and British influence, while resisted by the Iranians, was unchallenged elsewhere. A British emissary arrived in Teheran and presented a new proposal to the Iranian government: this was the ill-fated Anglo-Persian Agreement which was negotiated in August 1919. Like so many diplomatic documents, it seemed innocent in its purposes and terms. After reiterating respect for the independence and integrity of Iran, it provided that the British government would supply expert advisers to the Iranian government, whose powers and emoluments were, however, to be a matter of negotiation between that government and the advisers. The British government also undertook to supply officers, and such munitions and equipment as a joint commission should recommend, for the re-establishment of the Iranian army; to arrange for a loan to the Iranian government; and to co-operate in other ways in the restoration of Iranian economy and the development of Anglo-Iranian enterprise. In connection with the signing of the Agreement, a loan of £2,000,000 was offered, and the British government further undertook to co-operate in obtaining an indemnity for the losses sustained by Iran as a result of the war.

The announcement of the Agreement was received with hostility in Iran and with suspicion abroad, not only in the United States and France, but among the British public. It seemed an extension of British imperialism, and the British public in particular was weary of further adventure of this sort. Lord Curzon was at the time foreign minister of Great Britain and his imperialistic views were well known. What contributed further to this apprehension, no doubt, was the atmosphere in which the Agreement had been negotiated. It has been widely charged that the signatures to the document were obtained by bribery, and leaders of British opinion, among them Lord Grey of Fallodon, complained that the Agreement should have been submitted to the League of Nations.

While the Majlis, which still retained its constitutional prerogatives, dallied with ratification, Iranian public opinion began to ferment. Under pressure from home, the British government began to withdraw its forces from Iran. Meantime, the new Soviet government of Russia had become active in protecting its position in Iran. In June 1919, it had issued a declaration by which it renounced all imperialistic ambitions in Iran, abrogated all concessions held by the Imperial government or its subjects, with the exception of the Caspian fisheries concession, and annulled all debts of the Iranian government to the Russian. While denouncing tsarist imperialism, however, it began steadily to reoccupy the domains that successive tsars had brought under Russian suzerainty. In 1920 and 1921, the independent republics of Georgia, Azerbaijan,[8] and Armenia, which had been established in the Caucasus during the Revolution, were conquered and extinguished, and on 18 May 1920, a Red fleet appeared off Persian Enzeli,[9] bombarded the city, and forced the retirement of the British, who were still in occupation. On 6 June 1920, following the further withdrawal of the British, the city of Resht, capital of the province of Gilan, was occupied, and a Soviet Republic of Gilan proclaimed.

[8] Caucasian Azerbaijan, not to be confused with Iranian Azerbaijan, though at one time part of the Iranian Empire.
[9] Now Pahlavi.

It was at this point that Riza Khan, a colonel in the Cossack Brigade stationed at Kasvin, and a man of high intelligence and of imperial bearing, entered the scene of history. The situation in the capital was chaotic; the government was impotent; the British forces, upon which public order rested, were leaving the country; and the Russians were moving in. Early in 1921, fears of possible Russian occupation produced a state of panic. Riza Khan had attacked the Soviets with his forces and had been defeated. Emissaries—and according to reports, these emissaries were representatives of the British legation—[10] went to Kasvin and urged Riza Khan to move his forces to Teheran and take over the government.

While this was going on, the British legation was pressing the matter of the Anglo-Persian Agreement. The prime minister of Iran reluctantly summoned the Majlis to convene on 20 February 1921 to consider ratification.

On 21 February, Riza Khan appeared in Teheran with his troops, seized the government, and arrested the members of the cabinet. Seyyid Zia-ed-Din, a well-known Anglophile, was named prime minister, and Riza Khan became minister of war and commander of the army.

The unexpected, though not unprecedented, result of this *coup d'état* was that five days later the Majlis summarily rejected the Anglo-Persian Agreement, and on the same day the new government signed an agreement with Soviet Russia. This agreement reiterated the Russian self-denying declaration of the year earlier and confirmed the annulment of Russian concessions and other claims in Iran, with the exception of the Caspian Sea fisheries. It stipulated, however, that none of the surrendered concessions should be granted to any foreign interest without Russian permission. More significantly, as events revealed, it reserved the right to intervene in Iran, or occupy the country, if necessary for the defense of Russia.

The British completed their evacuation of Iran early in 1921, except for the southeastern desert, which was not evacuated

---

[10] See Filmer, Henry, *The Pageant of Persia*, Indianapolis, 1936, p. 344. Filmer quotes Emile Lesueur (*Les Anglais en Perse*, Paris, 1922), to the effect that an official of the British Legation distributed money to the troops under Riza Khan as an inducement to move. M. Lesueur was a professor teaching in Teheran at the time.

until 1924, and shortly afterwards the Soviet occupation of Gilan province ceased. Iran was now, for the first time in over twenty years, free of foreign troops on its soil, and though the country was prostrate from the effects of military devastation: famine, disease, disruption of communications, and governmental impotence, the national spirit was resurgent, and the scene was prepared for a new era of national development.

A summary of the history from 1900 to 1920 would indicate the following principal characteristics: (a) the gradual strengthening of democratic processes, accompanied by a renewed vitality of the national spirit of Iran; (b) a corresponding decay in governmental administration, a fact which may be attributed in part to unfamiliarity with democratic processes, in part to persistent foreign intervention; and (c) the continued pressure on the part of Russia, aided to a considerable extent by Great Britain, to reduce the people to a state of vassalage. The later political history of Iran will be surveyed in subsequent chapters.

IV

LIVELIHOOD

THE TRADITIONAL economy of Iran has been highly fortunate for the Iranian people, but that economy has been disappearing. That is to say, the Iranian people required little for their sustenance that they did not themselves produce, while on the other hand they produced certain articles that were highly regarded and in constant demand throughout the world. Today, Iran is rapidly approaching a condition in which its merchants demand everything from the outside world and have very little to offer in exchange.

A. PASTORAL LIVELIHOOD

Such generalizations of course require qualification. The mass of the Iranian people follows a primitive pastoral and agricultural pattern of life. Out of an estimated population of 16 million, not more than 20 per cent live in cities of more than 10,000 population, of which there are not more than 50. (In the United States more than 47½ per cent of the population lives in towns of 10,000 or more population.) Some 3 to 5 million of the inhabitants follow a pastoral life. These are the nomadic tribesmen. Because of the nature of their occupation, their mode of life is simple and their wants are correspondingly limited. While their living standards are low by comparison with those of the American town, village, and countryside, they are probably better fed and clothed than many cotton farmers of the Deep South, the miners of the remoter Appalachian valleys, or the hillmen of Kentucky.

The reason is that while their means are limited they have not lost the skill of hand to turn their few materials to account. For example, from the milk of their flocks they make a number of products: butter, cheese, and *mast*—this last, a fermentation of milk which has in recent years been introduced to the

77

American market as Bulgarian buttermilk or under its Turkish name of *yoghurt,* and which is often prescribed for infants and invalids because of its easy digestibility and nutritional qualities. Milk products are supplemented by goat's meat and mutton, eaten perhaps twice a week, and wild herbs. Many of the semi-nomadic tribes cultivate the ground for wheat, barley, and vegetables; the pure nomads obtain cereals by barter. Their chief requirement from the outside is tea to drink and sugar to sweeten the tea. For clothing, they weave interesting and durable fabrics of the wool from their flocks. While the brightly printed calicoes from abroad are popular among them, and may be preferred to their own hand-loomed fabrics, these are novelties that certainly are not equal in beauty or utility to their own weaves. Their goat's-hair tents are superior to any canvas the looms of the West can offer, and their carpets of course provide an adornment that would add to the beauty of the most comfortably established household of the West. Firearms and cutlery are in great demand among the tribesmen, but the firearms could well be foregone, if conditions of greater political security and justice prevailed.

Of the myriad interesting and useful objects of commerce which the West produces, few are designed for life among the tents.[1] A good portable radio, for instance, would be a great boon to life in the lonely hills, but an automobile cannot follow the paths the tribesmen must take with their flocks. Saddles and harnesses might find a market, except that these are made quite satisfactorily by the leather workers of the encampment. The nomads are desperately in want of good doctors—but doctors are not an article of trade—and medicines, but until they have physicians to administer the medicines they are almost as well off with the curative herbs familiar to them as with the patent nostrums that find their way into export trade.[2] They need education—but not the kind that is represented by books, magazines, advertising brochures that ordi-

[1] An equally valid statement would be, of course, that the nomadic life is not one designed to utilize the myriad interesting articles that industrialism produces.

[2] Some exceptions exist. A number of proprietary drugs are now finding their way to Iran which are self-administerable and which are specifics for numerous ailments, particularly skin diseases such as favus.

narily find their way into export trade. They need teachers and advisers who have a sympathetic understanding of their traditions and intellectual and moral requirements; they need a particular sort of books that so far have been sent by only one institution of the outer world, the Church.

On the other hand, the tribesmen produce much that has a ready market throughout the world. Their carpets are among the finest woven in Iran, and that means the finest in the world. And the precious lambskins known as Persian, of which the Iranian tribesmen are a substantial supplier, are the standard of fine furs.

Besides these better-known articles of commerce are others not so well known, but of considerable importance in various departments of civilized life. Sheep casings—or sheep intestine —importantly employed in sausage making and in other applications, have been exported largely from Iran. Gum tragacanth, found as an exudation of a wilderness bush,[3] and gum-arabic, extracted from the *konar* tree, are articles gathered by the Iranian nomads and villagers to satisfy a demand from abroad. Another product that civilization seeks of the tribesmen is licorice root, employed largely in tobacco manufacture. Besides these, there are numerous herbs employed in pharmaceuticals.

B. AGRICULTURAL LIVELIHOOD

The peasant class, which with the tribesmen composes the bulk of the population, exists by a simple and relatively self-sufficient system of livelihood in small villages, and farms the land by medieval methods of tillage. An ox is kept to draw the plow and to thresh the grain, a donkey to carry the produce to market, some sheep for wool and meat, some goats for milk, and always a flock of chickens. The stable is part of the house and the heat of the animals helps warm the home in winter. The flocks are pastured in common, and the oxen may be owned in common. The village, if substantial, may support a few craftsmen, such as the smith, the saddler, the potter, the barber, the baker, and the bath man. If large enough, it may also have a mosque and a mullah who, besides leading the

[3] The *astragalus*.

Friday prayers, will teach the children to recite the Koran (in Arabic) and to read and write. In the village there will also be the agent of the landlord, who supervises the gathering of the crops to make sure of the rental.

The land is farmed in strips, the strips being allocated afresh each year among the tenants. Crops are rotated, and the soil is fertilized with manure, ashes, and refuse. The grain is threshed on open floors by oxen treading the straw or by a primitive threshing machine, consisting of a roller about five feet long with wooden, or possibly iron, spikes spirally arranged on it; this revolves as the oxen draw it. Sometimes a machine resembling a sled, upon which is set a revolving paddle edged with flint stones, is used.

Despite these primitive methods, a wide variety of foodstuffs is produced. The diet of the villager and peasant consists variously of wheat and barley bread, millet porridge, eggs, milk and milk products, vegetables, and fruits.

The vegetables include beets, spinach, cabbage, cucumbers, asparagus, potatoes, as well as several varieties peculiar to Iran, such as the edible camel thorn, which is made into a sauce for *pilau* (steamed rice cooked with butter). The orchard crops have been mentioned earlier: almonds, walnuts, pistachios, and filberts among the nuts; peaches, pears, apricots, mulberries, quinces, cherries, pomegranates, among the fruits. The vines produce an abundance of melons, squash, pumpkins, and grapes. The grapes are either dried as raisins or pressed for the juice, which is boiled down into sirup to serve as sweetening or as a confection.

The peasants dress in cottons woven abroad or locally, and in cold weather, in woolens of their own weave, woolen felts, and sheepskins. The common shoe is a woven sandal, manufactured in the village.

Spinning and weaving dress goods, carpets, and other fabrics are common household industries. Though printed cottons from abroad are favored among them, as among the tribesmen, the typical wife still 'layeth her hands to the spindle, and her hands hold the distaff.' Wool is carded by pulling it over a pair of long-toothed combs. Wool and silk are still spun by a distaff whirled by hand, though a spinning wheel is sometimes used. In many villages in Gilan and Yezd, the principal silk-growing regions, there are little shops where the silk is spun on a small machine. It is prepared for spinning by throwing the cocoons into a caldron of boiling water mixed with sour milk. A man turns a wheel, about a yard in diameter, with a foot treadle, with one hand stirs the cocoons to loosen the fibers, while with the other he draws up the threads to be wound about the wheel.

Despite these primitive methods of cultivation, the peasants of Iran have managed to produce a surplus for the market, which, sold abroad, has provided the means to pay for many of the foreign luxuries demanded by the more fortunate in the cities. Iran is exceeded only by the United States in exports of raisins, dried fruits, and nuts.[4] A small wheat surplus is also sold abroad in normal times. Tobacco of exceptional quality is grown, with a flavor and aroma not exceeded by the best Turkish, Macedonian, or American leaf, but, unfortunately for tobacco users, little finds its way into world trade. The opium poppy, which is found throughout Iran, but is cultivated chiefly in the south, provides an article of commerce in both licit and illicit trade, and is a source of great profit to smugglers, besides providing considerable revenue to the government, which maintains a nominal monopoly in the trade. The importance and the effects of opium growing will be discussed later.

From the outside world, in exchange for these products, the peasant obtains little beyond sugar and tea, since they are not produced locally in sufficient quantity to supply the demand. There is much, however, that he could use of the production of the West. He stands in pitiable need of good hand tools and simple farm implements. A steel plow to replace his forked stick (which is generally shod nowadays with an iron tip) would be a great boon and immensely increase his productivity. One energetic American sewing-machine company has cultivated the household market in Iran, and sewing machines monogrammed with a large S are to be found in every village. But for the most part the products of the West that find their way to Iran consist of articles of metropolitan and govern-

---

[4] Trade statistics indicate that Turkey may be a larger exporter of these products than Iran, but the Turkish figures are said to include considerable amounts of Iranian products received in Turkey for re-export.

ment demand: steel for railways and highways, factory machinery, electrical goods and equipment, automobiles, cameras, radios, silk hose, and cosmetics. I have walked along the principal streets of Teheran and have seen in the shops a variety of articles sufficient to stock an American department store: pocketknives, coat hangers, tooth paste, razor blades, alarm clocks, typewriters, yard goods, ready-made clothing, top hats, kitchenware, china and glass, furniture, electric lamps—but not a hoe, a rake, or a steel plowshare. This is partly due to the higher profit that the merchant realizes on goods of metropolitan demand, partly to the greater ease with which the metropolitan market can be cultivated; very largely it is due to the general neglect of the agricultural economy and obtuseness to its importance on the part of the ruling classes.

c. Water Supply

Urgent among the agricultural needs of Iran is an adequate water supply. Everywhere, except along the Caspian coast, the rainfall is scanty. On the eastern tableland, as has been previously noted, the rain seldom exceeds 8 inches annually, while on the western tableland, the fall averages 15 inches. Most of this rainfall occurs in the autumn and winter months, though in the Urmiah plain in the northwest it is more evenly distributed. Winter wheat will generally head before the dry season, but for most crops irrigation is necessary.

In most parts of Iran, irrigation is the practice, but not water storage. Mountain streams, fed by melting snow, collect into small rivers; part of the water is diverted to the fields, while the balance flows into the desert and loses itself in saline marshes. Generally, however, the water flows off the mountains very much as water descends from a roof, and does not lend itself to collection or storage. In any case, as the season advances, the amount of water that courses down diminishes to a trickle. Cultivation accordingly is limited to crops that mature by midsummer. The principal method of water conservation and distribution, which has existed for centuries, has been to divert mountain springs into underground tunnels or water courses, called *kanats,* by which the water may be conducted as far as twenty-five miles into the plain. The cities all receive their water supply by numerous *kanats*. These *kanats* offer the advantage of avoiding evaporation that would take place in open ditches and serve also to protect the water from contamination.

The *kanats* are not lined, since the soil structure is such that only moderate loss by seepage is incurred. As they are somewhat subject to obstruction by caving, they are provided with openings at intervals along the course so that workmen can enter the channels to clear them. As the excavated material accumulates about the openings, it presents from a height the appearance of a row of huge ant hills stretching across the desert from the base of the mountains to the village or city.

The *kanats* are usually the property of private individuals or companies. Some enterprising person will tap a stream and lead the water into the town and sell it at so much a 'finger,' that is, by measure. Householders and gardeners buy their water just as they do here, except that in most cases the supplying of the water is a commercial undertaking. The water seller provides the service of keeping the *kanats* open and water flowing.

In the villages the provision of the water may be one of the services of the landlord of the village, for which he receives a share—usually a fifth—of the crop. Enterprising landowners open up new water supplies and enlarge their villages, or establish new villages. The soil is rich, and wherever water can be brought abundant crops can be grown. In some villages the *kanats* are a hereditary property of the community. Since one *kanat* may serve several villages, a great cause of dissension and feuds between villages is the allocation of water rights.

The problem of water supply has been one of considerable interest to observers of the Iranian scene, and two schools of thought are maintained. One view is that the government should undertake great water conservation works, on the order of Hoover Dam and Grand Coulee Dam. The spectacular nature of such projects has made them intriguing to the government and ruling classes. A number of sites exist—though few for a country so vast as Iran—where the results would warrant the expenditure. The principal and most promising is in Khuzistan, where a great barrage across the Karun has been under construction by the government as a result of

British interest and stimulus. This is used as a means of increasing the food supply in the districts in which the oil fields are located, and where the general poverty of the agricultural classes is extreme.

Incidentally, a dam was thrown across the Karun by Shapur I (A.D. 241-72), using Roman engineers and workers taken as prisoners with the emperor, Valerian. It was constructed of blocks of granite cramped together, and was 570 yards long. This dam still exists, though in disrepair.

The disadvantage of such construction schemes, from the standpoint of the individual peasant, is that they are adapted to large-scale mechanical farming, and hence tend to foster the increase of great estates and reduce the cultivators to the status of mere employees. As it is today, while the greater part of the tillable soil is owned by absentee landowners, the parcels are relatively small and dispersed: the villagers may live in poverty but at least they enjoy a modicum of independence.

The other view of the water problem is that the water supply should be increased by what is called in this country 'farm ponds.' Rather than attempt the expensive process of impounding water in great reservoirs, the available funds should be devoted to a system of small dams and an extension of the traditional system of *kanats*. Such a method would seem more in accord with the physical characteristics of the land and would permit a wider dispersion of water-conservation works. This is the view of the able Professor Luther Winsor, American agricultural adviser to the government of Iran, as well as of Dr. Harold B. Allen, director of education of the Near East Foundation, who has extensively surveyed the agrarian problem in Iran with the object of instituting a number of model or demonstration villages under the auspices of the Foundation.

A further method of increasing the water supply, which has been receiving increasing attention from students, is that of tapping the underground water table. The extent of this underground water has not yet been determined, but it appears that in many districts it is abundant and fairly close to the surface. Where artesian wells do not result from boring, but the water must be pumped, it is recommended that wind power or motor power be employed. The winds of Iran are fairly constant: the

Photo by author

VILLAGE HOT-POTATO SELLER

4. VILLAGE BARBER. In the background is the entrance to a bath house. Cakes of dr[...]
dung, used for fuel, are piled on the wall.

southwestern and southeastern districts are noted for the 'one hundred twenty day' wind, and in Seistan the wind blows from one quarter for as long as two hundred days in the year. Windmills are ancient in Iran and may have been invented there. Records of them exist as early as the tenth century, and possibly the seventh. In addition to wind power, there are the abundant motor-fuel resources from the oil fields and the refineries of the Anglo-Iranian Oil Company, and petroleum products are sold in Iran at prices cheaper than in Europe or Asia.

D. COMMUNICATIONS

A further need of the agricultural economy of Iran is roads. Since ancient times Iran has been a land of great trade routes. The first roads for wheeled traffic, as has been noted, were probably built in Iran. Among the works left for posterity by the early Achaemenian kings was a great system of imperial highways and post roads, and the rulers in subsequent eras of national resurgence, such as the Sassanian and the Safavid, have followed the Achaemenian road-building tradition. Road building became a dominant theme in the modern resurgence of Iran, the most ambitious undertaking having been a railway system, for which nearly nine hundred miles of rails were laid between 1925 and the outbreak of World War II. In addition, some fifteen thousand miles of motor highways were constructed.

Roads

The roads opened up the cities of Iran to the commerce of the world, and within two decades wisps of gasoline vapor were drifting across the wastes in all parts of Iran, and in remote hills the camels and donkeys were being driven off the roads by the honk of automobile horns.

What the peasants need, of course, more than highways by which their wheat and dried fruits may be borne to the ports and borders, and radios and pianos and glass chandeliers brought in (since they obtain few of the proceeds from the export and enjoy less of the articles of import), is a system of farm-to-market roads, by which they can reach the bazaar with their produce while it is still fresh ('with the flowers still on them' as the cucumber peddler is wont to chant), and so that a drought and a short crop in one village may be remedied by a surplus in another.

Air Transport

Of increasing importance in world traffic is air transport, and in this respect Iran possesses strategic values that are as yet unassayed. What routes the air traffic of the future will follow is still a matter of the new geography yet to be written, in which freight- and passenger-traffic potentials are balanced against 'great circle' distances, meteorological conditions, and, not least, the political configuration of the world. Certainly a territory as vast as Iran can hardly avoid being used one way or another in going from East to West, and one of the earliest air routes, that connecting the capital of the British Empire with India, which crossed the lower corner of Iran, produced a number of acrimonious negotiations between London and Teheran.

During World War II, when direct flying between western Europe and Russia was impossible, an enormous traffic to Russia was routed via Iran, but with normal conditions in Europe there would be no economic justification for this route. How important air routes to China via Iran will be in the future also remains to be seen.

So far as the livelihood of the Iranian people is concerned, however, though these great *rocs* of the present day may alight and rise at the principal cities, and their shadows glide swiftly over the Iranian landscape, it is not likely that this phenomenon will mean any more to the common man than possibly to frighten his lambs which mistake the shadows for those of preying eagles.

Telegraph

Though modern road building has as yet hardly begun in Iran, it is an interesting fact that for many years all the principal localities of Iran have been connected by State-owned telegraph, which is supplemented today, in many of the cities, by radio communication. Iran had indeed a telegraph system extending throughout the country before it had an adequate postal system. The first telegraph line, constructed by the government, was laid in 1859 between Teheran and Sultanieh; in 1870, with the completion of the Indo-European telegraph lines in Iran, communication was afforded with London, all of Europe, and with India; and by 1892, the capital was able to communicate by telegraph with every city of importance in Iran.

Postal service, until 1874, was handled on contract by *chaparchi-bashis,* or masters of the post houses, who collected postage at both ends of the line. In 1875, an official of the Austrian Post Office, G. Riederer, was commissioned to organize a postal service on European lines, and in the following year was appointed Postmaster General. As a result of his work, Iran was admitted, in 1877, to the International Postal Union.[5]

E. Livelihood of the Artisan

Despite the modern influences that have invaded the cities of Iran, the town economy is little better than the pastoral and agricultural.

The towns and cities are the principal center of a handicraft industry, the products of which were formerly of great demand throughout the world. Besides carpets, Iranian artisans produced such wares as leather goods, embroidery work, exquisitely engraved brass and silver work, all highly prized by connoisseurs for their quality and the artistry of their design.

This state of national economy, in which the world came to the bazaars of Iran to purchase rather than to sell, and the trade balance was favorable, began to disappear at the beginning of the century. As the world turned more and more to mechanical processes by which hundreds of articles of stereotyped design could be turned out in the time that a craftsman could produce one individualized article, Iranian craftsmen faced a shrinking market for their wares even among their own people.

Beyond carpets, lambskins, opium, and certain medicinal products, there is little the Iranian merchant can offer the world that cannot be obtained elsewhere, at cheaper price,

[5] Curzon, op. cit. vol. I, p. 466.

while at the same time he is proffered myriad products from overseas to tantalize his customers and to woo them of their substance. This condition has been aggravated rather than ameliorated by the efforts to achieve economic self-sufficiency through the modernization program that has been hectically pursued during recent decades.

Factory production is still an insignificant factor in Iranian economy, although the factories are supplying the major demand for cotton goods that were formerly imported and about half the sugar requirements of the country.

F. PETROLEUM

Of mineral production, while some coal and copper is mined, and various other minerals are found that may some day be significant, the principal item of present-day interest is petroleum. Iran is rich in oil resources and oil is a product of international interest and demand. Oil, however, is a dazzling chimera in Iranian economy. In current discussion, the word 'Iran,' when it is not linked with 'Russian imperialism,' is most frequently associated with the word 'oil'—and generally the three are linked together. The oil resources of Iran, both tapped and untapped, are immense, and though production is inconsiderable by comparison with United States production, it is greater than that of any other country except Russia and Venezuela.[6]

Deposits of bitumen, associated with petroleum, had been known in ancient times, when it was used for medicinal purposes and as a binder in brick construction. The flaming of natural gas seepages, ignited by lightning or other cause, was a miraculous manifestation that may have had much to do with the cult of fire worship, subsequently identified with Zoroastrianism. The modern story of oil begins in 1901, when W. K. D'Arcy, a British subject, obtained a concession for oil exploration and development covering the whole of the southern provinces of the country and a great part of central Iran. The vastness of this concession was not realized immediately.

---

[6] Production in 1939 was 78,151,000 barrels, compared with 1,264,962,000 barrels for the United States and 216,866,000 barrels for Russia. In 1945, Iranian production was 120,000,000 barrels.

For nearly seven years shafts sunk at great expense at various points proved to be only dry holes. The concession was on the point of being abandoned for lack of funds, but D'Arcy was one of those intrepid, unflagging spirits that make history. Pleading for time, begging for money, he finally persuaded his backers to finance one more well. This was bored at Masjid-i-Sulaiman, in desolate, inaccessible country some sixty miles north of Ahwaz, in southern Iran. On 26 May 1908, it came in a 'gusher' and opened up what has since proved to be one of the most prolific oil beds in all the world. The following year the Anglo-Persian Oil Company, Ltd.,[7] was organized to prosecute the concession, but even then the project faced up-hill going, and in 1913 application had to be made to the shareholders for additional capital.

The British government had for some time been exercised about fuel supplies for the Navy, which was seeking to convert from coal to oil. Winston Churchill, then First Lord of the Admiralty, proposed that the government advance the funds required by the company, and a bill was presented to this effect. The bill was vigorously opposed, largely because of the taint of imperialism it carried, but was eventually passed, and the British government became the major shareholder, by one share, in the Anglo-Persian Oil Company. During World War I, the Iranian fields became a principal supplier of fuel requirements to the eastern fleets, and to protect the fields from the Turks and Germans the Mesopotamian campaign was undertaken, which in 1917 succeeded in securing southern Iraq.

Royalties from the oil fields have ever since constituted a substantial share of the total revenue of the government of Iran, giving it a financial independence that it would not otherwise have possessed. By 1946, the annual royalty revenue to the government was at the rate of $20,000,000 annually, while expenditures by the company in Iran for goods and services amounted to around $50,000,000 annually.

So far as being a factor in solving the crucial economic problem of Iran, however, the oil workings and the revenues

[7] The name was subsequently changed to Anglo-Iranian Oil Company, Ltd., when the government officially changed the name of the country from 'Persia' to 'Iran.'

therefrom have been insignificant. The reasons for this are: first, the production of oil requires comparatively little labor or material from Iran; that is, outside the oil-field areas it creates only a minor degree of employment for Iranian labor and skill; second, since all subsurface wealth is the property of the government, the royalty revenue flows into the public treasury rather than in diffusion throughout the economy. Essentially, what contributes to the welfare and happiness of the individual is the sense of producing something the world wants; that is, something he can take to the market and exchange for that which he desires. While it may sound very fine that his government possesses an Aladdin's lamp, which it need only rub to bless the country with all the goods that the shops of the world offer, it does not solve his individual problem, except perhaps by reducing his tax burden.

Actually, as we shall observe later, the effect of this flow of revenue to the State was not to reduce the burden of taxes, but to increase it.

V

MORALS AND RELIGION

A. THE MALADY OF IRAN

IRAN cannot be called a happy country. Despite the introduction of modern culture from the West, despite the increasing flow of revenue to the State from oil royalties, despite political reforms and the spread of the tradition and processes of democracy, despite the improvement of communications, the embellishment of the principal cities, and the surface appearance of a greater material well-being, life in Iran remains affected with pessimism and with futility of spirit.

'We should not praise ourselves by saying that once upon a time Cyrus the Great conquered the whole world. In what other country can you find today so many traitors, adulterators and embezzlers, all immune from punishment?' was the dejected comment of Deputy Ali Dashti in the Majlis debates leading to the engagement of foreign advisers in 1942.[1]

A veil of sadness lies over life in Iran. The prevailing colors are somber. The typical outdoor dress of Iranian women, until recently, was the black *chaddar*, which enveloped them from head to foot. Their Friday custom was to gather in the cemeteries to mourn. In the mosques, the places of religious worship, no hymns are sung, but only wail-like chants. Music is not a part of Moslem worship. Except in the largest cities, parks and places of public recreation are rare, though now more frequent than before.

Loneliness is a characteristic of the ordinary Iranian. The high wall which is still a typical feature of both urban and rural construction, and the veil for women, only recently thrown aside, are evidence and symbol of the exclusiveness of the social spirit. Clubs and social organizations, so common in the West, are practically unknown in Iran. Associations

[1] Millspaugh, A. C., *Americans in Persia*, Washington, 1946, p. 54.

deteriorate under the corroding effects of a general suspicion
and distrust of others. One who moves among the people will
be struck by how few close friends or intimates the ordinary
Iranian enjoys, compared with the ordinary man of the West.
Even those who possess the advantages of wealth, education
abroad, and social rank are often the most prescribed in their
associations, and unable to claim a circle of intimates extending further than the range of family ties. These, and many
like them, come eagerly to the foreigner with their affection,
their confidences, and with their yearnings. Among them will
be found an acute loneliness and dejection, ill concealed by
parties and conversation and card leaving.

What are the causes of this pessimism of life, what virus
produces this *malaise* of the spirit?

This is a question the Iranians have asked as eagerly as
anyone.

Iran is not a hermit kingdom; the national spirit is not one
of exclusiveness and suspicion of other peoples. Unlike Japan,
Afghanistan, and the principalities of Arabia, Iran has never
been closed to intercourse with the world. While some xeno-
phobia exists, foreigners generally have been welcomed to its
bastioned uplands and freely admitted to its courts and revered
cities. Foreign counselors since the times of the brothers Sherley, of Queen Elizabeth's day, and earlier, have been honored
and consulted; particularly since the twentieth century, Iran
has welcomed the wisdom of the West in solving its problems.
More than that, shahs and the sons of nobles have gone abroad
to inquire into the secrets of well-being in the West and the
cure to the ills at home.

Materialistic Influences

What is the wisdom these students and patriots have brought
home? In Europe and America they learned, according to the
fashion of nineteenth-century thought, that education was the
universal panacea; that knowledge was the key to life; that
knowledge brought enlightenment, and enlightenment brought
universal peace, justice, and well-being. More recently, since
the twentieth century, they have brought home a new creed
from the West (and North): now, they learned, it was environment that conditioned happiness; material factors governed

the state of well-being; when the standard of living had been elevated, all men would be at peace, and social conflict would disappear.[2] The great objects of governmental policy, they were told, should be to increase the material resources of the nation, and to remove from its citizens the fear of economic insecurity.

How strange it must have seemed to these students from a land where a porter counts himself fortunate if he can have a little tea to go with his bread and cheese, and blessed indeed to have a little sugar to go with the tea, to discover that in a land so wealthy as America, where a carpenter rides to work in his own automobile, the preoccupation of statesmen and churchmen, of rich and poor, was that of the 'standard of living' and how it might be increased. No wonder they returned to their native land from a sojourn abroad with greater disquiet than before, convinced of the universal futility of existence, imbued with the dejected melancholy of their poet Omar who

> . . . did eagerly frequent
> Doctor and Saint, and heard great argument
> About it and about: but evermore
> Came out by the same door where in I went.

B. THE INFLUENCE OF ISLAM

The Christian view of life is that the elemental cause of man's unhappiness is sin, that is, that the fundamental problem of life is moral rather than economic.[3] The Christian emphasis on the moral aspects of life is one shared, if to a lesser degree, by the ancient faith of Iran, that of Zoroastrianism, in which the cosmos is viewed as an eternal conflict between the forces of righteousness, under Ahura Mazda, and the forces of evil under Ahriman, the power of darkness, in which man is called upon to wage battle under the banner of Ahura Mazda.

[2] 'With me . . . the ideal is nothing else than the material world reflected in the human mind, and translated into forms of thought.' (Karl Marx, *Das Kapital*. Preface to Second Edition.)

[3] 'Wherefore, as by one man [Adam] sin entered into the world, and death by sin; and so death passed upon all men, for that all have sinned.' (Romans v: 12.)

A consideration of the prevailing condition of Iran, from the Christian point of view, must inevitably take into account the moral values by which life is appraised, the prevailing standards of behavior, and the concepts held about man's relation to the Universe.[4] These are all bound up in, and a product of, the religious faith to which the inhabitants adhere. This faith is Islam.

Moslem Doctrine

Following the battle of Nehavend in A.D. 642, between the Persians and the Arabs, and the subsequent extinction of the Sassanian Empire, the religion of Zoroaster practically disappeared from Iran and was replaced by that of Islam, which the prophet Mohammed had proclaimed and under which the Arabs had been united and set upon a career of conquest and proselytization.

Among the Arabs, to whom the faith of Islam was first proclaimed, it brought many benefits. It supplanted a prevailing polytheism with a stern, uncompromising belief in one God; it abolished idol worship and priestcraft; it enjoined brotherly love among fellow believers, proscribed infanticide, and secured improvements in the status of women and slaves. It forbade wine drinking. As it spread from Arabia eastward to the borders of China and westward across North Africa and into Spain, it brought a political and religious unification of diverse peoples and a diffusion of the culture of the more civilized peoples within its embrace. Much of the culture that modern Europe inherited from the past was drawn from Islamic countries where it had been preserved from destruction at a time when conditions in Europe were adverse to its preservation.[5]

---

[4] Since Iran is a Moslem rather than a Christian country, it may, of course, be inappropriate to appraise the condition of the Iranian people from the Christian point of view. A Communist, appraising conditions from the point of view of dialectical materialism, might conclude that the basic problem was economic.

[5] Incidentally, much of this heritage of culture that passed into Europe under the name of Arabian or Saracenic was actually Persian, drawn into Islamic civilization following the conquest of Iran. The so-called *Arabian Nights Entertainment* (*The Thousand Nights and a Night*) was, for instance, a collection of Persian tales.

From a religious standpoint, a chief contribution of Islam was a purification of worship. All forms of deistic representation are strictly prohibited, images, ikons, or other symbols of deity being notably absent from any Moslem house of worship. There are, likewise, no altars in Islam and no complicated liturgy. The act of worship is refreshingly austere and simple: wherever the Believer may find himself at the stated hours of prayer, there he kneels—facing Mecca, the Prophet's birth-place—and makes his orisons to God the Compassionate, the Merciful. Priestly intermediation between God and man is not a part of Moslem doctrine; there exists no apostolic succession, no sacraments, and no one is ordained to pronounce even a benediction. The principal features of Moslem congregational worship are the reading of the Koran, sermons by clerics, and prayer rites in unison.

From the minarets of the mosques are chanted five times daily the *azan,* the Moslem call to prayer, and the minarets themselves are symbolic of the Islamic faith. 'As the minaret mounts into the sky, so must the soul seeking its God grope heavenward alone. Supported by buttresses, or joined to other structures, the minaret ceases to be a tower. And so it is with man. No priest can guide, no tongue but his alone can utter his soul's cry.'

And in this analogy of man's relation to God can be found an explanation of the democracy within Islam which so many travelers from Christendom have remarked. Within the following of the Prophet exists a brotherhood which, though it extends no further, is capable of bringing into union the Aryan Persian, the Semitic chieftain, and the savage from Africa, to kneel without let or hindrance side by side in the same mosque, or to marry their daughters with the others' sons. And in this same spirit one may often observe the *khan* and his servant sitting down together in the tea house to drink tea together or to smoke from the same *kalyan.*[6]

The holy book of the Moslem is the Koran, containing the

[6] This and the preceding quotation are from my 'The Mosque,' the *Atlantic Monthly,* November 1925. Paradoxically, while diverse races and colors unite in brotherhood within the mosque, no unbeliever is ordinarily permitted within its precincts, nor is it customary for women to enter.

words of God as revealed through his Apostle, Mohammed.
It comprises stories of the prophets and apostles from Adam
to Jesus; laws regulating family life, and personal, tribal, and
national affairs; exhortations to good works and admonitions
to evil doers; and vivid descriptions of the sensual delights of
Paradise and the torments of Hell. In its more exalted passages it reaches heights of sublimity approaching those of
some of the Hebraic psalms. The following is an example:

The Fatiha (opening chapter)

Praise be to God, Lord of the worlds!
The compassionate, the merciful!
King on the day of reckoning!
Thee only do we worship, and to Thee do we cry for help.
Guide Thou us on the straight path,
The path of those to whom Thou hast been gracious; with
whom Thou art not angry, and who go not astray.

Sura 1 [7]

Moral Code

The moral code of Islam is summarized in the five-fold
obligation of the Moslem to (a) keep the fast (to abstain from
food or drink from sunrise to sunset during the lunar month
of Ramazan); (b) to make the pilgrimage to Mecca (at least
once in a lifetime); (c) to pray (to make stated devotions five
times daily); (d) to bear witness to the Faith by recital of the
Creed ('There is no God but God, and Mohammed is His
Prophet'); and (e) to give alms (nominally a fortieth of one's
possessions).

Salutary as this code may be regarded, it falls short of the
ethical standards set forth in the Mosaic Decalogue, or the
summary of the Law as stated by Jesus.[8] It is generally considered as falling below the moral precepts of Zoroastrianism.

The Moslem moral code is a rigid system of rules of conduct
operating under the sanction of rewards and punishments,

[7] From J. M. Rodwell's translation of the Koran. This sura will be
found inscribed over doorways and on the title page of books; it is recited
daily at prayer.

[8] 'Thou shalt love the Lord thy God with all thy heart . . . and . . .
thy neighbor as thyself. . . On these two commandments hang all the
law and the prophets.' (Matthew XXII: 37-40.)

graded according to five categories: (a) obligatory acts (*vajeb*), (b) recommended acts (*mobah*), (c) permissible acts (*mostahab*), (d) disapproved acts (*makruh*), and (e) forbidden acts (*haram*). Obligatory and recommended acts are rewarded in Paradise if performed; omission of obligatory acts is punishable, while failure to perform recommended acts is not punishable. Permissible acts are neither rewarded nor punished, disapproved acts are not punished, while forbidden acts are punished and abstinence from forbidden acts is rewarded.

Sins are acts forbidden by God, regardless of the circumstances. There is no room for the operation of conscience. The ceremonial and the moral law are indistinguishable. It is as much a sin to pray without washing one's feet in the proper manner as to tell a lie. Adultery is no more sinful than eating a piece of bacon. Sins, however, are frequently divided into two main classes: great sins and little sins. The seven great sins are described as idolatry, murder, false charge of adultery, wasting the estate of orphans, taking interest on money, desertion from holy war, and disobedience of parents. Wine drinking and adultery are sometimes classified as great sins.[9]

Fatalistic Outlook

Supplementing this summary of the Moslem obligation is a great body of customary law and tradition, found partly in the Koran and partly in the commentaries of Moslem theologians, and similar to the Mosaic law and tradition in its applicability to the whole realm of human affairs, the effect of which was to create, in principle, a theocratic state. As a force in history, the Koranic law suffered from the defect that it was without the elements of growth; the standards it set were those adapted to the needs and conditions of primitive Arab tribes of the seventh century. The result is that today in Islamic countries the Koranic law represents an enclave of medievalism in the surrounding modernism, and in most Islamic countries it has been abrogated officially or its application has been severely limited.

Thus, while Islam may have ameliorated the condition of

[9] Titus, Murray T., *The Young Moslem Looks at Life*, New York, 1937, p. 81.

women and slaves among its earlier adherents, there was no moral dynamic at work to continue this amelioration. The result has been that while in Christendom slavery has been abolished and woman, as a child of God, is gradually achieving equality with man, in Islam slavery is still tolerated by the Koranic law, and the condition of woman, even in the more advanced countries, is still one of degradation by Western standards.

The absence of moral dynamic, or moral growth, which characterizes Islam, is traceable to the basic conception the religion indoctrinates concerning the relation between man and God. In Zoroastrianism, as has been remarked, man is accorded a highly important, if not crucial, position in the scheme of things. In the eternal warfare of the heavens, between good and evil, the powers of righteousness call upon man to lend his aid in defense of the right. In Christian theology, God, while infinite in attribute, renounces His infinitude for the sake of man in order that man may enter into communion with God.[10] In Islam no such bridge exists. God, being infinite in attribute, is unknowable by man, who is finite in attribute. The word *Islam* means, literally, submission (to the will of God). The predestination by God of good and evil, which is implicit in this conception, leads to the well-known Moslem doctrine of *Kismet,* or fate, expressed in the phrase, 'Every man's fate have we written on his forehead.'

The hopeless view of life, so far as spiritual growth and redemption is concerned, is aptly, if cynically, expressed in the couplet from the *Rubaiyat,* characterizing mankind as

> But helpless Pieces of the Game He plays
> Upon this Chequer-board of Nights and Days.

'As a goat or a duck cannot change its nature, being so created by Allah, neither can a man rise above his condition, nor should I aspire to be more than a clerk,' said my Moslem secretary to me one day.

[10] 'Forasmuch then as the children are partakers of flesh and blood, he also himself likewise took part of the same; that through death he might destroy him that had the power of death, that is, the devil.' (Hebrews II: 14.)

Mendacity

A Moslem doctrine, which received considerable development among Shi'a Moslems—the branch of the faith to which most Iranians adhere—is that of *taqia,* or dissimulation for self-preservation. Specifically, the doctrine of *taqia* granted the Faithful the indulgence of dissimulating their faith if, while on a pilgrimage, they were challenged by unfriendly infidels.[11] By logical extension of the doctrine, almost any form of deceit may be justified. Thus the teaching arose: 'Verily a lie is allowable in three cases—to women, to reconcile friends, and in war.'

Approbation of deceit permeates Persian literature and innumerable stories are told in praise of cleverness by ruse. The opening story of the celebrated *Gulistan* of Sa'di—probably the most popular literary work in Iran—is one that extols the 'white lie.' [12]

The effect of this teaching has been a development of mendacity as an Iranian characteristic remarked by most travelers to that country. The Iranians themselves acknowledge their failings in this respect.

Some years ago, the Reverend J. Christy Wilson was in conversation with a prominent official of Azerbaijan. The conversation turned to the respective contributions of various peoples to the sum of human culture. The official remarked that the world was indebted to the French for art, to the British for government and administration, to Americans for industry and mechanical science.

'And to what are we indebted to Persia?' inquired Dr. Wilson.

The official considered a moment.

'I suppose,' he said, 'that were it not for Persia, the world would be at a loss for liars.'

[11] Mohammed may have found his authority for this in the Biblical account of Abraham's journeys, during which the Patriarch, to avoid molestation, passed off his wife Sara as his sister. (Genesis XII: 11-20; XX: 2-8.) Abraham, as the father of the Arabs (through the offspring of Hagar) is revered as one of the prophets.

[12] The story ends with the following couplet:

> Words which beguile thee, but thy heart make glad,
> Outvalue truth which makes thy temper sad.

Deprecatory modesty may have been intended by this statement, but it remained a candid admission of a condition that is endemic in Iran.

The corrupting influence of Islam upon the Iranian national character may be illustrated by comparing the doctrine of *taqia,* as developed by Shi'a Moslems, with the corresponding teachings of Zoroaster, to which the people adhered prior to the Arab invasion in the seventh century.

Zoroaster identified all evil with the Lie—Druj it was called, or Ahriman, the Principle of Evil, against which all men should war. The importance of truth as a principle of behavior is illustrated by the following passages from the Avestic Gathas:

'In immortality shall the soul of the righteous be joyful, in perpetuity shall be the torments of the liars.' [13]

'The Liar stays the supporters of Right from prospering the cattle in district and province, infamous that he is, repellent by his actions.' [14]

'It is they, the liars, who destroy life.' [15]

'And there shall be for you the reward of this Covenant, if only most faithful zeal be with the wedded pair, that the spirit of the Liar, shrinking and cowering, may fall into perdition in the abyss.' [16]

Again and again these admonitions occur in the Gathas, the earliest Avestic hymns, which find their echo in the Biblical, 'He (Satan) is a lie and the father of it.'

How earnestly these teachings were taken to heart, how implicit they became in the standard of Persian virtue is well attested by Herodotus. Summarizing the fundamentals of Persian character, he wrote: 'Every boy is taught to ride, to draw the bow, and to tell the truth.' [17] And Darius, in his great Bisitun inscription, recounting his many conquests, reiterates '. . . I put down the Lie.'

How the Lie has corrupted the spirit of institutions in Iran today may be illustrated by the testimony of a certain Iranian woman who is now a professed Christian. She was, when I met her, about forty years of age, and a medical student at the

[13] Yasna XLV.
[14] Yasna XLVI.
[15] Yasna XXXII.
[16] Yasna LIII.
[17] *History,* Book I, ch. 136.

University of Teheran. I inquired about her conversion to Christianity. She explained:

While a student at the missionary school, I formed a great desire to be of help to my people. After leaving school, I did a number of things for which I was equipped by the education I had—such as teaching and office work—but there kept returning to me the call to a greater service. I had concluded that as disease seemed to be the greatest curse that afflicted our country I should become a physician. I enrolled in the University. I soon discovered, however, that I would never be able to complete my studies alone. I needed help. And so I went to the city of Hamadan, where I sought out Rev. Cady Allen, who had years before been my teacher, and told him my troubles. He suggested that I pray for help. I spent two weeks in the home of the Allens, and then the light dawned. It was not disease that was the curse of Iran, but sin, and for sin Islam offered no hope, but only further sin. Only Christ can redeem the world from sin. And so I accepted Christ as my Saviour.

I asked the woman why she had not been able to complete her studies without becoming a Christian. She answered:

Because I could not combat, without Jesus in my heart, the corruption and sin that everywhere assailed me. I was unwilling to bribe for marks, or to cheat for grades. That is the accepted method of obtaining a degree. Payments for marks are a chief source of income to the professors. It is in the order of things. We can have no true progress until we have honesty among our people and we can have no honesty among the people so long as deceit and corruption and bribery are taught them in the schools in which they are supposed to establish the principles of their lives. Here is the very fountainhead of corruption. The truth cannot be born of a lie, nor can a dishonest educational system produce honest men.

Degradation of Women

The position of women as a social class has already been described. The extent to which the sex was degraded by the tenets of Islam may be indicated by passages from the Koran, the sacred book and law of the Faith: 'Ye may divorce your wives twice. . . But if the husband divorce her a third time, it is not lawful for him to take her again, until she shall have married another husband.' (Sura II, *The Cow*.) 'And if ye be desirous to exchange one wife for another, and have given one of them a talent, make no deduction from it.' (Sura IV, *Women.*)

Moslems explain that what Mohammed intended by these injunctions was to elevate the status of women above that prevailing in his day, and to free them from the confinement of Judaistic law that was customary among the Arabs. The fact remains, however, that the Islamic domestic standard is an anomaly that is tacitly recognized by most Moslems themselves.

Religious Spectacles

A feature of Iranian life, tolerated by Shi'a Islam, and only recently abolished, has been the various religious spectacles, in which emotional excess reaches a depth of barbarity. The principal of these is the celebration of the Tenth of Moharram, which has both a religious and nationalistic character.

Moharram is the name of the first month in the Islamic lunar calendar, and the celebration takes place during the first ten days of the month, culminating on the tenth in a spectacle of sadistic frenzy. The occasion is one of mourning for Ali, Hussein, and Hassan, martyred claimants to the caliphate succession in the great political schism that divided the Islamic world into the *Sunni* and the *Shi'a*. Ali was the Prophet Mohammed's son-in-law, to whom, according to the Shi'a Moslems, the mantle of the Prophet should have passed. Instead, it went by election to Abu-Bekr, one of the Prophet's companions, and subsequently to Omar, and to Othman. On the death of Othman, Ali at last obtained the succession by election, but a schism developed; Ali was murdered by a dissident sectarian, and the succession passed by force to Muavia. The followers of Ali revolted and proclaimed as caliph Ali's son, Hassan, but Hassan soon renounced his claims under the threats of Muavia. After Muavia's death (A.D. 680) the Shi'a faction advanced Ali's second son, Hussein, as contender for the caliphate. A battle followed between the rival factions; Hussein and most of his followers were killed on the tenth of Moharram A.H. 61 (A.D. 680), and their heads were carried on lances through the streets of Kufa.

The cause of Ali disappeared, but did not perish, and Ali and his sons were revered as martyrs in Iran. The identifica-

tion of the cause of Ali with Iranian nationalism arose from
the submerged resentment at the Arabian conquest of Iran—
it was Omar, regarded by the Shi'as as an unlawful successor
to the caliphate, who sent Arab forces into Iran and destroyed
the Sassanian Empire at the battle of Nehavend, in A.D. 642—
and from the fact that Hussein had married a daughter of
the last Sassanian king, and so united in his succession the
blood of the Prophet with that of the Iranian royal house.

Shi'ism, as the party of Ali and Hussein came to be known,
continued to spread in Iran, and in 1502, with the rise of the
Iranian Safavid dynasty, it was proclaimed the national religion and the celebration of the martyrdom became a national
festival.

Celebration of Moharram

A principal feature of the celebration, which occurred in
every city and hamlet, was the procession of *flagellantes*—long
lines of men of all ages, including mere boys, gowned in black
with bared backs, bearing steel lashes and chains with which
they beat their backs to the intonation of '*Shah Hussein, Wah
Hassan*' ('King Hussein, also Hassan').

The spectacle reached a pitch of frenzy on the tenth day of
Moharram. In the cities the whole population turned out; no
work was done, and along the route of the processions the
streets and the roofs would be lined with watchers. The women,
in their black *chaddars,* kept to the roofs for safety where they
gave the appearance of rows of tightly packed starlings on a
ledge. On the Tenth of Moharram the lashes were abandoned
for a more ghastly form of self-mutilation. On the Tenth,
those who walked in the processions were gowned in white,
heads were bared and shaven; each man, each boy, carried a
sword, and at every intonation of the martyrs' names, would
strike his head. Blood flowed down the face; the white robes
were covered with blood; the intonation became a chant, a
wail that was taken up by the crowd, increased in tempo until
the syllables were blurred into a confused '*Shahsy, Wahsy,*' so
that the processions have been called the Shahsy-Wahsy processions. So frenzied did the participants become that to protect them, relatives and friends would walk along beside them,
carrying staves. When the blows became too intoxicated, they

would intercept them with the staff.[18] Many fainted from loss
of blood and were carried away on litters. At the head of some
of the processions walked those who were inured to torture:
they were almost naked, and into their bare flesh they would
thrust pins and flesh hooks to show their devotion to the
martyrs.

On the Tenth of Moharram it was unsafe for any but a
Moslem to appear in the streets: Armenians, Nestorians, Jews,
and foreigners, as a rule, kept indoors.

It was the custom for the governor or chief official of the
district to stand with his dignitaries in the principal *maidan,*
or square, and review the processions.

As late as 1922, when I last witnessed them, the celebrations
were carried on with official approval and with unabated
frenzy. In 1928, however, the Government forbade the infliction
of head wounds; subsequently officials were prohibited from
reviewing the processions; and in 1935 the celebrations were
prohibited entirely.

In 1935, also, the Id-i-Kourban, or Feast of the Sacrifice, in
which a gaily caparisoned camel was publicly butchered as a
sacrifice in the principal square, was abolished. This is a festival which, while celebrated both by Sunni and Shi'a Moslems, probably is a vestige of an ancient Magi and Arab
religious custom.

C. The System of Mudakhil

A corrupting factor in the official, commercial, and domestic
life of Iran which has been frequently commented on by observers is the system of *mudakhil.* The word may be freely
translated, 'what comes to me.' It implies, according to its
context, commission, perquisite, consideration, stealing, profit,
and it may be said to signify that balance of personal advantage, usually expressed in money form, that can be extracted
from any and every transaction. As Curzon said,

In no country that I have ever seen or heard of in the world is the
system so open, so shameless, or so universal as in Persia. So far from

[18] I have seen frenzied celebrants turn aside to avoid this protection and
strike with redoubled force. See my 'The Mosque, the *Atlantic Monthly,*
November 1925.

being limited to the sphere of domestic economy or to commercial
transactions, it permeates every walk and inspires most of the actions
of life. By its operation, generosity or gratuitous service may be said
to have been erased in Persia from the category of social virtues, and
cupidity has been elevated into the guiding principle of human
conduct.[19]

The consideration obtained for a favor or a service constituted the *mudakhil;* to the donor it was a *pishkesh,* or gift
(literally, 'that which leads or comes before'). It was the custom for every recipient of public office to make a gift to the
person from whom he received it. Each office holder in turn
required *pishkesh* from those who held office under him. This
requirement proceeded downward to the humblest clerk and
the policeman on his beat, who, having no one beneath from
whom to obtain his *mudakhil,* extracted it from any and every
one.

A friend of mine told me of a young Iranian who is employed in one of the State ministries. Recently he heard that
the young man had received a promotion. He hastened to
congratulate him. 'No, no, commiserate me rather,' said the
young man disconsolately. 'And why? Is it not a promotion?
Also do not you enjoy a higher salary, greater responsibilities
and honor?' 'Yes, yes,' sighed the young man, 'but not greater
perquisites.' 'What do you mean?' 'Why,' explained the young
man, 'now I am upstairs, in a large room, where I meet only
those who are shown to me, whereas formerly I sat at a little
desk in the antechamber, and could exact fees for the privilege
of showing people to the man whose chair I now occupy.'

An offense against the laws could be absolved by an appropriate *pishkesh,* which was a sort of unofficial fine, which
neither went into the public treasury nor carried the disgrace
of a fine. To be fined was an official humiliation not only for
the culprit but for his family and kinsmen. Iranian justice
was often swayed by such regard for the feelings of the accused.

The story is told that Aga Mohammed Shah, eighteenth-
century founder of the Kajar dynasty, hearing a peasant, whose
ears he had ordered to be cut off, promising the executioner
a few pieces of silver if only the tips were cut, notified the

[19] Op. cit. vol. I, p. 441.

peasant that if the *pishkesh* were doubled, in the shah's favor, he could save his ears entirely.[20]

In trade, a bargain was sealed by a *pishkesh*, a practice similar to that found in the West, in vestige, in the bonus. In addition to a stipulated, or customary, *pishkesh*, however, the transaction might be loaded with not so apparent *mudakhil*. An agent would extract a commission, or *mudakhil*, on every purchase made for his principal. A cook required his *mudakhil* on the food he bought for the table. A servant, on being engaged, would inquire how much rice was used in the house, in order to measure his *mudakhil*. The system reached its height in the annual New Year's presents to the shah. Every governor, minister, chief of a tribe, or official of any rank, then made his offering, the minimum amount of which was determined by custom, and the maximum left to the means or ambition of the donor. During the reign of the Kajars, in the nineteenth century, these presents often accounted for as much as a fifth to a third of the fixed revenue.

Curzon's comments on the system of *mudakhil* were written over fifty years ago. Most present-day observers make less mention of it, particularly in regard to governmental administration. In part, this has been due to the establishment of constitutional government in 1906, which, while weak, served to regularize the administration, provide more steady sources of revenue, and relieve somewhat the dependence of functionaries upon perquisites and illicit income. A more important factor has been a generally rising standard of official and personal conduct, of which more will be said later.

D. THE OPIUM PROBLEM

A survey of the moral condition of the Iranian people would not be complete without reference to the problem of opium.

In spring, upon the high Iranian plateau, particularly in the region of Isfahan, the traveler will come upon fields of tall, crimson flowers. These flowers produce a crop that is at once one of the principal sources of livelihood to peasant and merchant, and of revenue to the government, and the most serious

---

[20] Sykes, op. cit. vol. II, p. 295.

menace to the health, morals, and even the economic well-being of the country. These flowers are the opium poppy (*Papaver somniferum*). Its juice is opium, a powerful narcotic, a mixture of about twenty alkaloids, the most important of which is morphine.

Opium serves as a valuable component of medicines and as such is a boon to mankind; a good deal more opium is consumed directly, as a sedative, in which use it is a curse, since it weakens the body, destroys or perverts the senses, and corrupts the morals of the user. The greatest consumers of opium for this purpose have been among the peoples of Asia, principally the Chinese, to whom it was introduced by European traders, particularly the British, exporting the drug from India and Iran. Of recent years, the use of opium, in the more pernicious forms of its derivatives, morphine and heroin, has spread in Europe and the Western Hemisphere.

The history of opium cultivation in Iran is relatively recent. The story begins with the Anglo-Chinese opium war of 1840-42 when the Chinese emperor attempted to prohibit the importation of Indian opium into China by British and other foreign traders. As the result of that war, Hong Kong became a British possession, through which an enormous trade in opium developed. At that time, in Iran, the opium poppy was grown only to a limited extent, in the region of Yezd, and it was not until 1853 that opium as an item of export first appeared in the Iranian customs statistics. Cultivation of the opium poppy was stimulated in part by this demand, in part as a result of a blight, the pébrine, which in 1864 attacked the silkworm and all but destroyed the Persian silk culture. Until that time, Iran had been a principal source of silk in the European market. Attempts to introduce Japanese cocoons, and later Italian cocoons, did not fare well, and the Iranian peasants began to turn to poppy cultivation as a substitute crop.

The soil and climate of Iran are highly favorable to the growing of the opium poppy, and economic factors tend to foster its cultivation. The poppy is planted in the autumn for spring harvest, and thus it can be grown when the moisture content of the arid Iranian plateau is most abundant; it is harvested in time for summer crops such as melons and tobacco. Because of the concentrated nature of the product, and the high unit value (around $10 a pound in legitimate trade and many times that price in illicit trade), the grower is not troubled by the problem of transportation to market, so vital in a land of vast distances and poor roads as Iran.

The poppy is grown today in eighteen of the twenty-six provinces of Iran; its cultivation is an occupation engaging an estimated 20 per cent of the population. The value of the crop, until recent years, was exceeded only by that of wheat and barley; the revenue from the opium tax provided as much as 10 per cent of the government revenue.

Iran has become a principal source of opium in contraband trade. Formerly, it was in substantial demand by pharmaceutical houses, for medicinal use, because of its superior quality and high morphine content, which runs from 12 to 12½ per cent, compared with up to 10 per cent for the Chinese opium and 7 to 7½ per cent for the Indian; but the unwillingness of the Iranian government to place any effective control on its production and export led the legitimate trade, particularly that of the United States, to turn to Turkey, where such controls have been established, and the greater part of American imports now come from Turkey. It is estimated that Iran produces some 30 per cent of the world supply of opium, but because of the immense amount of contraband trade, any estimates are liable to be wide of the mark, as are figures for production and consumption.

The cultivation of the poppy is a natural inducement to the use of opium. After the flower has blown but before the seed has matured, peasants and townsfolk flock into the fields for the harvest. This is done by incising the seed pod. The juice exudes at these incisions, and collects in a reddish-brown, sticky, gum-like substance. The following morning the harvesters again go into the fields and gather this sap into copper bowls by means of spoon-shaped scrapers. These copper bowls are required to be delivered to the government warehouse in the village, where the peasant is paid for his produce; but much of this gum never reaches the warehouse. Wandering among the villagers will be mendicants with their wooden begging bowls who, in place of alms, may be granted the boon of dipping a spoon into the sap. Babies, when they cry, may be allowed to suck the sticky fingers of their mothers. Much of the crop is concealed for later sale through smugglers who offer a higher price than the government rate.

The international efforts that have been made to control the production and distribution of opium, and the attitude of the Iranian government toward these efforts, will be discussed in a later chapter. The gravity of the opium problem for the Iranians may be indicated by estimates, however tentative, that the number of opium smokers and opium eaters in Iran ran from 25 to 50 per cent of the population before World War II, and today runs as high as 75 per cent. The deleterious effect of such widespread addiction upon the health of the people can hardly be exaggerated.

E. CHRISTIAN MISSIONS

A constructive force among the Iranian people, combating the deteriorating influences above described, sowing the seeds of regeneration, is that of the Christian religion, the importance of which can hardly be ignored in any appraisal of the present situation. Christianity, once influential—though never predominant—throughout Iran, but long submerged and almost impotent during the ascendancy of Islam, has experienced a renascence, particularly during the past hundred years, since the advent of the modern missionary movement. A discussion of the impact of Christian missions upon the Iranian people must be reserved for a later chapter, but here a brief survey of Christian evangelism may be offered.

The earliest evangels to Iran were the Nestorians, the ancient Assyrians who in the first century accepted the Christ preached to them by the Apostles Thaddeus and Thomas and whose Church is known as the Church of the East. In succeeding centuries they sent their missionaries throughout Iran, Bactria, Tartary, India, and China; during the fourth and fifth centuries they maintained as many as thirty-two metropolitan sees, each see comprising from seven to fifteen bishoprics, stretching from the Mediterranean to the Pacific; the Church of the East at that time was greater in its number of adherents and its influence than the Western organizations of Christendom. To this day, in China, almost submerged by the surrounding Confucianism and Buddhism, are colonies of Christians who maintain, if feebly, the rites and traditions of the Church of the East.

During the Sassanian Empire (226-642), Christian influence was considerable throughout Iran, and some of the kings are said to have been adherents to the faith—among them Shapur I (241-72), and Chosroes II Parviz (591-628), who married a Christian, the Shirin of Persian legend—while translations of the Gospel into Persian exist from a date as early as 1282. This did not prevent serious persecutions of the faithful, however, since Christianity came to be identified with Roman influence. The rise of Islam and its spread throughout Iran after 642 was a further antagonistic influence.

Towards the end of the fourteenth century the scourge of Timur the Lame, the Tartar, fell upon the Church of the East, and its scattered and decimated adherents retired in poverty and distress to the mountain fortresses north of Mesopotamia.

From the seventh century on, as a result of the Islamic conquests, Iran had become almost wholly Moslem, and by the beginning of the twentieth century, the Christians, both of the Nestorian and the Armenian faith, numbered only a few hundred thousand.

Modern Missionary Effort

Missionary activity on the part of Western Christendom was begun in the early years of the seventeenth century, with the arrival in Isfahan of Augustinian friars, sent from Hormuz (under Portuguese control), and Carmelite friars, sent, by way of Russia, by Pope Clement VIII. These missionaries came originally in the dual capacity of political emissaries and Christian evangelists. The Carmelite mission was of the greater importance and established an evangelistic work that continued, with varying fortunes, until 1780, when it finally disappeared during the chaotic conditions in Iran following the death of Nadir Shah in 1747. Roman Catholic missionary work in Iran was not revived until 1850 when Lazarists began work in Tabriz.

The records of the Carmelite fathers in Iran have been generally neglected by historians of Iran, and the part they played in opening up diplomatic and cultural relations between Iran and the West has generally gone unrecognized.[21] Their dispatch to Iran was the result of letters received by Pope Clement VIII, brought from the Persian Shah Abbas by the English adventurer, Sir Anthony Sherley. Papal policy for many years had been directed towards a coalition of Christian powers to wage war against the Turks, whose empire was still expanding at the expense of Christendom. Shah Abbas had come to the throne in Persia and was waging successful warfare against the Turks from the East. He proposed, in the letters sent by Sherley, joint operations against the Turks, and offered in return hospitality and protection to Christians in his realm and freedom for evangelistic work.

The opportunity to organize a political and military coalition against the Turks, as well as to establish Catholic missionary work in Persia, appealed to the Pope, and to further these objects he requested the services of the Carmelites. The selection of Carmelites for such a mission was somewhat paradoxical. The Carmelites were pledged to poverty, obedience, and chastity. Until this time, moreover, they had confined themselves largely to contemplation and asceticism, and missionary evangelism was not regarded as within their sphere. They agreed, nevertheless, to undertake the mission, and three fathers of the Order,[22] accompanied by two lay brothers, one of whom was a military tactician, set forth in 1604, by way of Russia.

[21] In 1927 there appeared a volume, *A Chronicle of Events between the years 1623 and 1733 relating to the Settlement of the Order of Carmelites in Mesopotamia* (Oxford University Press, Sir Hermann Gollancz, ed., London, 1927), a transcription, accompanied by an English translation, of a manuscript from the archives of the Carmelite mission at Basra. Beyond a reference to the fact that the manuscript was acquired by purchase, no indication of its origin was given, but it appears to have been one of a number of manuscripts sold by Arab caretakers during a hiatus in the mission a quarter century earlier. The appearance of this work inspired an anonymous historian to make an exhaustive research of the archives of the Order at Basra and at Rome, as well as the secret Vatican archives, and in 1939 there was published in England, in two volumes, a work entitled *A Chronicle of the Carmelites in Persia,* giving a comprehensive survey, from original sources, of the establishment of the mission in 1604 until its final disappearance in 1780.

[22] Fr. Paul Simon, Fr. John Thaddeus, and Fr. Vincent. Fr. Paul Simon returned in 1608 with letters from the Shah to the Pope, and a little later

The monks were detained in Russia, then in political confusion because of the usurpation of the tsardom by Boris
Godounov, and did not reach the court of the shah until 1607.
The two lay brothers died en route. Throughout the reign of
Shah Abbas the Carmelite fathers continued to act as quasi-
ambassadors of the Pope, and meantime to press for the privilege of opening a church and of baptizing converts. They
translated the Gospels into Persian. The failure of diplomacy
to effect a coalition between the power of Persia and that of
Christendom against the Turk caused Shah Abbas' interest in
the Carmelites to cool, and in the latter years of his reign
they were subjected to considerable persecution, and but for
the high regard in which they were personally held by the
Shah—their asceticism and truthfulness seem to have made a
great impression on the monarch—they might have been expelled. Following the death of Shah Abbas and the development of other diplomatic relations between Persia and the
West, their role of diplomatists disappeared and they confined themselves to evangelism, more particularly among the
Armenians. During the 150 years of their major activity, some
150 Carmelite fathers were sent to Iran, and their average
tenure was fourteen and a half years.

The history of Protestant missions in Iran dates from 1811
when Henry Martyn, an English evangelist, translated the
New Testament into Persian. Henry Martyn left, however,
more than a translation of the Book; his life was a translation
of his Master's life in terms that the most unlettered could
understand. Though he died after only a year on the mission
field, such was the impression made by his character upon the
people that he is still remembered. Since Martyn's time, a
principal factor in Protestant missionary effort has been the

Fr. Vincent, discouraged by the obstacles to their mission, went off to
Hormuz to establish a convent there. Fr. John Thaddeus, however, remained, and, persevering in his missionary efforts, managed between his
diplomatic assignments to establish a church and win a number of converts.
On his return to Rome, in 1629, he was proposed as bishop to Isfahan, but
demurred on the ground that he was but a monk and not qualified for
ecclesiastical office. He was appointed, nevertheless, and in 1632 started on
his return to Persia to take up his duties. On the journey he died of
injuries sustained from a fall from his mule.

zeal in translating the Scriptures into Persian and the various subsidiary languages spoken by the tribes.

In 1829, the American Board of Commissioners for Foreign Missions established work in Urmiah (now Rizayeh) by sending out Messrs. Dwight and Smith, who were followed shortly by the Reverend Justin Perkins. This work was subsequently taken over by the Presbyterians, and in 1871 their activities were extended to Teheran, in 1873 to Tabriz, to Hamadan in 1881, to Resht in 1883, and in 1911, it became possible to establish work in such a center of Moslem fanaticism as the shrine city of Meshed. During the 1930's, before the government began to restrict missionary activity, there were more than a hundred Presbyterian missionaries in Iran, and their work included the operation of six hospitals, two colleges, and numerous secondary and primary schools.

Missionary work by the Church Missionary Society of the English Church was begun in 1869 in Isfahan, and in 1935 engaged some sixty missionaries.

In addition, several other Protestant denominations have carried on evangelism in Iran: the Lutherans formerly carried on a modest work among the Kurds, and the Seventh Day Adventists now maintain a mission in Teheran.

Official Attitude Towards Missions

Missionary activity in Iran has historically been much freer from restraint than it has in Turkey or Iraq. During the nineteenth century, because of opposition from the Islamic clergy, direct proselytization was confined largely to the Nestorians and Armenians, whose faith had survived the surrounding influences of Islam. The first Protestant churches were composed of adherents from these ancient Christian communities. The question naturally arises, and has often been debated, about the propriety of one Christian sect proselytizing among another, but the answer is only to be found in the degree of strengthening of the Christian testimony and the purification of morals and conduct that have occurred in the Christian community, where there are those adherent both to the ancient rites and to the newer.

For a long time, to preach among Shi'a Moslems was to incur risk of life for the preacher, and exile or death to those who listened. Nevertheless, there were always some who were eager to hear the Gospel message, and from the earliest days there have been instances of conversions from among Moslems. Missionary effort among them was, until the last fifty years, largely indirect, through schools and hospitals, where those who came were brought in touch with Christian influences and teaching and where Christian literature was available. By means of the depots and the traveling colporteurs of the British and Foreign Bible Society, also, whose work was established in 1812, the Bible, the Gospels, and Christian tracts have been distributed among the people in increasing numbers. In 1945, over a hundred thousand pieces of literature were sold.

The official attitude of the government has been one of tolerance towards missionary work, and in this connection it may be remarked that while American missionaries have been in Iran since 1829, it was not until 1883 that any diplomatic relations existed between the government of Iran and the United States. Missionaries have been hospitably received by all classes, and many of them have been confidants of the highest officials. Dr. W. S. Vanneman, for example, was frequently consulted by the *Vali Ahd,* or governor of Azerbaijan, a post always held by the heir apparent to the throne, and was admitted for professional calls into the royal *andirun,* or women's quarters, a trust accorded no Persian physician.

Recent Restrictions on Missionary Activity

While the government and the upper classes in general treated the missionaries with consideration, in the provinces, where the influence of the Moslem clergy was more powerful, the missionaries were often subject to annoyances and vexations, including occasional arrest.

An apparent setback to missionary work occurred during the era of reform and nationalistic fervor that followed the accession of Riza Shah Pahlavi in 1926. In 1928, perhaps as a means of weakening the influence of the Moslem clergy, perhaps in imitation of western secularization, the teaching of religion in schools was forbidden. In 1933, possibly in order to bring the Armenians and Nestorians of northwest Iran under greater control, the Urmiah district was declared a military zone and the missionaries were directed to leave.

Thus ended a missionary work that had existed for over a hundred years. Beginning in 1935, all foreign schools were closed by the process of forbidding their attendance by Iranians, and in 1938 the properties of the two Presbyterian colleges at Teheran were expropriated by the government.

This restriction on missionary work was no doubt a blessing in disguise. In the Urmiah district, where American missionary influence was extensive, the Armenians and Nestorians had come to look to the missionaries, rather than to their government, as their protector. There may have been justification for this.[23] In any case, an indigenous Christian Church now existed, and the Mission Board recognized that the time had come to allow this Church to find its own footing. The closing of the schools permitted the missionaries to focus their efforts on their main task, that of preaching the Gospel rather than disseminating the knowledge and material sciences of the West. Restrictions continued to be placed on preaching, however, but after the abdication of Riza Shah Pahlavi in 1941, missionary activity regained some of the freedom it was guaranteed under the Iranian Constitution.

[23] During World War I, when the district was in a state of anarchy, an American missionary, Reverend William A. Shedd, assumed a political status and practically ruled the Nestorian nation, of which some eighty thousand inhabitants had taken sanctuary in the mission compound from Turks and Kurds. Subsequently he led them out, under conditions of great confusion, to central Iran. Half the company perished from slaughter and disease on the way. Among those who fell victim to typhus was the intrepid Dr. Shedd.

PART THREE

THE REIGN OF RIZA SHAH PAHLAVI

THE ACCESSION OF RIZA SHAH PAHLAVI

FROM time to time in these pages reference has been made to Riza Shah Pahlavi and his reign. Riza Shah Pahlavi came into power in 1922 as Riza Khan, colonel in the Iranian army; he was crowned shah in 1926, and abdicated in 1941. He was, after Mustafa Kemal of Turkey, the first of the crop of dictators that were seeded by World War I—and he was the first of them to fall.

In the *coup d'état* of 21 February 1921, Riza Khan had taken the post of minister of war and commander of the army, leaving the prime ministry to Seyyid Zia-ed-Din. He obtained, however, the transfer of certain substantial sources of revenue from the ministry of finance to the ministry of war, for the purpose of re-equipping the army, and thereby secured his independence of the cabinet. It soon became apparent who was the power in the government: before a hundred days had elapsed, Seyyid Zia-ed-Din was hurrying out of the country into exile. During his early years in power, however, Riza Khan acted by strictly constitutional procedure, and there is every reason to believe that he was animated by patriotism and democratic ideals.

A. RESTORATION OF GOVERNMENTAL AUTHORITY

Riza Khan's first task was to restore the authority of the central government. The fact that this authority had practically ceased does not mean that complete anarchy prevailed. In a country so vast, and so poorly provided with communications, considerable authority had of necessity always been vested in the provincial governors, and the provincial governments had continued to function with varying effectiveness throughout the British and Russian occupation. The tribes, however, had grown increasingly restive and were now defiant, making the principal roads unsafe. Khuzistan under Sheik Khazal, Kurdistan under Ismail Agha (Simitko) and the Maku Sardars (the Ijlal-ul-Mulk family), Gilan under Kuchik Khan, the Karadagh under Amir Ashad, as well as several smaller areas, were all in revolt. All had to be subdued by military expeditions.

Riza Khan first proceeded to unify and re-equip the army. At that time the military forces of the realm consisted of the Cossack Brigade, an organization that had been created originally by Nasr-ed-Din Shah in 1882 but that had always been under Russian officers and Russian influence; the gendarmerie that W. Morgan Shuster had established, and that had been under Swedish officers; the South Persia Rifles that the British had organized, and that had never been recognized by the government; a small household troop about the shah, and the several tribal levies, officered by their own chiefs, of uncertain composition and strength.

The Cossack Brigade numbered some 14,000; the gendarmerie, around 12,000; the household troops about 2,000; while the South Persia Rifles totaled approximately 6,000.

Riza Khan had acquired command of the Cossack Brigade following the Russian Revolution and the withdrawal of the Russian officers; this became the core of his national army. The South Persia Rifles was disbanded without incident and its members incorporated into the army. An attempt to absorb the gendarmerie met with resistance, particularly in Tabriz.[1] It was necessary to besiege the city. The battle lasted nearly a week; a great deal of ammunition was expended, but few lives, and the principal losses were sustained by the Presbyterian mission compounds and the bazaars. The walls and upper stories of the mission school compound, where I was living at the time as a teacher, were riddled with gunfire, and the bazaars were looted from end to end by the victorious party.

By 1924, the military forces of the country had been consolidated into five principal armies and one independent brigade. In addition a separate force of highway patrol was

---

[1] The chief of the gendarmerie was Abol Qasim Lahuti, later known as a poet of revolutionary themes (see above, Part II, ch. I, *Modern Literature*). He later became a member of the Soviet Komintern and continued to carry on anti-shah propaganda from the safety of Moscow.

created to maintain security on the roads. In 1925, the national arms were further strengthened by the passage of a military conscription law, requiring two years' military service for all males reaching the age of twenty-one. The application of conscription was extended in 1926, and again in 1931, by limiting the exemptions from service.

By the end of the decade, the army had been built up to a force of between 70,000 and 80,000 troops, besides the highway-patrol force of around 12,000. Besides this, an embryonic navy of half a dozen gunboats was established on the Persian Gulf (Russia continued to forbid any Iranian forces on the Caspian); a small air force and several arsenals and munitions factories were also created.

Two officers' training schools were established at Teheran, and military students were sent to France and Germany for further military instruction. Another measure designed to enforce the authority of the new shah and the central government was the establishment of a secret police, modeled after the Italian and German, with informers and *agents provocateurs,* and secret executions. This, however, came later in Riza Khan's career.

Among the expenditures on the military establishment was an enormous sum for an officers' club in Teheran, the grand staircase, reception hall and furnishings of which would command admiration in any capital.

For a country of the resources of Iran, the cost of building up the military forces was tremendous, and constituted a serious drain on the economy; but while it served to maintain internal order, it did not deter the Russians and British from an eventual second occupation, in August 1941, during which the fleet was blown out of the water by the British, the Russians took over the munitions factories to supply their own needs, and Russians, British, and Americans all found the airfields a great convenience in their operations.

The immediate task of the new army was the reduction of the recalcitrant tribes. In Gilan, the Russians had set up a Soviet republic headed by Kuchik Khan, chief of the *Jangalis,* or Jungle Dwellers. Kuchik Khan had been a strong nationalist; at one time he had founded a brotherhood known as the *Ehtahad-ul-Islam,* or Union of Islam, which was sworn to driving out the foreigners, the members of which took a Nazarite vow not to bring scissor or razor to their heads until their oath had been accomplished.[2] Mostly, however, Kuchik Khan had supported himself and his followers by banditry; when the Russians occupied Resht in 1920, they found in him an apt tool for their purposes.

Following the signing of the Russo-Iranian Agreement on 26 February 1921, the Russians withdrew their support from Kuchik Khan. He was captured within the year and his head was cut off and placed on a spear above the gates of Kasvin.

The fertile Urmiah plain of Azerbaijan, the richest agricultural region of Iran, was in control of the Kurds, whose principal chief, the redoubtable Ismail Agha, familiarly known as Simitko, was seeking to establish an independent Kurdish state. Simitko had been at one time an officer in the Turkish army; he spoke excellent French. During the war he had marauded the Nestorians, and in the latter part of 1921, while a government force was seeking to reach him by a circuit around the northern end of Lake Urmiah, Simitko led a force of Kurds to the southern end of the lake and fell upon the city of Souj-Boulagh, garrisoned by a force of some seven hundred government troops. The whole garrison was captured and promptly massacred by being lined against a wall and mowed down with machine-gun fire.

In the pillage of the town that followed this success, the Kurds broke into the American Lutheran mission, murdered the principal missionary, Mr. Bachimont, and captured the three women missionaries. Fortunately, Simitko recognized one of the women as a missionary nurse whom he had once invited to teach his people; he set her to work looking after his wounded men, and a week later released the three to find their way to Tabriz, a hundred miles distant, as best they could.[3]

For some time it was feared that Simitko would follow up his success by an attack on Tabriz, but instead he shrewdly withdrew to the mountains. The Urmiah plain was eventually reoccupied in 1923, but the Kurds were not made tractable

---

[2] Sykes, op. cit. vol. II, pp. 489 ff.

[3] For an account of this massacre, see my *Blood of the Martyrs,* in the *Atlantic Monthly,* July 1922.

until some years later. Simitko took refuge in Iraq, and while the Iraq government refused to surrender him, on the grounds that his acts were political rather than criminal, he was subsequently induced to parley, and was seized and assassinated.

In the south, Sheik Khazal, who ruled the Muhaisin Arabs of Khuzistan, had enjoyed political independence for years under a subsidy of the Anglo-Persian Oil Company to keep peace. In 1924, he attempted to defy Riza Khan, but Riza Khan moved with an army against him. The Sheik surrendered and was brought to Teheran where, however, he was allowed to live in retirement. He died a few years later.

The Lurs and Kashgais were also gradually suppressed and disarmed, partly by force, partly by statecraft. Following an ancient policy of the shahs, Riza Khan induced or compelled numbers of the tribesmen to settle in villages, or to accept grazing privileges in other parts of the country, while their chiefs were courteously but firmly invited to take up their residence in the capital. When the Lurs had objected, by force of arms, to a highway that was projected through their mountains, Riza Khan resolved the question by building villages along the route of the highway and inducing the tribesmen to occupy them: this policy was, however, only moderately successful.

By 1925, the country was fairly quiet, though in 1929 the Kashgais again revolted, and once more in 1937, and still again in 1943. The 1929 troubles arose over resentment at the predatory practices of the military governor of the district, at attempts to apply conscription, at the imposition of European dress, and at the enforced residence of their chiefs in Teheran.

B. THE ACCESSION TO THE THRONE

Riza Khan assumed the premiership in 1923 in the general expectation that a republic would be established. Throughout Iran there was revulsion against the monarchy: the people were ready, psychologically if not politically, for the establishment of a republic. World War I had ended as a great triumph of political democracy, as formulated in Wilson's Fourteen Points, and the republican form of government was generally regarded as its ideal expression. The great monarchies of Europe had fallen—the Romanoff, the Hohenzollern, the Hapsburg—and in Turkey, in 1922, the Sultanate was abolished. The Shah of Iran, sensing the handwriting on the wall, and having no mind for government, was spending his time on the Riviera. It was generally understood, therefore, when Riza Khan became prime minister, that the anticipated republic would be proclaimed on the following New Year's Day (21 March, according to the Persian calendar).

At this juncture, however, support for the monarchy came from an unexpected source. The Moslem clergy, who had traditionally regarded the throne with suspicion, if not with contempt, and who had been instrumental in obtaining the Constitution, suddenly took fright at democratic institutions, and announced their opposition to a republic. What produced this change of heart was the action of the Turkish government, on 3 March 1924, abolishing the Caliphate, the spiritual headship of Islam, as it had two years before abolished the Sultanate.[4] The effect of this was profound throughout the Mohammedan world, and although the Moslems of Iran belonged to the Shi'a sect and had never recognized the caliphate, the clergy became alarmed lest under a republic their ecclesiastical prerogatives be shorn as they were being shorn in near-by Turkey.[5]

Three days before the meeting of the Majlis that was to make the change, demonstrations took place, and in order to quiet the agitation, Riza Khan publicly visited the holy shrine at Qum where he consulted the assembly of *mujtahids*. On 1 April 1924, he proclaimed that the republican form of government was contrary to the Islamic faith, and forbade further discussion of the matter. The following year, in February 1925, he requested and obtained dictatorial powers; on 31 October 1925, the Majlis formally deposed Sultan Ahmad Shah; and on 12 December Riza Khan was appointed shah by vote of the Majlis. On 25 April 1926, in accordance with the ancient

---

[4] The Ottoman sultans had assumed the title of Caliph, or Successor of the Prophet, in 1517, following the conquest of Egypt and the extinction of the Egyptian caliphate succession.

[5] It appears, also, that there was considerable conniving between Riza Khan and the leading clerics to bring about this eventuality.

custom, he placed the crown of the *Shah-in-Shah* on his head and founded a new dynasty. From then on his power grew more absolute, the character of his administration gradually changed, and the dictum of Lord Acton was justified that 'power corrupts, and absolute power corrupts absolutely.'

II

THE REGIME OF RIZA SHAH PAHLAVI

RIZA SHAH PAHLAVI's policy from the beginning was to restore the national spirit, consolidate the national unity, and strengthen the State to defend its sovereignty. Everywhere in the world, of course, nationalism was resurgent and seeking inspiration. In Turkey, Mustafa Kemal had boldly severed his nation from the past, seeking his new model in the democracies of the West. Riza Khan, however, returned to the ancient glories of his country, to the great empires of the Sassanians and Achaemenians for his example. Whether following this as a precedent or not, Mussolini, in Italy, revived the memory of the Caesars, and, in Germany, Hitler refurbished Valhalla and restored the Teutonic pantheon.

A. NATIONAL ATAVISM

It was natural that Riza Khan should turn to the past. He was from Mazanderan, the last Sassanian province to succumb to the Arab invasion, and a district in which the Persian tradition persisted at its purest. Moreover, throughout Iran, the recollection of the earlier glories had never been lost as they had been in Italy and Germany. This was largely due to Firdausi, whose epic poem the *Shah Namah,* or 'Chronicles of the Kings,' though written nearly a thousand years earlier, was still an integral part of the literature of the country, was still read and recited in the language in which it was written, as was not the case with the *Æneid,* the *Gallic Wars,* or the *Nibelungenlied.*

To signify the renascence of the earlier tradition and the purely Persian character of the new regime, Riza Khan not only assumed on his coronation the name Pahlavi, which is the name of the archaic Persian tongue in common use before its corruption by Arabic influences, but also instituted a movement to purge the Persian language of its Arabic incrustation. While the structure of the language was still substantially that of Firdausi, and the *Shah Namah* could still be understood, some half the words of common usage, it has been estimated, were of Arabic origin. A commission of scholars, the *Farhang*, was appointed to prepare a new dictionary, in which Persian words were substituted for their Arabic equivalents, and the Persian words were required to be used in all official com- munications.

For public constructions, architectural designs drawn from Persepolis, Susa, and other Achaemenian and Sassanian archi- tectures with modernistic adaptations were employed, together with purely modern styles imported from Germany, rather than the styles that had predominated since Islamic times.

Archaeological excavations were encouraged, and a magnifi- cent museum of archaeology was erected in Teheran.

Reference has been made to the Guebers, or Parsees, ad- herents to the ancient Zoroastrian faith, and of the considera- tion accorded them in recent years. Since Islamic times they had been outcasts in society, under greater disabilities than Christians or Jews, who were, despite their denial of the True Faith, regarded as 'People of the Book,' and entitled to a cer- tain toleration. Because of persecutions, and because they did not admit proselytes, the Parsees in Iran had diminished to only a few thousand, resident chiefly around Yezd, in southern Iran. As custodian of the ancient lineage and tradition, they were now visited with favor, and many of them became influen- tial in the government.

To signify to the world the changes that had occurred it was decreed that the country should henceforth be known by its traditional name of Iran, or Land of the Aryans, rather than Persia. This produced considerable confusion abroad, particularly in commercial circles, and especially in the rug trade, in which the name 'Persian' had become synonymous with the highest excellence in floor coverings.

B. Conflict with the Clergy

In centralizing all authority in the State, as well as in re- establishing pre-Islamic traditions, it was inevitable that Riza

Shah Pahlavi should come in conflict with the clergy. The actual opposition arose, however, over the efforts at modernization and the adoption of the current modes of the West. While the Shah returned to the past for inspiration, he faced forward and outward for his means. Coincident with a reverence for the great days of the Achaemenians and Sassanians was an equal reverence for the material achievements of modern civilization.

The first issue between the Shah and the clergy arose over the program to reform the legal administration of the country, a work that had first been undertaken following the establishment of the Constitution, but which had practically lapsed.

Prior to 1906, there existed in Iran, as in most Moslem countries, two systems of law, corresponding roughly to the common law and canon law of Europe during medieval times. The canon law, known as the *Qanun-i-shari'a*, was founded on the precepts and injunctions of the Koran, as amplified by the traditions and the commentaries; it was administered by the clergy. The term *Qanun-i-shari'a* means literally, 'the road to the watering place,' [1] a phrase which conveys an idea of its original purpose and scope. While the Koranic law theoretically applied to every act of man, it gradually was confined to questions of faith and morals, domestic relations, inheritance, and vows. The acknowledgment of vows, corresponding to notarial acts, gave the clergy considerable authority in commercial transactions, and the regulation of inheritances placed questions of land tenure largely in their hands.

The common law, known as *'ada*, or *'urf*, represented the body of local custom in any place, and governed transactions not specifically covered by the *Shari'a*, as well as relationships based on traditions that frequently antedated the *Shari'a*. Among these were water rights, landlord-tenant relations, grazing privileges, and frequently taxes.

In addition, there existed the laws promulgated by edict of the sovereign, which came to be known as the *Qanun*. These related to taxes, foreign affairs, public administration, and public security.

The administration of these three bodies of law was never

[1] Wilson, Sir Arnold, *Persia*, London, 1933, p. 218.

clearly defined. The shah was theoretically absolute, and held the life and property of his subjects in his hand. Violators of public safety, conspirators against the throne, robbers and malefactors, as well as officials and functionaries, could be put to death or otherwise punished as the shah or his ministers might decree. Fugitives from the sovereign's justice could, however, take sanctuary (*bast*) in certain shrines or mosques (which corresponded to the Biblical 'cities of refuge'), and in certain cases of death penalty the sentence required confirmation by the ecclesiastical courts. The legal administration was further complicated by the fact that the highest tribunal of ecclesiastical justice was composed of the *mujtahids* of the most sacred shrines of the *Shi'as,* which were in Kerbela and Najaf, outside the country, in adjoining Iraq. In this respect the shah's justice operated under a disability from which the sultan's was free, since the sovereign of Turkey combined the temporal authority of the sultan with the ecclesiastical and spiritual authority of the caliph.

A further element complicating the legal system was its concept of private rather than public justice. The idea of the State as a party in interest had never developed to any degree in juridical concepts. A crime was an offense against the injured party; the principle of *lex talionis,* or life for a life, prevailed, in which the injured, or his relatives, could demand blood money or satisfaction in kind. In civil cases, arbitration was the rule, with or without the interposition of the State.

Legal Reforms and Limitations on Ecclesiastical Privileges

In 1907, a Fundamental Law was enacted setting forth the general principles of criminal and civil procedure. This was followed in 1912 by a law setting up a judicial administration modeled upon European standards, with a hierarchy of courts, and rules of civil procedure; in 1914 a system of commercial courts was provided. These enactments remained, however, generally unenforced, owing to clerical opposition.

In 1922, shortly after Riza Khan came into power, a law for the voluntary registration of properties and documents was enacted as a beginning in administrative and judicial reform, but the violent opposition of the mullahs, who instigated rioting before the parliament building, prevented the enactment of a new commercial code which would have deprived them of jurisdiction in civil cases. After his accession to the throne, however, Riza Shah Pahlavi had more success: in 1926, a new penal code, abrogating the *lex talionis,* was instituted without incident. This was followed by other enactments that gradually abolished the *Shari'a.* In 1928, the application of the civil code was extended and the juridical opinions of the mullahs, given on the *Shari'a,* were declared to be without authority; in the same year, the authority of the clergy over titles was abolished by the establishment of a State Registration Bureau, and the requirement of its certification for all titles to property. By a law enacted 3 January 1929, the jurisdiction of the ecclesiastical courts was limited to domestic relations, personal status, and notarial acts. Two years later, on 14 August 1931, ecclesiastical authority over domestic relations was limited by a requirement that all marriage contracts and acts of divorce be registered with a civil official, and by an abrogation of certain provisions of the *Shari'a* regarding marital status. This law did not define marriage requirements, although by an administrative circular the civil notaries were instructed not to certify marriages in cases where the woman was less than sixteen years of age.

A further limitation on the power of the clergy was the seizure of the pious foundations (*waqfs*), representing estates dedicated by the pious to religious or charitable work. The revenues from the pious foundations, formerly used largely to defray instruction in the Koran, were now dedicated to State education, charities, and hospitals.

In 1931, certain of the more famous mosques were thrown open to foreign visitors. In 1935, laws or edicts were passed simplifying funeral ceremonies, further defining marital status, abolishing titles, abolishing the celebration of Moharram and Id-i-Kourban.

That year also marked the abolition of an ancient custom of reverence, that of keeping the head covered. On the opening of the tenth session of the Majlis, on 6 June 1935, the Shah removed his military cap on entering the parliament building, while at the same time, by pre-concert, all the deputies followed his example. On this occasion the Imam Suna', the principal *mujtahid,* and the other Moslem dignitaries were conspicuous by their absence.[2]

These various reforms were not achieved without considerable opposition from the clergy and the more fanatical of the Moslem faith. In 1927, in protest against the extension of conscription to theological students, the mullahs instigated the closing of the bazaars, and in further protest, a number of leading mullahs took sanctuary at the Qum shrine. So influential were they still that the Shah had to send the prime minister and the minister of court to treat with them.

The most violent opposition occurred in connection with what must be regarded as the most notable of Riza Shah Pahlavi's reforms, the removal of the veil and the partial emancipation of women. The clerical opposition to this was signalized by a diatribe delivered in the Qum mosque on the Persian New Year in 1928. The shrine, which encloses the tomb of Fatima, sister of the Imam Reza, eighth in the line of *imams,* is particularly revered by Moslem women, and is provided with a gallery where women may sit. The Queen of Iran had come to Qum to attend the services. During the sermon, as she sat in the gallery, she unveiled her face, advertently or inadvertently. The *mujtahid* turned from his sermonizing to reprimand her, and went on to excoriate the new tendencies and to denounce the Shah's encouragement of them. The result was that the crowd demonstrated against the Queen.

On this occasion, the Shah did not temporize, but proceeded immediately to Qum with two armored cars and a body of troops. He entered the mosque without removing his boots and proceeded to flog the *mujtahid.* To humiliate the clergy further, he ordered the arrest of several persons who had taken sanctuary in the mosque.

This incident marked the end of clerical influence as a major factor in government policy, though as late as 1935 violent opposition again was shown to the introduction of Western headgear.[3] In Meshed, under the incitation of one

[2] This summary of the Shah's legal and prescriptive reforms is drawn largely from the account by Henry Filmer, op. cit. pp. 360 ff.

[3] European dress, except for headgear, had already been prescribed by law some years earlier (1927). Headgear, however, is throughout the East a peculiar mark of one's nationality or religion.

Sheik Bahloul, a riotous demonstration occurred in the Shrine of the Imam Riza. Nothing better illustrates the contempt with which the clerical influence was now held than the manner in which the situation was met. Troops were brought into the sacred precincts and the mob ruthlessly dispersed by machine-gun fire.

III

FOREIGN RELATIONS

THE FOREIGN policy of Riza Shah Pahlavi was at the outset clear and explicit, but before the end of his reign it had become petty and equivocal.

Five days after his *coup d'état* in 1921, the Majlis had rejected the Anglo-Persian Agreement and effected a composition with Russia. The Anglo-Persian Agreement has generally been regarded, both in Iran and abroad, as an attempt on the part of British imperialism to take advantage of the collapse of Russia and to put Iran securely in the British pocket. British foreign policies were then being guided by Lord Curzon, long noted for his espousal of British interests in the Middle East as well as for his suspicions of Russia, and credited with the policy of 'encirclement' of Russia following the Revolution.

It is likely that at a future day, when the terms of the Anglo-Persian Agreement are examined more dispassionately, it will be concluded that it was less than nefarious and represented a reasonable effort at co-operation with the Iranian people with the object of establishing a strong and independent Iran. Lord Curzon always protested that Britain had no designs on Iranian territory, and that he never favored territorial aggrandizement in Iran. As early as 1892 he had stated his views of British policy in Iran as follows:

If then, I were asked what is the policy of Great Britain toward Persia, I should answer in the following terms. It is not now, nor at any time in this century has it been, one of territorial cupidity. England does not covet one square foot of Persian territory. In the war of 1856-57 British forces captured, and, for a short time, held both Bushire and Kharak Island, in the Gulf, and Mohammerah and Ahwaz on the Karun. It would have been easy to establish a permanent foothold on the Gulf, and to have settled the Karun question for all time by retaining these positions. In the absence of any reason rendering such a step compulsory, we gave them up. The Persians themselves, who had fully expected to lose Bushire, were bewildered at our clemency, and have come to believe that they ousted us by superior force. But the action remains an indisputable evidence of pacific purpose, and may appositely be contrasted with the Russian tactics at Ashurada in the North. . . In other words, the development of the industrial and material resources of Persia, the extension of her commerce, the maintenance of her integrity, the rehabilitation of her strength—these, under the pressure and by the aid of a friendly alliance, are the objects of British policy. The time for an offensive and defensive alliance has passed.[1]

The purposes and possible results of the Anglo-Persian Agreement are now, of course, an academic question. While refusing to ratify the Agreement, the Majlis, influenced by the fervid self-denying declarations of the Russian revolutionary government, concluded an agreement with that government by which the independence and integrity of Iran was guaranteed in even more categorical terms; at the end of World War II, however, it was the Russians, rather than the British, of whom the Iranians found themselves unable to rid their country.

A. RELATIONS WITH RUSSIA

The Russian Revolution had begun in November 1917. As early as 18 January 1918, Leon Trotsky, People's Commissar for Foreign Affairs of the Soviet Republic of Russia, handed a note to the Iranian minister in Petrograd, declaring null and void the Anglo-Russian Convention of 1907, and undertaking to secure the evacuation of all Russian troops from Iran. On 16 June 1918, and again on 19 June 1918, N. R. Brovine, the Soviet diplomatic agent, delivered notes to the Iranian foreign office, assuring the Iranian government of its anti-imperialistic intentions. The note of 19 June 1918, read as follows:

The weakness of the Persian Government has been due generally to the fact that her rights and her national wealth have fallen into the hands of foreign imperialism and capitalism. The revolutionary nation of Russia, after having done away with these internally in Russia, is convinced that its dear brother—the neighboring nation of Persia—should be free from the oppression of this same capitalism

[1] Op. cit. vol. II, pp. 619, 620.

and would like to see Persia free herself from the clutches of foreign capitalism. Therefore, it is stated that the Ministry is hereafter at liberty to consider all former concessions which the late Russian regime obtained for itself in Persia, including mineral, fishing, and transportation concessions (secured through the use of the bayonet or powerful men of Persia) as no longer under the protection of the Russian Republic. It is to be hoped that Persia will keep its interests for its own benefit and never deliver them into foreign hands.[2]

These notes were followed by one from Chicherin, Soviet foreign minister, on 26 June 1918, specifically setting forth the rights renounced. This renunciation made no reservation of the Caspian Sea fisheries, and declared moreover that the Caspian Sea should be freely open to the navigation of vessels bearing the Iranian flag. This declaration regarding the Caspian Sea was reaffirmed in a note of 31 May 1920, from the Russian Commissar for Foreign Affairs.

The treaty of 26 February 1921 confirmed most of these renunciations and was favorable enough in its terms. Nevertheless, by then the idealism of the earlier Russian declarations was already sicklied over with a strong cast of realism: while the Caspian fisheries concession was renounced, the Agreement provided that a new concession should be negotiated; it provided further that none of the concessions renounced should be granted to a third power, or to the subjects of a third power,[3] and, most importantly, reserved the right to Russia to occupy [4] Iran in case of a threat to Russia by a third power.[5]

[2] *Perso-Russian Treaties and Notes of* 1828-1931. Translation from the original Persian documents made by J. Rives Childs, 1934-5, while he was Secretary to Legation at Teheran. Typescript in Library of Congress.

[3] Art. 13. 'The Persian Government promises on its part not to place under the possession, authority, or use of any third government, or the subjects of any third government, the concessions and properties transferred to Persia according to this treaty, and to preserve all the abovementioned rights for the welfare of the people of Persia.'

[4] Literally, 'to send troops' into Iran. The language of diplomacy draws a distinction between 'occupation' and 'sending in troops,' but under the conditions the practical effects were the same.

[5] Art. 6. 'Both the High Contracting Parties are agreed that in case on the part of third countries there should be attempts by means of armed intervention to realize a rapacious policy on the territory of Persia or to turn the territory of Persia into a base for military action against the

Moreover, despite the solemn declarations of the Agreement, and despite the withdrawal of Russian support from the 'Soviet Republic of Gilan,' the Russians continued to occupy the port of Enzeli and used the occupation to compel an agreement in its favor on the Caspian fisheries question.

The importance of the Caspian fisheries arises from the fact that the sturgeon, prized both for itself and for caviar, is to be found only in the southern Caspian waters. A concession for the monopoly of these fisheries had been granted in 1876 to a Russian named Stepan Lionosoff, and renewed at various times subsequently; at the time of the Revolution, the under-taking employed several thousand persons and had equipment on the Iranian coast consisting of warehouses, docks, curing vats, refrigerators, and other installations valued at several million dollars.

In accordance with the Soviet declarations of 1918 and 1919, the Iranian government annulled the concession; but as the properties had fallen into the hands of the Soviet government, this government continued to operate them. In 1922, the Iranian government was induced to give a monopoly of the fisheries to one Hassan Kiadeh, an official of the Soviet Depart-ment of Trade, for an annual payment of 50,000 tomans, effec-tive for one year. Meantime, the Lionosoffs, who resided in Teheran, had protested the abrogation of the concession, and in 1922 an arbitration commission of Iranian jurists gave a decision that the cancellation of the concession had been illegal, and that in compensation for the damages sustained by the concessionaires the concession should be extended for fifteen years on condition that 50 per cent of the net profits be paid to the government.

In 1924, the Soviet government proposed to the Iranian gov-ernment that the fisheries be leased to a company, the shares

R.S.F.S.R. and if thereby danger should threaten the frontiers of the R.S.F.S.R. or its federated associates, and if the Persian Government after warning on the part of the Government of the R.S.F.S.R. shall prove to be itself not strong enough to prevent this danger, the Government of the R.S.F.S.R. shall have the right to send its troops into Persian territory in order to take necessary military measures in the interests of self-defense. When the danger has been removed the Government of the R.S.F.S.R. undertakes immediately to withdraw its troops beyond the frontiers of Persia.'

of which should be held equally by the two governments.

In 1922, however, the Iranian government had appointed an American, A. C. Millspaugh, as administrator general of the finances of Iran, with broad authority. Millspaugh, on examining the proposed contract, refused to approve it on the grounds that it offered no practical solution to the question. He refused, moreover, to receive into the treasury the check for one hundred thousand tomans which the Soviet government offered on account.[6]

In 1926, as a measure of coercing the Iranian government to accede to Soviet views, an embargo was placed on all Iranian exports to Russia, on the pretext of the necessity of conserving Soviet funds. This measure produced a great hardship on Iranian merchants, and when, in 1927, Millspaugh resigned over differences concerning his powers, the fisheries question was renewed with greater success. On 1 October 1927, a concession was granted to the Soviet government on substantially the terms it had originally laid down. The concession provided that the fisheries should be operated by a jointly owned company, that 80,000 tomans should be paid annually to the Iranian government as rentals, and that the profits of the company should be divided equally between the two shareholders. As, however, the product is sold almost exclusively to the Soviet government,[7] at terms dictated by the Soviet government, profits have been negligible or none.

At the time that the fisheries concession was signed, other outstanding questions between the two countries were cleared up—in four other agreements signed on the same date. Among these was one by which Iranian exports to Russia were limited to a maximum annual value of 50,000,000 rubles, and Soviet imports to Iran to 90 per cent of Iranian exports. The port of Enzeli was now returned to Iranian hands, and, to celebrate this diplomatic triumph, was renamed Pahlavi in honor of the Shah.

This diplomatic triumph—if such it can be called—was of short duration. Nominally, the Soviet government, now under the control of Joseph Stalin, had renounced the earlier Trot-

---

[6] Millspaugh, A. C., *The American Task in Persia*, New York, 1926, pp. 294 ff.

[7] Sturgeon are forbidden (*haram*) to Moslems as unclean.

sky doctrine of world revolution, and treated its eastern and southern neighbors as equals. Gradually, however, as the dream of world revolution faded, the spirit of Muscovite Russia revived, and the testament of Peter the Great was re-read, refurbished, and reapplied. The government had also turned back three hundred years for its commercial policies, adopting those of Elizabethan England, of granting rich monopolies to favored instrumentalities, as models of Marxian enlightenment. The system was now extended in 1930 to the south and east through the creation of a State agency known as the Eastern Trading Company, with a monopoly on foreign trade with Iran, Turkey, and Afghanistan. The Iranian merchants, who are above all individualistic and competitive, now found themselves under the disadvantage of dealing with an instrumentality enjoying perquisites and resources that they could not match.

The Eastern Trading Company employed all the tactics of large-scale capitalism, which the American government had long before outlawed and declared contrary to public policy. By dumping, withholding from sale, favoritism, and by other practices, it was able to control the market, purchase Iranian products at such prices as it cared to pay, and to exact the utmost for what it sold.

Consequently, in 1931, the Iranian government, to protect its economy, declared a monopoly on foreign trade, but it did not go further than to fix import quotas, which did not effectively meet the situation.[8] In 1932 and 1933, the bazaar instituted a boycott against Russian goods as a measure of self-defense and counter-reprisal. The Soviet government intervened on behalf of its instrumentality, and by pressure at Teheran forced the abandonment of the boycott. The Iranian government undertook now to meet the situation by the creation of its own State monopoly for trade with Russia, but to this the Russians objected that it would be discriminatory.

Meantime, however, Soviet policy towards Iran was in other respects conciliatory. The various agreements concluded in 1927 had assured Iran of transit rights through Russia for persons, merchandise, and the posts, and gave Iran the tariff

[8] Filmer, Henry, op. cit. p. 355.

autonomy which it had not enjoyed since the Treaty of Tur-komanchai. This treaty had fixed at a flat 5 per cent the import and export dues which the Iranian government could levy on goods interchanged with Russia, and under the principle of equality of treatment this rate had applied to trade with all other countries, except Turkey, with whom a special convention existed. In 1903, the rates fixed by the Treaty of Turkomanchai had been modified, but despite the renunciation of special interests in the Agreement of 26 February 1921, full tariff autonomy was not realized until 1927.

B. RELATIONS WITH GREAT BRITAIN

While Russo-Iranian relations were thus being adjusted to mutual satisfaction, Anglo-Iranian relations were less happy. The British had finally, in 1924, withdrawn the last of their troops from Iran; but in 1925 they gave moral support to Sheik Khazal, chief of the Muhaisin Arabs, in his defiance of the government's authority, which required the Shah to proceed against the sheik with an army before he surrendered.

With the defeat of the clergy over the reform of the legal system, and the introduction of Western legal codes, the government of Iran now undertook to abolish the Capitulatory rights which the nationals of various foreign powers enjoyed. Most of these rights had been obtained by the Treaty of Tur-komanchai with Russia and the extension of the provisions of this treaty under 'most favored nations' clauses in other treaties. In April 1927, the government promulgated its Judicial Regulations, which provided for certain legal safeguards for foreign subjects, including the right of foreign subjects to demand arbitration in cases of lawsuits with Iranian subjects, and on 10 May 1927, formal announcement was made of the abrogation of the Capitulatory rights, to take effect within twelve months.

While the French government promptly accepted the abrogation on behalf of French citizens, the British government objected, on the ground that the status of British subjects rested upon a legal basis quite apart from the Treaty of Turkoman-chai, namely, various rescripts of the shahs issued earlier than the Treaty of Turkomanchai, and upon general international law.

Interlocked with this dispute was the question of tariff autonomy, which the British were reluctant to concede, and the desire of the British government to obtain air-transit rights along the southern Iranian coast for the London-Bombay route of the British Imperial Airways Ltd.[9] The Iranian government had steadily refused to grant such rights.

On 10 May 1928, however, a treaty was concluded between the two governments by which these questions were settled to the satisfaction of the Iranian government, with the latter indicating its willingness to grant temporary landing rights to Imperial Airways. A permit for three years was in fact issued. Imperial Airways, however, unable to obtain a more extended lease, which would warrant the capital expenditures involved in constructing landing fields, hangars, and other installations, in 1932 shifted its route to the Arabian coast. By that time, airplanes had reached a development that rendered the cross-water route less hazardous than formerly, and the necessity for the Iranian-coast route largely disappeared.[10]

The oil fields of southern Iran, worked by the Anglo-Persian Oil Company, had flourished, and by 1930 production was running from 5½ to 6 million tons annually, upon which royalties paid to the government amounted to more than £1,250,000 annually, and provided nearly 20 per cent of the total revenue of the State. This compared with about $80,000 annually which the government was receiving from the Russians for the valuable Caspian Sea fisheries concession in the north. In 1931, however, production of oil suffered a sharp drop, as a result of world conditions, which brought a decline in the royalties paid.

On 27 November 1932, on the grounds that the company had violated the terms of the agreement, the government abruptly canceled the oil concession, an act celebrated by a two-day holiday throughout the country. The British government violently protested, going so far as to make a naval demonstration in the Persian Gulf, but since the Shah remained firm, the British adopted the more peaceful method

9 Now British Overseas Airways Co.
10 Wilson, Sir Arnold, op. cit. pp. 232 ff.

of an appeal to the League of Nations. The Iranian government made a spirited defense before the League Council, showing facts in support of its act and asserting that since this was an internal matter it should be dealt with by Iranian courts. The British government concluded to accept negotiations, and in May 1933, a new concession was negotiated, which gave much more favorable terms to the Iranian government, among which were a higher royalty rate, a restriction of the concession to an area of not more than 100,000 square miles, and the undertaking on the part of the company to distribute its petroleum products more generally throughout Iran. As a result of this last, the company erected a refinery at Kermanshah to exploit the marginal Iranian oil at the Naft-i-Shah field on the borders of Iraq, as well as to serve the Iranian trade.

A question that still colors relations between Iran and Great Britain is that of sovereignty over the island of Bahrein, off the western coast of Iran in the Persian Gulf, long famous for its pearl fisheries and of considerable importance for its oil resources, which were discovered in the early 1930's and which since then have been under development by two American companies.[11] Persian sovereignty had extended over Bahrein until 1783; Arabs then seized control, and held the island until 1906. In that year, Great Britain acquired sovereignty when British diplomacy induced the ruling sheik to place his domain under the protection and sovereignty of the British king. Iran never recognized this acquisition of sovereignty by Great Britain, particularly since the island was converted into a British naval base, and in 1929, and at intervals ever since, has made protests, asserting Iranian rights to sovereignty. In 1934, a protest was lodged with the League of Nations, but without results. The latest assertion of Iranian claims was made in 1946, apparently on the instigation of Soviet Russia.

c. Relations with Other Powers

A major achievement of Riza Shah Pahlavi's foreign policy was the establishment of more cordial relations between Iran

[11] The Texas Company and Standard Oil Company of California.

and its Moslem neighbors. Historically, relations with Turkey on the west and Afghanistan on the east had been unfriendly, if not hostile, partly because of political rivalries and largely because of the difference in religion, the Shi'a sect of Islam, to which Iranians adhere, being regarded as heterodox by the Sunnis of Turkey and Afghanistan. During the nineteenth century two wars had been fought between Iran and Afghanistan, in the second of which the British had intervened; the last war between Turkey and Iran had occurred in 1821-3, but in 1906, during the Constitutional revolution in Iran, Turkey had occupied the Urmiah plain in an attempt to secure control of this area, and during World War I had again invaded this territory.

Stimulated by Russian diplomacy, which was directed to securing peaceful relations among its southern neighbors, a treaty was signed with Afghanistan in 1923, and two years later the frontier between the two countries was delimited; in 1928, this was strengthened by a security pact. The following year, the Amir of Afghanistan, Amanullah, paid a State visit to Teheran, which, aside from its political significance, was notable for the public appearance of his Queen without the customary veil.

In 1926, a treaty of perpetual peace was signed with Turkey, which among other things regularized the customs and postal services between the two countries. It did not, however, settle the frontier question in Kurdistan, and the following year strain developed over Turkish operations against the Kurds which threatened for a time to rupture diplomatic relations. A new treaty of friendship was signed in 1932, and in 1934 the Shah paid a ceremonial visit to the President of the Turkish Republic—which was, incidentally, the only occasion during his reign in which he set foot outside Iranian territory. In 1937, and again in 1939, further accords were reached between the two governments, regulating judicial and extradition questions, communications, customs and quarantine problems, and finally defining the frontier.

With Iraq, which had been separated from the Turkish Empire following World War I, relations continued to be unsatisfactory until 1928. One source of dissension was the fact that the principal shrines of pilgrimage for the Shi'a Moslems of

Iran are located in Iraq, and the ecclesiastical authorities of these shrines continued to exert their reactionary influence against the program of reforms that was being instituted in Iran. The question of extraterritorial privileges for Iranian pilgrims also aggravated relations between the two governments, the Iranian government claiming for its nationals the same extraterritorial privileges that Iraq accorded to other foreigners. A further irritation was the drain on the Iranian monetary supply caused by the expenditures of the pilgrims in Iraq, as well as the smuggling out of silver by the pilgrims. The fact that Iraq was a British mandate, by right of which Great Britain continued to maintain military forces in Iraq, and hence on the Iranian border, was also annoying to the Shah.

Boundary questions also disturbed relations. The frontier had been defined in 1914, by an agreement between Turkey and Iran, by which the waters of the Shatt-el-Arab, which separate Iranian Khuzistan from Iraq, were assigned to Turkish jurisdiction. The development of the great oil refineries at Abadan, on the Shatt-el-Arab, required a reconsideration of the boundary, since it meant that the port of Abadan could be reached only by passing through the territorial waters of Iraq. As a result of these differences, Iran refused to accord recognition to Iraq or to maintain diplomatic relations with its government.

Following the agreement with Great Britain, by which Iran obtained British recognition of tariff autonomy and the abolition of the Capitulatory privileges, Iran consented to extend recognition to Iraq, and a treaty of accord was reached shortly thereafter; in 1932, following the withdrawal of the British and the establishment of Iraqian independence, King Feisal paid a State visit to Teheran. The problem of the Shatt-el-Arab remained, however, and in 1935 the matter was referred to the League of Nations. Meantime, the development of a new port at Bandar Shahpur, in Iranian waters, lessened the importance of Abadan, and in 1937 an agreement was reached which generally confirmed the 1914 boundaries but moved the line to the middle of the river opposite Abadan.

The greatest triumph of Riza Shah Pahlavi's diplomacy was the signing of a mutual pact of friendship and nonaggression by Iran, Turkey, Iraq, and Afghanistan. This took place in the Shah's palace at Saadabad on 8 July 1937. This treaty had been stimulated by the Italian invasion of Abyssinia and the fear of further European encroachments in the Middle East. It bound the signatories to forbid within their territories any foreign troops that would constitute a menace to any other signatory.

In his relations with other great powers of the West, Riza Shah Pahlavi followed an equivocal policy that did not further the country's best interests.

With Germany, there occurred a great increase in commercial interchange, and various German firms were given contracts and concessions in Iran; and German cultural and propagandist activities were intensified. The expansion of German interests in Iran was indirectly due to the policy of Imperial trade preference adopted for the British Empire at the Ottowa Conference, and by the enactment in the United States of the Hawley-Smoot tariff, the effects of both of which were to hamper British and American trade with Iran. Political relations between Germany and Iran, however, never became intimate, and several German official missions to Iran obtained only a moderately cordial welcome.

Towards the United States, which as a government had no territorial interest in Iran, and only slight commercial interest, but which through its citizens had poured out millions of dollars in philanthropy, Riza Shah Pahlavi manifested a puerile capriciousness that but for the American sense of humor would have reacted more unfavorably than it did. In March 1936, the Shah's minister in Washington, Ghaffar Jalal, while driving his car, was taken into custody by a Maryland police officer for violating the speed regulations. He was promptly released, under his diplomatic immunities, with appropriate apologies, but the Shah chose to regard the incident as an affront to the national dignity and withdrew his minister, and it was not until 1939, with the outbreak of World War II, that he resumed normal relations with the United States. From 1927 on, moreover, the activities of the missionaries in Iran had been gradually limited, through the closing of missionary schools, and by police regulations that placed restrictions upon missionary movements and preaching.

With France, also, a perverted sense of royal dignity led the Shah into a display of petulance. In 1937, a facetious French journalist published a reference to the Shah in which he made a pun upon *shah* and *chat*. It is highly offensive to a Moslem to be likened to any animal; the Shah took violent exception to the joke, directed his minister to protest, and ordered all the government-supported Iranian students in France to withdraw. The French government tactfully made such amends as it could, but the incident did not help Iranian prestige in French eyes.

ECONOMIC REFORMS

AMONG the major undertakings of Riza Shah Pahlavi was a program of economic reforms designed to give his country a greater measure of the material power enjoyed by the nations of the West. Of all the achievements of his reign, the economic reforms have been the most illusory, and they would warrant little discussion if it were not for the example they offer. They are of interest for the reason that they display, in microcosm, the problems of the larger sovereignties of the West, and permit their examination in perspective. It is possible to observe, in the economic history of modern Iran, the same tendencies that have appeared in Europe and America since the beginning of the century, and the same forces at work, stripped of their complexities, that have produced so much of the conflict and confusion of twentieth-century industrial civilization.

The characteristics of the change that occurred in Iran during the years 1921-41, may be summarized as follows: an increasing intervention of the State in the livelihood of its citizens; a growth of metropolitanism, and a hectic prosperity in the cities; finally, an increasing dependence on money as a tool of enterprise and means of subsistence, with a multiplication of financial institutions, financial instruments, monetary regulations, and the introduction and deterioration of paper money.

These events all went hand in hand and may best be described by a general presentation, mainly chronological, of the policies and programs followed. A separate section will, however, be devoted to the changes in the monetary system.

A. COMMUNICATIONS

Early in his regime, Riza Shah Pahlavi determined upon an improvement of the internal communications of the country, primarily directed to military needs in order to effect control over the distant provinces of the realm, but also designed to assist in the movement of internal trade. To this end, an extensive system of highways was projected, including a railway system. In 1921, the only railways of consequence in Iran consisted of an 85-mile, broad-gauge line connecting Tabriz with the Russian frontier, together with a 25-mile branch line to Lake Urmiah, and some 40 miles of narrow-gauge railway in the oil fields.[1] Riza Shah Pahlavi projected a standard-gauge (4′ 8½″) line running from the Persian Gulf northward to Teheran, with branches leading from Teheran to the Caspian and to Tabriz. In laying out the route, however, he had to compromise with political realities. For fifty years the project of a trans-Iranian railway had been a subject of correspondence between London and Moscow. Great Britain was unwilling to sanction any system that would connect with the Russian line and afford a means of communication from Russia to the Persian Gulf and India. Russia, likewise, would tolerate no system that would afford connections east and west between the Mediterranean and India. Iranian considerations for the independence of Iran agreed with both Russian and British views. The result was that a route neither north-south nor east-west was selected, but one running in a generally northeast-southwest direction. This route served also a distinctly Iranian political purpose in that while it touched no important city except Teheran, it did traverse the areas inhabited by the principal nomadic tribes, the control of which had always been a problem for the government.

The railway was largely completed by 1939; it constitutes today one of the most spectacular examples of railway building in the world. In the construction, the engineering skill of the principal nations of Europe and America was engaged— American, British, German, Swedish, and Danish, as well as Iranian. In the course of its 870 miles from the Persian Gulf to the Caspian Sea, it passes from sea level to an altitude of 9,500 feet, crosses 4,102 bridges, and passes through 224 tunnels, some of which corkscrew inside the mountain. At some

[1] A 50-mile railway line also connected Zahedan with the British-Indian railway system, but in 1931 trains ceased to operate over this line.

places, three levels of track are visible on the side of a gorge; in one notable location the railway traverses 6 bridges and 4 tunnels within a radius of 900 feet. Along one stretch, between Andimeshk and Dorud, 60 out of 90 miles consist of tunnels.

Along with the railway program was a similar program of modernizing the capital and the other principal cities by new public buildings, new streets, parks, and an extension of electric and telephone service.

B. FINANCES

All this, together with the demands of the army, called for large sums of money. Riza Shah Pahlavi was determined to avoid the mistake of his predecessors, who had mortgaged the country's resources and sovereignty for foreign loans, and proposed to finance his program by taxation. This required a reorganization of the financial administration in order effectively to collect the taxes levied, and to assure that the taxes collected did not evaporate while flowing from the taxpayer to the treasury. In 1922, while Riza Shah Pahlavi was still Riza Khan and minister of war, the government applied to the U. S. Department of State, as it had in 1910, for recommendations for a financial adviser. A. C. Millspaugh, economic adviser in the Department, was suggested, and was engaged as administrator general of the finances, together with a staff of assistants.

Foreign Advisers

The powers granted Millspaugh were extensive. Under their terms the government could neither grant any commercial or industrial concession nor take any decision on a financial question without consultation with him, and his approval was required for any expenditure or the assumption of any financial obligation. Millspaugh held the powers of a minister, and regularly attended the meetings of the council of ministers.

The mission remained in Iran for five years, when a disagreement arose between Millspaugh and the government over the powers conferred, and Millspaugh resigned. The results of his mission he subsequently characterized as 'partly illusory and almost wholly transitory.' [2] During the period, however, considerable order was brought into the tax system: antiquated and inequitable taxes were abolished and new taxes were introduced; the revenues were increased and the budget brought into approximate balance.

Riza Khan placed his authority as minister of war and the persuasive powers of the army behind the tax collectors, with the resultant collection of considerable sums of back taxes and disputed taxes. The accounts were unified and centralized so that the sums collected flowed without interruption into the treasury.

Millspaugh was led, however, to recommend financial measures destructive of the indigenous livelihood. Inbred with the idea of a balanced budget, he insisted on collecting back taxes, even though it entailed considerable hardship and promoted insurrection, and was willing to accept the aid of the army in establishing his financial agents throughout the country to enforce the payment. In spite of serious crop failures, he succeeded in increasing the internal taxes by 12 per cent in the third year of his administration, and almost succeeded in balancing the budget. Increasing revenues, however, stimulated expenditure, and increased expenditure created demand for more revenue. In 1924, Millspaugh proposed the levy of a tax on tobacco and a little later in the same year proposed a government monopoly on sugar and tea, the revenue from which was to be assigned to railroad construction, and a tax on matches, the revenue from which was to be assigned to sanitation. Indicative of the importance of these measures was the estimate that the sugar and tea monopoly would produce some 5 million tomans (approximately $5,000,000) a year. [3]

Sugar and tea were commodities of great importance to the peasants and the poor. The establishment of these monopolies meant that the burden of taxation was shifted to those least able to bear it. Millspaugh's tax originally was light, but the rates steadily increased under pressure for revenue, and by the end of 1939 were some fifteen times the original rates.

[2] *Americans in Persia,* Washington, 1946, p. 253.
[3] Millspaugh, A. C., *The American Task in Persia,* New York, 1925, p. 242.

c. State Enterprise

The government was learning how to squeeze money out of the country: by 1941, one could hardly find a samovar or a rug in the home of a peasant or an artisan, so severely had they been ground down by taxation.

The government now embarked upon other programs of expenditure. While the peasants were being taxed to pay for railroads that many of them would never see and from which they could derive no visible benefit, and for 'sanitation' to improve life in the cities where they would not live, the metropolitan population was receiving the benefits of a vast program of expenditure for streets, parks, and public buildings.

The capital was a particular beneficiary of embellishment. Besides several new palaces, a number of magnificent avenues were created, the principal of which, Avenue Shahriza, was later dubbed 'Park Avenue' by American soldiers. Besides avenues, parks, and numerous new buildings to house the ministries, construction was started on an opera house and a stock exchange.

With all this building, however, neither sewage systems nor water mains were constructed, and to this day no city in Iran is furnished with these utilities. The water supply flows down open channels in the streets, on the beneficent principle that it should be free to all and not the subject of monopoly by confinement to hidden conduits. There may have been something deep-rooted in the reluctance to place it underground for the sight of flowing water in the arid streets is refreshing to the spirit, however deleterious to the health.

The system of military conscription also aggravated the economic problem. The youth of the country were taken from their villages just at the age when they were becoming productive in the fields. The policy was to assign the conscripts to military centers, usually the cities, distant from their native districts, on the theory that their view would be broadened and their patriotism intensified by contact with the varied peoples and places of the realm. After their term of service, they were discharged where they were, without transportation home. The general effect of this was that the young men were left either without the means or without the desire to return to their homes, and instead sought livelihood in the city of their discharge, and added to the increasing number of proletariat.

In order to stimulate the local production of goods to supplant imports, the government created or subsidized companies to manufacture various products. Besides the State Railways, which was the largest of the State enterprises, the State undertook sugar refining, match manufacture, boot and shoe manufacture, button manufacture, fruit canning, jute extraction and processing, vegetable-oil extraction, tobacco manufacture, shipbuilding, glassmaking, paper production, as well as the operation of iron foundries, coal mines, cement works, copper mines, and smelters, soap and glycerine manufacture. Before the end of Riza Shah Pahlavi's reign, there were some 150 major undertakings, State owned, financed, or subsidized. In addition to these, projects were on foot for the manufacture of chemicals, rubber, soda, and creosote, but the abdication of the Shah in 1941 and the Russian and British occupation brought an abrupt end to the program.

Indicative of the extent to which State enterprise was carried was *Irantour,* a corporation to promote tourist trade, which built a number of magnificent hotels in various resorts, furnished in Pompeian luxury, equipped with chrome-plated plumbing (that seldom worked), ballrooms, and Hungarian dance bands.

The operation of the State enterprises eventually became a financial farce. While nominally under government supervision, actually they were the possession of the various managers who were placed in charge. No uniform system of accounting was established, and the government was seldom able to obtain an accounting of the operations. Balance sheets and income statements would be submitted, which always showed a profit, but the profits were usually shown to have been reinvested in extensions and capital additions. There was moreover a continual application to the government, on the part of the managers, for new funds for expansion of operations, accompanied by such glowing prospectuses that the government could not fail to grant the funds requested. Theoretically profitable, they actually constituted an increasing drain upon the treasury.

To find new revenue sources by which to finance these expenditures, the government extended the monopoly system. The sugar and tea monopolies, which Millspaugh had recommended, were followed by the establishment of State monopolies in tobacco, automobile imports, textiles and carpets, matches, opium, and others. All in all some twenty-seven monopolies were created by the end of the Shah's reign.

Monopolies were, however, not entirely new in Iranian experience. It had been traditional practice for the government to receive agricultural taxes in kind, and as a result the government was always a substantial holder of wheat and barley. These cereals were stored in government *ambars*, and were released, as necessity required, to maintain the bread supply in the cities.[4] The manipulation of government sales of the cereal stocks was a feature of the public administration that was both beneficial and deleterious. Powerful bakers or capitalists would often acquire a 'corner' in the market and force the price of bread to prohibitive levels. When the public outcry became loud enough the government would release enough of its wheat to break the price. Sometimes, however, the corners were acquired in connivance with the officials, and the government found itself without the stocks to sell. In such cases, when the public demanded relief, the practice frequently followed by the provincial governors was to arrest several of the leading bakers and nail them by the ears to the door of their shops. This expedient usually succeeded in effecting a reduction in the price of bread.

Operation of the Monopolies

The manner of operation of one of the monopolies created during Riza Shah Pahlavi's reign, that of tobacco, will illustrate their general effect upon the indigenous livelihood of the people. Formerly, the preparation of tobacco leaf for pipe or cigarette use had been an enterprise providing a living for individual shop owners throughout the country. In every covered bazaar they could be seen, squatting in tiny cubicles that were

[4] During Riza Shah Pahlavi's regime, government storage elevators (called 'silos' in Iran) were erected in Teheran, which are reputed to be among the largest in the world.

both work and sales rooms, surrounded by heaps of golden leaf—the proprietor and his sons or assistants busily filling paper tubes with tobacco, shearing the tubes and packing them in pasteboard boxes labeled with the particular brand name of the dealer. The shopkeeper prepared the blend to suit his customer's taste; he sold his product at the going price, or at such premium over the going price as he could command by the quality of his ware or his skill in bargaining. Competition was keen, and since the whole process of manufacture, from the raw product to the finished article, was open for all to see, success in business depended to a considerable degree on the superior quality the shopkeeper could give his product.

All this local trade and competition was now abolished, and the business became a government undertaking. A magnificent tobacco factory was erected in Teheran, equipped with all the modern machinery employed in American tobacco production. Two standard brands were produced for the general trade, and the customer took the one or the other. On the whole, the enterprise was well managed under the technical supervision of a British tobacco expert, and provided a substantial revenue to the treasury. Meantime, however, a gradual deterioration in the quality of the tobacco crop occurred. Since all tobacco produced, from whatever district, went into a common hopper, and emerged as a single blend, or two blends, the incentive to produce a finer and more aromatic leaf disappeared, and by 1942, a Persian cigarette was one of nondescript flavor and aroma, and wealthy Iranians were willing to pay up to fifty cents a package for American cigarettes filched from the army quartermaster.

The automobile monopoly operated somewhat differently. In theory the business was a government monopoly, but since the government was continually embarrassed for funds, the expedient was adopted of allowing private companies to purchase and import automobiles and parts, free of duty, and sell them at schedules fixed by the government, on condition that they be accountable to the government for the profits. Such was the demand for these products, however, that the companies were able to sell them at a greatly enhanced price while returning to the government only the scheduled price, less the costs of purchase and allowable fees and expenses. As these costs and expenses usually exceeded the sales price, the government was generally the loser. The business made numerous millionaires of those who were able to obtain the favor of the government. One particular merchant, learning that the government was about to investigate his accounts, forged his profits into golden tire chains, appropriately plated, and on the pretext of urgent business in Damascus, escaped with his gains.

D. EFFECTS OF REFORMS

The traditional livelihood system of the country was one resting on agriculture, animal husbandry, and handicraft. A factory system such as is familiar in Europe and America was nonexistent. Most articles of machine production were imported. The object the government set before it was to render the economy as independent of such imports as possible by establishing within the country the means of their production.

The dilemma that inevitably had to be confronted was this: as soon as one want was satisfied by local means, two new wants arose that could not be satisfied except from abroad. If a machine was imported to spin cotton thread, demand arose for parts and repairs that had to be imported, or for a new machine that would weave the cotton thread into fabric; this, in turn, created a need for modern bleaching, fulling, dyeing, and printing processes, as well as for power equipment to drive the machines. All these, in turn, induced a need for roads over which these machines could be transported, trucks to transport them, and in time all the paraphernalia of motorized transportation, from garages and repair shops to roadside filling stations. Once embarked upon the simplest program of industrialization, the economy was drawn irresistibly into the vortex of industrial civilization; there was no retreat; each forward step rendered the country not less but more dependent upon the West, increasingly mortgaged to its system, and bound to the wheel of its destiny.

The effect of this can be traced faintly in the customs statistics, which, though notoriously unreliable, show total exports, except oil, to have been 43,633,327 tomans in 1912-13, and total imports of 56,757,564 tomans. In 1930-31, exports, except oil, amounted to only 45,884,516 tomans, while imports had risen to 81,052,874 tomans.[5]

Of imports in the latter year, cotton piece goods constituted 21 per cent of the total; sugar and tea, 21 per cent, while machinery and iron and steel manufactures and semi-manufactures amounted to 20 per cent.

After 1931, when a new monetary system was introduced, secular comparisons lose significance, owing to the instability of the currency, but in 1938, the last prewar year, total exports, except oil, amounted to 671,152,000 rials, against total imports of 970,000,000 rials. Of imports, textiles accounted for 24 per cent; sugar and tea, 16½ per cent; and machinery and metal products, including automobiles and tires, 34 per cent. The remaining imports consisted of such articles as photographic film, writing paper, porcelain, glass, electric light bulbs, and watches.

Thus, the more fervidly the government sought to render the nation's livelihood independent of the world, the more dependent it became. The creation of factory industry, and the efforts to modernize the cities, brought people to the cities where their needs for things they could not make for themselves increased, while their desires mounted as they beheld the enticing displays in the shops. Increasing urban population brought increasing need for housing, streets, electric lights, and all the appurtenances of modern city life. This in turn created work, but not work the product of which could be exported; moreover, it increased the demand for products that could only be satisfied by importation. Trade was active, that of importers especially; a great show of prosperity was evident; everyone had money, and for this money wanted automobiles, radios, silk hose, cosmetics, imported plumbing and lighting fixtures.

[5] The adverse balance of trade was only partly made up by direct and indirect revenues from petroleum exports. Since the value of petroleum exports accrues directly to the concessionaire, the Anglo-Iranian Oil Company, and only indirectly and partially to the local economy, such exports are generally excluded from the trade statistics.

Effects upon Traditional Livelihood

While money grew plentiful in the cities, poverty increased in the hinterland. Exports, largely handicrafts and agricultural products, were not enough to provide the dollars and sterling needed to purchase all the articles that were insatiably demanded from abroad, and the balance was not met by the revenues from the oil wells.[6] In order to obtain foreign exchange for the purpose, the imports of the basic necessities, such as tea and sugar, were discouraged by increases in the import tax, and the cost of these articles to the peasant doubled and tripled. Meantime, export taxes were levied on articles that the peasant and artisan produced, the brunt of which fell on them. Finally, the government assumed the monopoly of foreign exchange. The effect of this was that an exporter of, say, dried fruits, which the peasants grew, had to turn over the dollar or sterling proceeds of the sale to the government, receiving in exchange a smaller amount of Iranian currency than was his due; the foreign exchange so acquired was distributed, at a premium, among the importers of automobiles, railway equipment, radios, and whatever else the government favored as necessary to modernize the country.

All this brought a new complexity into the economy—that of the money mechanism—and to solve the problems it created, a monetary revolution occurred that was in many ways more astounding than those by which the country had passed from a political state of absolutism to one of constitutionalism, and that was as unfortunate in its effects as the other had been salutary. To this revolution, some pages may well be devoted.

[6] The oil royalties accruing to the government were devoted almost exclusively to the purchase abroad (principally in Great Britain) of military supplies and equipment, and did not alleviate the demand for exchange for commercial transactions.

V

THE MONETARY REVOLUTION

A. MONETARY TRADITION IN IRAN

FROM the beginning of historical times until 1931 the medium of exchange in Iran had been metal coinage struck by the sovereign in units of uniform weight and fineness. Coinage, as a monetary device, had been an invention of Middle Eastern civilization, probably in Lydia, one of the kingdoms of what is now modern Anatolia, conquered by Cyrus in 546 B.C. Coinage in Iran was instituted by Darius the Great with the striking of a silver coin known as the *siglos,* of one-half-shekel weight, or about 86½ grains, together with a gold coin known as the *daric,* of 130 grains.[1] The *daric* was noted for its purity and became the standard of the ancient world.

In medieval times there occurred throughout Western civilization a revolutionary change in monetary usage. This was the introduction of paper money. In China, the art of paper making had been known as early as the sixth century, A.D., and paper money was probably used there as early as the ninth century. The Mongol conquerors of China found paper money a great convenience in their statecraft: they greatly expanded its use and carried it with them in their conquests of the Middle East, from whence it passed into Europe. Marco Polo, who visited China in the thirteenth century, describes the practice as follows:

In this city of Kanbalu is the mint of the grand Khan, who may truly be said to possess the secret of the alchemists, as he has the art of producing money by the following process. He causes the bark to be stripped from those mulberry trees the leaves of which are

[1] The *daric* was of one-shekel weight. The weight of the shekel differed according to whether gold or silver was being weighed. Sykes comments that the English sovereign and shilling correspond almost exactly in weight to the *daric* and *siglos* (123.2 grains and 87.3 grains gross). (Op. cit. vol. 1, p. 163.)

used for feeding silk-worms, and takes from that its inner rind. This being steeped, and afterwards pounded in a mortar, until reduced to a pulp, is made into paper. When ready for use, he has it cut into pieces of money of different sizes. . . The coinage of this paper money is authenticated with as much form and ceremony as if it were actually of pure gold or silver, for to each note à number of officers, specially appointed, not only subscribe their names, but affix their signets also . . . and the act of counterfeiting it is punished as a capital offense. When thus coined in large quantities, this paper money is circulated in every part of the grand Khan's dominions; nor dares any person, at the peril of his life, refuse to accept it in payment.[2]

Following the introduction of paper making into Europe, in the twelfth century, paper money came into general use, and has since remained the most important instrument of statecraft, the most baffling problem of economists, and the sword of Damocles hanging over all the institutions of commerce.

Traditional Monetary System

The peoples of the Iranian plateau, however, among whom may have persisted some memory of their ancient Prophet, seem to have regarded paper money as the manifestation of the Druj, the Eternal Lie; for among all the important nations from the Pillars of Hercules to the coasts of China, they alone resisted this innovation and temptation, and by 1930 were the only people in the world with a settled civilization that continued to adhere to the ancient doctrine of a 'sound sixpence.'

In A.D. 1294, during the Mongol dominion, an attempt had been made to introduce paper money in Iran. Kai Khatu, brother of Kubla Khan, whose paper money Marco Polo described, was ruler of Iran: finding himself embarrassed with debt and impressed by the success of his brother monarch in imposing paper money, he allowed himself to be persuaded by his vizier to make the experiment. The vizier pointed out that by issuing paper money for what the king owed, and requiring his subjects to pay in gold and silver what was owed the king, wealth would flow into the royal treasury, and the

2 *Travels*, ch. XVIII.

people, who would soon become accustomed to paper money, which they could have in great abundance, would be none the wiser, almost as happy, and certainly as prosperous. Accordingly, a royal edict was issued, forbidding the circulation of the precious metals as currency and substituting pieces of paper with the seal and signet of the sovereign beautifully printed thereon.

The edict was a fiasco. Mobs formed, the vizier was seized, torn to pieces, and thrown to the dogs. The throne itself tottered and the edict was repealed.[3]

For six hundred years, until the advent of Riza Shah Pahlavi, no ruler of Iran had dared to emit paper money,[4] and it is of interest that this ruler was compelled to abdicate within a decade after he began the issuance of paper money.

Thus, while Europe from the thirteenth century on gradually became accustomed to paper money and inured to its evils, and from the eighteenth century on became addicted to paper and credit and banks, Iran confined itself to opium as a narcotic and as a conjurer of dreams. It experienced no Mississippi Bubbles or tulip manias or South Sea frenzies, but continued its historical, if restrictive, tradition of metal money.

B. Advantages of Traditional System

Metallic Money in Handicraft

The preference for hard money, indeed the insistence upon it, rested upon the implicit needs of the country's livelihood and upon the necessities of the social and political conditions under which this livelihood was obtained. First may be mentioned the importance of a trustworthy metal coinage to handi-

[3] Malcolm, Sir John, *History of Persia*, London, 1815 (2 vols.), vol. I, ch. XII, pp. 430 ff. *See also* Curzon, op. cit. vol. I, pp. 477 ff.

[4] In 1889, however, a charter was issued to the British Imperial Bank of Iran which authorized it to issue paper money, but the notes so issued were limited in amount to £800,000 sterling value, and their validity was restricted to the town in which they were issued, with the result that they never became more than an insignificant factor in the total currency of the country. A similar right to issue notes was also given a Russian bank. A game played periodically by these institutions was to collect quantities of notes of the rival bank and present them for redemption with the object of embarrassing its operations.

craft economy. Gold, silver, copper, brass, and bronze, are highly prized for personal and household adornment, and metal work has been a major employment for skilled artisans. Metals workers have found not only an active local market for their wares but considerable foreign demand—the etched brass of Isfahan, for instance, being world famous, and surpassed, if at all, only by that of Damascus. Silver work, highly prized at home and abroad, is done in Zenjan and Kermanshah. Silver filigree work seems to have originated in Iran and the Zenjan work is unequaled.

Along with the exquisite workmanship to be found in Persian metal craft has continued the traditional purity of the metal. Gold and silver plating is unknown in Persian gold and silver craft. Coinage also has seldom been debased, and only infrequently has the standard been altered. This tradition seems to have characterized eastern Mediterranean civilization from the earliest times. Thus, after the Solonian reforms in Greece, a pledge not to tamper with the money was inserted in the oath of office taken by the *diakasts*.[5] The gold *solidus*, or bezant, struck at Byzantium first by Constantine the Great, was never altered in weight or fineness during a course of eight hundred years,[6] and in the sixth century, when Cosmas Indicopleustes visited Ceylon, he found the Persian coinage vying with the Byzantine in beauty and purity and in acceptance among the merchants.[7]

Much of the silver employed in Persian handicraft, as well as much of the copper and bronze, was obtained in the past from the melting down of coinage. Such a practice is of course forbidden in the United States and elsewhere, and while the loss to the State from the expense of coinage may be considerable, the practice was sanctioned in Iran for its salutary effect upon craft standards. It assured the trade a source of metal of

[5] See Grote, George, *History of Greece*, London, 1846-56, ch. XI; Boeckh, Augustus, *Public Economy of the Athenians*, trans. by Anthony Lamb, London, 1857.

[6] See my *Money: The Human Conflict*, Norman, 1934, Book IV.

[7] In Europe, a contrary tradition has prevailed, following the example set by the Roman emperors, of currency debasement as a means of increasing revenue, with the result that currency depreciation has been a characteristic of Western monetary history.

reliable content, and so long as the government continued to mint silver, the practice of melting down the coinage served to maintain and foster this important branch of economy.

The Practice of Hoarding

Secondly, metal coinage not only contributed to economic stability but it is a continuing necessity for political stability. Its chief service in this connection is to provide a means by which the individual can store wealth that is independent of the vicissitudes of circumstance for its value, and does not require the certification or guarantee of the government of its worth. The use of metal coinage as a store of wealth has come to be called hoarding, and is a practice that Western state-craft has invested with opprobrium, condemned as a sin against society, and in many countries, since World War I, has been outlawed in one form or another.[8] Hoarding, however, must be viewed in the East in the light of the conditions of life that have prevailed, in particular the absolutism and consequent instability of governments, and the feebleness of the protection the customary law has afforded the individual in the enjoyment of life and the possession of property.

Hoarding is the means by which the peasant, the artisan, the tribesman, assures his economic independence. A coin is tangible wealth, in a form that is more familiar to him, and more trusted, than the intangible forms of paper money, bonds, savings accounts, and shares, which have been the evidences of wealth in the West. It is something he can hide and keep against his old age when he can no longer toil, something the value of which is comparatively stable in a world of change, something that will not rot or wear, and that, if he grows prosperous, he can use to adorn wife and children.

In the cities, even among the classes that have in recent years become accustomed to Western modes, such as the merchants, who have learned to carry accounts in the banks or invest in government bonds and foreign shares, a private stock of precious metal is prized and contributes to their sense of inde-

[8] In the United States, the possession of gold coins by individuals was prohibited in 1934.

pendence. The continuing importance of metal coinage to meet the demand for 'hoards,' even assuming the existence of a relatively stable political regime, lies in the sense of security that its possession engenders in the possessor. A prime necessity of Iran, as of other countries, is a greater political stability. A prime cause of political instability is economic unrest. A prime cure for economic unrest is a diffusion of wealth. A prime method of diffusing wealth is the distribution of metallic money among the population.

On the other hand, a secondary cause of political instability is the concentration of wealth in the hands of a few, and in particular in State treasuries. Since the beginning of time, a principal lure of adventure and the spur to conquest have been the hoards that sovereigns have stored up in the treasuries of their capitals. It was the prospect of the piled wealth of Persepolis that inflamed the soldiers of Alexander; it was the Peacock Throne and the treasures of gems and gold that the Moguls had collected in Delhi that spurred Nadir Shah to the invasion of India; and there can be no doubt that not the least attraction to an imperialistic power invading Iran today would be the vast sums in gold and silver and jewels that have been assembled in the vaults of the national bank. If they are not a temptation to invasion from abroad, they constitute a continuing lure to unscrupulous men within the country to acquire control of the government.

Third, a metal coinage is a necessity for the political progress towards democracy of a country like Iran. Political democracy implies economic democracy. Political democracy cannot exist in a society where a large element of the population is both landless and propertyless. If distribution of wealth is to be achieved by evolutionary rather than revolutionary means, if the instruments of production are to be the possession of the people rather than the State, then individuals must have the means of storing wealth in small amounts until they can employ it for the purchase of the more substantial capital goods. Metal coinage, and its free employment as a store of wealth, through hoards, provides the bridge by which individuals can pass from a condition of destitution to one of possession, from vassalage to independence.

Metal Money Among the Nomads

The considerations presented above have been offered in general terms: their validity may be examined in the light of particular conditions in Iran. The first of these is the effect the introduction of paper money has had on the program of unifying the country.

A major political problem that faced the government was that of control of the nomadic tribes and of grafting them more firmly into the national life. This was done, in the first instance, by arms. But to hold the tribes in control, to render them loyal to the government, required a system of administration congenial to their natures and adapted to their habits. An important element of the administrative system is money in a form adapted to the necessities of nomadic existence. The tribesmen, in their dealings with the townsfolk, and with each other, like a money that they can bite, and hide, or use to adorn their womenfolk, or beat into plate for uses of their handicraft. Their complaisance with the regime, their acceptance of taxation, their general good will, are gained in large measure by payment for their wares and handiwork in good silver and gold, rather than in paper money, the value of which none of them can tell from day to day.

In their migrations in search of water and pasture for their herds and flocks, fording treacherous streams and battling through snow drifts, the tribesmen no doubt find the weight of coined wealth an encumbrance, and they should probably consider appealing the arguments of monetary economists for the 'greater convenience' of paper money; nevertheless, they prefer the heavy coin to the soluble paper, which may become a sodden mass in their baggage, unrecognizable, and rejected by merchant and banker when presented for redemption. Ordinarily, sultan and shah mean little to them; in the solitude of their tents or the security of their mountains they may cry 'Peace to Mahmud on his Golden Throne,' but as they find good silver and gold becoming scarcer and scarcer in their hands, such silver coinage as they receive debased in fineness, more and more compelled to accept the flimsy paper of the 'central bank,' as has become the rule, their grumblings mount. While this grumble may be only a murmur in the distant capital, and never reach the ears and disturb the serenity of monetary theorists sitting in the solitudes of classroom and conference chamber, eventually the guns begin to bark in the hills at the appearance of the tax gatherer, and the spirit of revolt against the government gathers strength.

Other factors are the relative novelty of paper money in Eastern economy and the doubtful capacity of governments generally to operate a managed currency system which paper money implies. It is no reflection on the capabilities of the Iranians to suggest that note-issue theory and practice are beyond their competence. When no government has succeeded for long in managing a paper currency in the three hundred years of European experience with central banking, when questions of note issue and credit control are still among the most baffling abstrusities with which economists and statesmen grapple, it is hardly to be expected that a country like Iran should fail to appreciate its implications or to solve the problems it presents.

Paper Money as Facilitating Conquest

A further factor, which the people of Iran, like the inhabitants of Europe, discovered to their sorrow, is that paper money provides an excellent pavement, and a broad highway, for the troops of an invader. Among a people accustomed to paper money, the problems of occupation an invader faces are simplified. The occupying army does not have to bring along gold or silver or commodities to finance its operations, nor is it compelled to the onerous and often hazardous task of local levy and taxation. It can, indeed, give its occupation the appearance of a boon, by lightening the tax burden and creating a sense of general prosperity. To do all this, it need only commandeer the printing presses of the national bank that emits the currency.

C. ADOPTION OF PAPER MONEY

All these considerations were overlooked or ignored by Riza Shah Pahlavi when in 1927 he obtained authorization from the Majlis to establish a national bank and in 1932 the further authorization for the bank to issue paper money. The bank

PERSIAN METAL WORK

6a. PUL-I-KHAJA BRIDGE, ISFAHAN. This bridge has footpaths on three levels, sm: chambers decorated with paintings, covered galleries cut through the sides of arches, a: heavy foundations that serve to dam the river.

b. SPRING PLOWING

so created was modeled along the best European lines; the law required that the managing director be an American [9] and the power of note issue was strictly limited. This institution, now named the Bank Melli, prospered from the beginning. In time it occupied a magnificent building on the Avenue Firdausi, executed in Achaemenian architectural traditions, and equipped with all the services and appointments found in the most elegant banking houses of the West: today the routine operations of the institution are punctilious; on the desk of the director stand two telephones, an interoffice communication system, and a row of push buttons; the Bank publishes a monthly statistical bulletin in Persian and in French (now English), bulkier in content than those published by most Wall Street banks; the gardens of the Bank are among the most beautiful in the city, and attract many visitors; the Bank maintains also a beautiful clubhouse for its employees, equipped with a swimming pool and gymnasium; the formalities of opening and closing the vaults, of issuing and retiring notes, are as ceremonious as those of the Federal Reserve Bank in New York.

Adoption of Paper Money

The Bank regularly shows handsome profits, for it charges interest to the government on its open-account loans, and receives a commission on all foreign-exchange transactions, whether such exchange is sold by it or by its commercial rival, the British-operated Imperial Bank. Its assets are invested in the capital stock of numerous State financial institutions, such as the Agricultural Bank, the State Insurance Company, and the like. It has instituted a savings-account system which is attracting increasing amounts of deposits from small and large investors.

In the course of its first ten years, it succeeded in replacing the greater part of the silver circulation of the country with

[9] In the naive confidence, no doubt, that Americans knew how to manage money as they knew how to manage great factories: this was before the crisis in 1933 when every bank in the United States was closed and the wheels of all industry stopped in consequence, and when, to remedy the conditions created by the credit system, the dollar had to be debased by 40 per cent.

its notes; the silver was withdrawn from circulation and piled up in the Bank's vaults in canvas sacks as cover for the note issue. The note issue is, according to accepted banking principles, eminently sound.

Nevertheless, a few facts regarding the changes in the currency and the note issue that followed the establishment of the Bank will illustrate the process by which the poison of fiat money infects the economy of a nation and spreads through the body of the national life.

The Bank Melli was created on 5 May 1927, with a capital of 15,000,000 tomans.[10] The charter stipulated that the Bank could make no loan to the government, or to any bureau or agency of the government, or to any municipality, without the approval of the Majlis.

Expansion of Note Issue

In 1930, the currency system, which had been based on a silver kran of 4.603392 grams .900 fine,[11] and which had been in effect throughout Kajar times, was abandoned in favor of a new system based on a gold rial containing .3661191 grams of fine gold, or roundly equivalent to $.29, valuing gold at its then official American price of $20.67 per ounce, or $.42 valuing gold at its present American statutory price of $35.00 an ounce.[12] The only coin of gold to be minted, however, was a gold pahlavi, equivalent to 20 gold rials, and struck from gold of a fineness of .900. The common medium of exchange for domestic transactions was a silver rial, containing 4.5 grams of fine silver, coined at a fineness of .900, and worth approximately $.08 at a price of silver of $.55 an ounce. The silver rial had only a nominal value, however, since the standard for payments was now gold.

Almost immediately, however, the world financial crisis brought a sharp change in the gold-silver ratio, which made this artificial standard unworkable. Silver prices began to decline, and from the average price of $.536 an ounce, which had prevailed in 1929, fell to an average price of $.311 an ounce

[10] A toman is the equivalent of 10 rials, and at the time had a value generally equivalent to one dollar, though this value fluctuated.

[11] Nine-tenths silver, one-tenth alloy.

[12] Act of 27 Esfand 1308 (18 March 1930).

in 1930, and to an average price of $.292 an ounce in 1931. Accordingly, by a law passed 13 March 1932,[13] the standard was modified by reducing the gold rial to one-fifth its previous value, or to .07322382 grams fine gold and the silver rial from 4.5 grams fine silver to 4.14 grams fine silver. This gave the rial now the same fine content as the former kran. The fineness of the silver coin was reduced from .900 to .828, which meant, as has been noted, a corresponding corruption of the silver content in articles of silver handicraft. These values corresponded to $.058 for the gold rial and $.04 for the silver rial, valuing the silver at $.30 per fine ounce.

The country was now embarked on a fictitious gold standard—fictitious from the fact that the gold rial was not coined and internal trade was based on the silver rial. This attempt brought the beginning of the complications of a managed money system, since the rial that the peasants received for their produce and gave for the sugar and tea and other articles they purchased had one value in the market and another value in the government accounts.

Incipient Inflation

At the same time that this change occurred, the Bank was authorized to issue notes up to an amount of 90,000,000 rials, plus an additional 250,000,000 rials of notes of large denominations (1,000 rials). The notes were to be secured in full by an equivalent amount of gold, silver, or foreign gold exchange (deposits in banks of countries that freely redeemed notes or deposits in gold), but a mystifying provision of the law was that the reserve 'might be in circulation.' Moreover, because of the monetary crisis, redemption of notes in gold was suspended, although the notes remained redeemable in silver. As the silver circulation of the country was estimated at the time to be approximately 550,000,000 krans, the effect of this was to increase the total purchasing media of the country by around 60 per cent.

Subsequently in the same year,[14] the introduction of the new coins was officially deferred owing to the inability of the government to mint the silver.

[13] Act of 22 Esfand 1310.
[14] Act of 5 Mehr 1311 (27 September 1932).

Two years later, on 11 September 1934, a further increase in the note issue was authorized, to bring the total authorization to 800,000,000 rials,[15] and the reserve requirement was reduced to 60 per cent in gold and silver, which reserve, however, had to be maintained in the vaults of the Bank.

These new increases in the note issue failed to meet the demand for currency, and on 8 November 1936,[16] a further note issue was authorized, bringing the total to 1,176,163,600 rials. The steady increase in paper money circulation may be visualized as follows:

Date	Notes in Circulation
20 March 1933	Rs. 194,999,700
20 March 1934	245,128,500
20 March 1935	421,653,500
19 March 1936	593,721,755
20 March 1937	813,186,220
20 March 1938	849,708,385
21 March 1939	999,819,620

Source: *Lois et decrets monétaires et bancaires,* Department of Economic and Financial Studies, Teheran, 1937; and *Annual Reports* of Bank Melli.

By the time World War II broke out, the country had generally become accustomed to paper money, and paper money was the common medium of exchange, except among the tribes and in isolated villages. The greater part of the silver stock had now been concentrated in the vaults of the Bank, as reserve against the note issue, and silver coins had ceased to be a source of supply for the silversmith.

The subsequent deterioration of the economy, and the effects upon the livelihood and standard of living of the people, as a result of paper-money issues, and the manner in which paper-money issue was employed by occupying armies, belongs to the story of the Russo-British occupation that began in 1941 and continued until 1946, and will be told as part of that record.

[15] Act of 20 Sharivar 1313.
[16] Act of 17 Aban 1315.

VI

DECAY OF THE REGIME

TOWARDS the end of his reign, Riza Shah Pahlavi, like the dictators that had arisen in Europe, became more autocratic, more capricious, more concerned with enlarging his personal fortune and securing his dynasty, less and less concerned with the essential welfare of his people. The movement towards political democracy, which had begun in 1906 with the establishment of the Constitution, and which for all the vicissitudes to which the process has subjected the Iranian people has been the most promising development in modern Iranian history, was almost fatally interrupted; there occurred a decay of public morals and standards of official conduct from which the country has not yet recovered and may not recover for a generation.

Absolutist Tendencies

Following the example of the regimes in Italy, Germany, and Russia, the Shah had created a secret police for political security; it was not long until, like all of these organizations, it became a terror to both the righteous and the unrighteous: free speech disappeared; the Majlis became a rubber stamp to authenticate the Shah's decrees.

Until 1933, the Shah's popularity had been unquestioned. Until then he had acted generally in accordance with the popular will and with the advice and consent of his ministers. The creation of various State enterprises had, however, presented too many opportunities for profit for those in the royal favor to miss—it became worth a fortune to be in the inner circle and to enjoy the Shah's confidence.

Financial Scandals

The minister of court controlled the audiences with the Shah. The incumbent of this office was one Abol Hossein Khan

Teymourtashe: it became necessary to win this minister's favor, by one means or another, to see the Shah. Teymourtashe began to grow wealthy. For some time, it seems, the Shah was unaware of the power that was being insensibly drawn from him and vested in Teymourtashe; when he did discover the fact, great was his vengeance.

What brought matters to a head was the affair of the opium monopoly. In 1928, the government had created a State monopoly for trade in opium, and in 1930 it gave the monopoly of opium exports to one Hadj Mirza Habibollah Amine, head of a wealthy trading firm of Isfahan, who was authorized to create a company to exploit the concession. The Shah became a shareholder of the company, as did numerous members of the royal court.

Amine soon discovered that his supposedly profitable concession was a liability. As it was generally assumed that he could now afford to dispense gratuities freely, he became the prey of various extortioners in royal favor. Thus, he was required to contribute 40,000 tomans ($10,000) towards the illumination of Isfahan on the occasion of a royal visit to that city. Teymourtashe, being required to accompany the royal princes to Europe on the occasion of their entering school there, applied to Amine for a sum to cover the expense to which he might be placed, and obtained £9,000 and 200,000 rials, or around $60,000 altogether. Amine concluded that the cost of his monopoly was too high, and gave it up in 1933. At the same time Teymourtashe was officially charged with bribery. He was sentenced to prison but died shortly afterward of what is commonly understood to have been poison or strangling.

Reign of Terror

The Shah now grew morose, aloof, and extremely suspicious. A little later Davar, the able and honest minister of justice, who had been largely responsible for the judicial reforms, fell into displeasure, and in order to avoid public disgrace, committed suicide by an overdose of opium.[1]

---

[1] Not everyone fell into disfavor, of course, and not everyone became tainted with corruption. Among those who escaped both, may be mentioned Taqizadeh, minister of finance, who had strongly opposed Tey-

The Shah now began to acquire estates wherever his fancy pleased, but chiefly in Mazanderan, his native province. Landowners whose properties he admired found it convenient to offer them as a present. The secret police became more and more oppressive, and a reign of terror developed which, according to observers, was little less sanguine than Hitler's. Formerly, persons incurring royal displeasure were given the appearance of a trial on some trumped-up charge; later, trials were dispensed with and clandestine executions became common. The highly respected Arbab Kai Khosroe, head of the Parsee community and a member of the Majlis, was thrown into prison, and, as was afterward testified during the trial of Muktarri, chief of police in Teheran, was put to death by the refined process of introducing air bubbles into his veins. The doctor who acted as executioner, testimony at Muktarri's trial brought out, executed some two hundred fifty persons by such means or by other medical malpractice.

Under the influence of the Shah's example, standards of public morality, which had experienced some purification and elevation during the early years of the regime, suffered a terrible deterioration. Corruption became general. The ancient system of *mudakhil,* previously described, became more vicious: functionaries, from ministers to clerks and the lowest *farash,* demanded a commission, perquisite, or advantage from their official acts. This decay of public administration remains a principal cause of government enfeeblement today, and the main retardent to national revival.

mourtashe, and who is now ambassador to Great Britain; Hussein Ala, head of the national bank and now the exceedingly respected and able ambassador to the United States; Hussein Pirnia; Ali Akbar Hekmat; Allahyar Saleh; Dr. Shafaq, all of whom have since rendered notable service to their country in various capacities. The list could be greatly extended.

VII

THE RUSSO-BRITISH OCCUPATION

A. THE OCCUPATION

THE APPARENTLY self-denying treaty of 26 February 1921, which Soviet Russia had negotiated with the government of Iran, had shrewdly provided that in case Russia were threatened by a third power, by way of Iran, it might send its troops into Iran to remove such threat.

In 1941, the Soviet government implemented this provision. During the previous decade, a good many German firms had entered business in Iran, as railway and electrical contractors and merchants, and possibly a thousand Germans capable of bearing arms were in Iran at this time. The Soviet government regarded these Germans as a menace, and began to make representations to the government of Iran, asserting that persons of German nationality or under German influence were storing munitions of war along the frontier and were organizing terrorists in Azerbaijan.

The British joined in these representations and in the second week of August 1941, sent 'friendly' warnings to the government.

Russo-British Invasion

A nation that had for a hundred years suffered continual interference in its affairs from a powerful neighbor might naturally view with satisfaction the humiliation of that neighbor and the curtailment of its military power, and the sympathies of the Iranian people were undoubtedly with Germany. The success of German arms had at that time been nowhere seriously challenged, and German armies were then marching towards the heart of Russia. Under these circumstances, Riza Shah Pahlavi replied in uncompromising terms to the Russian and British representations.

On 16 August 1941, a joint Russo-British note was addressed

to the Iranian government, as a result of which the Shah
reluctantly expelled a few Germans, but announced that any
Russian or British interference would be resisted. Since this
reply was not regarded as satisfactory, Russia and Britain, on
25 August 1941, sent forces into Iran, the Russians from the
north, the British from the south.

The government was in no position to resist invasion. Absolutism had gone into tyranny and tyranny had produced its
usual harvest of fear, both on the part of the ruler and ruled:
the Shah had found it necessary to keep the greater part of
the army around Teheran, rather than on the frontier.
Whether the army, had it been on the frontier, would have had
the will to fight is doubtful. In any case, on 26 August, the Shah
sued for peace, and a new government took office next day.
On 28 August firing ceased, though not before the British
had blown the puny Iranian navy out of the water and the
Russians had given the city of Tabriz a monitory bombing in
which, according to reports, several thousand innocent civilians were killed or wounded.

Abdication of Riza Shah Pahlavi

On 9 September 1941, an agreement was signed which put
the greater part of the country under Russian and British
control. On 16 September, Riza Shah Pahlavi, in order to
avoid his deposition and to save the throne for his dynasty,
abdicated in favor of his 22-year-old son, Mohammad Shahpur,
and on 20 September, the Constitution was restored to vigor
by the formal proclamation by the new Shah of a constitutional monarchy. Riza Shah Pahlavi retired to Johannesburg,
South Africa, where he died on 26 July 1944, at the age of 66.

On 29 January 1942, a formal treaty was entered into by
the three governments, by which the occupation was given a
juridical status. This treaty in its opening article reaffirmed
the independence of the country, and in the succeeding articles
established an alliance among the three powers, nominally
for the defense of Iran, but in fact to further the prosecution
of war against Germany. The Iranian government was not required to assist the other two powers, however, other than by
allowing them to occupy such parts of the country as they
pleased, and to place at their disposal any and all facilities

necessary for the movement of their troops, including censor-
ship of communications. It was stipulated that the presence of
the troops of these powers did not constitute military occupation, and that the internal administration of the country would
be subject to a minimum of interference. Finally, the two
powers agreed to 'safeguard the economic existence of the
Iranian people' and to withdraw their forces 'not later than
six months after all hostilities between the Allied Powers and
Germany and her associates have been suspended by the conclusion of an armistice or armistices, or on the conclusion of
peace between them, whichever date is the earlier.'

Appropriation of National Resources

The several agencies that Riza Shah Pahlavi had created to
assure his country's independence and security were now seized
by the occupying powers and employed, if not for an opposite
purpose, at least with an opposite effect. Promptly the splendid
railway and highway systems were devoted to the transport of
war supplies from the Persian Gulf north to the armies defending the Caucasus. All but an insignificant part of the automo-
tive transport of the country was likewise impressed into this
service. The people who had crowded into the cities during
the days of the great prosperity, drawn by the opportunities
for work in the factories and lured by the parks and public
buildings built for their pleasure, now began to feel the effects
of hunger. The trucks were busy carrying war materials to
Russia; camels, too slow and too feeble for such war service,
might have brought in food, but they had all but disappeared,
the Shah having banned them because they obstructed the
roads and seemed a sign of backwardness. In Teheran in the
winter of 1942-3, the Hotel Derbend, the magnificent resort
hotel which Irantour, the State tourist company, had erected
in near-by Shimran, had nothing better to serve its guests than
spinach and eggs and camel thorn, while in Ahwaz, for example, 600 miles distant by rail, dates were rotting in the
palm groves.

What the people needed, of course, was bread, but the chief
source of wheat for bread was in the northwestern provinces,
which were under Russian occupation, and this wheat, as well
as the rice of Mazanderan, was being taken to Russia. During

the winter of 1941-2, the British brought in 93,000 tons of wheat, part of which was supplied by the United States. The Russians now grudgingly agreed to bring in a similar quantity, though no positive evidence exists that this promise was ever fulfilled.

American Occupation of Railways

On 2 May 1942, the United States entered into an agreement with Iran whereby the American government agreed to supply Iran with goods and materials under the Lend-Lease Act, and later in 1942, in furtherance of its undertaking to supply Russia with war materials, under the Lend-Lease Act, established a military mission in Iran. Early in 1943, there was begun the organization of the Persian Gulf Service Command, a noncombat force composed primarily of transportation technicians. This force, which ultimately numbered from 20,000 to 30,000 persons, took over the task of operating the port facilities at Khorramshahr and Bandar Shahpur, in the south, together with the railways and the principal highways. The port installations were practically rebuilt, the railway line was strengthened and improved, and a great amount of rolling stock was added to the equipment. The highways were also improved to handle the huge volume of goods shipped north by truck convoy.

The American force, though confined to the railway line and the highways, and though unarmed in a military sense, was nevertheless in Iran in an anomalous position, since it came neither as a hostile occupying force, nor by right of any treaty or other agreement; nor was this status ever subsequently regularized by agreement or treaty, as was the Russian and British occupation.

By means of the railway and highway systems, which Riza Shah Pahlavi had built to serve his country, some 5,000,000 tons of war material were delivered to Russia, with the result that Russia was victorious over its enemies, and at the end of the war was still strong enough to continue its occupation of northern Iran in defiance of the expressed opinion of the rest of the world; and when it nominally evacuated this area, it was able to leave behind quantities of American tanks, trucks, and other war material in the hands of 'insurgents' who continued to defy the Iranian government and demand their independence of the rest of the country.

B. FINANCING THE OCCUPATION

Likewise, by means of the national bank and the institution of an Iranian paper currency, the major occupying powers were able to finance their military expenditures in Iran without the necessity of importing specie or other valuables, as had been the case during the previous occupation of the country by Russia and Great Britain in World War I. Had metal money been the standard of payment in Iran, and had the people been unaccustomed to any other, one or other of the following methods would have had to be followed: (a) to require the Iranian government to deliver such money from its own treasury or tax receipts, a process that would soon have exhausted the treasury without meeting the total requirements of the occupying powers; (b) to take over the administration of the country and make levies on the population, a course that would have required a full-scale occupation with all its attendant difficulties; (c) to barter for goods and services by bringing in goods; or (d) to import specie, that is, gold or silver, either to be minted into coin of the realm or to be exchanged for goods and services at its bullion value.

None of these alternatives was necessary. The legal tender in Iran was now the paper rial, and as by law the government held a monopoly of foreign exchange, it was not necessary to go into the market to purchase exchange.

From the beginning of the war, the value of the rial had been rising in relation to sterling, which dropped from 80 rials to the pound in 1939 to 65 rials to the pound before the occupation. But now the rial took a precipitate drop, to 142 to the pound. In order to protect the Iranian currency from a further depreciation, as well as to assure itself of a supply of rials, the British government negotiated a financial agreement with Iran, which was signed on 26 May 1942, which fixed the rial-sterling rate at 128-30 rials to the pound, and obligated the Iranian government to deliver unlimited quantities of rials at this rate. The agreement also fixed a corresponding rate for dollars of 32-32½ rials to the dollar (at the cross rate of $4 to the pound which had been set by the American and British governments). The sterling delivered for rials consisted of sterling credits set up in favor of the Iranian government (i.e. the Bank Melli) in the Bank of England, which credits could be drawn upon only for the purchases of goods in the 'Sterling Area' (that is, areas in which the value of sterling could be fixed by fiat), but could be used to purchase goods in North America after the Iranian government had exhausted all its supply of dollars. On its part, the British government agreed to convert 40 per cent of the sterling credits into gold at the official parity, which gold should, however, be kept either in Canada or South Africa.

Financial Agreements

Subsequently, on 5 January 1943, the agreement was modified at the insistence of the Iranian government, the British government agreeing to convert 60 per cent of the sterling balances into gold; subsequently, also, the transfer to Teheran of the gold portion of the credits was provided.

The fixing of the sterling-rial rate at 128-30 rials to the pound was an advantage at first to the British and American governments, but as a device to stabilize the cost of purchases it failed like most attempts at managed currency. While the price of rials was now fixed, the price of things that rials purchased was not fixed, and despite various attempts to control the price level by price fixing and rationing, the cost of occupation continued to mount with the mounting inflation.

The United States government also entered into negotiations for a financial agreement, as well as an agreement that would regularize the presence of American troops in the country, but the negotiations were never consummated. The American government, however, continued to sell dollars at the equivalent of the British rate for sterling, that is, 32 rials to the dollar, and in accordance with the Gold Reserve Act of 1934, made these dollars fully convertible into gold at the statutory rate of $35 an ounce.

When I examined this situation on my arrival in Teheran in January 1943,[1] I recommended that the American and

[1] As Treasurer General of Iran, by Parliamentary appointment (Act of 8 Dey 1321).

British governments sell gold directly in the market, and thereby relieve the strain on the printing press; not only would the process assist in stemming the inflation but it would reduce the costs of the occupation, since the bazaar price of gold was then $70 to $80 an ounce, as against the $35 an ounce, or its equivalent, at which dollars and pounds sterling were being sold to the Bank Melli. The British government was hesitant for fear the operation might set a precedent in other parts of the East and involve the British Treasury in gold commitments beyond its capacity. The American Treasury Department, which held abundance of gold, timidly followed the British lead, but offered to deliver gold to the Iranian government in lieu of dollar exchange. This offer was promptly accepted; I drafted a ministerial order for the Bank Melli to purchase a half ton of gold ($500,000) for immediate shipment by air. The gold, in small bars packed in sawdust-filled kegs, was delivered by the army air service within a fortnight, and promptly put on sale for the Iranian government account. The operation realized a profit of approximately 100 per cent for the government, and was instituted as a regular practice. Eventually, in March 1944, but too late to curb the inflation, the American and British governments concluded to follow the example set, and from then on until the end of the war the operations of these two powers in Iran were financed largely by open-market gold sales, made through the intermediary of and in account with the Bank Melli.[2]

On 10 March 1943, the Soviet government negotiated a financial agreement with Iran, following closely the British agreement, but with certain modifications of a peculiar nature. Since the Soviet government, as a result of its totalitarian economy, had no money with a recognized international value, the Russo-Iranian Agreement employed dollars as the unit of account, and the Soviet government agreed, in exchange for the rials received, to set up dollar balances in Moscow in favor

---

[2] Total U. S. disbursements in Iran from 1 July 1940, through 31 December 1945, amounted to $118,832,366 gross, and to $55,452,893 net. Sales of gold against rials (open-market sales) amounted to $5,595,232. In addition, sales of gold were made to the Bank Melli, either for resale or to add to the note reserve, of $11,499,874.

of the Iranian government. Such dollar balances were obviously bookkeeping entries.

Following meticulously the terms of the Irano-British Agreement, the Russo-Iranian Agreement further provided that 60 per cent of the credits so established should be convertible into gold, and that the gold would be transported on request to the Iranian border, providing, however, that the cost of insurance were borne by the Iranian government. The insurance rate was not specified. The Agreement also provided that the dollar credits might be used for the purchase of American goods, should the Iranian government's supply of dollars from other sources be exhausted. The final disposal of the dollar balances was to be determined at the termination of the Agreement, which would occur at the same time as the termination of the Agreement of 29 January 1942, governing the occupation.

Subsequently, the Soviet government notified the Iranian government that it would require 80,000,000 rials monthly for its occupation expenses. British occupation costs began to run at the rate of 300,000,000 rials monthly and American occupation costs substantially more.

c. The Spread of Inflation

The Bank Melli had begun to issue and deliver bank notes to the occupying powers,[3] and since the notes, once issued, remained in circulation (instead of returning to the Bank as customers' deposits), the Bank was continually under the necessity of issuing fresh quantities of notes. Moreover, the government, restricted in exercising its sovereign powers, particularly in the areas under Russian occupation, and unable to collect the taxes due, and faced also with mounting costs of administration, was compelled to borrow from the Bank to meet its budgetary needs. During the year 1942-3, tax collections dropped by around 670,000,000 rials, while expenditures increased by some 590,000,000 rials, compared with the year earlier. By 5 January 1943, the floating debt amounted to 3,400,000,000 rials, compared with 2,181,000,000 rials at the beginning of 1942.

[3] The notes were printed in England, and delivered by air.

Increase in Note Issue

The budgetary deficit, like the expenditures of the occupying powers, was financed by the Bank, by an increase of the note issue. The circulation, which stood at 1,550,000,000 rials on 21 August 1941, just before the occupation, mounted to more than 2 billion rials within a year. The subsequent increases may be shown as follows:

Date	Total Circulation	Net Circulation *
20 August 1941	Rs. 1,550,000,000	Rs. 1,377,101,665
22 October 1942	3,000,000,000	2,553,630,415
22 November 1943	5,998,625,600	5,024,442,440
21 November 1944	7,580,750,600	6,416,233,965
20 March 1945	7,662,000,000	6,662,783,500

* Notes not held by National Bank.

Along with this increase of notes went an increase in living costs, as follows, based on the year ending 21 March 1937 as 100.

Month and Year	Cost of Living Index
August-September 1941	154.1
August-September 1942	242.8
August-September 1943	392.1
November-December 1943	542.4
March-April 1944	910.
August-September 1944	993.
November-December 1944	1,076.
March-April 1945	1,108.

Source: Bulletins of Bank Melli Iran.

A principal effect of these emissions of paper money and the rise of prices was to induce a loss of confidence in the money and the government that issued it, and to add to the usual inducements to hoarding. Silver had long disappeared from circulation, and in the absence of silver or gold any commodity that could be stored was held off the market. This was chiefly wheat, which caused the food situation in the cities to grow increasingly serious.

The British government, more concerned than the Russian in the maintenance of the integrity of the Iranian government, and the independence of the people, early began to take such measures as it could to relieve the situation. Subsequently, on 4 December 1942, a Food Agreement was signed between the United States and Great Britain, on the one hand, and the Iranian government, on the other, by which the two powers agreed to make up any deficiency in the food supplies of the country resulting from the occupation.[4] In addition to the 93,000 tons of wheat which had been brought in during 1941-2, a further 30,000 tons of wheat and 24,000 tons of barley were promised for the ensuing year.

The Anglo-Iranian Oil Company, in order to assist the government in meeting the budgetary deficit, advanced several million pounds sterling against future royalties. During the summer of 1942, the British minister suggested that American financial advisers be engaged, in the hope that their presence might be of some assistance in maintaining public confidence, and that possibly they might devise some solution to the problem short of evacuation. It was a forlorn hope, of course, for chaos was implicit in a situation in which a country was visited with the troops of three foreign powers, two of which had been traditionally jealous of each other, the third of which, being neither an invader nor a visitor, and whose forces were neither troops nor civilians, was in the country under no law of war or peace, assuming none of the responsibilities, though enjoying most of the privileges, of a conqueror. In such a situation, order could be brought about only by a radical change in fundamentals.

D. AMERICAN FINANCIAL MISSION

To assist in solving the growing problems in the administration and finances of the country, the government requested the aid of foreign advisers. The United Kingdom Commercial Company (a British government agency which handled British transport and commercial transactions in Iran) lent advisers and gave assistance in the organization of an Iranian state transportation agency directed towards mobilizing all carrying facilities. Major General Clarence Ridley and a staff of

---

[4] This deficiency arose largely from seizures of grain and livestock by the Soviet occupation forces.

officers were sent by the United States Army to advise in the reorganization of the quartermaster and supply departments of the Iranian army. Another group of officers, headed by Colonel H. Norman Schwarzkopf, became advisers to the Iranian *Amniyeh,* or gendarmerie (internal police). Colonel L. Steven Timmerman was engaged as adviser to the Teheran police administration; J. P. Sheridan as adviser to a new food ministry, set up to deal with food supply and distribution; Dr. Luther Winsor, an expert on irrigation, as adviser to the ministry of agriculture; and Lt. Col. Alexander Neuwirth from the United States Army as adviser to the ministry of health.

In addition to these, a group of financial and fiscal advisers were engaged for service in the ministry of finance. The difference between this group, known as the American Financial Mission, and the other advisers, lay generally in the fact that they were conferred, either by law or by the nature of their appointment, with considerable executive powers in addition to their advisory functions. A. C. Millspaugh, who had previously (1922-7) served the government as administrator general of the finances, was, by act of the Majlis,[5] again appointed to the same post, and was vested with powers even broader than those he had previously exercised during his earlier service with the government.

By similar acts of the Majlis, Richard Bonneville was appointed chief finance inspector, Howard Shambarger as accountant general, Harold Gresham as director of customs, James G. Robinson as director of internal taxation, Paul Atkins as economic expert, and I as treasurer general.[6]

Mr. Bonneville did not take up his appointment. It soon became apparent to me that, in view of the policies and procedures being followed by the administrator general of the finances, I could render no effective service as treasurer general, and I resigned after six months. Messrs. Robinson, Shambarger, and Atkins likewise all withdrew before the end of the year.

[5] Act of 21 Aban 1321 (12 November 1942).

[6] All these posts, with the exception of that of economic expert, were statutory positions in the ministry of finance, with powers and duties generally defined by Iranian law.

The mission arrived in January 1943. In his first monthly report the administrator general of the finances summarized the economic condition of the country in the following words:

The economic situation at the present moment is of the gravest character. The various factors in the situation are complicated and interwoven, and because some of the most important of these factors are beyond the control of the Iranian Government the task of coping with the situation is one of extreme difficulty. The most serious and urgent aspects of the economic situation should be considered under two heads: (1) the food problem and (2) the rising cost of living.[7]

To meet this situation, the mission proposed the following measures:

1. Price-fixing and rationing of essential commodities.
2. Revision of the income-tax law, so as to draw off as much as possible of the excess purchasing power and cover the Government deficit.
3. Reduction of the Government budget and of Government borrowing from the National Bank.
4. An internal Treasury loan, intended to provide a means of saving and also draw off a portion of the excess purchasing power.
5. Increase of agricultural and industrial production within the country.
6. The increase of imports to meet Iran's need for essential goods, so far as such action may be possible in view of the shortage of shipping.
7. Better means of distributing imported goods.
8. Sale of Government properties.
9. Bringing gold into the country and better means of handling exchange transactions.
10. Sale of silver for rials.
11. Selling of obsolete coins at the Mint.
12. Minting of token money.[8]

The administrator general of the finances concluded that even more extensive powers than had originally been conferred on him were necessary in order to deal with the crisis. These were granted. He was authorized also to engage a staff

[7] *Monthly Report of the Administrator General of the Finances,* Bahman 1321.
[8] Ibid.

of sixty Americans, besides Iranian assistants. He now came to the conclusion that only dictatorial powers would save the situation, and in a letter to the American ambassador wrote: 'Although the actual status of the mission may be camouflaged to some extent to save Iranian feelings, the mission will have to be in effect the government of the country in financial, economic, and social affairs.' [9] This was a view that the American government could not properly support in the light of its known position, and one that the Iranian government could not accept with dignity. Relations between the administrator general and the government became less and less cordial, and when the former finally attempted to assert authority over the powerful Bank Melli, its managing director challenged him. The question now came to the Majlis for determination. Opposition to the administrator general and the policies he had been following had been growing. The Majlis resolved the question in favor of the Bank manager, and at the same time repealed a number of the powers that had been conferred upon the administrator general. Millspaugh thereupon, in February 1945, resigned his post. He went to England, where he stayed until the end of the year, returning to the United States in time to issue a statement, on the eve of the meeting of the Security Council to consider the Soviet-Iranian question, sharply criticizing the Iranian government as incapable of self-government, and proposing in effect a joint Russo-British-American protectorate.

E. RUSSIAN OCCUPATION POLICY

British policy, as stated, was directed towards the maintenance of the integrity of Iran, so far as was consistent with the military purpose of the occupation. This was a policy in accord with British long-range interests in the Middle East, which were to keep a buffer state between Russia and the Persian Gulf. After the British victory at El Alamein in October 1942, and the German defeat at Stalingrad in January 1943, the Middle East was relatively secure, and military reasons for British occupation ceased to exist. The only interest

[9] *Americans in Persia*, p. 220.

of the Western Allies in Iran was the usefulness of the country as a corridor for shipments of war material to Russia. This interest could have been served without a military occupation. There is reason to believe that Great Britain would gladly have withdrawn its troops at this time, which could have been used to greater effectiveness in the European theater, but Soviet Russia had other designs, and the British were required to remain as a counter-check upon their ally.

In the northern areas, under Russian occupation, no effort was made to assist the Iranian government in maintaining its sovereignty. In the words of an official observation made in January 1942, 'On the one hand the Russians treat the people individually in a considerate and kindly manner, and on the other have utter contempt for the government and social system.'

Some instances of the manner in which the Russians ignored and flouted the Iranian government, and arranged affairs so as to reduce it to further impotence may be cited:

(1) While the Iranian customs in the south were maintained, and American and British imports (except goods en route to Russia) paid the stated customs tariff, the customs frontier in the north was ignored, and the Russians brought in goods for sale in Iran without the formality of declaring their value. They also declined to pay the internal road tax, or the railway tariff for the transportation of war material to Russia. The result was that the Americans and British had to pay these charges. It should be explained in this connection that while the Americans operated the railways, the legal control remained in the Iranian State Railways, and the stated tariff was paid to the State Railways which in turn paid the costs of operation.

(2) The Soviet government, invoking the terms of the Agreement of 29 January 1942, required the Iranian government to provide facilities of various sorts, and to defray the expense of upkeep of these facilities, while, contrariwise, requiring the Iranian government to pay the cost of any facilities or goods made available by the Russians for the maintenance of Iranian security and economy. Thus, the State munitions factory was taken over and devoted to manufacturing machine guns and ammunition for the Soviet army. All the operating expenses of

this factory continued to be borne by the Iranian government, which was compelled to include in its budget sums for this purpose. A similar requirement was made in regard to the canning factories turned over to the Soviet authorities.

(3) The Caspian fisheries were operated at a loss owing to the refusal of the Soviet government to fix a price at which the products were sold.

(4) The Soviet government took the output of the copper mines without reimbursement.

(5) The Soviet government required the Iranian government to advance (up to June 1943) 22,500,000 rials to rebuild roads used by the Soviet forces, 88,200,000 rials for maintaining the portion of the railway operated by Soviet forces, 80,-000,000 rials for maintenance of roads used by Soviet forces, 5,500,000 rials to maintain the port facilities at Bandar Pahlavi, operated by Soviet forces, 1,850,000 rials to maintain the port of Noo Shahr.

(6) The Soviet authorities took the product of the State military shoe factory, at a time when Iran was obtaining shoes for its own army from the United States under the Lend-Lease Agreement.

(7) The Soviet authorities took the greater part of the rice crop in Mazanderan and Gilan, drove out 150,000 sheep and goats, but imported a little wheat, which it sold for cash. At the same time, it required the Iranian Agricultural Bank at Shahrud to advance 10,000,000 rials for the harvest and purchase of wheat, which wheat it took out of the country.

American forces evacuated Iran at the end of 1945, and early in 1946 the United States negotiated an agreement with the Iranian government in settlement of the accounts. While under the Lend-Lease Agreement with Soviet Russia goods were to be delivered to Russia at American ports, and the cost of shipment was to be borne by the Soviet government, the United States government, taking the realistic view that the Iranian government would never collect the railway tolls from Russia, paid them instead. Installations, equipment, and surplus property left in Iran were valued (at cost to the United States) at $60,776,747. A good deal of this property, such as locomotives and cars, as well as other supplies, were subsequently removed and sold to the United Nations Relief and Rehabilitation Administration and others. The balance was disposed of to the Iranian government for $27,000,000, of which $11,000,-000 was paid in cash from dollar balances in the United States, and the remainder in rials which, under the Agreement, were required to be spent gradually. The transaction, which was negotiated by Colonel John B. Stetson, was one not disadvantageous to the American government.

The British evacuated before 2 March 1946, which was the date of termination of the Agreement of 29 January 1942, being six months after the signing of the instrument of surrender by the Japanese. The Russians, however, did not leave the country, as promised. The situation this created is left for discussion in a later chapter.

PART FOUR

IRAN TODAY

I

LIVELIHOOD

A. CONDITION OF COUNTRY AT END OF WORLD WAR II

THE END of World War II left Iran in a condition of
monetary inflation which had lifted the general cost of
living to ten times the average for the year 1936-7. The poor
had grown poorer, for wages had not kept abreast of rising
prices; speculators and traders had grown rich, and many of
them had transferred themselves and their gains to Cairo, England, and the United States, where they hoped to find more
security for both life and property than existed in Iran. The
government budget was unbalanced, a mass of floating debt
had accumulated, and the internal administration had deteriorated. As of 20 March 1945, the government owed the Bank
Melli a total of 4,407,370,271 rials (approximately $132,000,-
000) of which 1,400,000,000 rials had been funded as the unre-
deemable portion of the note issue.

Financial Position

On the hopeful side, however, the country emerged from
the war with no foreign obligations and with substantial balances to its credit abroad.

The 60 per cent of the sterling credits, which had been set
aside in gold in South Africa were now transferred to Iran.
A substantial part of the dollar credits still held were also
taken in gold and transported to Iran as note reserve. All this
gold was obtained at the American statutory rate (and its
English equivalent) of $35 an ounce, which compared with an
open-market rate in Iran that ran as high as $70 to $80 an
ounce at the rate that had been fixed for the rial. The effect
of this was that despite an increase in the note circulation to
7,762,000,000 rials as of 20 March 1945, the Bank held 113,-
980,474 grams of gold of a current value of $128,256,520, repre-
senting 53.57 per cent of the note issue; in addition, silver was

held to the extent of 786,254,436 grams standard, worth approximately $12,500,000 at $.50 per ounce, and constituting 4.14 per cent of the issue. By all standard banking practices, this represents a high reserve for the note issue, and in the view of the Bank itself:

. . . the use of the word 'inflation' with regard to Iranian currency is not justifiable and in view of the unfavorable psychological effect which it has on the people, it is hoped that both official authorities and private individuals will refrain from using it in connection with the country's currency.[1]

Moreover, on 18 November 1943, the government began anew the issue of silver coins, of 1-, 2- and 5-rial denomination. These coins were substantially reduced in weight and fineness from the standards set when the rial was introduced, the new rial piece now consisting of .96 grams of fine silver, compared with 4.14 grams originally, and the fineness was reduced from .828 to .600, which was in effect creating a coin not silver but almost half base metal.

Oil Resources

More important than the yellow gold in the bank vaults is the black gold of the oil fields. Here is an immense and spectacular resource the value of which was not impaired, but rather increased by war. The refineries at Abadan and Kermanshah were enlarged, and oil is at present flowing in greater quantities than ever before, carrying with it a steadily increasing stream of royalty revenue to the government. Production is now running at around 120 million barrels annually, with the royalties yielding as a fixed minimum £4,000,000, or approximately 512,000,000 rials, annually. Immense oil reserves still remain to be developed, both in the north and in the south, and if the government is able to obtain the same terms for their development as it now enjoys from the Anglo-Iranian Oil Company, these reserves will constitute an important means of improving the national well-being.

[1] *Report of the Bank Melli for the year* 1322 (22 March 1943—20 March 1944). Teheran. The ratio of 53.57 per cent gold was obtained of course, by a revaluation of the gold at a higher rate: i.e. a devaluation of the rial from its former equivalent of .07322 grams fine gold to .027411 grams fine gold, or to about 37 per cent of its former value.

Aside from the revenue it provides, the oil affords a means of carrying forward the program of industrialization which as yet has been attained only to an insignificant extent. Of current oil production, about 5 per cent is used in Iran. Besides the oil, gas is produced, but cannot be exported, and sound economy would dictate its greater utilization locally. While as much gas is conserved as possible, and is employed in repressuring wells, enormous quantities are allowed to escape: the flames from their combustion illuminate the desolate Bakhtiari hills and at night give the landscape an appearance suggestive of Dante's Inferno.

Agriculture and Crafts

Agriculture, grazing, and handicraft, upon which the livelihood of some 90 per cent of the population still depends, had further deteriorated as a result of the war, government policy, and the impact of foreign industrialism. During the latter years of Riza Shah Pahlavi's reign, the tax on agricultural produce, which had been abolished on the recommendation of A. C. Millspaugh in favor of a tax on the land, was reimposed. The effect of this had been again to place the incidence of taxation upon the peasant rather than upon the landowner. In addition, the price of sugar, tea, and matches had been increased by the State monopolies on these articles. Moreover, Riza Shah Pahlavi, following a policy of statecraft as old as the Romans, of making bread cheap in the cities, had kept the price of wheat low, with the practical result of reducing the yield; wherever the opium poppy could be grown it replaced wheat as an article of commerce.

The war effected a further decline in agriculture, particularly in the fertile north. The production of dried fruits is today about half of the prewar normal, due to the indiscriminate cutting down of orchards by the Russians for firewood.

Fortunately, towards the end of Riza Shah Pahlavi's regime, some recognition had been given to the agricultural problem, and certain efforts were made to meet it: an agricultural school was established; an agricultural loan bank was created to assist small landowners in purchasing and improving their properties; the sale of State domain to the peasants was begun; State-fostered locust-control measures were undertaken; several small dams and irrigation projects were undertaken or projected; some progress was made in supplying improved seed to farmers; experts were brought in to improve the culture of silk cocoons.

Most of these measures, however, fell far short of the realities of the situation. Most of them were to the advantage of landowners rather than to the peasants themselves. It was in the nature of things, for instance, that only those who were already possessed of land borrowed money from the agricultural bank. Irrigation projects opened up new land but the land was still burdened with the landlord's rent. The agricultural school, at Karaj, a few miles from Teheran, spent most of its funds on beautiful grounds, and in teaching the theory of agriculture to sons of landowners rather than the practice of agriculture to the peasants who tilled the soil.

Industrialization in the cities and the competition of machine-made foreign wares had been effecting a gradual decline in handicraft industry, and to these forces were added, during the war, monetary inflation. Silver and copper became almost unobtainable for the metal handicraft industries, and the great demand for labor by the occupying forces drew artisans away from the bench. Moreover, because of the artificial price level, the prices of these articles were higher in Iran than abroad, and this, combined with the dislocation of markets, discouraged production.

War-Time Policies and Measures

Following the abdication of Riza Shah Pahlavi, but while the war was still in progress and the government was laboring under the handicaps of an occupation and a restricted sovereignty, a number of measures were taken in the direction of improving the livelihood of the people. The American financial mission has already been discussed. In 1941, the government invited a mission from the United States to survey the educational needs of the people, and to recommend a program. Dr. Luther Winsor carried on a survey of irrigation possibilities, and some steps were taken in the direction of a public health program. In 1943, the statutes of the Bank Melli were revised by which the note-issue functions were separated from the banking functions in accordance with Bank of England practice.

Most of these measures bore little fruit during the war, but they served to clarify the main problems that confronted the country and paved the way for the program of economic reforms subsequently announced in 1946.

B. AGRICULTURAL NEEDS

Because of war dislocations and other difficulties, the only member of the educational mission to reach Iran was Harold B. Allen, Director of Education of the Near East Foundation. Allen is a leading authority on village and rural rehabilitation, and he took with him the interest of the Foundation, which for some fifteen years had been carrying on a valuable work in village and rural rehabilitation in Bulgaria, Greece, and Syria.

The Allen Survey

Allen arrived in Iran in 1943, and following a survey made under the auspices of the Foundation, presented a series of reports to the Iranian government. The findings and recommendations he made, in summary, are as follows:

(1) The unquestioned fertility of the soil, and the productivity of the soil wherever water is available.

(2) The relative ease with which the water problem can be improved under proper handling. Allen recommends, as the simplest and least expensive method of providing water, the restoration and extension of the ancient *kanat,* or underground canal, system. Because of the nature of the water sheds, soil structure, and other factors, only a few areas exist where large dam and irrigation projects are feasible; moreover, greater good would be gained by a diffusion of expenditure.

In addition to extending the *kanat* system, the possibilities of the underground water table should be explored. Vast areas exist, too distant from the mountain springs for the use of *kanats,* where underground water can be tapped. In some cases, artesian wells are possible; in other cases the water must be lifted. Advantage should be taken of the constancy of the winds on the plateau, through the introduction, or rather reintroduction, of windmills to operate pumps. Besides windmills, motor-driven pumps, employing the fuel-oil resources of the country, might be widely used.

(3) The question of ownership of the *kanats* must be dealt with. Generally, the construction of a *kanat* is an undertaking beyond the means of the peasant, and since one *kanat* will serve to irrigate more land than a single family can till, there seems to be some place for a limited form of land capitalism. Allen is of the opinion, however, that the peasants are fully capable of operating the *kanats* as a co-operative project. His view, accordingly, is that the policy of the government should be to build *kanats,* or to assist in their building, in order to open new land for cultivation. This land should be sold to individual peasants, and the *kanats* should thereupon be turned over to the peasants to manage.

(4) The problem of land tenure and absentee landlordism must be solved before the country can hope for any real agricultural progress. Allen thinks that this land reform should be evolutionary rather than revolutionary; that in villages that have long been under the control of landlords a sudden dispossession of the landlords would find the peasants unprepared to assume the responsibilities of ownership. He believes, however, that the peasants are fully capable of independence, and it was his observation that wherever the peasants have acquired ownership of the land an immediate improvement in conditions resulted. He advocates a progressive program of pre-empting estates by purchase and their resale on favorable terms to the peasants.

Allen found the government generally aware of the seriousness of the land-tenure problem, and even among the landowning classes, he states, he encountered an increasing willingness to accept the necessities of reform.

My observations and conclusions relative to this problem of land tenure are quickly stated. The peasants who farm their own small plots utilize their land just a little more effectively; they grow a little more food; they secure slightly better yields; have somewhat more liveable homes; are more insistent on demanding educational facilities for their children and medical attention for their families. They show more independence of thought and action, more spirit. Even where their conditions were miserable they stated emphatically that

MAN AND HIS SONS WITH HOES, NEAR DORUD

8a. RUG WEAVING, HAMADAN

b. RUG WEAVER TRIMMING RUG

they would not change places with compatriots of theirs who are in more productive areas but working under the feudal system.[2]

Allen goes on to say:

A government that is thoroughly committed to a policy of protecting and developing its greatest resource (the land and the peasant population), a proper system of land tenure and a constantly increasing supply of water are, in my opinion, the foundation stones of all rural progress in Iran. With these factors assured we are in a position to give serious consideration to other important aspects of village welfare.[3]

(5) The fundamental need, Allen points out, is adult education, both social and technical, that is, the need to instruct the peasant in improved processes of agriculture, sanitation, housing, and co-operative living.

League of Nations Survey

Prior to the Allen survey, a League of Nations Opium Commission, which visited Iran in 1925, made recommendations regarding the development of agricultural crops in substitution for the opium poppy, and the findings of this Commission, long ignored, may profitably be recalled.

The Commission pointed out that much could be done to revive the silk industry, which until the middle of the nineteenth century, when it was all but destroyed by the pébrine blight, was a principal supplier to the European market. Subsequently, the world market was largely pre-empted by the Japanese, who adopted modern techniques of growing, preparing, and reeling for the trade. Persian silk possesses, however, distinctive characteristics that still make it prized by connoisseurs, but the industry would need to be reorganized to meet modern trade requirements, particularly in regard to reeling.

The Commission also pointed out that the Iranian climate is especially favorable to the growing of other products, by which it could assume a unique position in world trade. It

[2] Allen, H. B., *Studies in Rural Education (Rural Welfare) in Iran* by authority of the Imperial Government of Iran, Teheran, 1943.
[3] Ibid.

recommended that attention be given to the cultivation of aromatic plants, such as the rose, jasmine, mint (*Mentha pipperita*), tarragon, anise (*Pimpinella anisum*), the rose geranium, lavender, saffron (*Crocus sativus*), iris (*Iris pallida*), and others. Formerly, the extraction of these oils was an extensive industry. (The word *attar* is the English equivalent of the Persian *atr* by which these oils were originally known in the trade.) There is no reason, the Commission stated, why this industry should not again be more extensively developed, as it is in the Balkans, where it is highly profitable. Other products that are in world demand, for the growing of which the soil and climate of Iran are highly favorable, are various oleaginous plants, such as the mandab (*Eruca sativa*), sesame (*Sesamum indicum*), castor-oil beans (*Ricinus communis*), soy beans (*Soja hispida*), colza (*Brassica campestris*), and rape (*Brassica napus*).

Need for Farm Implements

One of the most useful things the government could do to improve agriculture would be to encourage the importation or local manufacture of simple farm tools and implements. The import statistics contain an item of agricultural implements, but examination of the components of this item reveal them to be chiefly machine cultivators, threshing machines, and other equipment used in large-scale farming. What the peasant needs today are steel hoes and spades, a hand cultivator, a steel plow suitable for an ox, and other elementary equipment.

In 1934, the United States exported to Iran goods to the value of $3,686,515, of which $1,243,629 consisted of trucks, while exports of farm implements amounted to $20,396, of which the principal item was machines. In 1936, Iran purchased from the United States $1,584,888 worth of trucks and $20,199 worth of implements of cultivation. In 1937 and 1938, no exports of farm implements from the United States are recorded, but there was sent $1,485,485 worth of trucks, in addition to passenger automobiles and parts. In 1939, American exports to Iran of implements of cultivation amounted to $6,499, and in 1940 to but $29 out of total exports of $2,398,559 and $4,406,199.

C. HANDICRAFT

The twentieth century has witnessed the gradual extinction in Iran of a number of famous industries which have been unable to withstand the impact of the machine. Formerly, marvelous fabrics of silk, wool, and cotton were produced on the Persian looms and sold throughout the world. This weaving industry has now practically disappeared. Embroideries have almost vanished, while the industries of inlaying, carving, enameling, and metal work, once famous, are falling into desuetude, or show evidence of deterioration in design because of the vain effort to meet the competition of machine-made articles. Even the interesting hand-printed cottons (*kalamkar*) are now made of imported rather than native cotton and are of inferior design.

'There is every reason why these native industries should be saved,' says the Opium Commission Report, 'and saved while there are yet artisans to teach the younger generation.' As Western civilization becomes more and more surfeited with stereotyped machine-made wares, it will seek the refreshment and inspiration that is to be found only in the individuality of handicraft, and it will return to those lands where the highest traditions of handicraft have been maintained. Furthermore, the maintenance of handicraft provides an independence and security from the periodic convulsions that are seemingly the inevitable accompaniment of highly organized, mass-production industry. The Opium Commission Report states further that,

India has had some success in introducing improved hand looms, and there is no contribution which would do more to revive the village and cottage industries of Iran than the introduction of simple machines for ginning, carding, spinning and weaving the various tissues which abound and are native to the country.

An industry, formerly of considerable importance, and which the Commission regarded as susceptible of revival as a result of the development of the oil fields, is that of tile and pottery work. Iran does not possess the resources of kaolin that China enjoys, which are so necessary for the finest porcelains, but glazed tiles and glass work have been famous from antiq-

uity. The great handicap has been the lack of fuel to burn
in the kilns. The abundance of fuel oil and the existence of
coal and lignite in various parts of the country offer a means
of correcting this deficiency.

d. The Carpet Industry

There remains the question of the future of the Persian
carpet industry. It has been the least affected by the impact
of industrialism and today provides the largest single item of
export apart from oil. Despite the development of machines
that are capable of producing carpets in such close imitation
of the hand-made article, not only in the complexity of design
and variety of color but in the nap itself, that they deceive
any but an expert, the hand-woven Persian carpet continues
to find a steady demand throughout the world. It is the standard of excellence and artistry, and is not surpassed by the
Chinese, Turkish, Indian, or the North African.

Government Policy Towards Carpet Industry

Whether craft standards are seriously impaired today is a
debatable question. In 1921-3, during my earlier stay in Iran,
A. C. Edwards, head of a large carpet export firm, and a leading authority on carpets, gave the opinion that carpets then
being woven were not inferior in design, color, and texture to
the finest productions of the past. A general opinion held today,
however, is that standards have since deteriorated, and whether
this is temporary or not would seem to depend upon (a) the
policies adopted by the government, and (b) the continued
independence of Iran.

Concerning the carpet industry directly, the government
has shown a keen interest and has endeavored to maintain
craft standards. Where standards were threatened by the
development of synthetic (analine) dyes, and the substitution
of these for the locally extracted vegetable dyes, the importation of such dyes for carpet making was forbidden. Analine
dyes continued to be imported for the textile-weaving factories,
however, and whether they will eventually corrupt the carpet-
weaving industry will depend upon the continued care with
which the government regulates this traffic.

A deteriorating influence that has not been eliminated has been the establishment of 'factories' by the principal carpet importing houses. In these factories, the carpets are still hand-woven—since this is the essential characteristic of such carpets —but the patterns are provided by the importer, and are usually the simpler, bolder designs which are more easily executed and which at the same time are popular among the trade. 'Factory'-made carpets are usually of looser texture, a factor also tending to cheapen the price, and the nap is left long rather than close sheared as in the finest productions.

Among the measures taken by the government to preserve the native handicraft industry was the establishment of an Institute of Arts and Crafts in Teheran, the purposes of which were to revive and preserve the ancient designs and to foster finer standards of craftsmanship. The results of this effort have been somewhat abortive. While standards of precision are probably as high today as ever, and carpets of unsurpassed fineness of texture are still being made, the effect upon design has been negligible.

Sources of Artistic Inspiration

The weaving of a carpet is essentially an artistic rather than a commercial undertaking. The finest carpets are produced in the tents of the nomads and in the villages, where the weaving is a part-time occupation and largely in the nature of an artistic expression. If the product is sold it is because the household possesses a surplus, and the proceeds of the sale will purchase a samovar, a piece of silk, or, in time of need, some article of necessity.

The best evidence of this characteristic of the industry is that among the people carpets are prized for themselves, and in the most remote tent can be found the finest carpets, woven for the owner's satisfaction, rather than for the market.

The importation of foreign wares exercises an influence on craft standards. When the weaver discovers a preference for the articles of the bazaar, and his product acquires in his eyes a monetary rather than artistic value, his standards of workmanship decline. The inspiration deteriorates. Contact with foreign civilization, with its bewildering variety of articles creating desire for possession, fosters this tendency to commercialization.

Another factor leading to deterioration in rug weaving is the decay of the religious spirit in Iran, particularly the decay of Islam. The stimulus to employ the creative talents in the embellishment of mosques with marvelous and unsurpassed faïence work, with intricately pierced and engraved brass lamps, inlaid furniture, carpets of unimaginable texture and design, no longer exists. Design, which is the principal characteristic of Persian art, is a mode of expression particularly adapted to convey the abstract conceptions of God which are emphasized in Islamic theology. When the Islamic spirit merged with the cultural traditions of Iran there resulted a magnificent florescence of art in materials, textiles, and poetry, which reached its heights in Sufi poetry, the Persian mosque, and the Persian rug. One cannot gaze at one of the mosque rugs without being imbued with an inner exaltation, all the more pervasive and mysterious because of its lack of concreteness. The only approach in mood to these works of art is a symphonic composition, with which they have, in their design, much in common.

Capacity and aptitude for design, though it reached its finest expression in association with Islamic inspiration, both antedates and survives Islam. Thus it was that this artistic development reached its apex during the Safavid dynasty, roughly from the end of the fifteenth century through the seventeenth century, when Islamic inspiration was fortified by a great burst of national glory which culminated in the reign of Shah Abbas the Great (1587-1629).

The people are no longer imbued with the religious fervor and faith that have in the past stimulated the production of great art, and the country no longer enjoys the material power and grandeur that during the Safavid and earlier periods were an encouragement and stimulus to artistic creativeness. The creative instinct, however, is not dead, nor have the people yet lost the sense of national identity and the cultural tradition which are the fountainhead of their creative artistry. The latent sources of creativeness still exist, and are preserved, and find such expression as the times permit. To the continuing independence of the nation may be attributed in large measure the continued production of Persian rugs and handicraft that are still supreme in their field. It is a fair conclusion that should the national independence be extinguished, either in fact or by economic and political pressures by which the people were reduced to subservience to another power, there would result an eclipse of a splendid cultural tradition, which would be a supreme loss not only to the Iranian people but to the world.

E. NEW ECONOMIC PROGRAM

In April 1945, following the dissolution of the American financial mission, the council of ministers created a Supreme Economic Council charged with formulating economic policies for the country. This Council was composed of twenty-five members, of whom nine represented various ministries and State organizations and the remainder were appointed by the prime minister. On 30 March 1946, the prime minister, then Ahmad Ghavam Saltaneh, announced the following policy of the government:

(1) to raise the standard of living by increased production and increased consumption;

(2) to assure a just distribution of wealth produced.

To carry out this policy the following program was laid down:

(1) The retention and strengthening of the foreign-trade monopoly as the basis of the country's economic policy.

(2) Efforts to increase exports by better methods of preparation and packaging, increased production, and adjustment of the internal price level to the world price level.

(3) Maintenance of the quota on imports to prevent competition with domestic products, except on certain products currently in short supply, such as sugar and tea.

(4) Support and stimulation of industrialization by economic planning and other measures. Existing industries, whether State-owned or not, born of the foreign-trade monopoly, to receive continued support and protection.

(5) Labor relations to be given especial consideration, and application to be made to the International Labor Office for assistance and counsel in the development of a legal code.

(6) A five-year plan for municipal improvements. The report pointed out that the sixty cities in Iran having a munici-

pal status, including the capital, are without water, sewage, or sanitary systems, and largely without lighting or telephone service.

(7) The actual production and the living requirements of the peasant to be determined, and the traditional distribution of the produce of the land according to the ownership of the factors of production to be abolished; instead, the product to be distributed primarily with regard to the well-being of the peasant and his family.

(8) A plan for the division and sale of State domain on term payments to be rapidly executed for the purpose of encouraging the creation of a class of small landowners.

(9) A program of irrigation to be adopted.

(10) Communications to be improved.

(11) A program for development of mineral resources to be prepared.

Prevailing Tendencies

How effective this program will be remains to be seen. As the Majlis was not in session, the program rested on ministerial fiat, and much will depend upon the support it receives from the people and the vigor with which it is executed. It is of interest, however, as representative of the present governing tendencies in Iran. It will be noted that the program is almost exclusively economic in its objects, and while it recognizes the moral imperative of a more equitable distribution of the fruits of enterprise, it ignores such problems as child labor, status of women, education in citizenship, public health, and, in particular, a system of justice and public administration giving assurance that the fruits of economic reform will be realized.

Increased Government Intervention

The views of the Economic Committee, the recommendations of which had led to the establishment of the Supreme Economic Council, are of interest as indicating prevailing thought among the governing classes on the subject of the government's functions in the economy of the country.

Government intervention in economic affairs began ten years ago. The normal course of the economic life was changed in various ways by measures taken by the Government; namely, the establishment of monopolies, the taking over by the Government of the direct charge of sales and purchases, production and transportation of goods and the enactment of laws and regulations. This intervention in many cases was either deemed unavoidable or thought to be beneficial to the Government.[4]

Among the reasons assigned for State intervention were the following: (a) the need for setting up an organization to deal with countries where both internal and foreign trade were under government monopoly; (b) to increase State revenues; (c) to limit imports in order to conserve the foreign-exchange resources; (d) to protect home industries and improve the quality of goods made locally either for consumption or export; and (e) to obtain better terms in the world markets for goods sold or purchased.

The report conceded that these objects had not been attained, largely because of mismanagement and lack of proper studies, and that had the war not intervened, the policy would have been abandoned or restricted. A policy of minimizing government intervention was indeed adopted after 1941, but the trend of events neutralized its effect, and government intervention actually expanded. 'Thus, today by far the greatest part of imports and exports of this country is being either handled directly by the Government, or controlled and supervised by it,' says the report, which goes on to say:

The decision to set up a new organization . . . would not seem at first glance to be conducive to a great improvement, considering the drawbacks and disadvantages of the Government's direct economic activities, and it would look as though the best arrangement would be one which encouraged the freedom of action by individuals in the economic sphere and restricted, as far as practicable, any restriction imposed on it.

After surveying the condition of the country and the general trend abroad, however, the report concluded that it was both impossible and contrary to the public interest for the government to discontinue its economic activities. Concerning external factors, the report commented, significantly:

[4] 'Report of the Economic Committee,' in *Bulletin of Bank Melli*, February-March 1945.

Further, the war economy in other countries is so organized that foreign trade everywhere is under State management, and governments are not generally willing, nor even prepared, to do business with individuals. . . Again, it should be noted that the world is going through a great economic transition, and it is probable that after the war the economic structure of the Great Powers, particularly so far as foreign trade is concerned, will be re-built on a new basis widely different from the pre-war structure.

Land-Tenure Program

Subsequent to the announcement of 30 March 1946, Premier Ghavam made (on 6 June) a further pronouncement on the program of land-tenure reform. The extent to which liberal tendencies have taken root in the political consciousness of the governing classes is suggested to some extent by the language accompanying the declaration.

Iran will be great only when its inhabitants are people who have gained knowledge, strength, freedom, and health. In my opinion, the transfer of State land to peasants without compensation is the first and main step. By strengthening and increasing the small holders among the peasants a true right of property will be established throughout the country. I must point out that I do not intend to abolish private property as such. Only those persons can be considered rightful owners of land who make an effort to cultivate the land.

The existing order throughout the world cannot tolerate that any person under the pretext of the so-called right of ownership should leave hundreds of thousands of square meters of land untilled, or that estates of hundreds of hectares should remain unexploited and lie waste.

He then announced the intention of the government to place into effect measures establishing the relations between landlords and tenants, and guaranteeing freedom and legal rights to tenants; giving landowners a time limit within which to place land in cultivation, on penalty of confiscation; and defining the duties of landlords.

Along with this program of land reform, the government concluded an understanding with the Near East Foundation whereby the Foundation would establish, with government assistance, a program of rural education through model villages and adult education.

II

THE OPIUM QUESTION

A. IRAN AND THE INTERNATIONAL TRAFFIC

THE GOVERNMENT of Iran has not been noted for co-operation in international efforts to control the opium trade, or for efforts to restrict the use of opium among its own people.

Iran has never adhered to any of the opium treaties, with the result that opium produced in that country has been sold to any and all buyers. Iranian opium has been found in almost all seizures of illict opium smuggled into this country and Canada. It was a major source of difficulty in the Far East, when the government monopoly systems were attempting to prevent opium from being smuggled into their territories, as 'bootleg' competition for government sales. Shipments of many tons left Bushire, consigned ostensibly to Vladivostok, but actually appeared in every port where there was a smuggling market. These facts were made public year after year in the meetings of the Opium Advisory Committee at Geneva, but without effect on Iranian policy.[1]

As a result of Iranian official complacence towards opium traffic, opium consumption among the Iranian people has become one of the most serious problems confronting the country today.

The view that opium is a curse is of course not one shared by all authorities, and Iranian dalliance with the opium question has had its defenders abroad. The late Lord Curzon, writing in 1892, spoke of the government's 'wise and resolute interference' in the opium trade, as a result of which 'under strict supervision the trade revived, and has now reached very large dimensions.'[2]

And Sir Arnold Wilson, writing in 1933, speaks of opium indulgently in the following language:

[1] *Foreign Policy Bulletin*, 21 July 1944.
[2] Op. cit. vol. II, p. 499.

As in India, it is the soldier's emergency ration, the muleteer's tonic and the starveling's solace; it is daily used to ease the pain of thousands of sick and injured men who cannot hope to obtain skilled medical assistance. Physically and mentally the Persian nation as a whole need not be afraid to challenge comparison with the polyglot communities of the New World, for whose sake it is apparently desired to impoverish and to circumvent the liberties of Eastern races who can, for the most part, use without abusing stimulants. The existence in Western countries of a few weak-minded drug addicts is a poor excuse for under-mining by harassing legislation the sturdy individualism that is one of the most enduring assets of the Persian race.[3]

Early Attempts to Restrict Opium Cultivation

Although the Iranian government has generally been indulgent towards the opium traffic, it is of interest that during those periods in modern Iranian history when public sentiment was vocal and the government was responsive to such sentiment, efforts were made to cope with the problem. In the early days of the Constitution, in 1908, when the government was momentarily in possession of the people, among the reforms undertaken was the reduction of opium culture. This was the Opium Limitation Act, which imposed a tax of 3 shahis per miscal [4] on opium production, the tax to be increased each year by 3 shahis until 1917, by which time, it was expected, the prohibitive tax would have eliminated its culture. The act failed of its purposes, of course, though the tax did reach a figure of 21 shahis per miscal, at which figure it was fixed until 1928.

Thus, Iran was the first of the opium-producing countries in modern times to attempt administrative action looking towards the limitation of opium cultivation.

International Efforts at Opium Control

In 1909, under the stimulus of the United States government, which had had to deal with the opium question in the Philippines and which was concerned with the spread of the traffic to the Western hemisphere, an international conference on the opium traffic was convened in Shanghai. In 1912,

[3] Op. cit. p. 59.
[4] A miscal weighs 4.64 grams.

a second conference, convened at The Hague, resulted in an agreement by which the signatory powers bound themselves not to export opium to countries having prohibitions against its import except on import licenses granted by that government. The government of Iran was a signatory to The Hague Convention, but it made a reservation regarding this provision.

In 1909, the British government, which had forced the opium trade on China by the Opium War of 1840-42, reversed its policy and concluded with the Chinese government an agreement whereby opium exports from India would be reduced one-tenth each year; such exports actually terminated in 1913. In a note to the American government, dated 9 January 1925, the British government requested the United States to support the representations it was making to the government of Iran regarding more effective control of illicit trade in opium. In 1935 Great Britain took further steps to restrict the Far Eastern opium traffic by prohibiting British vessels from carrying opium, except opium licensed for medicinal use or for sale to the opium monopolies in British possessions. (It did not, however, restrict to medicinal uses the sale of opium by the opium monopolies in these possessions.) In 1926, the government of India announced that all exports of opium for other than medicinal purposes would be reduced by one-tenth each year and terminated entirely by 1936, and in 1940 reported that all such exports had ceased by 1 January 1936.

B. OFFICIAL POLICY

As a result of the British withdrawal from the opium-carrying trade, and the refusal of the Iranian government to adhere to the licensing system created by The Hague Convention, a great deal of this trade, which had formerly had its source in the Indian crop, now passed to Iran, and Iran became the principal source of opium for illicit trade in the Far East.

League of Nations Opium Commission

In 1923, the opium question was renewed before the League of Nations, at the instance of the United States, and by a Convention, signed in 1925, effective in 1928, the Permanent Central Opium Board was established, together with a mandatory licensing system. In the discussions leading to the Convention, the Iranian delegate protested his government's interest in the question, but pointed out the difficulties of restricting opium production without foreign assistance. He complained in particular of import duties levied by other governments (indicating the United States) upon Iranian products, such as rugs, and of the necessity of developing substitute crops and industries. Specifically, the delegate announced that his government would withdraw its reservation to the Opium Convention of 1912 as soon as a practical scheme for replacing opium cultivation by other industries or crops had been drawn up. The significance of the delegate's statement may be found in the opium statistics of Iran. In 1924-5, exports of opium amounted to 1,077,290 pounds, and represented 16.4 per cent of total exports exclusive of oil, and the taxes on opium amounted to 9 per cent of the total revenue. At that time it was estimated that around one-third of the total opium crop escaped governmen scrutiny and passed into illicit trade for domestic consumption or for export.

As a result of the delegate's statement, the League of Nations dispatched to Iran a commission headed by Frederic A. Delano of the United States to look into the production of opium and to recommend steps for its control. The Commission visited Iran in 1926, and as a result of its investigation reported that 'while difficult of accomplishment, it is possible, and to the economic interest of Persia, to adopt a program for the gradual diminution of the cultivation of the opium poppy,' and went on to recommend a number of practical measures for the development of substitute crops and of industries which would absorb the energies of the people and provide an equivalent livelihood. These recommendations have been discussed in the preceding chapter.

Reservations of the Iranian Government

The government accepted the recommendations of the Commission and announced its intention of reducing production of opium to medicinal requirements:

It is our conviction that the production of opium can be curtailed . . . nevertheless the Persian Government will take immediate measures to reduce the production of opium to medicinal requirements and will prosecute these measures as rapidly as circumstances permit. The Government is likewise determined to put a stop to the smoking of opium within the country as rapidly as possible.[5]

The government, however, hedged its acceptance of these recommendations with the qualification that it could not undertake the program until the government had obtained tariff autonomy, and unless other governments were prepared to reduce import duties on Iranian goods. Despite the fact that tariff autonomy was obtained in 1928, no measures were adopted to put into effect the recommendations of the Commission, or, for that matter, to impose controls on the export of opium.

Opium Monopoly Created

The government had for many years maintained a certain supervision over the production of opium, mainly because of its importance as a source of tax revenue, and in 1928 an opium monopoly was established by which the government assumed control of all internal trade in opium, while continuing, nevertheless, to permit its export to any destination, provided the government dues were paid.

Indicative of popular opinion in Iran on the opium question was the lively debate in the Majlis over the establishment of the monopoly, many of the deputies arguing that its effect would be not to restrict opium culture but simply to increase the government's revenues from this source. The Shah, however, who is reported himself to have been a user of opium, rejected these views, through his ministers, and the monopoly was established.

In 1929, as has been mentioned earlier, the monopoly of exports was ceded to a company organized by the Amine family of Isfahan, in which the Shah is reported to have held an interest. Under the terms of this monopoly the company was required to export a minimum of 6,500 chests of opium per annum, upon which it was required to pay an export tax ranging from £83 to £117 per chest. As a chest weighs approximately 160 pounds, the total minimum export provided for

[5] League of Nations Commission of Inquiry into the Production of Opium in Persia. *Report to the Council*, Geneva, 1926, p. 54. *Letter from Persian Prime Minister to President of Commission*, dated 1 June 1926.

by this concession was over 500 tons annually. The significance of this quantity may be indicated by the fact that total world requirements of opium for medicinal purposes do not exceed 400 tons annually.

The Monopoly Act required growers to obtain a license to cultivate the opium poppy, and required them to deposit the estimated amount of the crop in government warehouses, where it was prepared in sticks, for internal trade, or cakes, for export trade. A grower obtaining such a license was under no supervision so long as he delivered the estimated amount of the crop to the government warehouse. The tendency was to underestimate the crop. So far as is known, no limits were ever placed on the amount of ground that could be put into cultivation.

The Amine concession was canceled in 1933, and foreign trade in opium thereafter was free to anyone who paid the government export tax. Internal trade was handled by the Monopoly. Opium cultivation increased, partly as a result of the shift from the cultivation of cereals, which the government endeavored to keep cheap, partly as a result of indulgence shown by the government towards opium cultivation and use, and largely because of the stimulus of foreign demand, accompanied by higher prices for opium. With the British withdrawal from the opium trade, the Japanese had entered the market, and after 1931, following the occupation of Manchuria, had begun to buy opium in tremendous quantities and to encourage its use among the conquered peoples of China. Japanese takings of Iranian opium became enormous in 1937 and 1938. One Japanese ship, the SS *Muko Maru,* loaded 1,500 chests (240,000 lbs.) on 29 December 1937; in the first quarter of 1938, orders were placed by the Japanese for 2,900 chests, of which 1,128 chests were shipped in the first 17 days of March 1938.[6]

C. INCREASE IN OPIUM CONSUMPTION

Meantime, the government of Iran did little to restrict consumption of opium among its people. Opium was freely obtainable from the Monopoly and could be purchased for smoking

[6] *U. S. Legation reports.*

or eating at every pharmacy and tea house. The tax was indeed raised from 21 shahis per miscal (equivalent to 1.05 rials) to 2.50 rials per miscal, and a register of opium smokers was established with the idea of limiting the sale to registered users, but no one would voluntarily admit being a user, nor would he pay the high tax so long as opium could be obtained illicitly. In 1931, the tax was reduced to .50 rials per miscal in the poppy-growing areas, with the result that more of the traffic now flowed through the Monopoly. Monopoly sales increased as follows: [7]

OPIUM MONOPOLY SALES IN IRAN
1930-34

Year Ended 20 March	Kilograms
1930	18,132
1931	29,131
1932	88,510
1933	132,560
1934	155,486

The most authoritative figures on the total production of opium in Iran are those submitted to the Permanent Central Opium Board of the League of Nations, but how much contraband production is not represented in the figures is hard to say. In 1924-5, as stated, the Commission of Inquiry into the Production of Opium in Persia was officially advised that an estimated one-third of the crop escaped government scrutiny, but it is generally understood that after the establishment of the Opium Monopoly, a larger percentage of total production was under government control. The officially reported production is as follows:

OPIUM PRODUCTION IN IRAN
1929-40

Year Ended 20 March	Kilograms
1929	686,662
1930	556,617
1931	898,338
1932	547,726
1933	461,414

[7] League of Nations, *Reports of Advisory Committee on Traffic in Opium and Other Dangerous Drugs*, Geneva.

Year Ended 20 March	*Kilograms*
1934	459,243
1935	833,499
1936	1,346,712
1937	521,715
1938	—
1939	672,058
1940	752,250

Effect of World War II

In 1941, the Far Eastern market for Iranian opium was suddenly cut off as a result of the entry of Japan into the war, and at the same time domestic controls of opium production were seriously relaxed owing to the disintegration of the administration following the Russo-British occupation. Total reported production of opium showed a sharp decline, as follows:

OPIUM PRODUCTION IN IRAN
1941-4

Year Ended 20 March	*Kilograms*
1941	210,200
1942	214,900
1943	130,500
1944	192,000

Indicative of the effect of the occupation are the figures for government opium collections in 1943 and 1944. While total collections increased from 130,500 kilos in 1943 to 192,000 kilos in 1944, collections dropped in Meshed, which was under Russian control, from 76,000 kilos to 41,000 kilos.

There is no reason to believe, however, that actual production declined to the extent indicated by the official figures. Reliable estimates are that production continued at a rate of 600 to 700 metric tons annually. This production now began to seek a demand locally and in near-by countries, and a certain amount was smuggled to the United States and elsewhere by small operators, Chinese seamen, and others, on the ships engaged in carrying war material to Persian Gulf ports. A substantial amount is believed to have gone overland to Cairo and Palestine by way of the Kurdish mountains. Domestic consumption increased enormously. In 1925, the Commission of

Inquiry obtained estimates indicating that from 25 to 50 per cent of the population consumed opium in one form or another. Estimates given me in 1943 by the medical adviser to the Iranian Ministry of Health, Lt. Colonel Alexander Neuwirth, were that probably 75 per cent of the population were opium consumers. In some large establishments, it was reported, employees were given fifteen-minute rest periods for smoking opium.

D. NEW GOVERNMENT POLICY

One of the reassuring features of the situation, however, was the reversal of government policy towards opium following the abdication of Riza Shah Pahlavi and the return to Constitutional government and free speech. Almost immediately after the abdication, in November 1941, the government issued a decree forbidding the further cultivation of opium in the provinces of Kirman, Baluchistan, and Yezd, and while these provinces today produce only a minor portion of the total crop, and although the decree was ineffective owing to the impotency of the government, it was indicative of the attitude now being adopted.

In the middle of December 1941, a further order was issued restricting the sale of Monopoly opium to pharmacies and to holders of coupons issued by the government, which coupons could be obtained only by persons forty years of age. This measure was also ineffectual, due to the fact that control of the trade had passed out of the hands of the Monopoly.

On 9 March 1942, the prime minister, Ali Soheily, presented to the Majlis a program for the gradual prohibition of the cultivation and consumption of opium, but no steps were taken to implement the program because of the breakdown of government authority.

In 1943, there was organized in Teheran an Anti-Opium and Alcohol Society, which began to publish estimates of opium production and consumption and to agitate for prohibition of opium culture. This Society estimated that 500 metric tons of opium were consumed in Iran in 1943 by addicts totaling 1,000,000, of whom 700,000 were believed to be smokers and 300,000 eaters of opium. In 1944, the Society estimated the production to be 800 tons.

On 28 January 1945, a bill was introduced in the Majlis by Hassan Ali Farmand (Farmand-Garagozlou), deputy from Hamadan—the same deputy, incidentally, who had led the opposition in the Majlis in 1928 to the establishment of the Opium Monopoly—providing for the prohibition of the cultivation and use of opium. This bill was accompanied by a petition signed by 66 of the 136 deputies in the Majlis.

In 1943, the governments of Great Britain and the Netherlands announced that upon the freeing of their Far Eastern possessions, then under Japanese occupation, opium smoking under government license (the monopoly system) would be abolished, and trade in opium for other than medicinal purposes would be prohibited. In 1944, the United States government, as a result of a joint resolution of the Congress, sent a circular note to all opium-producing countries, urging them to take effective measures to reduce opium cultivation to legitimate needs. The government of Afghanistan, in response, announced that it was prohibiting, after 21 March 1945, the further cultivation of the opium poppy.

In Iran, the Majlis session expired in March 1946, and pending elections to the new Majlis, the government was under the control of the prime minister, Ahmad Ghavam Saltaneh. On 10 April 1946, the Prime Minister issued a decree instructing the governors of all provinces to stop the cultivation of the opium poppy as of this year and at the same time instructing the ministries of finance and agriculture to prepare regulations for the enforcement of the decree. Until the decree has been ratified by the Majlis and activated by administrative application, it is only a statement of policy, and it remains to be seen whether the production of opium will be effectively stopped.

III

TENDENCIES AND INFLUENCES

A. WANE OF ISLAM

THE MOST significant change observable in Iran in an interval of twenty-five years is the wane of Islam. During this period Islam ceased to be the official religion of the State; the Koranic law was largely abrogated in favor of European legal concepts, and in those areas in which it still retains applicability its force has been greatly reduced. The status of women has been redeemed from much of the degradation it suffers under Islamic teaching, though women still do not enjoy the equality and respect accorded them in Christian communities. The Moslem clergy have been deprived of much of the influence and many of the prerogatives they enjoyed in former times, and great estates held by pious foundations have been brought under State control. The revolting spectacle of Moharram described in an earlier chapter, which has been the principal religious festival in Iran for at least four hundred years, has all but disappeared.

Significant also of the declining influence of Islam among the people is the increasing receptivity to Western modes of thought and action. The Islamic clergy are conservative, and though many of them have been leaders in the movement against monarchical absolutism and have supported reform of various sorts, generally their influence has been against change, particularly innovations from outside Islam.

New Moral Spirit

The interest in Western civilization that can be seen has largely arisen from a desire to possess the greater material well-being of the West, and is concerned with those modes that will bring a greater prosperity to the country. More and more, however, the social philosophy of the West is finding recognition in public policy, in a greater political democracy, in concern for agriculture, in elevating the status of women. Standards of official morality have generally improved, though on this subject no statistics are available, and I have only my personal observation from residence in Iran after an interval of twenty-five years. During the latter 1930's, during the closing years of Riza Shah Pahlavi's reign, it is true, a terrible deterioration occurred in public morality. Under the example of the Shah, who became preoccupied with enlarging his private wealth, a veritable mania of profiteering, bribery, and peculation possessed the governing classes, infected the ranks of clerical employees, and spread to the bazaar, generally the most trustworthy element of the community. The disasters that overtook the country during World War II, however, exercised a chastening influence: standards of honesty and probity revived; during my experience as a principal official of the Iranian ministry of finance, in 1943, I found everywhere a high sense of patriotic duty and scrupulousness of official conduct, men eager to serve and trustworthy in action, if somewhat lacking in courage, men firm in their idealism, if as yet soft in conviction.

The weakness that can be observed is not so much the weakness of corruption, but the weakness of virtue that is without discipline or perspective. Officials are unwilling to accept responsibility for their acts, where blame or ridicule might follow; they are afraid to be unpopular with their friends or class. When courage is required, they will insist upon anonymity by acting through a 'commission.' Men who are themselves honest will condone dishonesty in others, particularly if friends or family are involved. Out of an abundance of affection or generosity, they will veer from official impartiality to do a favor. An arrant peculator of government funds will be allowed to escape prosecution out of regard for his family and the shame that would fall upon them.

B. SOCIAL OUTLOOK

An encouraging feature in the outlook for the Iranian people is the evidence of an increasing awareness on the part of the government and the privileged classes of the need of fundamental reform in the social system of the country.

Land Tenure

In regard to land tenure, the observations of H. B. Allen of the Near East Foundation are of interest. He states:

All of my observations relative to this matter were verified by many intelligent students of this problem who are themselves large landowners. They tell me that they are part of an ancient system that must go . . . and the landowners who emphasize this point of view are, in the main, the altruistic, philanthropic citizens, of whom there are many in Iran, who have constructed model villages for their people, established schools, provided medical facilities. But notwithstanding their sincere efforts in helping to create a better world, they state emphatically that they are part of a system which must pass away.[1]

Education

Popular education has been receiving increasing attention. The principal emphasis during Riza Shah Pahlavi's regime was upon higher education, on the theory that institutions of higher education were necessary in order to prepare teachers for the elementary schools, and considerable pride was taken in the establishment of the University of Teheran in 1935. Nevertheless, a considerable extension of elementary education took place. During the first ten years of Riza Shah Pahlavi's regime appropriations for education increased by seven times the amount for 1924. In 1940, there were reported to be 8,237 schools of all kinds, with 496,960 students, but of the schools only 1,516 were State schools, the balance being private schools including the antiquated *Mektabs* (mullah schools). Public education on the elementary level is thus still rudimentary. Allen reported that in one district he visited of about 800 villages there were not over 30 schools; in another district of 500 villages there were 20 schools.

A serious blow to education was the closing of the missionary schools, beginning with the elementary schools in 1935 and culminating in the closing of the colleges in 1938, of which the most important were Alborz College for men and Sage College for women conducted by the Presbyterians, and the Stewart Memorial College conducted by the English Church

[1] Op. cit.

Missionary Society in Isfahan. Since the abdication of Riza Shah Pahlavi, however, some restrictions have been relaxed, and as the charters of the institutions were never annulled, hope is at present entertained by the missions that they may be permitted to resume educational work.

Public Health

An effective public health program is as yet nonexistent in Iran, although the government has taken steps in this direction through the establishment of several elaborate hospitals in the cities, the establishment of a Pasteur Institute in Teheran for the production and distribution of vaccines, and the establishment of a medical school in the University. In the provinces, the principal source of competent medical attention has been the hospitals maintained by the missionaries and the itinerant missionary physicians. Iranian medical graduates, on the whole, prefer to establish their practice in the cities where life is pleasant rather than to accept the ardor of village or itinerant practice.

Emancipation of Women

The reform of dress in Iran, including the abolition of the veil and the granting of freedom of movement to women has been treated in an earlier chapter. A legal emancipation of women also took place, though less decisive in character. The Koranic law, as has been noted, gave the husband almost complete power over his wife, and in particular permitted him to divorce her at will. Moreover, by fixing the age of puberty for women at nine years, it had encouraged the institution of child marriages. By law enacted on 4 August 1931, which required marriages and divorces to be registered with a civil official, the government was able to establish a minimum age of sixteen years for marriage. In 1935, the minimum age for marriage was legally fixed at sixteen years for women and eighteen years for men, and women were permitted to institute divorce actions in limited cases. A wife could sue for divorce if the husband failed to reveal, at the time of marriage, the existence of other wives, or if he married a second wife without her consent. Limited as was this reform, it represented a notable advance in women's rights since, while it did not prohibit polygamy (authorized by the Koran) or the Shi'a institution of *muta'a,* or temporary marriage, it had the effect of discouraging these practices.

Nevertheless, the status of women still remains inferior to that of men, in that the husband may, in instances of persuasion or coercion, take more than one wife; he may still divorce his wife on any grounds by payment of the divorce settlement which was fixed at marriage; the husband is head of the family and has legal control over the children; a woman's inheritance rights are less than a man's; and women do not enjoy the privileges of voting and many other civil rights. Moreover, effective legal safeguards were not set up, and a woman without means or influence still is very much at the mercy of her husband.

The Press and Politics

A feature of Iranian life following the abdication of Riza Shah Pahlavi was the revival of free speech and discussion and the mushrooming of newspapers and periodicals. While the journalistic ethics of these papers are low, by Western standards, and the editors employ such language in their attacks on public figures as would bring the authors into court for libel if written here, nevertheless, the general influence of their fervid discussion is salutary. The press is not entirely free, of course, for publications may appear only under license, and they are frequently suspended for their intemperate language. It is always a simple matter, however, to obtain a license, and generally the enterprising publisher simply adopts a new name for his sheet, obtains a license for its publication, and goes on his way with hardly a day lost in circulation.[2]

Along with publications came a burst of political parties, of which the most influential soon came to be the Tudeh (Masses), which had its adherents chiefly among factory employees and other workers in the larger cities, but also among the professional and intellectual classes. The Tudeh party enjoyed the support of Soviet propaganda and probably Soviet money, and it has been noted that it was strong in the areas under Soviet control, and after the Soviet evacuation it tended

[2] In 1946 there were about 250 licensed newspapers, but seldom more than a dozen were published at any one time.

to go underground except in the neighborhood of Soviet consulates. Nevertheless, even under foreign stimulus, the fact that the depressed classes should find vocal expression of even the most feeble sort must be regarded as a sign of political awakening.

c. CHRISTIANITY

Foreign observers come and go, and many shake their heads in despair at what they find, and some of them hopelessly consign the country to perdition, or recommend a foreign protectorate as the only hope of salvation for Islam.

Among the Christian missionaries in Iran, who spend their lives among the people and know them most intimately, a reassuring optimism will be found. Of all foreigners in Iran they are the most hopeful, the most positive in their trust in the Iranian people, the most confident of the ability of the Iranians to solve their problems and to put their houses in order without aid of foreign intervention.

The optimism of the missionaries is paradoxical. It would appear that of all foreigners in Iran they should be the most discouraged. Their business is to win converts to the Christian faith. Despite a hundred years of missionary effort there exists as yet no widespread evangelical movement in Iran, no substantial Christian Church (apart from the ancient Armenian and Syrian rites). The number of Christian converts is infinitesimal.

The missionaries, however, can point to considerable fruit of the Christian spirit working in Iran. Characteristic of Iran today is the increasing acceptance of Christian ethical and moral teachings as a standard of conduct, and a marked, if more reserved, interest in the theological claims of Christianity as a way of personal salvation from sin and death. Acceptance of the ethical and moral teachings of Christianity as a basis of national life is found most generally among the educated classes, among whom exists a growing recognition of the importance of the moral question in Iran, and the necessity of reforming the institutions of the country according to a higher ethic. Social questions, such as land tenure, the proletariat, public health and education, domestic relations, opium production, commerce, public administration, justice, and the relations between the government and the governed, are all being re-examined in the light of Christian moral teachings.[3]

Christian evangelists, however, are primarily interested in winning acknowledgment of their Christ as the Mediator between God and man, and acceptance of His Sacrifice as the atonement for human sin, and their optimism for the future of Iran is based upon the increasing receptiveness to the Gospel that they find among those who are seeking personal rather than national salvation. This receptiveness is found more and more among those classes of the population that formerly constituted the bulwark of resistance to change and the chief support of Islam: peasants, nomads, and workers.

A Case Example

As an illustration of Christian evangelism at work, and the fruit it is bearing both in terms of personal regeneration and a more secure national existence, an instance in the experience of Bill Miller [4] of Teheran may be offered.

Bill is an ardent apostle of the Gospel, and is constantly touring among the villages distributing Scriptures and Gospel tracts and preaching the Word in season and out. He has been an evangelist in Iran for a quarter century.

In 1943, Bill made a missionary journey to eastern Iran, a part of the country he had not visited since a brief sojourn there some twenty-two years earlier, when he was a young man fresh from seminary. In those earlier days he traveled by horseback, by high-wheeled Russian droshky, or by springless *fourgon,* or wagon. Now he journeyed eastward by motor car, over a highway on which passed long caravans of motor trucks carrying war material to Russia, and making immense clouds of dust in the desert air.

Bill came to Seistan, which is inhabited by Baluchi nomads. At a roadside tea house, he made inquiry about conditions in

[3] The materialistic teachings of Communism, however, which regard the moral forces of the universe as subordinate to the material, and human existence as a struggle between opposing material forces (rather than as the warfare of good and evil, as taught by the Prophet Zoroaster) exercise considerable influence among certain classes of Iranians.

[4] The Reverend William McE. Miller of the Presbyterian Church in the U.S.A.

the mountains, since he intended, if possible, to leave his car at Zahedan and to go up into the hills and preach.

He was told that conditions were tranquil. Thanks to one Sardar Nazar Khan, he was assured, he could now travel anywhere in the hills in peace and security.

Sardar Nazar Khan

In the old days, before Sardar Nazar Khan became chief—the gossips at the tea house told him—conditions were otherwise. Then the roads were unsafe for travelers, and the firman of the Shah was much ignored in the valleys. The armies of His Majesty had often bivouacked in the foothills, but the tribes were never awed; sometimes the imperial armies would march in for a distance, and then the bullets would sing against the rocks, and even blood might flow; thereupon they would march out, and the tribes would resume their quarrels, and their pillage of the villages for grain and brass samovars and wives.

But now it was different. Sardar Nazar Khan had been elected chief of his tribe, and he had made changes. He had forbidden his young men to go on raids and had persuaded the old men of the wisdom of his view. He had settled the ancient feuds with the rival tribes. Finally, at the council of the tribal chieftains, he had urged them to compose their differences with the Shah. There should be, he proclaimed, an end to strife and rapine and bloodshed; men should live in unity and brotherly love. Persuasive was his plea, but more persuasive was the evidence of its results in his own tribe. The tribal chiefs accepted his views; negotiations with the government were authorized, and Sardar Nazar Khan was delegated to represent the tribes. The emissaries of the Shah, accustomed to wile, were likewise impressed by the young chief's fairness and sincerity; they reached with the chief a composition of their differences: the terms included a settlement of the imperial taxes due and a confirmation of the prescriptive rights and privileges of the tribes.

Sardar Nazar Khan, Bill was told, was a Christian.

This was extraordinary and joyful news to a man of Bill Miller's profession, and he expressed the hope of meeting this

Sardar Nazar Khan and of hearing the statement confirmed from his own lips.

Seed and Harvest

As chance would have it, while Bill tarried in Zahedan, Sardar Nazar Khan, hearing of the missionary, journeyed down from the hills to see him. Bill expressed his delight at meeting a fellow-believer and brother in Christ, and then inquired how long his brother had been in the Lord, and by whom he had been baptized.

Thirteen years before, the chief explained, an English missionary had come into the mountains preaching, and had baptized him. For thirteen years he had not been in the company of a fellow Christian, nor had he received the sacraments of the Church. Still, he protested, he was a believer, and a follower of the Christ. Moreover, he assured Bill, he had been a Christian long before the coming of the English missionary. The Englishman had baptized him, but he had long known and loved the Christ.

Bill wanted to know how he had heard of the Christ.

'From reading the Bible,' responded Sardar Nazar Khan.

'But,' asked Bill, in perplexity, 'from whom did you obtain the Bible? Have you traveled to India; have you been in the cities?'

The chief regarded Bill fondly.

'No, my brother,' he said patiently, and with a beatific smile. 'Do you not recall how two and twenty years ago you visited our encampment on the slopes, how you gave me—I was a small boy then—a Bible, and asked me to read it? I have read it daily since, and more and more increase in faith and love toward Jesus, who is the peace of the world and the hope of the life to come.'

The Case of Red Beard

This is only one of the more romantic of the stories of the Gospel road in Iran. The missionaries, if one will listen, have many others to tell. There is the case of the henna-bearded villager who had gone from his village to the town of Kashan to sell his cotton. There he met a man selling books and purchased one. It was a copy of the Bible in Persian. He took it home and read it. He was moved to become a Christian. For several years he read and prayed, and then one day, hearing that there was in the capital, two hundred fifty miles away, a community of Christians, he set out to meet them, traveling by donkey and by bus. He reached the city and was directed to the mission. A service was in progress; he stood outside and listened, fearing to enter lest the Christians drive him from their house of worship as an infidel and unclean. After the service he waited, hoping to be spoken to, but no one seemed to notice the villager with the red beard and the frayed dress. He returned sadly to his village. 'I am not a Christian,' he thought, 'else they would have known me and would have spoken to me.' He read his Bible with renewed devotion, desperately anxious to be a true Christian. A year passed. Again he made his way to Teheran, and again he ventured to the steps of the church. On this occasion Bill Miller was present, returned from one of his evangelistic tours. As Bill stood on the steps, speaking to those that came, he caught sight of Red Beard, went to him and offered his hand in welcome, and asked him if he would like to attend the service. Red Beard was overjoyed. 'That is what I have come for,' he exclaimed. Later, Bill took the villager before the elders of the church, who examined him about his knowledge of the Scriptures and his faith. So familiar was he with the Bible, so evident his faith, that the elders recommended that instead of the customary year of probation he be granted baptism at once.

The missionaries are indeed hopeful. The doors, they say, are opening. Everywhere, they testify, there is a new willingness, or rather an eagerness, to hear the Gospel. Sales of the Bible in the Persian tongue, so the British and Foreign Bible Society reports, are breaking all records. There is more attention paid to preaching; inquirers form a steady stream to the doors of church and mission; converts are multiplying; and a strong, if small, indigenous Church has arisen.

Among all non-Christians, Moslems have historically been the most difficult to proselytize, the most adverse to evangelism. In Iran, however, mission board secretaries report, evangelistic effort is remarkably free, and missionary work regarded with greater tolerance by government and masses than is found in any other Moslem land. Dr. W. N. Wysham, Secretary of the Presbyterian Board of Foreign Missions, wrote as follows:

In Iran today, a Moslem can become a Christian and be publicly baptized, yet retain the esteem of his friends. Usually he can continue his former occupation with no more than petty persecution. Iran is unique also in having churches largely composed of Moslem converts and with much of the lay leadership in their hands. . . In one Moslem land at least, the incredibly difficult preparatory period has ended and the era of the indigenous Christian Church has begun.[5]

The Christian Missions

The missionaries have on the whole maintained their detachment from political partisanship and the differentiation of their purposes in Iran—as evangelists of Jesus Christ rather than as protagonists of Western civilization—and this policy has borne fruit. In 1942, when the tides of war were rolling into the Caucasus, and it appeared that Iran might be invaded by Germany, and the nationals of the governments at war with Germany were beginning to leave the country, the missions debated whether the missionaries should follow suit. The action they took is noteworthy. It stated:

The Mission in Iran believes in the light of facts now before it that the evacuation or abandonment of any one of our stations as a unit would result in serious if not irreparable damage to the work. . . We can prove the sincerity of our professions to have come to Iran to serve the people here in no better way than by standing by them in such a time. . . But it should be understood once and for all that all those who do not immediately ask for government transportation facilities have decided to remain in Iran for the duration, bring what it may in famine, suffering, persecution, and even death.

While a number did return home, chiefly women and children, enough remained on the field—some forty-five out of little more than a hundred—to keep all stations open.

The general effect of keeping the mission work going has been the most salutary. As stated by one missionary: 'Never

[5] *On This We Build in the Near East.* Publication of the Presbyterian Board of Foreign Missions. New York.

has the field been so ripe, never has there been so much
freedom.'

Criticisms of Missionaries

The missionaries have been frequently criticized, particularly by casual travelers, for the relative luxury in which they
live. They have been charged with affecting superiority to the
life of the common people and with failure to adopt the modes
and customs of the country. Some basis exists for this complaint. Coming, as they do, from a civilization of so much
greater material wealth, and more particularly from an
atmosphere in which the prevalent conception of the good
life is a clean and comfortable life, it is perhaps inevitable
that they should bring with them, and be unwilling to forego,
standards of physical environment far higher than those they
meet. On the other hand, the question may properly be raised
about the advantages of their acting in a manner that is un-
natural to them, or of adopting the modes of life with which
the people of the country themselves are dissatisfied, and
which they are seeking as rapidly as possible to discard. How
little would have been gained by the practice, say, of wearing
the ancient *kola,* and the loose-flowing *aba,* or outer robe,
which the government itself by decree subsequently prohibited its own people to wear.

More pertinent would be the charge that many of the missionaries have missed their true calling and the object of their
endeavor, namely, the propagation of the Christian faith, and
have become rather propagandists of a civilization that, however identified with Christianity, is in many respects as pagan
as that of ancient Greece. Too many of the missionaries are
still of the nineteenth-century cast of thought, which regarded
the spread of education as the panacea to human ills and the
Tree of Knowledge as the object of worship rather than God.

Perhaps unfortunate also for the spread of the Gospel
was the apparent transfer of allegiance from Christ to Caesar,
which occurred during World War II in the case of many former missionaries. In the prosecution of the war in the Middle
East, the American government engaged many of these persons
in its service because of their familiarity with the country, the
language, and the customs of the people. Numerous former

missionaries, either retired or unable to return to their missionary work for other reasons, accepted such employment and returned to Iran, no longer as missionaries, but as officials and servants of the State, the effect of which was to cause lifted eyebrows and mild cynicism on the part of Iranians. 'Here,' they were inclined to say, 'are your true purposes and allegiances revealed. In the final test, you are not Christians, but Americans. You came among us proclaiming Christ your King, and the Cross your banner, but all the time your true king was Caesar, your banner the eagle.'

Despite these failings and frailities, the missionaries have been, and remain, the truest friends the Iranians possess; what they offer is the surest hope for the future, and from their mission stations shines the brightest light in the pervading gloom. Not many of them are martyrs, but martyrdom has been their lot, and even in modern times, men like Dr. Shedd and Mr. Bachimont have offered their blood as the seed of the Kingdom. And many others have toiled patiently for years, in loneliness and devotion, that the Iranian people may be brought to the knowledge and love of God through His Son Jesus Christ, and in the end have found their graves, if in a field distant from their native land, among a people they have loved and served.

IV

IRAN AND RUSSIA

A. Soviet Reluctance to Evacuate Iran

BY THE terms of the three-power agreement among Soviet Russia, Great Britain, and Iran, signed 29 January 1942, governing the occupation of Iran, Soviet Russia and Great Britain agreed to evacuate Iran within six months after the end of hostilities. It has been generally understood that this limit was 2 March 1946.

Towards the end of 1945, however, it became apparent that Soviet Russia was reluctant to fulfill its obligations. This may have been due to concern over the increasing influence of the United States in Iranian affairs, as a result of the presence of American forces in Iran, American advisers to the Iranian government, and American economic assistance to Iran. In May 1942, the United States had extended the benefits of the Lend-Lease Act to Iran, as a result of which the United States supplied Iran up to the end of 1945 with goods and services of a value of $4,525,511, in addition to financial aid totaling $2,606,300. In December 1942, the United States with Great Britain had agreed to supply Iran with food; following this, American advisers in increasing numbers began to take up positions in various government ministries. In September 1943, largely on American counsel, given by the President's special ambassador, Major General Patrick J. Hurley, Iran had declared war on Germany. This act had had no military significance, but it gave Iran a stronger juridical position in international councils.

At the meeting of the Big Three—Roosevelt, Churchill, and Stalin—in Teheran in November and December 1943, at the instance of President Roosevelt a joint statement regarding Iran was issued by which the three governments 'recognized the assistance which Iran had given in the prosecution of the war,' and declared themselves to be 'at one with the Government of Iran in their desire for the maintenance of the sovereignty, independence, and territorial integrity of Iran.' In February 1944, the United States, in concert with Great Britain, raised its legation to an embassy, and in March 1944, negotiated a reciprocal-trade agreement with Iran.

Soviet Demands for Oil Concession

In August 1944, representatives of three different groups of British and American interests appeared in Teheran seeking an oil concession in southeastern Iran. The Iranian government entered into negotiations with these representatives and engaged an American consulting firm [1] to advise it in the negotiations. While these negotiations were in progress, in mid-September 1944, a Soviet delegation, headed by Sergei Kavtaradze, vice-commissar for foreign affairs, and accompanied by a staff of over ninety persons, specialists in all branches of public administration, appeared in Teheran and demanded a concession in the north.

From an economic and political point of view, Russian participation in the northern developments would seem almost necessary, since the oil in this area would find its principal markets either in Russia or in world markets by transportation across Russian territory. In 1922, the Sinclair interests had negotiated a concession in this area, but when it became apparent that Russian co-operation in providing transit facilities would not be forthcoming, Sinclair abandoned its concession. Some time later another American group, organized as the Amiranian Oil Company, negotiated a concession in northeastern and eastern Iran, but this was subsequently abandoned for the same reason.

It was obvious from the imposing character of the Soviet delegation, and the extensive character of the concessions sought—not only oil but all mineral deposits, together with extraterritorial rights in exploiting these resources—that what the Soviets proposed was not a purely commercial enterprise but actually the grant of an economic monopoly over all northern Iran, an area of some 216,000 square miles. In order to

[1] Herbert Hoover, Jr. and A. A. Curtice of Hoover, Curtice and Rubey. The oil interests that engaged in negotiations were the Royal-Dutch Shell, Sinclair, and Socony-Vacuum.

escape the embarrassing necessity of treating with the Soviets on a matter of such gravity at a time when Soviet troops were in effective occupation of the territory in question, Premier Sa'id Maraghei broke off negotiations with the British and American representatives, and Hoover and Curtice left the country on 7 October. On 16 October Premier Sa'id announced, after consultation with his cabinet, and a secret session of the Majlis, that the government would not consider any grant of concessions to foreigners so long as foreign troops were on its soil.

This announcement produced prompt repercussions. On 17 October there occurred tremendous demonstrations by the Soviet-fostered Tudeh party, which were followed by a virulent press campaign against the prime minister, in which the prime minister was accused of planning to destroy the working-class movement. The climax to this campaign came on 24 October 1944, when Kavtaradze declared: 'The disloyal and unfriendly attitude of Premier Sa'id excludes any possibility of further cooperation with him.'

A few days later (4 November), the Soviet organ, *Izvestia* of Moscow, raised the question of the legality of the presence of American troops in Iran. Finally, on 9 November, Premier Sa'id Maraghei resigned with his cabinet, and was succeeded on 20 November by Mustafa Goli Khan Bayat. Shortly thereafter, 3 December, a law was passed by the Majlis 'prohibiting any Iranian official from negotiating or signing any oil agreement, or even discussing the subject of oil with official or unofficial representatives of neighboring states or states which are not neighbors.'

Soviet Russia did not consider the question closed, but, on the contrary, made the grant of the concession a prerequisite to a renewal of friendly relations between the two governments. In order to conciliate its powerful neighbor, the Iranian government undertook to explore the idea of an Iranian corporation to exploit the northern oil resources with the help of Soviet capital, machinery, and technical advice. The Soviet delegation now responded by expressing its great appreciation of this spirit of co-operation, and insisting that the Soviet government be permitted to express its appreciation and good will by providing the Iranian government with experts in all branches of public administration to assist in administering the country.

The Soviet delegation also requested the right to build a pipe line to the Persian Gulf, and to be permitted to guard the pipe line by maintaining troops along a corridor through which it would pass.

The Iranian government could not bring itself to accept or extend such generosity, and negotiations ceased.

Soviet-Sponsored Uprisings

The displeasure of the Soviet government was manifested in due course. In November and December 1945, there occurred Soviet-fostered uprisings in Azerbaijan, and in an endeavor to compose the trouble, Bayat, who had been succeeded as premier by Ebrahim Hakimi, was appointed governor of Azerbaijan on the strength of his pro-Soviet tendencies. In a further effort to appease Russia, the 76-year-old Hakimi announced on 12 December that he would go to Moscow to negotiate a settlement. On 16 December, however, the Moscow radio announced that a revolutionary 'national government of Iranian Azerbaijan' had been established in northwestern Iran. The head of this government was one Jaafar Pishevari, head of the Soviet-supported Tudeh party in Azerbaijan. A quarter century earlier, Pishevari had been involved in the establishment of the 'Soviet Republic of Gilan,' and since 1921 had been a refugee in Russia. In 1937, after the invasion of Abyssinia, Pishevari had been sent back to Iran to organize a labor movement, but was arrested and imprisoned until released by Soviet forces when they occupied Iran in 1941. The Tudeh party in Azerbaijan now took the name of Democratic Party.

At the same time, additional Russian troops were dispatched to Iran, and Iranian troops sent to quell the 'insurrection' were forbidden to enter the Russian zone.

B. INTERNATIONAL CRISIS

These events occurred on the eve of the meeting in Moscow of the foreign ministers of Russia, Great Britain, and the United States, and were perhaps hastened to avoid a discussion of the situation by presenting the conference with a *fait accompli.* Previously, in November, the Iranian government had addressed a note to the Soviet government, but receiving an unsatisfactory reply, it now made a plea, through its ambassadors in London and Washington, to have the question placed on the agenda of the foreign ministers' conference. When the Soviet foreign minister, Vyacheslav M. Molotoff, protested his government's 'strict attachment' to its treaty obligation, and pointed out that some months remained before Soviet troops were required to evacuate under the treaty, the matter was laid aside. On 24 November, however, the American government proposed to Russia and Great Britain that since the war was over and no need existed for the occupation, the date of evacuation be advanced to not later than 1 January 1946. This proposal was declined by Soviet Russia, and the British followed suit; but the American government announced that all American forces would be evacuated by 1 January 1946, and such forces were so evacuated.

Premier Hakimi had not been permitted by the Soviets to go to Moscow. On 17 January 1946, therefore, he instructed that an appeal be presented to the Security Council of the United Nations at its first meeting, in London, and immediately resigned to avoid the reactions that inevitably followed. On 19 January, the Iranian ambassador to London, Taqizadeh, presented the appeal, which charged Soviet Russia with interference in Iranian internal affairs, and with creating a situation that might lead to international friction. The Soviet delegate, Vishinsky, now challenged the validity of the appeal as coming from a government no longer in existence, but so impressive was the recital of facts presented by Taqizadeh that the Council admitted the appeal and placed the case on the agenda.

On 23 January, Ahmad Ghavam Saltaneh, a wealthy landowner with estates in Azerbaijan, who had served intermittently as premier since 1922, and who was generally regarded as pro-Russian, took the reins of government. As he indicated a more pliant attitude and a willingness to negotiate, the Security Council, on 30 January 1946, referred the dispute to 'direct negotiations' between the parties, in accordance with one of the Charter provisions, but directed the parties to advise the Council of the progress of the negotiations.

It was not until the middle of February that Ghavam was able to form a cabinet satisfactory to the Majlis, but finally, on 26 February, Ghavam went to Moscow to negotiate with Soviet Russia in accordance with the suggestions of the Security Council. On 1 March, while he was still in Moscow, the Moscow radio announced that evacuation of Russian troops would begin on 2 March from 'districts where the situation was relatively quiet'—namely the eastern part of Iran—but that 'as to Soviet forces in other parts of Iran, they will remain in Iran until the situation has been elucidated.' This last phrase implied that the troops would remain until Soviet demands upon Iran for political and economic concessions had been met. Ghavam thereupon cabled the Iranian ambassador in Washington, Hussein Ala, to announce that the Soviet government had not complied with its treaty obligations. Actually there were no indications of preparations for departure on the part of Soviet forces, and, meantime, the 'autonomous' government of Azerbaijan was steadily strengthening its power with local levies armed and equipped by the Russians with material, much of which had been manufactured in the Iranian government arsenals and taken by Soviet Russia during the occupation for use in the war against Germany.

United States' Representations

On 7 March, therefore, the United States formally addressed Soviet Russia, requesting that Soviet troops in Iran be withdrawn. At the same time a parliamentary crisis occurred in Iran. The term of the 14th Majlis was about to expire, but by law the expiration could be postponed pending an election. Mass demonstrations before the parliament building now took place under Tudeh auspices, with such violence that the Majlis was prevented from convening and passing the legislation necessary to extend its life; on 11 March the session expired, and the premier became in effect a dictator under his interim powers. The purpose of this maneuver is not clear, except by the interpretation that the Soviet government expected that it would find dealing with Ghavam easier than dealing with the Majlis, and that perhaps Ghavam preferred to see the Majlis expire, in order to have a freer hand in dealing with the crisis. In any case, it is of interest to note that Ghavam, who had left Moscow, arrived in Baku on 10 March, but deferred his return to Teheran until 11 March, after the Majlis had been intimidated from sitting, and had expired.

Upon the expiration of the Majlis, Soviet troop movements in Iran began to assume alarming proportions, apparently with the purpose of forcing a *coup d'état* in Iran. The American government announced on 12 March:

> The Department of State has received reports to the effect that during the last week additional Soviet armed forces and heavy military combat equipment have been moving southward from the direction of the Soviet frontier through Tabriz toward Teheran and toward the western border of Iran. This Government has enquired of the Soviet Government whether such movements have taken place, and, if so, the reasons therefor.

No reply was received to the note of 7 March.

C. APPEAL TO THE SECURITY COUNCIL

On 19 March, the Iranian government again made an appeal to the Security Council of the United Nations, to meet in New York on 25 March. There now began a series of maneuvers before that body. The Soviet delegate, Andrei Gromyko, proposed that the meeting of the Council be deferred until 10 April on the ground that negotiations were still proceeding between Soviet Russia and Iran, but upon the protest of the American delegate, Edward R. Stettinius, no action to defer was taken. On the eve of the meeting, 24 March, the Soviet government announced that an agreement had been reached with Iran by which evacuation of troops would be completed within six weeks, or by 6 May, and at the meeting of the Council, on 26 March, the Soviet delegate formally moved that the Iranian plea be taken from the agenda. This was voted down after extended debate, and on the following day the Council received a statement from the Iranian representative, Hussein Ala, the Iranian ambassador at Washington, summarizing the status of the negotiations that had been taking place between the two governments. This summary disclosed the conditions that the Soviet government had been seeking to impose upon Iran as a price for peace:

(1) Soviet troops to continue to stay in some parts of Iran for an indefinite period.

(2) The Iranian government to recognize the autonomy of Azerbaijan.

(3) In lieu of a Soviet oil concession, an Irano-Soviet joint stock company to be set up with 51 per cent of the shares to be held by the Soviet government.

The Iranian representative, Ala, ended his statement with a formal denial that any negotiations had been concluded, or an agreement reached, between Soviet Russia and Iran, as had been announced by Moscow.

As a result of this statement, the Security Council, on 29 March, called on the Soviet and Iranian governments to advise the Security Council not later than 3 April (a) as to the actual state of negotiations between the two governments, and (b) whether the reported withdrawal of Soviet forces from Iran was conditional upon agreements regarding other subjects.

Considerable doubt existed whether the Soviet government would respond to this request, for its delegate had ceremoniously walked out of the Council meeting at its 27 March meeting when the Council voted to hear the Iranian representative. However, shortly before the Council convened on 3 April, the secretary general, Trygve Lie, was handed a communication from that government stating that the withdrawal of Soviet troops had begun 24 March and would be completed within a month and a half, and that the other questions between the two governments were not connected with the question of withdrawal, as the question of the oil concession had been raised in 1944 independently of the evacuation question.

The Iranian reply stated that Soviet interference in its internal affairs was continuing, and further that the Soviet government had presented three memorandums on 24 March, the first of which dealt with the withdrawal of troops, the second with a joint stock company for the extraction of oil, and the third with autonomy for Azerbaijan. It added that on 27 March the Soviet ambassador had declared orally that if agreement were reached on the second and third subjects, 'no un-

forseen circumstances' would arise in connection with the
evacuation of troops.

As a result of these statements, the Security Council adopted
a motion postponing until 6 May further consideration of the
Iranian case.

Soviet Attempts to Quiet Discussion

Almost coincident with this action, on 5 April, a joint com-
munique was issued from Teheran by the Iranian premier
and the Soviet ambassador announcing a conclusion of negotiations between the two governments and a 'complete agreement
on all points.' The agreements were to the effect that (a)
Soviet forces would evacuate all Iranian territory within one
and a half months from 24 March; (b) an agreement for a joint
Irano-Soviet oil company and its terms would be submitted
to the Majlis for approval within seven months after 24
March; and (c) the Azerbaijan question, being an internal
matter, would be settled between the government and the
people of Azerbaijan, in accordance with existing laws and in
a benevolent spirit towards the people of Azerbaijan.

The Soviet delegate to the Security Council now demanded
that the Council formally dismiss the appeal of Iran, on the
strength of the agreements reached, and attacked the legality
of the proceedings. The Iranian representative announced,
however, that his government wished the matter to remain on
the agenda, and in consequence the Soviet move was rejected
by the Council.

The Soviet government now placed heavy pressure on the
Iranian government to withdraw its case from the Council.
Soviet troop movements increased, without evidence of withdrawal, and the 'autonomous' government of Azerbaijan began
to move troops in the direction of the capital. Until then, the
government had avoided any armed clashes between its forces
and the forces of the 'autonomous' government in Tabriz, but
fighting in various localities now developed. As a result, Ala
was instructed on 15 April to advise the Council that 'the
Iranian government has no doubt that this agreement [regard-
ing troop withdrawals] will be carried out,' but added significantly, 'but at the same time has not the right to fix the
course which the Security Council should take.'

Action of Security Council

The Council again rejected the Soviet move to take the Iranian case from the agenda. On 7 May, the Council assembled to hear the reports of the two governments regarding the fulfillment of the agreement. The Soviet government ignored the Council by making no reply. The Iranian representative advised the Council that certain evacuations had occurred but that his government was still unable to exercise its authority in Azerbaijan and could not ascertain whether the province had actually been evacuated or not.

The Council now voted, with the Soviet delegate absenting himself, to defer until 20 May further consideration of the Iranian case, and requested the Iranian government to submit at that time a further report of the status of the situation.

Soviet pressure on Iran was now further increased, and press dispatches told of armed clashes between government troops and troops of the Azerbaijan 'autonomous' government. Nevertheless, the Iranian government resisted this pressure and advised the Council on 20 May that it was still unable to exercise any effective authority in Azerbaijan and was unable to confirm the withdrawal of Soviet forces.

The following day, however, Ala announced, on instructions from his government, that the Soviet forces had presumably evacuated certain points in Iran on 6 May, and the Soviet government, while continuing to ignore the Council, issued a press release announcing that the evacuation had been completed by 9 May.

The Security Council still declined, however, to remove the matter from the agenda. The Iranian government, under Soviet pressure, now formally requested the Security Council to remove its appeal from the agenda. After extended debate in the Council whether its authority to consider an appeal could be abrogated by the withdrawal of the appeal, the Council concluded that its authority continued, and declined to remove the matter from the agenda.

There the question rested. It appeared that Soviet troops did actually evacuate Iran, but left a number of Soviet personnel behind in civilian clothes, estimated at 2,500 to 3,000, to aid the 'autonomous' government of Azerbaijan, and also left considerable quantities of war material by which the Azerbaijan government was able to continue to defy the Iranian government.

The evacuation, however, substantially lessened the tension; negotiations were entered into between the government and the representatives of Azerbaijan, and in June, an agreement was concluded whereby the 'autonomous' government was dissolved and Azerbaijan was reincorporated into the structure of the Iranian state, but with a grant of considerable powers of local administration and tax collection.

D. AFTERMATH

This agreement remained without effect, however, and the Iranian government was without authority in the area until about the middle of December, largely because of Soviet support of the Azerbaijan government, when the course of events elsewhere produced apparent changes in Soviet policy. American opinion had gradually been growing restive over the aggressive diplomacy of Soviet Russia and the intransigence manifested towards American views regarding the peace settlements, and as the result of various irritating or threatening acts on the part of the puppet governments that Soviet Russia had established in Central Europe. This opinion hardened in August when an ultimatum was sent to Yugoslavia over the shooting down of American planes that inadvertently had flown over Yugoslav territory. World opinion coalesced behind the American position. The American government announced that American naval contingents would be maintained in Mediterranean waters and visits of American war vessels to Mediterranean ports became more frequent.

At the same time Great Britain instituted a more active diplomacy in southern Iran. When Tudeh-inspired strikes threatened in July to obstruct operations of the Anglo-Iranian Oil Company, a counter-movement developed, and in resultant fighting some seventeen persons were killed and one hundred fifty persons were wounded. The Iranian government dispatched forces and brought the situation under control by expelling the Tudeh leaders.

In September occurred a revolt of the Kashgais and other

tribesmen in the south. Shiraz and the port of Bushire were captured, and autonomy for the southern provinces similar to that accorded to Azerbaijan was demanded. The Soviet *Tass* charged that this revolt was fomented by the British and conducted with aid of British arms supplied to the tribes. It may have been that this revolt was engineered as a warning to Soviet Russia of the consequences of a policy of dismembering Iran, for the revolt subsided after some small fighting and considerable negotiating, with the result that the government's authority was restored in the south and, in exchange, a cabinet reorganization occurred in which Tudeh members of Premier Ghavam's government were displaced. The southern provinces were also guaranteed a larger degree of self-government.

Soviet Russia had continued to urge execution of the oil concession, but on 2 October, Ghavam was reported to have rejected a Soviet proposal for a provisional grant. However, shortly thereafter, Ghavam announced that elections to the new Majlis would begin on 7 December, and subsequently declared the intention of the government to send troops to Azerbaijan to supervise the elections. The determination to send troops to Azerbaijan seems to have been at the insistence of the Shah, who demanded that the government take a firmer stand against Soviet imperialism. The Azerbaijan government threatened warfare if central government troops crossed the provincial border.

On 23 October, the General Assembly and the Security Council of the United Nations convened in New York, and on 4 November, the Council of Foreign Ministers. At these meetings the differences between Soviet Russia on the one hand and Great Britain and the United States on the other became more accentuated. For weeks the question of the statute of Trieste was argued, and it appeared that all hope of international agreement was foredoomed over this issue. And then, dramatically, in the week of 25 November, there came a series of Russian concessions.

Soviet Russia acceded to American and British views on Trieste, and this was followed by Soviet concessions regarding freedom of navigation of the Danube. The Soviet government also indicated a conciliatory attitude towards questions of disarmament and atomic control, and on other issues.

The reasons for this reversal of policy were not clear at the time, and were variously attributed to the state of Premier Stalin's health and concern in Russia over the succession, to unrest in the Ukraine, and to recognition of the loss of world influence produced by Soviet foreign policy.

Whatever the reasons, the effects were promptly felt in Teheran. Despite a warning from the Soviet ambassador that the Soviet government could not countenance disturbances along its frontier, the Iranian government undertook to execute its decision to send troops to Azerbaijan. The moment the Iranian government troops crossed the borders of Azerbaijan on 10 December, the resistance of the Azerbaijan government melted, and on 11 December, the Iranian government troops, to the accompaniment of celebrations throughout the city, entered Tabriz.[2] Pishevari, leader of the Azerbaijan autonomous movement, fled to Russia. All Iran was united again under the sovereignty that emanated from Teheran.

Following these events, Soviet political activity in Iran subsided, and Iranian nationalism reasserted itself. The Tudeh party was driven underground, elections to the new Majlis were called and finally held in 1947, and the government showed increasing indifference to the question of an oil concession to Soviet Russia. Additional American military advisers were engaged, and the purchase of quantities of American surplus war materials was negotiated. An ambitious program of national rehabilitation was projected, involving a large loan for economic undertakings from the International Bank for Reconstruction and Development, and an American engineering firm was engaged to draw up plans.

Meantime, despite the retreat in Iran, it soon became apparent that Soviet foreign policy had not changed but was more and more directed towards implementing the will of Peter the Great, by enlarging its hegemony or influence on

[2] The story, obtained from authoritative sources, is that Salamullah Djavid, governor general of 'autonomous' Azerbaijan, realizing the lack of popular support for the regime, secretly telegraphed to Teheran the surrender of his government. This telegram arrived about two hours before the Soviet ambassador called on the Shah to warn him of the consequences should warfare break out along the Soviet frontier. The Shah was able to assure the Soviet ambassador, much to that official's consternation, that the occupation of Azerbaijan would occur without disturbances.

all its frontiers. This became evident, as 1947 advanced, in Soviet unwillingness to reach peace settlements in Europe and the Far East, in its efforts to hamper the economic reconstruction of Western Europe, in the various political revolutions it engineered in Central Europe, and in its maneuvering to overthrow the independent Greek government.

Whether, or how long, Iran will be able to pursue its independent existence without molestation by its northern neighbor remains, therefore, in the words of Abol Qasim Lahuti, one of the secrets 'locked in the Kremlin.' Much will depend upon the force of the international will to peace; much more, upon the vitality the Iranian national spirit can demonstrate, the success of the government in purifying and elevating standards of administration, and the degree to which the Iranian people accept the moral requirements of independent existence.

BIBLIOGRAPHY

Ali, Sayyid Maulavi Amir, *Spirit of Islam*, London, new ed., 1925

Browne, E. G., *A Year Amongst the Persians*, Cambridge (England), 1927

—*A Literary History of Persia*, 4 Vols., London, 1906-24

—*The Persian Revolution 1905-1909*, Cambridge (England), 1910

—*The Press and Poetry of Modern Persia*, Cambridge (England), 1914

Bulletins of the Bank Melli, Teheran

Cambridge Ancient History, Vol. IV, *The Persian Empire*, Cambridge (England), 1926

A Chronicle of the Carmelites in Persia, London, 1939

Curzon, G. N., *Persia*, 2 Vols., London, 1892

Donaldson, Dr. D., *The Shi'ite Religion*, London, 1933

Elwell-Sutton, L. P., *Modern Iran*, London, 1941

Farmer, Henry George, 'The Old Persian Musical Modes,' in *Journal of the Royal Asiatic Society*, January, 1926

Filmer, Henry, *The Pageant of Persia*, Indianapolis, 1936

Haas, William J., *Iran*, New York, 1946

Herbert, Thomas, *Travels in Persia* (1627-1629), Sir William Foster, ed.. New York, 1929

Herzfeld, Ernst, *Archaeological History of Iran*, London, 1935

Huart, M. Clement, 'Musique Persane,' in *Encyclopédie de la Musique et Dictionnaire du Conservatoire*, Vol. 5, Paris, 1922

Ishaque, Mohammed, *Modern Persian Poetry*, Calcutta, 1943

Jackson, A. V. Williams, *Zoroaster*, New York, 1899

—*The Ancient Persian Doctrine of a Future Life*, Chicago, 1896

—*Ormazd, or the Ancient Persian Idea of God*, Chicago, 1899

—*Persia, Past and Present*, New York, 1906

League of Nations Commission of Inquiry into the Production of Opium in Persia, *Report to the Council*, Geneva, 1926

League of Nations, *Reports of Advisory Committee on Traffic in Opium and Other Dangerous Drugs*, Geneva

Macdonald, D. B., *Aspects of Islam*, New York, 1911

Malcolm, Sir J., *The History of Persia*, 2 Vols., London, 1815

Marco Polo, *Travels*

Millspaugh, A. C., *The American Task in Persia*, New York, 1925

—*Americans in Persia*, Washington, 1946

Morier, James, *Hajji Baba of Isfahan*

Old Testament, Books of Daniel, Esther, Ezra, and Nehemiah

Pope, Arthur U., ed., *A Survey of Persian Art,* London and New York, 1938

Rawlinson, G., *The Five Great Monarchies of the Ancient Eastern World,* 4 Vols., London, 1862-7

Richards, Fred, *A Persian Journey,* London, 1932

Ross, E. Denison, ed., *Sir Anthony Sherley and His Persian Adventure,* London, 1933

Sacred Books and Literature of the East, Vols. 7 and 8, *Ancient and Medieval Persia,* London, 1917

Shuster, W. Morgan, *The Strangling of Persia,* New York, 1912

Skrine, F. H. B., *Expansion of Russia 1815-1900,* Cambridge (England), 1903, 3rd ed., 1915

Sykes, Sir Percy, *A History of Persia,* 2 Vols., London, 1930

Titus, Murray T., *The Young Moslem Looks at Life,* New York, 1937

Vital Forces of Christianity and Islam, Six Studies by Missionaries to Moslems, New York, 1915

Williamson, J. W., *In a Persian Oil Field,* London, 1927

Wilson, A. T., *Persia,* New York, 1933

Wilson, S. G., *Persian Life and Customs,* New York, 1895

Xenophon, *Anabasis*

Zwemer, Samuel, *Islam: A Challenge to the Faith,* New York, 1907

INDEX